ALSO BY THE EDITORS AT AMERICA'S TEST KITCHEN

The Science of Good Cooking

The Cook's Illustrated Cookbook

The America's Test Kitchen Menu Cookbook

The America's Test Kitchen Quick Family
Cookbook

The America's Test Kitchen Healthy
Family Cookbook

The America's Test Kitchen Family Baking Book

The America's Test Kitchen Family Cookbook

THE AMERICA'S TEST KITCHEN LIBRARY SERIES:

Pasta Revolution

Simple Weeknight Favorites

Slow Cooker Revolution

The Best Simple Recipes

THE COOK'S COUNTRY SERIES:

From Our Grandmothers' Kitchens

Cook's Country Blue Ribbon Desserts

Cook's Country Best Potluck Recipes

Cook's Country Best Lost Suppers

Cook's Country Best Grilling Recipes

The Cook's Country Cookbook

America's Best Lost Recipes

THE TV COMPANION SERIES:

The Complete Cook's Country TV Show
Cookbook

The Complete America's Test Kitchen TV Show
Cookbook 2001–2013

America's Test Kitchen: The TV Companion
Cookbook (2009, 2011, 2012, and
2013 Editions)

Behind the Scenes with America's Test Kitchen

Test Kitchen Favorites

Cooking at Home with America's Test Kitchen

America's Test Kitchen Live!

Inside America's Test Kitchen

Here in America's Test Kitchen

The America's Test Kitchen Cookbook

AMERICA'S TEST KITCHEN ANNUALS:

The Best of America's Test Kitchen
(2007–2013 Editions)

Cooking for Two (2010–2012 Editions)

Light & Healthy (2010–2012 Editions)

THE BEST RECIPE SERIES:

The New Best Recipe

More Best Recipes

The Best One-Dish Suppers

Soups, Stews & Chilis

The Best Skillet Recipes

The Best Slow & Easy Recipes

The Best Chicken Recipes

The Best International Recipe

The Best Make-Ahead Recipe

The Best 30-Minute Recipe

The Best Light Recipe

The Cook's Illustrated Guide
to Grilling and Barbecue

Best American Side Dishes

Cover & Bake

Steaks, Chops, Roasts & Ribs

Baking Illustrated

Italian Classics

American Classics

**FOR A FULL LISTING OF ALL OUR BOOKS
OR TO ORDER TITLES:**

CooksIllustrated.com

AmericasTestKitchen.com

or call 800-611-0759

PRAISE FOR OTHER AMERICA'S TEST KITCHEN TITLES

"There are pasta books . . . and then there's this pasta book. Flip your carbohydrate dreams upside down and strain them through this sieve of revolutionary, creative, and also traditional recipes."
SAN FRANCISCO BOOK REVIEW ON *PASTA REVOLUTION*

"The perfect kitchen home companion. The practical side of things is very much on display. . . . cook-friendly and kitchen-oriented, illuminating the process of preparing food instead of mystifying it."
THE WALL STREET JOURNAL ON *THE COOK'S ILLUSTRATED COOKBOOK*

"If this were the only cookbook you owned, you would cook well, be everyone's favorite host, have a well-run kitchen, and eat happily every day."
THECITYCOOK.COM ON *THE AMERICA'S TEST KITCHEN MENU COOKBOOK*

"This book upgrades slow cooking for discriminating, 21st-century palates— that is indeed revolutionary."
THE DALLAS MORNING NEWS ON *SLOW COOKER REVOLUTION*

"Forget about marketing hype, designer labels, and pretentious entrées: This is an unblinking, unbedazzled guide to the Beardian good-cooking ideal."
THE WALL STREET JOURNAL ON *THE BEST OF AMERICA'S TEST KITCHEN 2009*

"Expert bakers and novices scared of baking's requisite exactitude can all learn something from this hefty, all-purpose home baking volume."
PUBLISHERS WEEKLY ON *THE AMERICA'S TEST KITCHEN FAMILY BAKING BOOK*

"Scrupulously tested regional and heirloom recipes."
THE NEW YORK TIMES ON *THE COOK'S COUNTRY COOKBOOK*

"If you're hankering for old-fashioned pleasures, look no further."
PEOPLE MAGAZINE ON *AMERICA'S BEST LOST RECIPES*

"This tome definitely raises the bar for all-in-one, basic, must-have cookbooks. . . . Kimball and his company have scored another hit."
THE OREGONIAN ON *THE AMERICA'S TEST KITCHEN FAMILY COOKBOOK*

"A foolproof, go-to resource for everyday cooking."
PUBLISHERS WEEKLY ON *THE AMERICA'S TEST KITCHEN FAMILY COOKBOOK*

"The strength of the Best Recipe series lies in the sheer thoughtfulness and details of the recipes."
PUBLISHERS WEEKLY ON *THE BEST RECIPE SERIES*

"These dishes taste as luxurious as their full-fat siblings. Even desserts are terrific."
PUBLISHERS WEEKLY ON *THE BEST LIGHT RECIPE*

"Further proof that practice makes perfect, if not transcendent . . . If an intermediate cook follows the directions exactly, the results will be better than takeout or Mom's."
THE NEW YORK TIMES ON *THE NEW BEST RECIPE*

"Like a mini–cooking school, the detailed instructions and illustrations ensure that even the most inexperienced cook can follow these recipes with success."
PUBLISHERS WEEKLY ON *BEST AMERICAN SIDE DISHES*

"Makes one-dish dinners a reality for average cooks, with honest ingredients and detailed make-ahead instructions."
THE NEW YORK TIMES ON *COVER & BAKE*

"Sturdy, stick-to-your-ribs fare that deserves a place at the table."
THE OREGONIAN ON *COOK'S COUNTRY BEST LOST SUPPERS*

"The best instructional book on baking this reviewer has seen."
THE LIBRARY JOURNAL (STARRED REVIEW) ON *BAKING ILLUSTRATED*

THE AMERICA'S TEST KITCHEN
DO-IT-YOURSELF
COOKBOOK

100+ FOOLPROOF KITCHEN PROJECTS
FOR THE ADVENTUROUS HOME COOK

BY THE EDITORS AT

America's Test Kitchen

PHOTOGRAPHY BY

Anthony Tieuli

AMERICA'S TEST KITCHEN
17 Station Street, Brookline, MA 02445

Library of Congress
Cataloging-in-Publication Data
The America's test kitchen do-it-yourself
cookbook: 100+ foolproof kitchen projects for
the adventurous home cook / by the editors
at America's test kitchen ; photography by
Anthony Tieuli — 1st ed.
    pages cm
 Includes index.
 ISBN 978-1-936493-08-1
1. Cooking, American. I. America's test
kitchen (Television program) II. Title: Do-it-
yourself cookbook.
 TX715.A54884 2012
 641.5973--dc23
                    2012022144
Manufactured in the United States

10 9 8 7 6 5 4 3 2 1

Distributed by America's Test Kitchen
17 Station Street, Brookline, MA 02445

EDITORIAL DIRECTOR: Jack Bishop
EDITORIAL DIRECTOR, BOOKS: Elizabeth Carduff
EXECUTIVE FOOD EDITOR: Julia Collin Davison
SENIOR EDITORS: Louise Emerick, Suzannah McFerran
ASSOCIATE EDITORS: Adelaide Parker, Dan Zuccarello
TEST COOKS: Rebecca Morris, Kate Williams
ASSISTANT EDITOR: Alyssa King
RECIPE CONTRIBUTORS: See pages 348–351
DESIGN DIRECTOR: Amy Klee
ART DIRECTOR: Greg Galvan
DESIGNERS: Taylor Argenzio, Beverly Hsu
FRONT COVER PHOTOGRAPH: Carl Tremblay
FRONT COVER FOOD STYLING: Marie Piraino
INTERIOR PHOTOGRAPHY: Anthony Tieuli
PHOTOGRAPHY EDITOR: Stephen Klise
STAFF PHOTOGRAPHER: Daniel J. van Ackere
PRODUCTION DIRECTOR: Guy Rochford
SENIOR PRODUCTION MANAGER: Jessica Quirk
SENIOR PROJECT MANAGER: Alice Carpenter
PRODUCTION AND TRAFFIC COORDINATOR: Kate Hux
WORKFLOW AND DIGITAL ASSET MANAGER: Andrew Mannone
PRODUCTION AND IMAGING SPECIALISTS: Judy Blomquist,
Heather Dube, Lauren Pettapiece
COPYEDITOR: Cheryl Redmond
PROOFREADER: Christine Corcoran Cox
INDEXER: Elizabeth Parson

PICTURED ON FRONT COVER: Seville Orange Marmalade (page 63),
Marinated Artichokes (page 37), Fresh Goat Cheese (page 149),
Lavash Crackers (page 243)
PICTURED OPPOSITE TITLE PAGE: Wine Jelly (page 83)
PICTURED ON BACK OF JACKET: Bacon (page 180), Sour Dill Pickles
(page 104), Ginger Beer (page 306)

Contents

Welcome to America's
Test Kitchen
viii

Introduction
1

Stock the Pantry:
Staples Made Fresh
3

Preserving the
Seasons: Jams,
Jellies, and Spreads
57

Pickle It: From
Cucumbers to Kimchi
103

Milky Ways: Cheese,
Yogurt, and Curds
131

Cured, Smoked, and
Terrined: Preserving
Meat and Fish
179

Snacks from Scratch:
Everyday Favorites
and Gourmet Goodies
227

The Sweet Kitchen:
Cookies, Candies,
and Dessert Sauces
257

The Beverage
Center: Sips, Brews,
and Spirits
301

Meet the D.I.Y. Test Kitchen
348

Index
352

Welcome to America's Test Kitchen

This book has been tested, written, and edited by the folks at America's Test Kitchen, a very real 2,500-square-foot kitchen located just outside of Boston. It is the home of *Cook's Illustrated* magazine and *Cook's Country* magazine and is the Monday-through-Friday destination for more than three dozen test cooks, editors, food scientists, tasters, and cookware specialists. Our mission is to test recipes over and over again until we understand how and why they work and until we arrive at the "best" version.

We start the process of testing a recipe with a complete lack of conviction, which means that we accept no claim, no theory, no technique, and no recipe at face value. We simply assemble as many variations as possible, test a half-dozen of the most promising, and taste the results blind. We then construct our own hybrid recipe and continue to test it, varying ingredients, techniques, and cooking times until we reach a consensus. The result, we hope, is the best version of a particular recipe, but we realize that only you can be the final judge of our success (or failure). As we like to say in the test kitchen, "We make the mistakes, so you don't have to."

All of this would not be possible without a belief that good cooking, much like good music, is indeed based on a foundation of objective technique. Some people like spicy foods and others don't, but there is a right way to sauté, there is a best way to cook a pot roast, and there are measurable scientific principles involved in producing perfectly beaten, stable egg whites. This is our ultimate goal: to investigate the fundamental principles of cooking so that you become a better cook. It is as simple as that.

You can watch us work (in our actual test kitchen) by tuning in to *America's Test Kitchen* (AmericasTestKitchenTV.com) or *Cook's Country from America's Test Kitchen* (CooksCountryTV.com) on public television, or by subscribing to *Cook's Illustrated* magazine (CooksIllustrated.com) or *Cook's Country* magazine (CooksCountry.com). We welcome you into our kitchen, where you can stand by our side as we test our way to the "best" recipes in America.

Introduction

Growing up on a farm, just about everything was "Do-It-Yourself" or "D.I.Y." You milked the cow, picked the blackberries, and made your own Anadama bread using molasses and cornmeal. You changed your clutch, welded the snowplow, sharpened the chainsaw, and hunted for most of the meat in your freezer; almost always venison, with the odd rabbit or wild turkey thrown in for good measure.

These days, virtually nothing is D.I.Y. You can't adjust the timing on your distributor or replace a fuse, and most folks have even forgotten how to bake a cake or make biscuits.

All that is about to change.

With *The America's Test Kitchen Do-It-Yourself Cookbook*, we want to put the fun and the "homemade" back into home cooking. Did you know that wine vinegar is nothing more than wine, water, and a store-bought culture left to sit on the counter? You can ferment your own hot sauce in a French press coffee maker with no daily skimming. Believe it or not, American cheese can be made in a food processor in just minutes, without the flavorings, colorings, and emulsifiers.

Yes, we show you how to make pickles and jams, but you will also learn to make recipes like marshmallows, graham crackers, homemade versions of Thin Mints, Nutella, Fritos, and Ritz crackers, plus cocktail bitters, root beer, tonic water, and ginger beer. This cookbook demonstrates, step by step, how to make homemade bacon, mozzarella, Greek yogurt, marinated artichokes, preserved lemons, salted caramels, and even your own tofu and harissa.

Some of these items are quick and easy, others are more complicated, but we have thoroughly tested each and every one of these recipes and photographed every step of the process (we include more than 700 large color photos) so you can be sure that they will turn out as advertised.

In Vermont, nobody tells you what to do. You learn by example, by watching others do something the right way. In fact, the only time I earned a rebuke was when I took a tractor and baler out of gear going downhill. The farmer, Charlie Bentley, allowed as how I might not want to do that a second time given the poor state of the brakes! So, we are offering to show you, not tell you, how to make your foods from scratch the smart way. We've made the mistakes so you don't have to.

Years ago, an old farmer was tinkering with a rusty harrow on a back road in Marshfield and was accosted by a bright-eyed young man peddling a new manual on improved farming techniques. After the sales pitch, the young man asked if the farmer was interested in buying a copy. The old man replied:

"Reckon not, son. I don't farm now half as good as I know how to. Got to catch up on what I know before I take on any more ideas."

Hopefully you're more open than the farmer to a fresh recipe and a new notion. So get busy this weekend and start a batch of vinegar or perhaps throw together a jar of whole-grain mustard. Who knows what ideas we might put in your head?

CHRISTOPHER KIMBALL
Founder and Editor,
Cook's Illustrated and *Cook's Country*
Host, *America's Test Kitchen* and
Cook's Country from America's Test Kitchen

Stocking the Pantry: Staples Made Fresh

4   **Almond Butter**

Peanut Butter

6   **Chocolate-Hazelnut Spread**

8   **Whole-Grain Mustard**

11   **Ketchup**

15   **Hot Sauce**

19   **Sriracha**

22   **Wine Vinegar**

26   **Worcestershire Sauce**

29   **Harissa**

32   **Prepared Horseradish**

34   **Preserved Lemons**

37   **Marinated Artichokes**

40   **Oven-Dried Tomatoes**

43   **Big-Batch Summer Tomato Sauce**

47   **Dukkah**

50   **Candied Ginger**

53   **Vanilla Extract**

Almond Butter

✔ **WHY THIS RECIPE WORKS:** Making almond butter is dirt simple— raw almonds go into the oven and then into the food processor. Nevertheless, recipes proliferate. A surprising number call for vegetable oil. The thinking seems to be the almonds need help turning into paste, but really, all you have to do is wait. With each minute the processor's metal blade whirs, it coaxes out oil from inside the almonds, and that is all it needs. Could you add flaxseed, or honey or brown sugar? Probably. Shards of dark chocolate tempt me, definitely. But I think one taste of still-warm homemade almond butter, simple, rich, and creamy, is its own argument.

—AMY GRAVES, Associate Editor, America's Test Kitchen

Get toasted: Almond butter starts with arranging raw almonds in a single layer on a sheet pan and toasting them at 375 degrees for 10 to 12 minutes, just until they're slightly darkened and fragrant. But the roasting can be a dangerous game: You want that roasted, toasted taste because it adds depth, but if toasting is taken too far, the oven will churn out a popcornlike aroma, and guess what? Time to start over. Trust me, nuts go from perfectly toasted to burnt in seconds, so if anything, err on the side of underroasting them, just to be safe.

Process while warm: Let the almonds cool awhile, just so you can touch them without wincing, and then they can go into the processor. This is the fun part. Let 'er rip, stopping after the first minute or so to scrape down the bowl. At this point you should have a dusty almond meal.

It can't get much easier: After one or two more minutes more the meal starts to clump together. In another minute, it's sticky from the bit of oil that the almonds have released. Let it whir around for one more minute into a creamy paste that's almost a puree (like you see here). I like the barest minimum of salt in my almond butter: 1 teaspoon kosher salt per 4-cup batch of almonds. Add the salt and give it a few pulses in the machine. And guess what? That's it.

Almond Butter

Makes 2 cups
Make today, enjoy immediately

4   cups (1¼ pounds) whole almonds
1   teaspoon kosher salt

1. Adjust oven rack to middle position and heat oven to 375 degrees. Spread almonds in single layer on rimmed baking sheet and roast until fragrant and darkened slightly, 10 to 12 minutes, rotating sheet halfway through roasting. Transfer sheet to wire rack and let cool until almonds are just warm, about 20 minutes.

2. Process almonds in food processor until their oil is released and they begin to form loose, pastelike texture, 5 to 7 minutes, scraping down bowl often. Add salt and pulse to incorporate, about 3 pulses. Transfer to jar with tight-fitting lid. Almond butter can be stored at room temperature or refrigerated for up to 2 months.

TO MAKE PEANUT BUTTER: Substitute 4 cups (1¼ pounds) dry-roasted, unsalted peanuts for almonds. Decrease roasting time in step 1 to about 5 minutes.

Chocolate-Hazelnut Spread

✔ **WHY THIS RECIPE WORKS:** Nutella and I have been through a lot together, so I felt like a bit of traitor when I recently bought a jar of another similar spread. Its texture was a bit plasticky, but it was chock full of hazelnut flavor. It highlighted my Nutella's one shortcoming: lack of real nuttiness. Could my favorite food be made better? The answer was yes. Toasted hazelnuts and cocoa powder provided the backbone, while a food processor and some oil brought it together. Mix in confectioners' sugar, vanilla, and salt, and you've got a no-joke winner. If you think Nutella is addictive, just wait until you try this stuff.

—MARI LEVINE, Associate Editor, Web Editorial

Shake things up: Toasting the hazelnuts deepens their flavor. But keep a close eye on them—they can go from a pleasant caramel color to burned black in just a few minutes. To skin them, nothing gets the job done like making a maraca with them—shaking the nuts vigorously between two mixing bowls until their peels can't hold on any longer. I usually shake the bowls for a few seconds, transfer the nuts that have lost their skins to the food processor, then re-cover the bowl and shake some more. This can seem a bit tedious, but the skins will give your spread a bitter edge.

Smooth operator: Processing the hazelnuts is my favorite part because you get to just sit back and watch your food processor work its magic. Plus, it gives my spread a great natural nut butter texture you won't get from store-bought versions. You'll go through a range of emotions: After the first minute or two, you'll feel doubtful that the nuts will ever get smooth. Then the processor's blade starts to draw out the nuts' oil, and you'll feel more positive (and guilty for ever doubting the recipe). And finally, you'll see the smooth, loose paste you've been waiting for, and you'll feel relieved (and hungry).

Spread the love: Once you've added the cocoa powder (it doesn't matter if it's Dutch-processed or not), sugar, vanilla, salt, and oil, and processed the whole lot, it will start to look like a glossy, smooth, chocolate cookie dough. I prefer using hazelnut oil for obvious reasons, but you could substitute walnut or even vegetable oil if you really wanted to. The hazelnut oil works wonders at loosening the entire mixture and bringing it into spreadable territory. Slather the spread on a piece of bread, dip pretzels in it, or just grab a big old spoonful. Share it and you'll make instant friends.

Chocolate-Hazelnut Spread

Makes 1½ cups
Make today, enjoy immediately

2	**cups (8 ounces) hazelnuts**
1	**cup confectioners' sugar**
⅓	**cup cocoa powder**
2	**tablespoons hazelnut oil**
1	**teaspoon vanilla extract**
⅛	**teaspoon salt**

1. Adjust oven rack to middle position and heat oven to 375 degrees. Place hazelnuts in single layer on rimmed baking sheet and roast until fragrant and dark brown, 12 to 15 minutes, rotating baking sheet halfway through roasting. Transfer hazelnuts to medium bowl. When hazelnuts are cool enough to handle, place second medium bowl on top and shake vigorously to remove skins.

2. Process peeled hazelnuts in food processor until their oil is released and they form a smooth, loose paste, about 5 minutes, scraping down bowl often.

3. Add sugar, cocoa powder, oil, vanilla, and salt and process until fully incorporated and mixture begins to loosen slightly and becomes glossy, about 2 minutes, scraping down bowl as needed.

4. Transfer spread to jar with tight-fitting lid. Chocolate-hazelnut spread can be stored at room temperature or refrigerated for up to 1 month.

Whole-Grain Mustard

SEED SEARCH

This recipe calls for both brown and yellow mustard seeds. You can find brown mustard seeds in some high-end grocery stores, spice shops, and Indian markets, or order them online from penzeys.com or kalustyans.com.

✓ **WHY THIS RECIPE WORKS:** At last count, there were seven opened jars of mustard in my fridge (and that doesn't include the bright yellow stuff my kids slather on hot dogs). And it's not just because I forget I already have an opened jar—mustard has many faces. Sharp or sweet, subtle or super-spicy, there's a mustard out there to complement any type of food.

There was a time when I would scour specialty food markets for interesting mustards, and there was no limit on what I would spend on those that sounded appealing. That was until I discovered that I could buy a pound of mustard seeds at my local wholesale store for about five bucks. I soon found that making mustard is not as mysterious as I once thought.

A basic mustard involves soaking mustard seeds in vinegar (or other liquid) for a couple of days, and then grinding this mixture to the desired consistency. Since a food processor or blender can be used for the grinding step, making mustard at home is really quite easy. Once you've mastered the basics, you can start adding sweeteners, herbs, spices, dried fruit—the possibilities are almost endless.

Homemade mustard will keep for several months, but if you are like me it will be gone in a couple of weeks. And don't worry about filling up your refrigerator—there's always room for one more of those little jars.

—KEITH DRESSER, Senior Editor, *Cook's Illustrated*

The perfect bite: My favorite basic mustard starts with four ingredients: yellow and brown mustard seeds, vinegar, and beer. Yellow (also called white) seeds have the mildest flavor. Brown mustard seeds are a little harder to find than yellow mustard seeds, but their hotter, more pungent flavor is (I think) crucial to a good mustard. For a mustard with a subtle bite, I like to use a 50/50 combination of yellow and brown seeds, but you can alter the ratio to suit your taste.

Vinegar and a touch of beer:
Cider vinegar, with about 5 percent acidity, stands up to the pungency of the mustard seeds. Generally, combining equal parts mustard seed and vinegar provides a nice balance. If you choose a slightly more acidic vinegar, you might want to use a little less, and vice versa if using a milder vinegar. The next addition is my favorite part of making mustard: beer. A quarter cup adds a malty sweetness to the mustard—and also leaves some in the bottle to drink! Don't like beer? Wine, brandy, apple cider, and water are all good alternatives.

Bringing out the softer side:
Cover the bowl with plastic wrap and let the seeds soften at room temperature for at least eight hours. Word of warning: Heat activates an enzyme that kills the flavor of mustard, so don't be tempted to hurry the soaking process by adding hot liquids.

Hitting the sweet spot: Once the seeds have soaked, transfer them to a food processor. Alternatively, you can use a blender if you are looking for a smoother, Dijon-like mustard. A little bit of brown sugar will help temper the mustard's bite. And if you like honey mustard on your turkey sandwich, add ½ cup of honey instead of the brown sugar at this point. This is also the time to add some salt.

Mustard in a minute: Process the mustard to the desired consistency. A minute will get you mustard that is spreadable, but still has plenty of whole seeds that pop with flavor as you eat it. If you are interested in trying out some add-ins, add them to the workbowl and blend with everything else (though sometimes I add spices, like pepper, to the mustard seeds when they soak).

Aging for the better: Transfer the mustard to a glass container. Why glass? I've had mustards that have picked up off-flavors from metal and plastic containers. That's it. You're done—well, not quite. You'll have to wait for the mustard to "ripen" for a few days. Sampled right after mixing, the mustard might taste a little bitter; however, this will dissipate with age. Leave the mixture at room temperature (provided it has no perishable add-ins) to age. Refrigeration will halt the formation of the spicy compounds, so once the mustard is at your optimum heat level, transfer it to the fridge.

Whole-Grain Mustard

Makes 1 cup
Make today, enjoy in 1 to 4 days

- ½ **cup cider vinegar**
- ¼ **cup yellow mustard seeds**
- ¼ **cup brown mustard seeds**
- ¼ **cup beer**
- 2 **teaspoons packed light brown sugar**
- ¾ **teaspoon salt**

1. Combine vinegar, mustard seeds, and beer in medium bowl. Cover with plastic wrap and let stand at room temperature for at least 8 hours or up to 2 days.

2. Process soaked mustard seeds with sugar and salt in food processor until coarsely ground and thickened, about 1 minute, scraping down bowl as needed.

3. Transfer mustard to jar with tight-fitting lid and let stand at room temperature until it achieves desired spiciness, 1 to 2 days. Transfer to refrigerator. Mustard can be refrigerated for up to 3 months.

Ketchup

WHY THIS RECIPE WORKS: Imagine a world without ketchup: All those lonely French fries mourning the loss of their life partner, and dejected burgers in an endless search for a saucy companion. Phew. That was scary, huh? Americans love their ketchup, so we can probably rest easy tonight knowing that it's not going anywhere. But the crusade against processed foods has certainly caused me to think twice about what's inside the bottle of my beloved Hunt's. (Sorry, Heinz.)

Now, some naysayers might argue that ketchup is simply slow-moving, tomato-flavored sugar full of preservatives and syrups. But store-bought isn't your only option; the reality is, ketchup is pretty easy to make at home. I found a surprising number of recipes on the web, but most were just too trendy. Every restaurant I've been to lately has its own version: smoky, curried, spicy, or truffled. Sadly, these all, well, kind of stink. And I'm left eating my fries nude with a cartoon bubble of a smiling bottle of Hunt's over my head.

Apparently, those commercial ketchup-making people know what they're doing; I wanted to duplicate their product. Up to this point, I'd never thought much about what went into a bottle of ketchup. Tomatoes, salt, sugar, and vinegar, right? It was the mysterious "spice" and "natural flavor" listed on the bottle's ingredient list that tripped me up. Natural flavor of what?

Once I figured out the secrets, though, making ketchup was not all that complicated, and, I'm happy to report, all the ingredients needed to make it are things you probably already have on hand. Just make sure to buy whole tomatoes packed in juice, not puree, for this recipe.

—LYNN CLARK, Associate Editor, *Cook's Country*

"Now, some naysayers might argue that ketchup is simply slow-moving, tomato-flavored sugar full of preservatives and syrups. But store-bought isn't your only option; the reality is, ketchup is pretty easy to make at home."

The right spices are in the bag: Peppercorns, mustard seeds, bay leaves, and allspice are pretty standard fare for most homemade ketchup recipes. I also add cinnamon. Wrap everything in cheesecloth—a sachet, if you will—and tie it with kitchen twine. Leave several inches of extra twine on the end. You'll see why later.

D.I.Y. clove oil: Clove or, more specifically, clove oil is said to be Heinz's "secret ingredient." I liked the idea of clove, but whole cloves in the sachet were too aggressive and the resulting ketchup reeked of bad mulled cider. You can buy clove oil in natural foods stores, but I prefer to just make my own by first heating some cloves in vegetable oil. Let the cloves steep for a few minutes in the oil before straining them out. What's left: infused oil with just a hint of clove.

Thicken with tomato paste: Next, put the clove oil back in the pot and use it to sauté some onions and garlic, which together serve as the savory elements in our ketchup. Tomato paste—a full can, at that—makes the ketchup thicker. I heat it with the onion and garlic to help deepen its flavor.

I say (whole) tomatoes: Put the tomato paste mixture in a blender and add 2 cans of whole tomatoes. Whole tomatoes work better than diced or crushed; when cooked, the gelatinous centers give the ketchup more structure so it stays put on hot dogs and burgers. And tomatoes packed in juice are best; the puree is just too thick. Process the whole thing until smooth. You might need to do this in batches if you have a small blender. The color of the resulting puree is probably lighter than what you expect; it'll get darker later when it cooks down.

Simmer away: Pour the tomato mixture back into the pot, add brown sugar, vinegar, and salt, then submerge your spice sachet. Tie the sachet to the handle of the pot, which will make it easier to fish out later—just make sure to trim any loose edges. Now just let 'er simmer. (To avoid scorching, make sure the heat is turned down low enough to keep the sauce simmering gently.) Other than an occasional stir, it won't need you for a couple of hours. So, watch *Glee* (as I might) or do the laundry (as I might not). After a couple hours the ketchup should be really thick and dark red. Untie your sachet and say goodbye.

The bad seeds: Technically, you could call it a day here. But my people are a little more finicky so I strain out the seeds and tomato solids. A fine-mesh strainer will do the job; just press on the solids to extract as much ketchup as possible.

A tidy transfer: Transfer the ketchup to whatever adorable little vessel or vessels you'd like. I'm partial to the classic plastic squeeze bottles. Using a funnel to do this job is a good idea. What with the whole preservative-free thing I was going for, this ketchup won't last quite as long as that bottle you've probably had in your fridge since Manny Ramirez played left field for the Red Sox. (If you don't get this, I'm not sure we can be friends.) One month in the fridge is the limit.

Ketchup

Makes about 4 cups

Make today, enjoy immediately

- 1 teaspoon black peppercorns
- 1 teaspoon mustard seeds
- 2 bay leaves
- 1 cinnamon stick, broken in half
- ½ teaspoon allspice berries
- 2 tablespoons vegetable oil
- 1 teaspoon whole cloves
- 1 small onion, chopped
- 1 (6-ounce) can tomato paste
- 2 garlic cloves, minced
- ⅛ teaspoon cayenne pepper
- 2 (28-ounce) cans whole peeled tomatoes
- ½ cup packed dark brown sugar
- ½ cup cider vinegar
- Salt and pepper

1. Bundle peppercorns, mustard seeds, bay leaves, cinnamon stick, and allspice in small piece of cheesecloth and tie with kitchen twine to secure, leaving about 5 inches extra twine on 1 end.

2. Heat oil and cloves in large saucepan over medium-low heat until oil begins to bubble. Continue to cook 5 minutes. Remove from heat, cover, and let steep for 5 minutes. Strain oil through fine-mesh strainer set over bowl and discard cloves.

3. Return strained clove oil to now-empty saucepan and heat over medium heat until shimmering. Add onion and cook until softened, 5 to 7 minutes. Stir in tomato paste, garlic, and cayenne and cook until fragrant, about 1 minute.

4. Transfer to blender, add tomatoes, and process (in batches if necessary) until smooth, about 30 seconds. Return tomato mixture to now-empty pot, and stir in brown sugar, vinegar, and 1½ teaspoons salt. Secure twine of spice bag to handle of pot and submerge bag in tomato mixture.

5. Bring mixture to boil over medium-high heat, then reduce heat to medium-low and simmer, stirring occasionally, until mixture is dark red, thick, and reduced to about 4 cups, about 2 hours.

6. Remove spice bag. Strain ketchup through fine-mesh strainer set over large bowl, pressing on solids. Let ketchup cool to room temperature, then season with salt and pepper to taste. Pour cooled ketchup into jars or plastic squeeze bottles with tight-fitting lids and refrigerate. Ketchup can be refrigerated for up to 1 month.

Hot Sauce

✔ **WHY THIS RECIPE WORKS:** I've never really liked Tabasco, with its vinegary, flat flavor. Honestly, no store-bought hot sauce is exactly what I want. I want a seriously hot hot sauce. I want to be able to taste the vegetal flavor of the chiles, plus a kick from vinegar and sweetness from sugar. I would just have to make my own.

The process involves pulling the liquid out of chiles (using salt), fermenting that liquid, then adding flavorings like vinegar and sugar. Commercial sauces are usually fermented for good reason; the process adds complexity and helps prevent spoilage. But it turns out, fermenting peppers is kind of a pain. Because the peppers must be kept submerged in their own juices or a brine (when exposed to air they can mold and ruin the batch), most recipes call for checking your ferment daily to scrape off any mold or yeast. I didn't necessarily mind these long timelines, but the fact I needed to check the peppers so frequently was a real turn-off.

To speed up fermentation, I landed on a secret ingredient (I add whey strained from yogurt) and turned the peppers into a "mash" using the food processor. But these bits of pepper were even more apt to float to the top. I tried weighing them down with plates, rocks, fishing and pie weights, and bags of brine. They all still required regular adjustment and scum removal.

Then I eyed my French coffee press. Putting the pepper mash in the pot and pressing gently on the filter allowed the liquid to rise and kept the solids submerged. The press may be "French," but given the personal liberty and hands-off, incredibly tasty batch of hot sauce it gave me, I'd say it's all-American. Note that cleanliness for the vegetables and utensils is critical when fermenting.

—ADDY PARKER, Associate Editor, Books

"The press may be 'French,' but given the personal liberty and hands-off, incredibly tasty batch of hot sauce it gave me, I'd say it's all-American."

Use hot and mild chiles: I wanted my sauce to feature the bright, fruity, floral flavor of Scotch bonnets (or habaneros, which are closely related and more available). They are intensely hot; they're not the hottest of all peppers, but they are hottest among those that are widely used. Of course, a sauce with all Scotch bonnets would peel the paint off the walls, so I soften the blow by adding red jalapeños (find them at better grocery stores or produce markets, or order through your supermarket's produce department) and mild red bell peppers.

Prep the peppers: Fermenting is not the time to be frugal or empty your fridge—a bad chile can ruin the batch by introducing harmful bacteria. Snip the chiles' stems, leaving behind the aromatic stem base. Get rid of the bell pepper stems and seeds, which are bland and bitter. Clean, dry, and inspect the chiles and peppers, tossing any duds. (If just part of a chile is moldy, you can cut it off. Note cleanliness is important for your utensils as well.) Weigh the trimmed chiles, then add several garlic cloves and bell peppers, as needed, to get 3 pounds.

Do the pepper mash: Make a "mash" by pulsing the chiles, peppers, and garlic in batches with salt in the food processor. This really works the salt into the vegetables and jump-starts the process of pulling liquid out. As for the salt, too little and the vegetables will go bad, but too much will slow down the fermenting process too much. I found that adding enough salt to equal about 6 percent of the trimmed weight of the peppers, chiles, and garlic, or 3 ounces, was just right.

Cheat (just a smidge): Next I stir in my recipe's secret ingredient. What is it? Well, I found that adding the whey (the strained liquid) from yogurt inoculates the mash with lactic bacteria, which in turn jump-starts the fermentation process. Instead of taking months, it takes just a week or two. To get the amount of whey required (⅓ cup), line a fine-mesh strainer with a triple layer of coffee filters, then set it over a liquid measuring cup. Spoon 1 cup of yogurt into the strainer, then cover it and put it in the fridge to drain. It takes about two hours, so just make sure you plan for this step.

Press and relax: Now I combine the mash, vinegar, and the whey in my French press and press down on the plunger just enough to submerge the solids. Now the press goes to a dark place, like a cabinet. You could also wrap it with towels and put it in a dark corner. As the bacteria produce lactic acid, carbon dioxide is created. Air pockets will likely appear in the mash and you'll see the liquid level slowly rise; fermentation has started. When gases aren't being produced anymore, the liquid level will settle back down close to its starting point, telling you it's wrapping up. This should take 12 to 16 days.

Spoon and strain: Once the fermenting is finished, spoon off just the very top of the liquid. (Even if there are no visible mold colonies on it, I figure it can't hurt to be extra safe.) Scoop the remaining mash and liquid into layers of cheesecloth set over a fine-mesh strainer. Wearing gloves while prepping chiles is optional, but gloves are NOT optional here: This stuff is hot. Be careful of fumes and don't get the sauce in your eyes. Squeezing through cheesecloth is quick, easy, and very effective at getting all the liquid out of the mash.

Balance, then bottle the heat: Next whisk the remaining vinegar and sugar into the strained sauce to add some balancing flavor and complexity. Finally, bottle it up. (Sometimes the sauce separates after a while, but just shake before using.) After washing my French press, it was ready to go back to its old coffee-making job.

Makes about 4 cups

Start today, enjoy in 12 to 16 days

1	**cup plain yogurt**
1	**pound red bell peppers**
1½	**pounds red jalapeño chiles**
1	**pound Scotch bonnet or habanero chiles**
8	**garlic cloves, peeled**
½	**cup Diamond Crystal kosher salt (see page 70)**
½	**cup white wine vinegar**
¼	**cup sugar**

1. Line fine-mesh strainer with triple layer of coffee filters and set over liquid measuring cup. Spoon yogurt into strainer, cover, and refrigerate until yogurt has released ⅓ cup liquid, about 2 hours.

2. Meanwhile, stem and seed bell peppers, then cut into 2-inch pieces. Using scissors, trim stems off jalapeños and Scotch bonnets, leaving caps intact. Wash jalapeños, Scotch bonnets, and chopped bell peppers thoroughly under cold water; using clean chiles and peppers is essential. Trim away all bloated, softened, or moldy spots on jalapeños or Scotch bonnets (discard any beyond salvaging). Weigh trimmed chiles and garlic, adding bell peppers as needed to reach 3 pounds. (Set aside any remaining bell peppers for another use.)

3. Working in 2 batches, pulse peppers, chiles, garlic, and salt in food processor until mixture is finely ground (pieces no larger than seeds), 12 to 15 pulses, scraping down bowl as needed. Transfer mixture to large bowl.

4. Stir ⅓ cup liquid exuded from yogurt (whey) and 3 tablespoons vinegar into chile mixture until well combined (save strained yogurt for another use). Spoon chile mash into large (about 2-quart) sterilized glass French press. Stir to remove air pockets. Place lid on press and slowly and evenly press plunger down until top of filter is covered in thin layer of liquid, about ¼ inch. Wrap plastic wrap around sides of lid and cover spout.

5. Store French press in dark place at room temperature (about 70 degrees) to ferment until liquid level has risen and then settled back down, signaling fermentation has slowed, at least 12 or up to 16 days.

6. Set fine-mesh strainer over 4-cup liquid measuring cup and line with triple layer of cheesecloth that overhangs edges. Remove plastic wrap and lid from press, then carefully spoon off top surface of liquid and discard. Pour remaining mixture into prepared strainer. Wearing gloves, gather corners of cheesecloth and twist into a ball, pressing to extract liquid and pulp, leaving behind only skins and seeds; you should have about 3½ cups strained liquid.

7. Whisk remaining 5 tablespoons vinegar and sugar into strained liquid until well combined. Transfer hot sauce to jars or bottles with tight-fitting lids. Hot sauce will last indefinitely in refrigerator.

Sriracha

✔ **WHY THIS RECIPE WORKS:** There's a commercial for hot sauce on TV with the tagline, "I put that #%★& on everything." That's how I feel about Sriracha. Sriracha is a fiery-red Thai-American hot sauce fondly known by its loyal followers as rooster sauce (just look at a bottle). The condiment's popularity means that it can be found everywhere, from mega-marts and convenience stores to truck stops and four-star restaurants. Chiles, sugar, salt, garlic, and distilled vinegar are the main ingredients. Then comes potassium sorbate and sodium bisulfate. I wanted to figure out how to make my own rooster sauce, minus the preservatives.

I found a few recipes that called for cooking a mixture of chopped red jalapeños with a little sugar, garlic cloves, a few tablespoons of vinegar, water, and fish sauce. After I simmered and pureed the ingredients in the blender, strained it, and pressed out all the seeds, I gave it a taste. It was ripping hot, for sure, but tasted more like a spicy red bell pepper sauce and was the wrong color; more orange than the deep red I was looking for.

Then I found a recipe that pureed the peppers raw, along with significant amounts of water and vinegar. The mixture was pressed through a fine-mesh strainer, simmered until thickened, and aged for about a week. The balance was better, and the consistency was the ketchup-y thickness of the original. But I wanted to make it easier.

By removing the seeds before blending, I can skip the straining step later, so it only needs to refrigerate for a day before using. It's hot (but not searing), spicy (if you want it spicier, add up to 1 tablespoon of the chile seeds), salty, sweet, sour: the perfect condiment. And yeah, I will put it on just about anything.

—DIANE UNGER, Senior Editor, *Cook's Country*

> *"By removing the seeds before blending, I can skip the straining step later, so it only needs to refrigerate for a day before using. It's hot… spicy… salty, sweet, sour: the perfect condiment. And yeah, I will put it on just about anything."*

Pick a pepper: I call for red jalapeño chiles; you can usually find enough at better grocery stores or produce markets, or order them ahead of time through your produce department. Choose chiles that are bright red, firm, and ripe. They're not the hottest peppers, but it's still a good idea to wear gloves when cutting them to protect yourself from their oils. Start by cutting the stems off. Next, scrape out any remaining seeds; using the tip of a teaspoon is helpful for this. You can hold on to up to 1 tablespoon of the seeds if you want a spicier sauce.

Blend and sweeten: Put the chiles and garlic cloves in the blender, then add the liquids. I like to use both water (for easy blending) and vinegar (for a sour bite). Blend the mixture until very smooth; it takes about 2 minutes. Transfer the puree to a large saucepan. Stir in the sugar and salt and bring it to a boil. I found a cup of sugar and a full 3 tablespoons of salt gave the sauce the balance I was after.

Lose the foam: As the mixture starts to boil, foam will rise to the surface (and may cause it to boil over if you're not paying attention— this has happened to me, so beware and adjust the heat as necessary). Use a large spoon to skim the foam and discard it.

Make it thick, make it smooth: Let the mixture simmer until it has thickened and reduced to about 2 cups (this typically takes about 25 minutes), at which point it will have turned a deep fire-engine red color. Transfer the mixture back to your clean blender. Blend the Sriracha again on low speed (so you don't incorporate too much air) until the sauce is as smooth as ketchup (about 20 seconds).

Sit tight: Transfer the Sriracha to a glass measuring cup, which will make it easier to transfer to a squeeze bottle or glass jar, and let it cool. Refrigerate it for at least 1 day before using. Sure, it's *possible* that you could use it right away, but I found that the flavors deepen and get better with age. Honestly, it's best to just sit tight for 24 hours before you indulge in your Sriracha's spicy kick. It's good on rice, great in stir-fries, or delicious in soup or . . . on just about anything.

Sriracha

Makes about 2 cups

Make today, enjoy tomorrow

1½	**pounds red jalapeño chiles, stemmed, seeds reserved**
12	**garlic cloves, peeled**
1	**cup water**
¾	**cup distilled white vinegar**
1	**cup sugar**
3	**tablespoons salt**

1. Process jalapeños, up to 1 tablespoon reserved jalapeño seeds, if desired, garlic, water, and vinegar in blender until smooth, about 2 minutes. Transfer mixture to large saucepan and whisk in sugar and salt.

2. Bring to boil over high heat, then reduce heat to medium-low and simmer, stirring occasionally and skimming any surface foam, until mixture is thickened and reduced to about 2 cups, about 25 minutes. Remove pan from heat and let cool 5 minutes.

3. Return mixture to blender and process on low speed until smooth, about 20 seconds. Transfer to large liquid measuring cup and let cool to room temperature. Pour cooled mixture into jar or plastic squeeze bottle with tight-fitting lid and refrigerate for at least 1 day before using. Sriracha can be refrigerated for up to 3 weeks.

Wine Vinegar

WHY THIS RECIPE WORKS: The process of making vinegar seems to be shrouded in mystery. There's talk of mothers, bacteria, feeding schedules, oak barrels, botched batches, sterilization, and the smell of acetone. You'll find online rants debating the value of a watered-down wine stock or whether you should add quantities of wine as a vinegar ages.

All of that intimidating lingo obscures the fact that, really, vinegar is just wine that's been encouraged to go bad. Sure, there are plenty of variables, but do you really need anything more than a little wine and some patience? We found the answer is no. The one key is using a mother. In theory, you could let wine turn to vinegar on its own, but the timeline is long and the results inconsistent. It's far better to start with a "vinegar mother," a culture that helps acidify the wine, whether it's store-bought or gifted from an industrious vinegar-making friend. Throw in some wine and water, and you're in business. We prefer vinegars made with full-bodied wines like Syrahs or Chardonnays, but honestly, just use a wine you like since the vinegar will echo its flavor. Vinegars made with organic, low-sulfite wines fermented slightly faster for us, but the difference was mostly negligible over a few months.

Many D.I.Y. wine vinegar recipes call for complicated steps like feeding (with additional wine) or aerating, but we found the simplest method gave us the best vinegar and was the most reliable. After mixing the wine, water, and culture together, all you need to do is wait. Note that white wines take about a month longer than reds since they usually have more sulfites in them that need to dissipate before the fermentation process can begin.

—ADDY PARKER, Associate Editor, and
KATE WILLIAMS, Test Cook, Books

FINDING YOUR MOTHER AND CROCKS

You can find mother of vinegar cultures at homebrew stores or online at beer-wine.com. Crocks are ideal for fermenting and pickling since their wide openings and thick, opaque walls keep out light and minimize temperature changes. They are available at hardware stores and Sur La Table, as well as through online resources like amazon.com.

It starts with a mother: Wine could turn to vinegar on its own, but we jump-start the process by adding a "vinegar mother" culture, which is basically a blob of starch filled with the acetic acid bacteria needed to acidify the wine. There's a near-direct correlation between the percentage alcohol you start with and the vinegar's final acid concentration, so we dilute the wine with water using a 2:1 ratio. That will give you a vinegar with around 5 to 7 percent acidity. We use an opaque ceramic gallon-size sterilized crock, but a glass container wrapped in a towel to keep out bacteria-killing light also works.

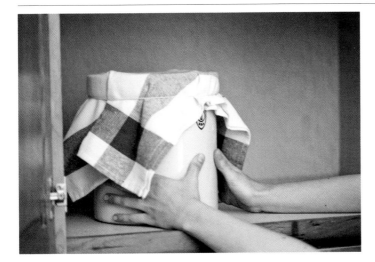

Let it breathe: The bacteria need oxygen to flourish, so don't completely seal off the crock. Instead, cover it with a clean kitchen towel, which will keep fruit flies out, then place it in a relatively warm space. The ideal temperature for fermenting vinegar is around 75 to 80 degrees; cabinets above the fridge, stove, or oven work best. Temperatures slightly below or above this target range will work, but the fermentation time will vary slightly.

Beginning to grow: After 10 days, the mother should be starting to form. Usually it looks like an oil slick, but if it's very active bacteria, you may see larger pieces. The mother will be opaque and slightly lighter in color than the wine. If you're working with white wine, you may not see much until almost a month has gone by. White wine generally has more sulfites than red, and therefore can take longer to turn to vinegar. It could take a week longer than these estimates to see something, but if the slick never appears, there's likely something wrong with the mother and you should start over with a new one.

Turning wine into vinegar: After three months, the mother should have grown substantially. The vinegar should be ready by this point, although the only way to know if it's ready is to taste it. Depending on how much your crock has been moved around during fermentation, and depending on when you harvest your vinegar, you may see tiny pieces of mother floating on the surface instead of a flat sheet. Don't worry; that's normal and safe. You'll also notice there's been some evaporation, which will vary depending on several factors, like room temperature and your crock's dimensions.

Mother removal: It's time to remove the mother from the crock. You can simply pull it out with your hands (wear gloves if you're squeamish). There will still be some bits floating in the crock, but we'll take care of those momentarily.

Saving up for the next batch: Rather than throw it out, we always save our mother for making future batches (or to give away to fellow vinegar makers); it will keep for three months at room temperature. If you're ready to make more vinegar right away, you can simply break off a piece of mother and start all over. For later use, break off a 2-inch piece from the mother and transfer to a 4-ounce jar with a tight-fitting lid. You'll cover it with some vinegar for storage, but you need to strain the vinegar first. (You can prep more of these if you want to give some away.)

Clean it up: The small floating pieces of mother left in the crock are totally harmless, but they aren't pretty to look at. We like to strain them through a coffee filter–lined fine-mesh strainer to ensure clean, clarified vinegar before bottling. At this point, you should take some of that strained vinegar and pour it over the bit of mother you just put in the jar until it's covered (around ½ cup for a 4-ounce jar).

Fill 'em up: Despite the straining, there are still bacteria in the vinegar. To prevent the vinegar from continuing to ferment, you want to fill your bottles all the way to the brim. Since you introduce oxygen (aka food for acetic acid bacteria) each time you open the bottle, and it takes a while to go through a large amount of vinegar, divide the final product between a couple of bottles for storage. This way, you will have just one bottle in use and can keep the other closed and oxygen-free. Chances are, you will still see a little bit of new mother forming in your vinegar after it has been opened. This is normal.

Wine Vinegar

Makes 4 to 5 cups red wine vinegar or 2 to 3 cups white wine vinegar

Start today, enjoy in 3 to 4 months

- **2 (750-ml) bottles full-bodied red or white wine**
- **3¼ cups filtered water**
- **8 ounces red or white wine mother of vinegar**

1. Combine wine, water, and mother of vinegar in sterilized 1-gallon ceramic crock. Cover top of crock with clean kitchen towel and secure with rubber band. Place in warm, dark space to ferment, undisturbed, until mixture no longer tastes alcoholic and has a strong vinegar flavor, about 3 months for red wine or 4 months for white wine. After about 10 days for red wine and about 1 month for white wine, mother should be starting to form on surface of mixture (surface will look oily and wine will look cloudy). Oil slick will gradually transform into thick, gelatinous sheet; do not disturb crock during fermentation or mother will break up and become harder to remove.

2. Using your hands, gently transfer mother to separate bowl. Break off 2-inch piece and transfer to 4-ounce jar with tight-fitting lid; discard remaining mother.

3. Line fine-mesh strainer with double layer of coffee filters and set over 8-cup liquid measuring cup; pour vinegar through strainer. Pour enough strained vinegar over mother in jar to cover completely; cover jar and store at room temperature for up to 3 months for next batch of vinegar. Pour remaining vinegar into glass bottles with tight-fitting lids. Vinegar and mother of vinegar can be stored in cool, dark place for at least 6 months.

Worcestershire Sauce

TAMARIND

A mainstay of Indian, Middle Eastern, and Southeast Asian cooking, tamarind is the vitamin-rich tangy pulp that can be extracted from the pods of the tropical Asian tamarind tree. Tamarind is commonly sold as a paste or pulp and in concentrate form. You can find it in Asian and Indian markets and some gourmet stores as well as online.

✔ WHY THIS RECIPE WORKS: I usually have a bottle of Lea & Perrins Worcestershire sauce hanging out in my pantry, ready to go when I crave a Caesar salad or a Bloody Mary. However, on one recent occasion, I reached for the Worcestershire, only to discover, with dismay, an empty bottle.

My recent dabbling in reconstructing French's yellow mustard and Heinz's neon green pickle relish gave me confidence. It was time I gave Worcestershire sauce a shot.

After inspecting the ingredient list—distilled white vinegar, molasses, water, sugar, onions, anchovies, salt, garlic, cloves, tamarind extract, natural flavorings, and chile pepper extract—I realized, no, really, I can make this.

A little further research revealed that Lea & Perrins uses a long fermentation process to develop its distinctive flavor, but that wasn't something I was willing to undertake. I wanted a version that I could put together quickly. It took some patience, but after adjusting ratios, trying different spices, and tasting, tasting, tasting, I got something that was similar to Lea & Perrins, yet distinctly my own. Ingredients like anchovies and fish sauce might raise some eyebrows, but trust me. My Worcestershire sauce is deep, robust, and tangy. And I gotta tell you, it makes one great Bloody Mary.

—CHRIS O'CONNOR, Associate Editor, America's Test Kitchen

Flavor without fermentation: Lea & Perrins relies on fermentation for its distinctive taste; my version relies on spices—pepper, ginger, cinnamon, cloves, onion powder, and cayenne—plus other boldly flavored ingredients. Anchovies and fish sauce add a critical savory depth (and zero fishiness). Molasses lends smoky sweetness; vinegar, brightness; garlic and shallots, earthy bite. Tamarind extract isn't sold at grocery stores, but tamarind paste, a staple for pad Thai recipes, is available at Asian markets and larger supermarkets.

Toast the spices: To boost intensity and flavor, toast the dried spices for about a minute in a skillet. The spices are done when you can smell them and wisps of smoke rise from the pan. At this point, immediately transfer them to a small bowl so they don't burn.

Make the base: Sauté the shallots until softened and nicely browned, deepening their flavor. Once the shallots are browned, add the anchovies, garlic, and the toasted spice mixture. After about 30 seconds in the pan, the heat will draw out their flavors and aromas.

Boil, then cool: Now add the white vinegar, water, molasses, fish sauce, and tamarind paste. (Whisking these ingredients together before you start cooking will make their addition at this point quick and easy.) Bring the whole mixture to a boil, then remove it from the heat and allow the sauce to cool. During this time the flavors will combine and deepen—I like to give it an hour or so.

Strain it: Once cooled, strain the Worcestershire sauce through a fine-mesh strainer and discard the solids. You can use the condiment right away, but day by day, the flavors will mellow and become more complex and balanced.

Worcestershire Sauce

Makes 2 cups

Make today, enjoy immediately

1	**teaspoon pepper**
1	**teaspoon ground ginger**
½	**teaspoon ground cinnamon**
½	**teaspoon ground cloves**
½	**teaspoon onion powder**
¼	**teaspoon cayenne pepper**
1	**cup distilled white vinegar**
½	**cup water**
½	**cup molasses**
2	**tablespoons fish sauce**
1	**tablespoon tamarind paste**
1	**tablespoon vegetable oil**
2	**shallots, minced**
5	**anchovies, rinsed and minced**
4	**garlic cloves, minced**

1. Toast pepper, ginger, cinnamon, cloves, onion powder, and cayenne in 8-inch skillet over medium heat until fragrant, about 1 minute. Transfer spices to small bowl. Whisk vinegar, water, molasses, fish sauce, and tamarind paste together in medium bowl.

2. Heat oil in small saucepan over medium-low heat until shimmering. Add shallots and cook until softened and browned, 5 to 7 minutes. Add toasted spices, anchovies, and garlic and cook until fragrant, about 30 seconds.

3. Whisk in vinegar mixture, scraping up any browned bits. Bring to boil, remove from heat, and let cool for 1 hour.

4. Strain sauce through fine-mesh strainer set over 4-cup liquid measuring cup, pressing lightly on solids; discard solids. Transfer to jar with tight-fitting lid. Worcestershire can be refrigerated for at least 6 months.

Harissa

✓ WHY THIS RECIPE WORKS: Harissa first came on my radar when two of my favorite bloggers started sneaking the spicy North African staple into sauces and dressings. I thought making my own might be a challenge, but I soon realized I had most of the ingredients (cumin, coriander, olive oil, lemon), and the rest I could easily pick up at the store. Plus, I could whip up a batch in about 30 minutes. Harissa doesn't just slap you with heat; it's smoky, spicy, and complex. I've bridled it with a little honey and mint. It's traditionally eaten with hummus, lamb, and couscous; it's also at home on eggs, in potato salad, spread on a sandwich, or rubbed on a whole chicken.

—SHANNON HATCH, Assistant Editor, America's Test Kitchen

Firepower (but not too much): Dried chiles are harissa's backbone. Ancho are on the milder end of the chile spectrum, but I still find their firepower quite strong, so I remove most or all of the seeds (I've learned to respect all chiles, so I wear gloves for the job). Cut off the tops with kitchen shears, then open them up, pull out the core, and shake the seeds out (if you want a spicier version, leave in the seeds and the membrane). Next, pour boiling water over the chiles to rehydrate them. After about 20 minutes, they should be softened but not mushy.

More peppers, more flavor: While traditional harissa doesn't contain fresh chiles or peppers, I've found that raw serranos add fresh heat and roasted poblano chiles and bell peppers add brightness, heat, and smoky depth. While you still have the gloves on, seed the fresh chiles. Then trim the peppers and poblanos and lay them on a foil-lined baking sheet, pressing them as flat as possible (for even charring). Pop the sheet under the broiler. I keep a close eye on things to avoid setting off the smoke alarm, and keeping the peppers 6 inches from the element ensures they don't go from blistered to burnt too quickly.

Skins off: When the skins start to blister and blacken, place the poblanos and bell peppers in a bowl and cover with plastic wrap. After 10 to 15 minutes of steaming, you should be able to pull the skins right off.

Toast and grind: Cumin, coriander, and caraway are the holy trinity of harissa spices, and toasting them brings their flavors front and center. After toasting, grind the spices in a spice grinder (an old coffee grinder works as well, or you could muscle it out with a mortar and pestle) until finely ground. Transfer them to your food processor with the remaining ingredients. Fresh mint adds clean flavor, and honey tempers the heat and fights any bitterness. Olive oil gives it the right consistency (an Alice Waters recipe uses clarified butter instead, but I found this made a less versatile harissa).

A quick process: Now it's time to give everything a quick zip in the food processor. I think processing the ingredients for 10 seconds is a good start. Then scrape down sides and process again until smooth. You will end up processing the mixture for a total of 45 seconds or so.

Store it: Transfer the harissa to jars and drizzle with a little olive oil before tightening the lids and refrigerating. More cosmopolitan than most condiments, harissa is so versatile, it's even great with a burger and fries. (I've given ketchup and hot sauce my notice.)

Harissa

Makes 1½ cups
Make today, enjoy immediately

2	**ounces dried ancho chiles (5 to 7 chiles), stemmed and seeded**
2	**poblano chiles, stemmed, halved, and seeded**
1	**red bell pepper, stemmed, halved, and seeded**
1	**teaspoon cumin seeds**
½	**teaspoon coriander seeds**
½	**teaspoon caraway seeds**
2	**serrano chiles, stemmed, halved, and seeded**
2	**tablespoons chopped fresh mint**
1	**tablespoon extra-virgin olive oil, plus extra for storing**
1	**tablespoon lemon juice**
2	**garlic cloves, peeled**
2	**teaspoons honey**
1	**teaspoon kosher salt**
¼	**teaspoon ground nutmeg**

1. Place ancho chiles in medium bowl, add boiling water to cover, and let sit until softened, about 20 minutes. Drain chiles, discarding water; transfer to food processor.

2. Meanwhile, adjust oven rack 6 inches from broiler element and heat broiler. Line rimmed baking sheet with aluminum foil. Arrange poblanos and bell pepper on prepared baking sheet, skin side up. Broil until skins start to blister and blacken, 8 to 12 minutes, rotating sheet halfway through broiling. Transfer poblanos and bell pepper to bowl, cover with plastic wrap, and let sit until skins peel off easily, 10 to 15 minutes. Peel and discard skins; transfer poblanos and bell pepper to food processor with ancho chiles.

3. Toast cumin, coriander, and caraway in small skillet over medium-high heat until fragrant, 3 to 5 minutes. Transfer spices to spice grinder and process until finely ground, about 10 seconds; then add to food processor along with serranos, mint, oil, lemon juice, garlic, honey, salt, and nutmeg. Process mixture until smooth, about 45 seconds, scraping down bowl as needed. Transfer harissa to jars with tight-fitting lids, leaving ¼ inch space at top, then cover with additional oil. Harissa can be refrigerated for up to 3 weeks.

Prepared Horseradish

WHY THIS RECIPE WORKS: Originally praised for its medicinal purposes and around since 1500 BC, horseradish is often considered the world's first condiment. Today, people swear it helps with everything from headaches to respiratory issues. Me? I just think it tastes delicious. My favorite ways to use it are in cocktail sauce and Bloody Marys, but you could also mix it with mayo for a sandwich spread, spread it on pork or beef, or mix it with sour cream for a dip. I have friends who add it to applesauce and risotto. Making horseradish is easy, which is good because once you try homemade, you'll never want to get the store-bought stuff again.

—CAROLYNN PURPURA MACKAY, Test Cook, *Cook's Country*

Gather your ingredients: All you need is horseradish, salt, and vinegar. Because of this recipe's simplicity, be sure to buy fresh horseradish root. Once peeled (simply use a vegetable peeler), the horseradish should be creamy white in color (whiter roots are generally fresher). I prefer using cider vinegar, but you can also use white vinegar. And while some people like to add a little granulated sugar to their horseradish, I tend to use mine in strictly savory turns, so I have never felt the need to sweeten it.

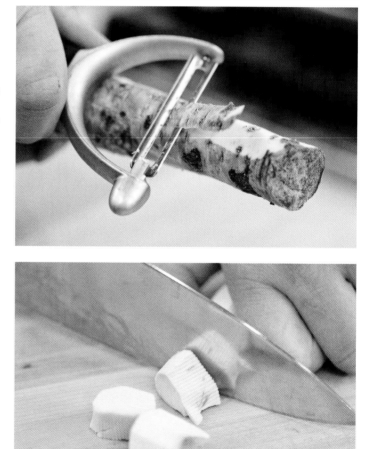

Make it food processor-friendly: After peeling off the dark, rough (and often dirty) skin, chop the horseradish root into small pieces so that the food processor can handle it.

Pulse, add vinegar, then run with it: Put the root and the salt in the bowl of the food processor and pulse until roughly chopped. Then, with the food processor running, slowly add the vinegar through the feed tube. The vinegar preserves the prepared horseradish and keeps it from discoloring (in addition to adding some flavor, of course). Continue to run the processor until the horseradish has a pulplike consistency.

Store it, use it: Transfer the horseradish to a jar. It will stay good for up to 3 weeks in the refrigerator.

Prepared Horseradish

Makes 1 cup
Make today, enjoy immediately

5   ounces horseradish root, peeled and chopped coarse (1 cup)
¼   teaspoon kosher salt
½   cup cider vinegar

1. Pulse horseradish and salt in food processor until coarsely chopped, scraping down bowl as needed, about 15 pulses.

2. With processor running, slowly add vinegar until incorporated and mixture has pulplike consistency, about 1 minute. Transfer to jar with tight-fitting lid and refrigerate. Horseradish can be refrigerated for up to 3 weeks.

Preserved Lemons

FINDING MEYER LEMONS

The Meyer lemon, a hybrid of a lemon and an orange, is less acidic and more floral than the common supermarket lemon. Look for them from August through March at higher-end markets and gourmet shops.

WHY THIS RECIPE WORKS: I discovered preserved lemons when I was working in the kitchen at Rialto, a restaurant in Cambridge, Massachusetts, where I had my first cooking job. On one of my first days, I spied Taleeb, a food runner who originally hailed from Morocco, in the kitchen with a case of lemons and a large box of kosher salt. Curious, I went over to find out what he was doing. He was preserving lemons. He began by pouring salt into a lemon that had been cut in half almost all the way. After he filled the cavity with salt, he would rub the lemon halves together to get the juices flowing, then add the lemon to a large tub, where he already had a layer of similarly prepared lemons piling up. Taleeb had learned how to preserve lemons in salt as a child in Morocco, he told me. Whenever we had preserved lemons in a dish on the menu, it was his job to make them. To this day, I think of him every time I make a batch.

Preserved lemons are a staple of Moroccan cuisine. Typically the rinds, which become soft in texture and mellow in flavor once preserved, are sliced thin or minced before being added to a recipe. Their bright citrus flavor, balanced by brininess and sourness, can add depth and nuance to all sorts of dishes, perhaps most famously to Moroccan tagines. But I go beyond the expected, adding them to simple pan sauces, combining them with a garlicky yogurt for serving with grilled meats or fish, and incorporating them into vinaigrettes. Plus, you can flavor the lemons by adding a cinnamon stick, bay leaf, coriander seeds, and/or various other spices to the jar while they preserve. The possibilities are endless.

Make sure you don't substitute table salt for the kosher salt.

—SUZANNAH MCFERRAN, Senior Editor, Books

X marks the spot: I use Meyer lemons because they are thin-skinned and a bit sweeter and mellower than common supermarket lemons, but either will work. Wash, scrub, and dry the lemons well (important since it's the rinds that you eat). Next, you'll cut the lemons so that you can pack them with salt. Start by slicing a lemon in half lengthwise, stopping about 1 inch from the bottom. Rotate and slice again (creating an X with the bottom intact). Gently pull the quarters slightly apart, being careful not to detach them at the base.

Sufficiently salty: Some recipes pack the whole jar with copious amounts of salt. However, I found that filling the cavity of each lemon with about 2 tablespoons of kosher salt is enough to cure the lemons in about six to eight weeks and avoids making them overly salty.

Get the juices flowing: Over a bowl, rub the sections of each lemon together, grinding the salt into the flesh to get the juices flowing. Then place the lemons in a clean 1-quart glass jar and pour any of the accumulated salt and juice from the bowl into the jar with the lemons. Now pour about 1½ cups lemon juice (you'll need to juice around 8 lemons to get this much) over the salted lemons, until they are submerged, then gently press them down. Cover the jar with the lid to seal tightly, then place the jar in the refrigerator.

Wait for the cure: Now be patient and wait. The lemons will soften, deflate a bit, change texture, and begin to glisten. When the lemons are ready (start checking around six weeks) they should look like this. If they don't, put them back and let them cure a little longer. As they deflate and become softer, the lemons might start to float above the liquid. This is fine; just shake the jar occasionally to rearrange them so the same bit isn't always above the surface.

Prep and use: When I'm ready to put a little to use, I first remove the flesh and pith with a knife and use just the rind. Some folks I know use all parts of the lemon; experiment and learn what you like. To rinse or not to rinse is another personal preference; rinsing gives a slightly cleaner flavor. Lastly, I slice the preserved lemon rind into thin strips or mince it, depending on the dish. Use as much or as little as you like; I find a quarter of a lemon adds just the right touch of flavor to a vinaigrette or pan sauce.

Preserved Lemons

Makes 4 preserved lemons
Start today, enjoy in 6 to
8 weeks

**12   Meyer lemons (4 whole,
        scrubbed and dried,
        8 juiced to yield 1½ cups),
        plus extra juice if needed**
**½   cup Diamond Crystal
        kosher salt (see page 70)**

1. Cut 4 lemons lengthwise into quarters, stopping 1-inch from bottom so lemons stay intact at base.

2. Working with 1 lemon at a time, hold lemon over medium bowl and pour 2 tablespoons salt into cavity of lemon. Gently rub cut surfaces of lemon together, then place in clean 1-quart jar. Repeat with remaining lemons and salt. Add any accumulated salt and juice in bowl to jar.

3. Pour 1½ cups lemon juice into jar and press gently to submerge lemons. (Add more lemon juice to jar if needed to cover lemons completely.) Cover jar tightly with lid and shake. Refrigerate lemons, shaking jar once per day for first 4 days to redistribute salt and juice. Let lemons cure in refrigerator until glossy and softened, 6 to 8 weeks. Preserved lemons can be refrigerated for up to 6 months.

4. TO USE: Cut off desired amount of preserved lemon. Using knife, remove pulp and white pith from rind. Slice, chop, or mince rind as desired.

Marinated Artichokes

WHY THIS RECIPE WORKS: Marinated artichokes have the reputation for being a "specialty item," and it's true that these beauties, ensconced in olive oil, spices, and herbs, seem luxurious. (Their high price tag only adds to this impression.) But at the same time, I view marinated artichokes as a legitimate pantry staple; they have so many uses, perfect for everything from throwing on pizzas to tossing into a salad or pasta to eating on an antipasto platter, one of the simplest yet most elegant of appetizers.

Yet every time I invest the money in a jar of marinated artichokes, I find myself disappointed, even with the highest-end brands. The artichokes themselves tend to be mushy and almost flavorless, and there are never enough aromatics. In developing my own recipe, I wanted to right these wrongs by using fresh springtime artichokes, a gentle cooking method, and a truckload of fresh aromatics.

Sure, fresh artichokes take a little extra time to prep, but to make the ultimate gourmet convenience product as delicious as possible, it's worth rolling up your sleeves. And I promise, the tender yet meaty texture, true sweet, nutty artichoke flavor, and elegant, complementary mix of seasonings in this recipe will prove it to you.

—REBECCA MORRIS, Test Cook, Books

"Sure, fresh artichokes take a little extra time to prep, but to make the ultimate gourmet convenience product as delicious as possible, it's worth rolling up your sleeves."

Babies are best: I opt for baby artichokes here because they are not only easier to clean (while you have to remove the fuzzy "choke" from the middle of mature artichokes, the choke isn't fully formed in babies, so no removal is necessary), but they are also the perfect size for an antipasti platter or for tossing in pasta or salad. Look for those between 2 and 4 ounces with tight, green leaves. Don't worry about brown or black spots; that is just oxidization and is harmless.

Time to trim: Start by cutting off the top quarter of the artichoke, which will allow for a better grip. Then snap off leaves until you reach the inner light green, more tender petals. Trim away any dark spots and peel and trim the stem. Halve each artichoke, then rub each half with a cut lemon to stave off browning (this imparts flavor too) and immediately place it in a large saucepan filled with 5 cups extra-virgin olive oil. This process is the most time-consuming part. It takes 30 to 45 minutes to prep them all, but it's easy going from here.

Simmer, then sit: Cook the artichokes by bringing the oil to a rapid simmer, then reduce the heat and cook them for about five minutes, until they can be pierced with a fork but are still firm. You don't want to simmer them much longer since overcooked, mushy artichokes are exactly what we're trying to avoid here. At this point, take them off the heat and let them sit in the oil until they become fork-tender, about 20 minutes. This cooks them through while keeping their tender leaves intact. Keep the artichokes completely submerged in the oil; any exposed leaves will discolor and become tough.

Fold in the flavor: Next, you'll gently fold in a handful of carefully chosen ingredients to enhance the artichokes' delicate flavor: lemon zest for brightness, ½ cup lemon juice for acidity, minced garlic for depth, and freshly chopped mint for a refreshing herbaceous note. Stir in these ingredients as gently as possible since the artichokes' leaves have a tendency to flake off if manhandled. Note that the acid present might cause the garlic to turn blue; this reaction is normal and the garlic is perfectly fine to eat.

Extra oil? It's extra good: Next, transfer the artichokes to jars. Since a lot of the seasonings will fall to the bottom of the saucepan, strain the oil and then evenly distribute those aromatics among the jars. Topping the jars off with that flavorful strained oil is the last step. I always end up with some extra oil left over; definitely don't throw it out. It offers a bounty of intoxicating flavor and aroma; you'll be surprised how many uses you can think of for it, from sautéing and drizzling over vegetables to maybe just plain bathing in it. So really, you get two great things from this one recipe.

Marinated Artichokes

Makes four 1-pint jars

Make today, enjoy immediately

- 3 **lemons**
- 5 **cups extra-virgin olive oil**
- 6 **pounds baby artichokes (2 to 4 ounces each)**
- 16 **garlic cloves, peeled (12 smashed, 4 minced)**
- ½ **teaspoon red pepper flakes**
- 4 **sprigs fresh thyme**
  Salt and pepper
- ½ **cup minced fresh mint**

1. Using vegetable peeler, remove six (2-inch) strips zest from 1 lemon. Grate and reserve 1 teaspoon zest from second lemon. Halve and juice lemons to yield ½ cup juice, reserving spent lemon halves.

2. Combine oil and lemon zest strips in large saucepan. Working with 1 artichoke at a time, cut top quarter off each artichoke, snap off outer leaves, and trim away dark skin. Peel and trim stem, then cut artichoke in half lengthwise (quarter artichoke if large). Rub each artichoke half with spent lemon half and place in saucepan.

3. Add smashed garlic, pepper flakes, thyme, 2 teaspoons salt, and ½ teaspoon pepper to saucepan and bring to rapid simmer over high heat. Reduce heat to medium-low and simmer, stirring occasionally to submerge all artichokes, until artichokes can be pierced with fork but are still firm, about 5 minutes. Remove from heat, cover, and let sit until artichokes are fork-tender and fully cooked, about 20 minutes.

4. Gently fold in reserved grated lemon zest, reserved lemon juice, remaining minced garlic, and mint, and season with salt to taste. Using slotted spoon, transfer artichokes to four 1-pint jars with tight-fitting lids. Strain oil through fine-mesh strainer set over 8-cup liquid measuring cup. Discard thyme stems, then spoon strained solids evenly into jars. Cover artichokes with strained oil and let cool to room temperature (leftover strained oil can be refrigerated and used as desired). Marinated artichokes can be refrigerated for up to 3 weeks.

Oven-Dried Tomatoes

"Roasting the tomatoes for hours is a pretty hands-off process, and it works wonders with the summer fruit, concentrating the tomatoes' flavor and turning them into rich, flavor-packed morsels."

WHY THIS RECIPE WORKS: TMT—Too Many Tomatoes—is a painless affliction that flares up when one has an overabundance of beautiful summer tomatoes (countertop clutter is a common side effect). I'm no stranger to this condition. Growing up, our family garden produced bushels of tomatoes every August. Today, friends come to dinner proudly gifting bags of colorful, oddly shaped heirloom tomatoes from their gardens. And, well, it's possible that I might have a slight addiction to buying tomatoes (and corn, and arugula, and shell beans, and…) at farmers' markets.

Is there a cure for TMT? Yes: Putting the tomatoes up. Since I'm too lazy to can whole tomatoes or turn them into sauce, I've learned to use my oven to help me cope with TMT by making oven-dried tomatoes. Roasting the tomatoes for hours is a pretty hands-off process, and it works wonders with the summer fruit, concentrating the tomatoes' flavor and turning them into rich, flavor-packed morsels. The seasoning required is minimal: some herbes de Provence, salt and pepper, and a little olive oil. It's best to let the tomatoes do the talking. I eat them straight as part of an antipasto plate; add them to sandwiches, sauces, soups, and stews; chop them fine and add them to mayonnaise; and use them as a pizza or focaccia topping. Really, they have countless uses, and since they keep in the fridge for several weeks, it's a great way to preserve your summer bounty. Even if you feel like you have the worst case of TMT on record, I think you'll quickly discover you just can't have enough of these oven-dried tomatoes.

—SCOTT KATHAN, Managing Editor, *Cook's Country*

Bring on the flavor: Once the tomatoes are cored and halved, toss them with extra-virgin olive oil, kosher salt, freshly cracked black pepper, and dried herbes de Provence. Thyme and oregano make good substitutions for the herbes de Provence here (mint and rosemary do not).

Rack them up: For easy cleanup, line two baking sheets with parchment paper or aluminum foil. Roasting the tomatoes on a greased wire rack set inside a rimmed baking sheet increases air circulation, resulting in drier tomatoes. Place the seasoned tomatoes on the racks cut side down, then top the tomatoes with any oil and seasoning remaining in the bowl.

Blister and skin: Blistering the tomatoes' skins in a hot oven makes it easy to remove the skins. Place them in a preheated 425-degree oven for 20 minutes (or until the skins wrinkle). Carefully remove the baking sheets from the oven and immediately turn the temperature down to 300 degrees. Use tongs to remove and discard the hot tomato skins, then return the tomatoes to the oven. After 30 minutes back in the oven, use a spatula to flip the tomato halves cut side up (they'll stay this way for the remainder of cooking). Return them to the oven, switching and rotating the sheet pans.

Roast, roast, and roast some more: The rest of the process takes three or four more hours of oven time (depending on the size and ripeness of your tomatoes). I found it was necessary to switch and rotate baking sheets twice during this stage to ensure even cooking. Eventually, the tomatoes will look like this—visibly dried with some dark edges. At this point, pull them from the oven. The roasting concentrates their flavor, turning the tomatoes into savory, tender little umami bombs. It will require real willpower to resist the urge to eat them all immediately. (And who am I to stop you?)

Keeping them fresh: Let the tomatoes cool to room temperature on the wire racks. Then transfer them to jars and cover them completely in extra-virgin olive oil. I think they keep best this way, and they should last up to three weeks in the refrigerator.

Oven-Dried Tomatoes

Makes 4 cups

Make today, enjoy immediately

6	**pounds ripe plum tomatoes, cored and halved lengthwise**
1¾	**cups extra-virgin olive oil**
1	**tablespoon dried herbes de Provence**
½	**teaspoon kosher salt**
¼	**teaspoon pepper**

1. Adjust oven racks to upper-middle and lower-middle positions and heat oven to 425 degrees. Spray 2 wire racks with vegetable oil spray and set in 2 rimmed baking sheets lined with parchment paper. In large bowl, combine tomatoes, ½ cup oil, herbes de Provence, salt, and pepper and toss gently to coat. Place tomatoes cut side down on prepared wire racks and top the tomatoes with any oil and seasoning remaining in bowl. Roast until skins have loosened, about 20 minutes.

2. Remove tomatoes from oven and reduce oven temperature to 300 degrees. Using tongs, carefully remove and discard tomato skins. Return tomatoes to oven and continue to roast for 30 minutes.

3. Remove tomatoes from oven. Using spatula, carefully flip each tomato half cut side up, then return to oven, switching and rotating baking sheets. Roast tomatoes until visibly shrunken, dry, and slightly dark around edges, 3 to 4 hours, switching and rotating sheets twice more during cooking. (Remove smaller tomatoes as they finish cooking as needed.)

4. Remove tomatoes from oven and let cool to room temperature. Transfer tomatoes to jars with tight-fitting lids, lightly packing them into jars. Cover tomatoes completely with remaining 1¼ cups oil. Oven-dried tomatoes can be refrigerated up to 3 weeks.

Big-Batch Summer Tomato Sauce

☑ WHY THIS RECIPE WORKS: When I think of my summers growing up in rural Virginia, I remember all the times I would ride with my mother and siblings down hot, dusty back roads looking for the tomato-and-corn man or the peach man; their idea of setting up shop was to load up a pickup truck with their wares and wait for people to drive by. Back home, I watched my mother can tomatoes for the winter or make quarts of her summer tomato sauce. It was light, garlic- and basil-infused, made with the sweetest, largest field-grown tomatoes.

Many years later, settled in Boston with small children of my own, I coerced a colleague into re-creating my mother's recipe with me. My mother gave me the rough formula, which involved only a handful of ingredients. We took a morning ride to Haymarket, Boston's historic open air market, legendary for rock-bottom prices and rough Italian vendors who would scream at you if you so much as touched their produce. We bought more than 60 pounds of tomatoes and countless bunches of basil. After a day (and evening) spent blanching, peeling, grinding, and cooking pots and pots of tomatoes until they reduced down into sauce, we had a counter full of beautiful jars of sauce flecked with basil and chopped garlic. We felt rich and proud. Not to mention how heavenly it was to open up a jar on a dreary February night and conjure up the summer day of our expedition.

Since then, I have continued to make this sauce, but with fewer tomatoes so it would be more manageable, and you can also easily halve the recipe if you want a smaller batch.

—ELIZABETH CARDUFF, Editorial Director, Books

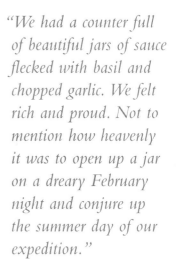

"We had a counter full of beautiful jars of sauce flecked with basil and chopped garlic. We felt rich and proud. Not to mention how heavenly it was to open up a jar on a dreary February night and conjure up the summer day of our expedition."

Go shopping: This tomato sauce makes great use of an end-of-summer tomato bounty. I like to process about 30 pounds of tomatoes when I make this sauce. These days, for the best results I buy my tomatoes at the farmers' market, but I envy those who grow their own. In addition to the tomatoes, I gather tomato paste, a dozen garlic cloves, basil, red wine vinegar, and sugar.

Skins off: While many rustic tomato sauce recipes include the skins, I find them distracting in the final product. To peel the tomatoes, use a paring knife to remove the stem end and core from each tomato, then cut a small X on the base. These prepped tomatoes take a quick bath in a large pot of boiling water until the skins start to wrinkle and peel off on their own (which takes 15 to 45 seconds). Transfer the hot tomatoes to an ice bath to quickly cool before removing the skins with your fingertips.

Faster than a garlic press: Before I puree the tomatoes, I like to mince the garlic using the food processor. Twelve cloves is a fair amount of garlic, and since I'll be using the food processor to puree the tomatoes, it's easy enough to use it first to quickly mince the garlic. Ten seconds in the food processor is enough to transform the cloves into a pile of (almost) perfectly minced pieces. Once the garlic is done, scrape it into a bowl but don't bother to wash out the workbowl.

Puree before you simmer: I like to puree my tomatoes before cooking to prevent the inevitable dangerous splatter that goes hand in hand with hot, juicy tomato chunks. Process them in small batches in the food processor until they turn into a chunky puree. Thirty pounds of tomatoes should give you about 14 quarts of puree.

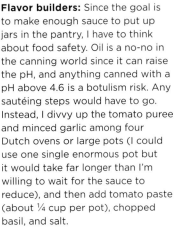

Flavor builders: Since the goal is to make enough sauce to put up jars in the pantry, I have to think about food safety. Oil is a no-no in the canning world since it can raise the pH, and anything canned with a pH above 4.6 is a botulism risk. Any sautéing steps would have to go. Instead, I divvy up the tomato puree and minced garlic among four Dutch ovens or large pots (I could use one single enormous pot but it would take far longer than I'm willing to wait for the sauce to reduce), and then add tomato paste (about ¼ cup per pot), chopped basil, and salt.

Simmer it, season it: Bring this all to a simmer and then let it bubble away for the better part of two hours, giving it a stir every 15 minutes or so to prevent any sticking. Once the sauce has cooked down to 2 quarts in each pot (8 quarts total), season the sauce with vinegar, sugar, salt, and pepper. The amount of vinegar (2 tablespoons per pot) may seem high, but it's hard to guarantee a safe level of acidity with tomatoes, and this amount of vinegar ensures the sauce's pH is in the sweet spot. The sugar helps balance the flavor out.

Store it: Since this is such a large batch of sauce, I think it's essential to process the jars in a boiling water bath to preserve them for long-term storage. Pour the sauce into quart jars (the perfect amount for saucing a pound of pasta), wipe the rims clean, and place them in boiling water for 20 minutes (quart jars need a relatively long processing time because it takes awhile for all of the contents to sterilize at the proper temperature; see page 71 for step-by-step canning directions). Now you can have a bright taste of summer even in the cold depths of February.

Put it to use: My favorite way to
serve this sauce is simple: I boil
1 pound of spaghetti or linguine in
a large pot of salted water. While
the pasta cooks, I heat up one jar
of sauce in a Dutch oven. Once the
pasta is cooked and drained, I toss
it right into the pot of sauce, give
it a good stir, and shower it with a
handful of fluffy grated Parmesan.

Big-Batch Summer Tomato Sauce

Makes 8 quarts

Make today, enjoy immediately

30	**pounds tomatoes**
12	**garlic cloves, peeled**
1	**cup tomato paste**
1	**cup chopped fresh basil**
	Salt and pepper
½	**cup red wine vinegar**
	Sugar

1. Bring 4 quarts water to boil in large pot over high heat and prepare
ice bath in large bowl. Remove core from tomatoes and score small X
in base. In batches, lower tomatoes into boiling water and cook just until
skins loosen, 15 to 45 seconds. Using slotted spoon, transfer tomatoes to
ice bath to cool, about 2 minutes. Remove tomatoes from ice bath and
remove loosened tomato skins.

2. Process garlic in food processor until minced, about 10 seconds.
Transfer to small bowl. Process peeled tomatoes in batches in now-
empty food processor until almost smooth, 15 to 20 seconds. Transfer
to large bowl.

3. Combine 3½ quarts tomato puree, one-quarter of minced garlic, ¼ cup
tomato paste, ¼ cup basil, and 1½ teaspoons salt in each of 4 Dutch ovens
or large pots and bring to simmer over medium heat. Continue to cook,
stirring occasionally, until sauce in each pot has thickened and reduced
to 2 quarts, 1½ to 2 hours. Stir 2 tablespoons vinegar and 1 teaspoon
sugar into each pot, seasoning with additional sugar to taste. Season with
salt and pepper to taste.

4. Following Canning 101 steps on page 71, transfer hot tomato sauce
to 8 hot, sterilized quart jars, leaving ½ inch of headspace at top, and
process. Processing times depend on your altitude: 20 minutes for up to
1,000 feet, 25 minutes for 1,001 to 6,000 feet, and 30 minutes for above
6,000 feet. Store in cool, dark place for up to 1 year. Opened jars of
tomato sauce can be refrigerated for up to 1 week.

Dukkah

WHY THIS RECIPE WORKS: Until recently, I had never heard of dukkah, but once the robust and crunchy mix of nuts, seeds, and freshly ground spices crossed my lips a few months ago, I was hooked. The spice blend usually appears in the carts of street food vendors in the countries in North Africa, served atop bread kissed with olive oil for an addictive afternoon snack. Stateside, dukkah sightings are a rarity, but when the mix makes an appearance, it's generally hiding between dips and spreads on an overpriced appetizer platter or crusted on a pan-seared fish fillet. And when I occasionally happen upon the stuff in a neighborhood gourmet shop, it has usually been hanging out on the shelf for some time and the flavor has inevitably turned lackluster. So what is a nut-and-seed-ophile like myself to do? Raid a well-stocked grocery store bulk section and get to work, of course.

As a temperamental nut lover (I'm addicted to most tree nuts but am severely allergic to cashews, as well as peanuts, plus I have a taste aversion to hazelnuts), I needed to tread carefully when concocting my blend. Luckily, my research turned up as many recipes for dukkah as there are restaurants in Manhattan; the key was making sure the trademark ingredients of cumin, coriander, and sesame seeds made the final list. Keeping my options open, I tested a wide variety of mixtures, finally landing on the blend here. Just remember, fresh spices are crucial so don't use anything that has been sitting in your pantry for too long.

—KATE WILLIAMS, Test Cook, Books

BLACK SESAME SEEDS

Black sesame seeds add nice color contrast to this recipe. You can find them at Indian markets, spice shops, some higher-end grocery stores, and online at penzeys.com.

A nutty, spicy start: Making dukkah is about finding the right balance of nuts, seeds, and spices. Instead of using hazelnuts or cashews (which you find in many American versions), I use chickpeas, an ingredient that, although a legume, appears in traditional recipes. Once roasted, they provide an earthiness and nuttiness that is the perfect complement to the spices: cumin, coriander, fennel, and black pepper. To add color and sweetness, I include pistachios. Black sesame seeds and a generous amount of salt round it out.

Roast and toast: To turn canned chickpeas into crisp, nutty nuggets, I rinse and dry the beans, toss them with 1 teaspoon olive oil, and place them in a 400-degree oven for 40 to 45 minutes. Shaking the sheet every 5 to 10 minutes makes sure they brown evenly. While they roast, toast the remaining ingredients on the stovetop. First up: pistachios. Toast them until they are golden brown to bring out every last bit of their flavor. Then toast the sesame seeds until fragrant, wipe out the skillet, and give the spices a quick stint in the pan as well.

Keep 'em separated: Next, bring out your food processor. It's best to grind each component separately; you want them all to have the same texture in the end, but it takes a different amount of time for each ingredient to get there. The spices go in first, and they take a good two to three minutes to turn into a coarse powder, while the chickpeas take 10 seconds.

Color contrast: Next up are my most colorful ingredients: the pistachios and sesame seeds. They also happen to be just a tinge more fussy because they are softer and therefore easier to overprocess (you can turn them into nut butter if you don't watch it). As a result, I pulse both the pistachios and the sesame seeds (with a hefty dose of salt added to the latter) rather than process them continuously. I like to use black sesame seeds for an added pop of contrast in my finished dukkah, but you can certainly substitute white.

Go for a dip: All you have to do now is mix all the components together in a bowl, then your dukkah is ready for all kinds of uses: as the traditional bread dip, a crunchy coating for goat cheese, a soup garnish, a white rice enhancer, and even a topping for deviled eggs.

Dukkah

Makes 2 cups

Make today, enjoy immediately

1	**(15-ounce) can chickpeas, rinsed**
1	**teaspoon olive oil**
½	**cup shelled pistachios**
⅓	**cup black sesame seeds**
2½	**tablespoons coriander seeds**
1	**tablespoon cumin seeds**
2	**teaspoons fennel seeds**
1½	**teaspoons freshly ground pepper**
1¼	**teaspoons salt**

1. Adjust oven rack to middle position and heat oven to 400 degrees. Pat chickpeas dry with paper towels and transfer to rimmed baking sheet. Drizzle oil over chickpeas, toss to coat, and spread in even layer. Roast until browned and crisp, 40 to 45 minutes, stirring every 5 to 10 minutes. Transfer to wire rack and let cool completely.

2. Meanwhile, toast pistachios in 8-inch skillet over medium heat, stirring frequently, until lightly browned and fragrant, 3 to 5 minutes; transfer to small bowl and let cool completely. Add sesame seeds to now-empty skillet and toast, stirring frequently, until fragrant, about 1 minute; transfer to separate small bowl and let cool. Add coriander, cumin, fennel, and pepper to now-empty skillet and toast, stirring frequently, until fragrant, about 30 seconds; transfer to food processor.

3. Process spices in food processor until finely ground, 2 to 3 minutes; transfer to medium bowl. Process chickpeas in now-empty food processor until coarsely ground, about 10 seconds; add to bowl with spices. Pulse pistachios in now-empty food processor until coarsely ground, about 15 pulses; add to bowl with spices and chickpeas. Pulse sesame seeds and salt in food processor until coarsely ground, about 5 pulses; add to bowl with nuts and spices.

4. Toss dukkah together until well combined and transfer to jars with tight-fitting lids. Dukkah can be stored at room temperature for up to 3 months.

Candied Ginger

"For just a few dollars and in just a few short hours (the majority of it hands-off), I had a half-pound of glimmering, spicy-sweet ginger coins."

✓ **WHY THIS RECIPE WORKS:** While some of my coworkers use their kitchens as at-home culinary labs, mine is definitely more low-tech. The wares from my pantry could be described as *Little House on the Prairie* meets the 21st century: tomato-port jam and jalapeño pepper jelly, a blushing red onion marmalade, turmeric-laced zucchini pickles. My philosophy: Why buy it if you can make it (and make it better)?

However, it didn't occur to me to make my own candied ginger until I let my eyes wander to the ingredient list on the packaging of some candied ginger at my neighborhood grocery store: ginger, sugar. Simple enough. So I walked over to the produce aisle, dropped a hunk of the gnarly rhizome in my basket, then set off for home to get to work.

For just a few dollars and in just a few short hours (the majority of it hands-off), I had a half-pound of glimmering, spicy-sweet ginger coins. Unsurprisingly, starting with the fresh stuff amps up the peppery heat compared to what you find in the store, so be prepared. Today if I want to toss a handful of my new favorite staple into homemade granola, crumble topping, or mashed sweet potatoes, all I have to do is open my pantry door. Be aware that simmering and drying times may vary depending upon humidity and the freshness of your ginger.

—SHANNON HATCH, Assistant Editor, America's Test Kitchen

It doesn't take much: Sugar and ginger (plus water)—that's all you need to make candied ginger. Most markets carry ginger in its mature form, but if you're looking for a little less bite, seek out young ginger, also called spring ginger (Asian markets often carry it). You'll know it by its thin, nearly translucent skin. I like to use a spoon to peel ginger. Its edge removes the skin just as well as a peeler or a knife, but it's easier to navigate around all of the bumps and knobs. Once the ginger is peeled, slice it crosswise into thin coins.

It's just that simple: Next, make a simple syrup—equal parts water and sugar. This is not just your cooking liquid but also what enables the sugar granules to "glue" themselves to the ginger coins by giving the ginger a sticky exterior. Add the sliced ginger to your simple syrup and cook for about 45 minutes, or until the ginger is tender and translucent.

Save the syrup: Instead of draining your tenderized ginger over the sink, place a large container (like a 4-cup measuring cup or a bowl) underneath. This allows you to capture the ginger-infused syrup and refrigerate it for later use. I've made mock ginger ale with it. It also goes great with rum and is perfect for sweetening iced tea, tossing with sliced fruit, or even brushing over a just-baked pound cake.

Drying time: It's important to spread the ginger in a single layer on a wire rack and allow it to dry completely for 6 to 12 hours (it can vary quite a bit, depending on the humidity and the freshness of your ginger). It should just be tacky to the touch; don't rush it. The first time I tried to make candied ginger, I was in a hurry and tossed the slices with sugar after an hour—big mistake. The sugar melted into the ginger instead of sticking to the surface, creating a sticky, gooey mess.

Sugar coated: After your ginger is sufficiently dried, combine it with granulated sugar in a bowl and toss or stir until the slices are completely covered. It's OK if you end up with extra sugar in the bottom of the bowl—you can save that to flavor tea or sprinkle on top of cookies. Stored in an airtight container, the candied ginger should keep for a few weeks, unless, like me, you keep a stash at work within arm's reach.

Candied Ginger

Makes ¾ cup

Make today, enjoy immediately

2¼	**cups sugar**
2	**cups water**
8	**ounces fresh ginger, peeled and sliced thin**

1. Set wire rack in rimmed baking sheet. Combine 2 cups sugar and water in small saucepan over medium heat. Bring to simmer, stirring occasionally, until sugar dissolves. Add ginger and simmer until tender and translucent, about 45 minutes. Strain through fine-mesh strainer set over medium bowl or large liquid measuring cup. Reserve syrup for later use.

2. Transfer ginger to prepared wire rack and let dry until ginger is tacky and no longer damp, 6 to 12 hours.

3. Combine dried ginger slices and remaining ¼ cup sugar in medium bowl, and toss until ginger is lightly dusted with sugar. Transfer ginger to airtight container. Candied ginger can be stored at room temperature for up to 2 weeks.

Vanilla Extract

✔ WHY THIS RECIPE WORKS: Store-bought vanilla extract ranges from the cheap imitation stuff to fancy bottles so expensive you would think they contained liquid gold. Vanilla beans aren't exactly cheap, so I was surprised when I recently learned that making vanilla extract at home can actually produce a top-quality product at a very reasonable price. Basically, you just let vanilla beans steep in alcohol for several weeks and *voilà*, you've got extract. Buying the beans in bulk and using a basic (we're talking well stuff, not the top-shelf) liquor keeps it affordable—it ends up being about $2.50 per ounce, compared to $3.74 per ounce at the store.

I did come up with a few tricks to speed up the process a bit, but still, with around two months of waiting time, this is certainly not a project for the impatient. However, I will attest to the fact it's well worth the wait. Pop off the lid of your homemade vanilla and you'll find the scent is pure and unadulterated. The taste? A full-bodied, well-rounded flavor that makes the best of the store-bought pure vanilla extract taste like the cheapest stuff on the shelf. Plus, there's room to play. Using a different variety of bean—say classic Madagascar or floral Tahitian or bolder Mexican—will give you a slightly different end product, and you'll discover each one has roles it fills better than the others (whipped cream hits a whole new gourmet level when you add a little Tahitian vanilla extract). Homemade vanilla extract: cheaper, better, it lasts forever—and now you have a recipe. You're crazy if you don't start making your own vanilla extract today.

—REBECCA MORRIS, Test Cook, Books

BEANS IN BULK

To save money, order vanilla beans online from sites such as beanilla.com. You'll end up spending a lot less ($13 plus shipping for 10 Madagascar beans) than you would buying them from a supermarket. And of course, the more beans you buy, the cheaper they are. Beanilla also sells amber glass bottles for storing your vanilla. If you can find them, Grade B beans, labeled "extract beans," contain less water and are ideal for homemade extract.

Maximum extraction: You've probably noticed vanilla extract tastes a little boozy; that's because alcohol enables maximum extraction of flavor from the beans. Some people use bourbon, brandy, or rum, but I prefer using a neutral liquor, vodka, to allow for a pure vanilla flavor. You can use Smirnoff—a premium brand isn't necessary. To get maximum flavor quickly, start by splitting the pods lengthwise and scraping out the seeds, then chop the pods into pieces (this step also helps them fit more easily in a jar for the steeping phase).

Heat things up: The extraction process will go faster if you heat everything together first. Add the pods and seeds to a saucepan. Now pour in 1 cup of vodka, cover the pan, and heat it over medium-low, just until wafts of steam are rising from the liquid (you don't want it to boil, so err on the side of less time rather than more). Make sure to cover the saucepan so none of the alcohol burns off, and be careful not to open the lid while it is still on the flame—it will ignite!

Let 'er steep: Next, immediately pour everything into a clean jar (using a canning funnel keeps it tidy but isn't a must), then let the mixture cool to room temperature before covering and placing it in a dark cabinet. Because the tiny seeds will settle in a pile at the bottom of the jar along with the pods, I shake the jar once a week to redistribute them.

Filtered and finished: I found six weeks was the minimum amount of time necessary to get an extract with well-rounded vanilla flavor; you can keep aging for up to ten weeks for even stronger extract (if you have extremely moist beans it might take a bit longer). You can taste a little bit along the way, and when the flavor is just where you want it, strain the vanilla extract through two coffee filters to remove the seeds and pods. Be warned though: Once you strain the vanilla, the flavor won't change, so make sure you are happy with what you have.

Adventures with extract:
Stored in a cool, dark place like a cabinet, your homemade extract will keep forever. Because of its shelf life and because it's such an easy process, you might want to experiment with vanilla bean varieties. Madagascar and Bourbon are classic choices, but I particularly love Tahitian beans for their floral, fruity flavor. Meanwhile, Mexican has a slightly dark flavor, making it particularly nice for chocolate desserts and ice cream. Build up an arsenal of all the varieties and you'll have the perfect vanilla ready for every recipe.

Vanilla Extract

Makes 1 cup
Start today, enjoy in 6 to 10 weeks

8 **vanilla beans (1 ounce)**
1 **cup vodka**

1. Cut vanilla beans in half lengthwise. Using tip of paring knife or spoon, scrape out seeds and transfer to small saucepan. Cut bean pods into 1-inch pieces and add to saucepan.

2. Add vodka, cover, and cook over medium-low heat until mixture is hot and steaming, about 2 minutes. (Do not open lid while pot is over flame or alcohol will ignite.)

3. Pour mixture into jar with tight-fitting lid and let cool to room temperature. Cover with lid and store in dark place for at least 6 weeks or up to 10 weeks, shaking jar gently once a week.

4. Line fine-mesh strainer with 2 coffee filters and set over liquid measuring cup. Strain vanilla through filters, then transfer from measuring cup to clean jar with tight-fitting lid. Vanilla extract will keep indefinitely.

TO DOUBLE: Increase vanilla beans to 16 beans and vodka to 2 cups. Increase cooking time in step 2 to about 3 minutes.

Preserving the Seasons: Jams, Jellies, and Spreads

58   **Easy Refrigerator Jams**

         Strawberry Refrigerator Jam

         Raspberry Refrigerator Jam

         Blueberry Refrigerator Jam

60   **Raspberry-Peach Spreadable Fruit**

63   **Seville Orange Marmalade**

67   **Fig-Balsamic Jam**

72   **Spicy Tomato Jam**

75   **Caramelized Onion Jam**

77   **Bacon Jam**

80   **Red Pepper Jelly**

83   **Wine Jelly**

86   **Mango Chutney**

88   **Green Tomato Chutney**

90   **Peach Mostarda**

94   **Apple Butter**

98   **Marmelada (Quince Paste)**

Easy Refrigerator Jams

✔ **WHY THIS RECIPE WORKS:** During my Boston childhood, the closest I came to experiencing nature's bounty was when I planted Popsicle sticks in our tiny backyard. I had to venture to Maine to get my dose of nature; there, with a friend and her wild raspberry bush, I experienced the wonders of jam making. In the morning, the raspberries were on the bush; by afternoon we had jam. The beauty was in the simplicity, both in terms of pure fruit flavor and that it took just 30 minutes to make. I recently decided it was time I developed my own jam recipes, making a small amount that didn't need to be processed and could be kept in the fridge a few weeks.

—ADDY PARKER, Associate Editor, Books

Chop into chunks: My first decision was to bar sliced strawberries from my jam because I've never liked stringy pieces of fruit in the final jam. So after hulling the berries, I chop them into ½-inch chunks. I add lemon juice not just for flavor—it (along with the proportion of sugar used) helps this jam set up without the need for adding pectin.

Strong heat, strong hand, good jam: It may seem counterintuitive, but to avoid destroying the freshness of fruit, one has to have a strong hand with the heat. This is because extended cooking actually dulls flavor. It also destroys the naturally occurring pectin in the fruit, which is necessary for proper gelling. So I simmer the fruit vigorously for just 15 to 20 minutes. To further expand on the "strong hand" theme, I also beat the berries with a potato masher before cooking. This jump-starts the release of pectin and further decreases the cooking time, ensuring maximum fresh fruit flavor.

Is it done yet?: Again, rather than rely on subtleties to test for doneness, I went for the direct, literal approach. If you want to see how jam will set once chilled, then chill it. A little jam cools quickly on a pre-frozen spoon, preventing any surprises in texture when your jam cools down. If it seems runny (see photos page 61 for photos showing the difference between a jam that's not quite ready and one that is), just bring your jam back to a simmer and repeat the test. The great thing about this jam is it makes just enough for a few weeks; there's no need to fuss with canning.

Strawberry Refrigerator Jam

Makes about 2 cups

Make today, enjoy immediately

1½	**pounds strawberries, hulled and cut into ½-inch pieces (3 cups)**
1	**cup sugar**
3	**tablespoons lemon juice**

1. Place metal spoon in freezer to chill. Combine strawberries, sugar, and lemon juice in large saucepan. Bring to boil over medium-high heat, then reduce heat to medium. Mash fruit with potato masher until fruit is mostly broken down. Simmer vigorously until fruit mixture thickens to jamlike consistency, 15 to 20 minutes.

2. To test for set point, remove saucepan from heat. Dip chilled spoon into jam and allow jam to run off spoon; jam should slowly fall off spoon in one thickened clump. If jam is runny, return to medium heat and simmer 2 to 4 minutes before retesting. Transfer finished jam to jar with tight-fitting lid, let cool to room temperature, then cover and refrigerate. Jam can be refrigerated for up to 3 weeks.

TO MAKE RASPBERRY REFRIGERATOR JAM: Substitute 1 pound raspberries for strawberries and leave fruit whole. Reduce sugar to ¾ cup and lemon juice to 2 tablespoons.

TO MAKE BLUEBERRY REFRIGERATOR JAM: Substitute 1 pound blueberries for strawberries and leave fruit whole. Reduce sugar to ¾ cup and lemon juice to 2 tablespoons. In step 1, simmer mixture for 8 to 12 minutes.

Raspberry-Peach Spreadable Fruit

"The first time I opened his freezer, I noticed that it contained little more than fruit (and ice cubes). This summer, as I made crisps, cobblers, and pies, and yet still watched our freezer fill up, panic set in and I said, 'Enough.' It was time for jam."

✔ **WHY THIS RECIPE WORKS:** I married into fruit. My husband, Ken, moved into our house over a decade ago in a city full of skinny little yards—most of them no bigger than your average driveway. Yet in that time he's managed to create a thriving urban orchard that includes apples, peaches, cherries, pluots, and apricots, as well as grapes, blueberries, and raspberries.

Before I came into the picture, Ken shared his bounty with his housemates, made a lot of pies, and tossed the rest into the freezer—in fact, the first time I opened his freezer, I noticed that it contained little more than fruit (and ice cubes). This summer, as I made crisps, cobblers, and pies, and yet still watched our freezer fill up, panic set in and I said, "Enough." It was time for jam.

I hadn't made jam in years, partly out of laziness and partly because I love Sarabeth's Spreadable Fruit. This stuff is great—it actually tastes like fruit, not sugar—but it's not cheap and the way we go through it (spread on toast and scones and even stirred into yogurt), I thought that making my own version might not be a bad idea. Plus, I could reclaim space in the freezer. Sarabeth's jam isn't very thick—in fact, it's on the thin side. I checked out her website and learned that her preserves don't contain added pectin, which probably accounts for their fluid texture. My goal was to approximate her preserves using raspberries and peaches. What you'll find here is just that, a loose spreadable jam with bright fruit flavor that isn't too sweet. It's perfect for toast, scones, and, of course, yogurt.

—LORI GALVIN, Executive Editor, Books

A berry sweet start: I made batches with varying ratios of sugar to fruit and the best of the lot was 1 cup sugar to 10½ cups fruit. Warm the sugar (so that it will melt more evenly) in a saucepan over medium heat, giving it a few stirs, for about a minute. Add the raspberries, stir until coated with sugar, then let the mixture cook until the sugar is dissolved and the raspberries have released their juices. Be careful not to let them cook too long because you still want them to hold some shape.

Prep, cook, mash: Traditionally, peaches are peeled by scoring and blanching before being cooked into jam. Who has time for this? Instead, I use a vegetable peeler (if your peaches are very juicy, peel them over a bowl). After peeling them, halve, pit, and slice the peaches about ¼ inch thick. I prefer smaller pieces of fruit in my jam, so I then stack the slices together and cut them in half crosswise. Add the peaches to the pan, let the fruit cook for about five minutes, and then give it all a mash to help break things down.

Put it to the spoon test: Let the fruit boil for about 10 minutes. To check to see if the jam is properly thickened, I like to use the spoon test. Before you start cooking, place a metal spoon in the freezer. When you think the jam is ready, dip the chilled spoon into the jam and let the jam run off. If it runs off slowly (as shown on the right), it's ready. It will also be darker in color. If it runs off in a fast stream (left), it needs more time—try testing again after cooking the jam for a few more minutes.

Froth free: Once it's cooked, you'll notice a white froth across the jam's surface. It doesn't taste bad, but it doesn't look nice—and if you're going to process the jam for storage, skimming the froth off is recommended since it contains a lot of air that can inhibit headspace in the jar and promote molding. Use a large, shallow spoon to remove the froth from the surface of the jam. After skimming, add fresh lemon juice for a bright boost.

Get fresh: Remember, jam isn't just for toast; try stirring a few spoonfuls into plain yogurt—it's a whole lot fresher tasting than the preflavored store-bought variety.

Raspberry-Peach Spreadable Fruit

Makes about five 1-cup jars

Make today, enjoy immediately

- **1 cup sugar**
- **12 ounces (2½ cups) raspberries**
- **3 pounds peaches, peeled, halved, pitted, sliced ¼ inch thick, and each slice halved crosswise (8 cups)**
- **3 tablespoons lemon juice**

1. Place metal spoon in freezer to chill. Heat sugar in large saucepan over medium heat, stirring frequently, until warm, about 1 minute. Add raspberries and continue to stir until raspberries release their juices, about 1 minute. Stir in peaches, bring to boil over medium-high heat, and cook until peaches are just tender, 5 to 7 minutes. Coarsely mash fruit with potato masher.

2. Return fruit mixture to boil and cook until mixture thickens to jam-like consistency, 8 to 10 minutes. To test for set point, remove saucepan from heat. Dip chilled spoon into jam, and allow jam to run off spoon; jam should slowly fall off spoon in one thickened clump. If it is runny, return jam to medium heat and simmer 2 to 4 minutes before retesting. Using large spoon, skim foam from top of jam. Stir in lemon juice.

3. Transfer jam to jars with tight-fitting lids, let cool to room temperature, then cover and refrigerate. Jam can be refrigerated for up to 3 weeks.

TO DOUBLE: Double ingredients and substitute Dutch oven for large saucepan. In step 1, increase cooking time of peaches to 10 to 15 minutes. In step 2, increase cooking time to 15 to 20 minutes.

TO PROCESS FOR LONG-TERM STORAGE: In step 3, transfer jam, while still hot, to hot, sterilized 1-cup jars, leaving ¼-inch of headspace at top, and process following Canning 101 steps on page 71. Processing times depend on your altitude: 5 minutes for up to 1,000 feet, 10 minutes for 1,001 to 6,000 feet, and 15 minutes for above 6,000 feet. Store in cool, dark place for up to 1 year.

Seville Orange Marmalade

✔ **WHY THIS RECIPE WORKS:** Authentic marmalade—the kind made from bitter, sour Seville oranges—is not for wimps. Its sweet, tart, astringent, and spicy notes battle fiercely for supremacy on the palate; it is the fruit preserve of choice among those who love a good fight. No surprise, then, that marmalade is most closely associated with Scotland.

I lived in Scotland for several years and, in my experience, the Scots are a smart, tough-minded, practical lot who readily embrace a challenge. This is a country in which mountains are referred to as "hills," where the natives express their cultural pride by donning kilts and throwing telephone poles around, and where the ability to hold one's own in a pub debate is the most admired of social traits. So marmalade is, in my opinion, an excellent culinary emblem for the Scots. A smear of Nutella on your morning toast might gently coax you into a difficult day, but a spoonful of Seville orange marmalade slaps you upside the head and admonishes you to get on with it.

My recipe reflects the nonessential step of warming sugar in the oven. I've seen this in many traditional recipes, and I think I've figured out the reason behind it. A Scottish kitchen can be a chilly place since many homes in rural areas are still not centrally heated, and adding cool sugar to a bubbling pot of marmalade would slow the process considerably. Out of deference, I haven't changed this step even though my kitchen is fairly warm.

To eat real marmalade, I slice a thick piece of sourdough and spread it with unsalted butter. Then I sprinkle that butter with flaky sea salt. I spoon a generous amount of marmalade over the butter and spread it to the edges. Each bite is sweet, salty, spicy, bitter, and chewy—"gorgeous," as the Scots would say. You should try it, if you're tough enough.

—ANDREA GEARY, Associate Editor, *Cook's Illustrated*

SOURCING SEVILLES

Like the Scots, Seville oranges are a rugged, persnickety lot. They (the oranges, not the Scots) are available for about three weeks in January and can be frozen whole for several months before using.

Begin with boiling: Start by weighing out 2 pounds of Seville oranges (it's OK if they're a bit green or blemished, but I throw out any that have soft spots). Add two lemons for their flavor and higher pectin content (it helps the marmalade set up properly). Since all these peels are going into the marmalade, make sure to clean them well, then place the fruit in a Dutch oven with 10 cups of water and bring it to a boil over high heat.

Simmer until tender: Once the fruit has come to a boil, turn the heat down until the water is just simmering. Cover the Dutch oven with heavy-duty aluminum foil (or a double layer of regular foil) to minimize the evaporation, then place the lid on top. Let it simmer away for 2½ to 3 hours, until the fruit is so soft it can be easily pierced with a skewer. Then take the Dutch oven off the heat and let everything sit overnight to cool.

A good squeeze: Remove the fruit from the pot (leave the cooking liquid, now thick with pectin, behind). Sometimes the fruit's skin breaks during cooking; that's not a problem. Quarter each piece (both oranges and lemons) and scrape the pulp and seeds back into the Dutch oven and reserve the peels. There's still more pectin-y goodness to be extracted from the pulp and seeds, so when all the guts are in the pot, I squish them up just to make sure all the pectin is as exposed as possible. Then bring it to a boil and let it bubble away for 10 full minutes.

Strain and press: After the pulp and seeds are finished simmering, strain the liquid into a bowl, stirring and pressing the solids lightly, just to get all the good stuff out. Discard the guts and return the liquid back to the pot.

Chop chop: While the pulp simmers, you can take care of chopping the lemon and orange peels. Yep, I'm that person; I like to stack them for this step. I take each stack and slice them lengthwise into four or five strips, then cut them crosswise into pieces. A lot of people complain about the chopping part of marmalade production, but since the fruit is cooked until soft, it's actually really easy—you could almost do this with a plastic spoon. Some might prefer to chop the peel in the food processor. I couldn't possibly comment on that.

Add peels, then sugar: Add the chopped peels to the pot of strained liquid and bring it to a boil again. (This is starting to seem a bit repetitive, I know, but we're entering the home stretch.) Add the sugar (yes, 9 cups of it, which is about 4 pounds), which, following tradition, has been warmed through in a roasting pan in a 250-degree oven. I add the sugar off the heat (this guards against sugar recrystallizing once melted) and stir until the sugar is fully dissolved. Return the pot to the heat and bring the mixture to a boil. Now turn the heat down and let everything simmer for about 30 minutes.

Wrinkles are good: After 30 minutes, it's time to start checking whether the marmalade has reached the set point. I like to put a teaspoonful on a cold plate and place it in the freezer to chill for a couple of minutes. Take the plate out of the freezer and push at the jam with your finger. If it wrinkles (like you see here), it's done. If it doesn't, let the marmalade cook for another five minutes and test it again. Repeat the process until the marmalade wrinkles on the cold plate.

Makes about four 1-pint jars
Start today, enjoy tomorrow

- **10 cups water**
- **2 pounds Seville oranges, scrubbed**
- **2 lemons, scrubbed**
- **9 cups sugar**

1. Combine water, oranges, and lemons in Dutch oven and bring to boil over high heat. Reduce heat to low, and bring down to gentle simmer. Cover pot with heavy-duty aluminum foil, crimping at edges to seal tightly. Cover with lid and simmer until fruits can be easily pierced with skewer, 2½ to 3 hours. Remove pot from heat and let cool overnight at room temperature.

2. Adjust oven rack to middle position and heat oven to 250 degrees. Place sugar in roasting pan, cover tightly with foil, and transfer to oven to warm.

3. Remove fruit from cooking liquid and set pot aside, leaving liquid in pot. Cut fruit (both oranges and lemons) into quarters and, using spoon, scrape pulp and seeds back into pot, reserving peels. Mash pulp lightly with hands or potato masher. Bring to boil over high heat and boil for 10 minutes. Strain liquid through fine-mesh strainer set over large bowl, pressing lightly on solids with rubber spatula; discard solids. Return strained liquid to now-empty pot.

4. Place small plate in freezer. Slice orange and lemon peels lengthwise into thin strips, then crosswise into ½-inch pieces. Transfer chopped peels to pot and bring to boil, then remove pot from heat. Add warm sugar to pot and stir gently until sugar is completely dissolved, 1 to 2 minutes. Return pot to medium-high heat and vigorously simmer marmalade, stirring occasionally, until slightly thickened and darker, about 30 minutes.

5. To test for set point, place 1 teaspoon of marmalade on chilled plate and place in freezer for 2 minutes. Gently push cooled marmalade with finger; marmalade should wrinkle around edges when set. If not set, return marmalade to medium-high heat and simmer 5 minutes longer before retesting.

6. Transfer marmalade to jars with tight-fitting lids, let cool to room temperature, then cover and refrigerate. Jam can be refrigerated for up to 2 months.

TO PROCESS FOR LONG-TERM STORAGE: In step 6, transfer marmalade, while still hot, to hot, sterilized 1-pint jars, leaving ¼ inch of headspace at top, and process following Canning 101 steps on page 71. Processing times depend on your altitude: 5 minutes for up to 1,000 feet, 10 minutes for 1,001 to 6,000 feet, and 15 minutes for above 6,000 feet. Store in cool, dark place for up to 1 year.

Fig-Balsamic Jam

WHY THIS RECIPE WORKS: Figs have always seemed exotic to me. Perhaps because they make a fleeting appearance in New England stores and farmers' markets during late summer and early fall. But also because, even though I've always admired their beauty, I've been at a loss for what to do with them other than serve them on a cheese board.

That changed when I discovered fig jam. My path to fig jam was a recipe a former test cook gave me many years ago: a simple tart slathered with fig jam and topped with caramelized onions, blue cheese, thyme, and prosciutto. If you have bought fig jam before, my guess is that you have bought a jar of the Turkish fig jam found at most supermarkets. While it works fine in some recipes, it's definitely lacking when spread on toast or used in any more pure way. I've found jams at gourmet stores, but they can be really pricey. All this led me to try my hand at making it myself.

Since figs and balsamic vinegar have a natural affinity for one another, my starting point was simple: figs, sugar, water, and balsamic vinegar. Adding mustard and rosemary lent some defining savory notes, giving me a jam that could feel just as at home at breakfast as it would at dinner.

This recipe is much easier than just about any jam I've ever made: There's no pectin required, no hours standing at the stove nervously watching for that moment when a giant pot of simmering, foaming fruit magically gels into jam. Basically, it's foolproof. It pairs perfectly with just about any crusty bread and cheese: goat cheese, Manchego, or soft, ripe Brie. And it also tastes great served alongside roast pork.

—ELIZABETH CARDUFF, Editorial Director, Books

"My path to fig jam was a recipe a former test cook gave me many years ago: a simple tart slathered with fig jam and topped with caramelized onions, blue cheese, thyme, and prosciutto."

Prep first: Place 1½ pounds figs in a colander and wash them gently. Next, stem the figs and chop them roughly. You should have about 4 cups.

Sugar, balsamic, and savory seasonings: Place the chopped figs in a large nonstick skillet over medium-high heat and add 1¼ cups sugar. Then add ½ cup good balsamic vinegar and an equal amount of water. Bring this mixture to a boil. Reduce the heat to low and mix in the seasonings. I like to use mustard seeds to further enhance the savory notes of the jam and give it some bite—they lend subtle heat and a little texture, too. Some lemon juice, chopped fresh rosemary, salt, and pepper round out the jam's flavors.

Test for the trail: Simmer, stirring occasionally, until the mixture is just thickened and jamlike, 35 to 40 minutes. A spatula will make a trail through this mixture when you're done.

Process for perfect texture: Transfer the mixture from the skillet to a large liquid measuring cup (this will keep you from making a mess), then pour it into the food processor. Pulse until the mixture has a uniform, but still slightly chunky, texture.

Jar it: If you're not going to can the jam for long-term storage (I don't think it's necessary unless you do a double batch), simply pour it into jars (a canning funnel makes this task mess-free), let it cool, then cover and refrigerate for up to one month.

Fig-Balsamic Jam

Makes about three 1-cup jars
Make today, enjoy immediately

1½	**pounds fresh figs, stemmed and chopped coarse**
1¼	**cups sugar**
½	**cup balsamic vinegar**
½	**cup water**
2	**tablespoons lemon juice**
1	**tablespoon yellow mustard seeds**
1	**teaspoon minced fresh rosemary**
	Salt and pepper

1. Combine figs, sugar, vinegar, and water in 12-inch nonstick skillet and bring to boil over medium-high heat. Reduce heat to medium-low, and stir in lemon juice, mustard seeds, rosemary, pinch of salt, and ¼ teaspoon pepper. Simmer, stirring occasionally, until rubber spatula or wooden spoon leaves distinct trail when dragged across bottom of skillet, 35 to 40 minutes.

2. Transfer jam to food processor and pulse until uniform but still chunky, about 4 pulses. Transfer jam to jars with tight-fitting lids, let cool to room temperature, then cover and refrigerate. Jam can be refrigerated for up to 1 month.

TO DOUBLE AND PROCESS FOR LONG-TERM STORAGE: Double ingredients and substitute Dutch oven for skillet. In step 1, increase simmering time to 50 to 55 minutes. In step 2, increase pulses in food processor to 8 pulses. Then transfer jam, while still hot, to hot, sterilized 1-cup jars, leaving ¼ inch of headspace at top, and process following Canning 101 steps on page 71. Processing times depend on your altitude: 5 minutes for up to 1,000 feet, 10 minutes for 1,001 to 6,000 feet, and 15 minutes for above 6,000 feet. Store in cool, dark place for up to 1 year.

Canning 101

Canning is a fantastic way to preserve foods you love, from jams and jellies to all manner of pickles, so that you can enjoy them throughout the year. You might hesitate to jump into canning, but it is actually a very simple and safe process, especially if you stick with water-bath canning, as we do in this book. Here is a quick overview, including the equipment you'll need and a walk-through of how to can recipes using a water bath.

Equipment

It pays to have the right equipment for water-bath canning. You don't need anything too fancy or expensive. You can typically find everything you need at a good kitchen supply or hardware store, and they often sell all-in-one canning kits to make the shopping that much easier.

1. A LARGE (18- TO 21-QUART) CANNING POT is key for processing and sterilizing the jars (you can also sterilize the jars in the dishwasher).

2. A CANNING INSERT WITH HANDLES (OR A RACK) that fits inside the pot makes pulling the jars out of boiling water a snap. Often canning pots are sold with a rack, but we prefer the insert, since it makes the canning process easier.

3. GLASS CANNING JARS (AKA MASON JARS) are sold with flat metal lids and threaded metal screw bands that hold the lids in place during processing.

4. A CANNING-SPECIFIC JAR LIFTER works better than tongs when pulling filled jars out of a water bath because it allows you to grasp the jars firmly.

5. A WIDE-MOUTH STAINLESS STEEL FUNNEL makes pouring liquids, like jams, into jars tidy and easy.

Types of Salt

When using a significant amount of salt in a recipe, as is the case in many pickling and curing recipes, the type of salt you use matters. First, don't use iodized salt. Second, note that kosher salt has a coarser crystal structure and packs fewer ounces into each cup compared with table salt. In fact, even the volume measurements between the two major brands of kosher salt—Morton and Diamond Crystal—vary significantly. We use Diamond Crystal, but you can easily adjust for Morton. Here's how they measure up:

1 CUP TABLE SALT = 1½ CUPS MORTON KOSHER SALT = 2 CUPS DIAMOND CRYSTAL KOSHER SALT

Step-by-Step Water-Bath Canning

1. PRE-STERILIZE

It's easiest to sterilize jars using your dishwasher. Or, wash them in hot, soapy water, then simmer them in your canning pot, covered with water, for 10 minutes. The jars should still be

warm, when it's time to fill them. To avoid damaging lids, simmer them separately in a small pan of hot water over medium heat. You don't have to sterilize the bands or tongs, but dipping the funnel and ladle in the pot of boiling water is quick and simple.

2. HEAT WATER, MAKE THE RECIPE, FILL THE JARS

Because boiling the large amount of water necessary for processing takes time, fill your canning pot with water and start heating it well in advance.

Your recipe and the jars should both be warm when it's time to can, so if your recipe takes more than 30 minutes, you can prepare it before sterilizing the jars; otherwise prepare it after sterilizing the jars. Fill the still-warm jars with the prepared recipe, leaving headspace at the top as specified in the recipe (typically ¼ or ½ inch). If pickling, make sure the fruit or vegetable is fully covered by the pickling liquid. Stir the contents to release air bubbles, wipe the rim of each jar clean, then put on the lids and screw on the bands fingertip-tight (don't completely tighten them so air in the jar can escape).

3. PROCESS

Place the filled jars in the canning insert and lower the insert into the pot of boiling water (or lower the jars into the pot and onto the rack using a jar lifter), making sure the jars are

covered by at least 1 inch of water. Process the jars for the amount of time prescribed in the recipe, making sure the water is at a rapid boil before you start the clock. Processing times vary not only based on the size of the jars you are using but also altitude. As elevation increases, water boils at lower temperatures that are less effective for canning. We specify the times for various elevations in each recipe. After the processing time is up, turn off the heat and let the jars sit in the water for 5 minutes.

4. COOL

Remove the cans from the pot using the canning insert and jar lifter (or just use a jar lifter to remove the jars if you are only using a rack) and let the jars cool on a wire rack or towel for 24 hours.

During cooling, you should hear a popping noise, which is the sign that the jars are sealed airtight and the process is complete. You can check the seal by removing the bands; the lid should be taut and should adhere tightly to the rim of the jar. Store sealed jars in a cool, dark place; they will keep for at least 1 year.

Can You Can It? Food Acidity and Water-Bath Canning

When processing foods using the water-bath canning method, the food being canned must possess a certain acidity level. If the food is not acidic enough, there is a risk bacteria can grow. We include directions for water-bath canning with those recipes that have the proper acidity level; recipes such as our Mango Chutney (page 86) are too low in acidity and should be stored in the refrigerator.

Spicy Tomato Jam

✔️ **WHY THIS RECIPE WORKS:** The next time you are seduced into buying several pounds of tomatoes, consider this spicy tomato jam. My inspiration came from Darina Allen, who runs the world-renowned Ballymaloe Cookery School in Ireland. In her book *Forgotten Skills of Cooking*, I spotted a tomato-chile jam. A simple recipe: tomatoes, red chiles, garlic, ginger, sugar, vinegar, and something totally unexpected—fish sauce. I had to try it, then came up with my own version. You'll find yourself spooning it over eggs, spreading it on sandwiches, topping burgers with it, slathering it on meatloaf, and eating it on crackers with your favorite stinky cheese.

—ELIZABETH CARDUFF, Editorial Director, Books

A plum choice: I start by coring, halving, and then chopping 2 pounds of plum tomatoes. Although you could use any variety, plum tomatoes are meatier; plus, you can get away with not peeling them. Even in the dead of winter, you can usually get your hands on decent plum tomatoes, putting this jam within reach year-round.

The secret's in the (fish) sauce: For the jam's spicy base, puree the following in your food processor: a large stemmed, seeded, and minced jalapeño (if you want your jam to be spicier, add the jalapeño seeds too), a half dozen minced garlic cloves, grated ginger, and ¼ cup fish sauce. I know this sounds like a lot of fish sauce, but trust me—your jam will not taste fishy. As the jam cooks down, it will take on a mysteriously deep, earthy, and spicy flavor.

All in the skillet: Scrape this mixture out of the food processor into a large nonstick skillet with the tomatoes, sugar, and some red wine vinegar. It's not required, but I also like to add a couple of star anise pods; they add some depth of flavor to the mix.

Mash and jam: The mixture will look loose at first, but don't worry; it will hit just the right consistency after some time on the stove. Bring the mixture to a boil over medium-high heat, then lower the heat to keep it simmering. Cook for about half an hour, until it turns a dark red color and looks jammy. At this point, remove the star anise pods if you've added them, get out your potato masher, and mash around in the skillet to give the jam a smoother, silkier consistency.

Cook it down: Then continue to cook it down just a bit more. You will know it's done when you can see a trail when you run your spatula or wooden spoon down the middle of the skillet.

All done: This recipe makes a small amount and you'll certainly want to start using it right away, so there's no need to can it (unless you opt to make a bigger batch). Simply transfer the jam to a liquid measuring cup (for easy pouring) and pour the jam into sterilized jars. Let it cool, then cover with a lid and store it in the refrigerator—or why wait? Bring out the cheese and dig in.

Spicy Tomato Jam

Makes about two 1-cup jars
Make today, enjoy immediately

¼ **cup fish sauce**
6 **garlic cloves, minced**
1 **large jalapeño chile,
   stemmed, seeds reserved,
   and minced**
1 **tablespoon grated fresh
   ginger**
2 **pounds plum tomatoes,
   cored and cut into ½-inch
   pieces**
1¼ **cups sugar**
¾ **cup red wine vinegar**
2 **star anise pods (optional)**

1. Process fish sauce, garlic, jalapeño, reserved jalapeño seeds, if desired, and ginger in food processor until combined, scraping down bowl as needed, about 10 seconds. Transfer mixture to 12-inch nonstick skillet, add tomatoes, sugar, vinegar, and star anise, if using, and bring to boil over high heat. Reduce heat to medium-high and simmer, stirring often, until mixture has thickened and darkened in color, 25 to 30 minutes.

2. If using them, remove and discard star anise. Mash jam with potato masher to an even consistency. Continue to simmer until rubber spatula or wooden spoon leaves distinct trail when dragged across bottom of skillet, 5 to 10 minutes longer. Transfer jam to jars with tight-fitting lids, let cool to room temperature, then cover and refrigerate. Jam can be refrigerated for up to 3 weeks.

TO DOUBLE AND PROCESS FOR LONG-TERM STORAGE: Double ingredients and substitute Dutch oven for skillet. In step 1, increase simmering time to 50 minutes to 1 hour. In step 2, increase simmering time to 10 to 20 minutes. Then transfer jam, while still hot, to hot, sterilized 1-cup jars, leaving ¼ inch of headspace at top, and process following Canning 101 steps on page 71. Processing times depend on your altitude: 5 minutes for up to 1,000 feet, 10 minutes for 1,001 to 6,000 feet, and 15 minutes for above 6,000 feet. Store in cool, dark place for up to 1 year.

Caramelized Onion Jam

✔️ **WHY THIS RECIPE WORKS:** Caramelized onion jam is a test-kitchen favorite—it pairs well with numerous dishes and its savory sweetness and rich color belie its simplicity. The key to keeping it truly simple is moving the bulk of the time spent caramelizing the onions to the oven. With 4 pounds of onions in the pot, this saved us from a lot of stirring. Returning it to the stovetop, we added sugar, port, and vinegar and turned our onions into jam, ready for topping burgers, stirring into onion dip, accompanying cheese platters, or garnishing pizzas. For just the right consistency, make sure you let the jam come to room temperature before using.

—THE TEST KITCHEN

Opt for the oven: We use the oven to caramelize the onions since it's effective and virtually hands-free. Using yellow onions is key; sweet onions, such as Vidalia or Walla Walla, will turn gummy. Slicing the onions "pole to pole," or from the root to the stem, gave us better results than slicing them crosswise along the equator, which, once cooked, produced unappealing stringy pieces. Lastly, we cook the onions covered for the first hour to keep them moist. Then we crack the lid to let excess moisture evaporate and encourage browning. Once browning begins, it's key to stir the onions every half hour.

Add flavor: Once the onions have caramelized, pull them from the oven, dump the whole mess onto a cutting board and chop into 1-inch pieces, then transfer them to a large saucepan. When we first made this recipe, we used a simple combination of port and sugar to build the jammy base, but the finished product was a clumpy mess and too sweet. In the end, we found that adding water loosens the mixture, white wine vinegar balances the sugar, and a sprinkling of fresh thyme adds depth.

Cook it down: You'll know the jam is finished when it turns thick and glossy and a spatula or wooden spoon leaves a trail when dragged across the bottom of the saucepan. Serve this versatile jam alongside a wedge of cheese, as part of a sandwich, spread on pizza, or stirred into a dip.

Caramelized Onion Jam

Makes about 2½ cups

Make today, enjoy immediately

- 3 **tablespoons olive oil**
- 4 **pounds onions, halved and sliced through root end into ¼-inch-thick pieces**
  Salt and pepper
- ¾ **cup ruby port**
- ½ **cup water**
- ⅓ **cup sugar**
- ¼ **cup white wine vinegar**
- 2 **teaspoons minced fresh thyme**

1. Adjust oven rack to lower-middle position and heat oven to 400 degrees. Coat inside of Dutch oven with vegetable oil spray. Heat oil in prepared Dutch oven over medium heat until shimmering. Stir in onions and 1 teaspoon salt. Cover, place pot in oven, and cook for 1 hour. (The onions will be moist and slightly reduced in volume.)

2. Remove pot from oven and stir onions, scraping bottom and sides of pot. Return pot to oven, partially covered, and continue to cook, until onions are deep golden brown, 1½ to 1¾ hours, stirring onions and scraping bottom and sides of pot every 30 minutes. Transfer onions to cutting board, let cool slightly, and then chop into rough 1-inch pieces.

3. Transfer chopped onions to large saucepan, stir in port, water, sugar, vinegar, and thyme and bring to simmer over medium heat. Cook until liquid is reduced and rubber spatula or wooden spoon leaves distinct trail when dragged across bottom of saucepan, 8 to 10 minutes. Season with salt and pepper to taste.

4. Transfer jam to jar with tight-fitting lid, let cool to room temperature, then cover and refrigerate. Jam can be refrigerated for up to 2 weeks. Bring to room temperature before using.

Bacon Jam

✔ WHY THIS RECIPE WORKS: After I tell someone I'm in a book club, I can almost guarantee the response: "What are you reading now?" That's when I explain that we haven't read a book since our first meeting two years ago, at which point we realized we were all more interested in eating than reading. At every get-together since, we've been far too concerned with our latest cooking and dining adventures to talk about anything else.

It was at one of our meetings that I was first introduced to bacon jam. At the time, bacon was the hot new ingredient on dessert menus, the inspiration behind dozens of bacon-lovers' websites, and the main component in wacky products like bacon mayonnaise and bacon lip balm. I'd always been a fan of bacon, but I'd never had it in this jammy form: smoky-sweet, with a spreadable texture. I was hooked.

Bacon jam isn't exactly what it sounds like. (Although if you're thinking it sounds delicious, then yes, it's exactly what it sounds like.) It's essentially bacon simmered in its fat along with a lot of flavorings, then processed to a spreadable texture. After making a few batches inspired by bacon marmalade (a mouth-watering, chewy, sweet version from a Brooklyn-based company) and recipes on various blogs, I settled on my own.

Bacon, onions, garlic, coffee, vinegar, maple syrup, and brown sugar make up the foundation, while shallots, honey, allspice, and chili powder help complete the rich, meaty, sweet, and smoky profile. It's amazing on a burger or egg sandwich, in a grilled cheese (or paired with any stinky cheese), or used as the bacon in a BLT, for starters. And as for the book club, we recently decided to break from tradition and assign some actual reading—a cookbook, of course.

—MARI LEVINE, Associate Editor, Web Editorial

"I'd always been a fan of bacon, but I'd never had it in this jammy form: smoky-sweet, with a spreadable texture. I was hooked."

Let it fry: Allowing the bacon to properly crisp before transferring it to a paper towel-lined plate is the first step—and a difficult one for me since I am not a patient cook. It can take almost 20 minutes to crisp up because there is so much of it. To keep myself from removing the bacon from the pot prematurely, I slice the onion, garlic, and shallots while the bacon cooks. It's an efficient use of time, and it keeps my hands busy so they don't touch the bacon before they should.

Put the fat to work: Once the crisped bacon has been set aside, the rendered fat left in the pot serves two purposes beyond being a cooking oil. First, it boosts the bacon flavor. Second, it gives the final jam a smooth, almost creamy, consistency. So into the pot go the onion, garlic, and shallot, which I cook in the fat until they're softened.

Cook it down: Once the onions have softened, return the crisped bacon to the pot and add the liquids and sweeteners—coffee, water, vinegar, maple syrup, and honey—plus allspice and chili powder for some smoky, warm depth. This recipe takes a couple of hours to prepare, but the bulk of that happens here, waiting for the mixture to cook down to a glazy, jammy consistency. The mixture will thicken and start to darken in color. I know it's just about ready to puree when the rubber spatula I'm using to stir the pot leaves a distinct trail.

Keep some fat, lose the rest: Simmering the ingredients in the rendered bacon fat infuses them with meaty flavor, but pureeing the whole mixture would make the jam overly greasy. Use a slotted spoon to transfer the bacon mixture to a food processor. Let the mixture drain pretty well before you put it in the food processor; it should just be glistening with fat but not swimming in the stuff. Some fat will still make it to the processor workbowl, but that's what you want. It is key to have a little in there to get the right texture once the jam is pureed.

Just the right process: The final texture depends completely on personal preference. I like my bacon jam on the chunky side, when it's got texture but is spreadable. Pulse it a few times, then check the consistency. If the bacon pieces are still a little too big for your liking, pulse it another few times. Just remember, you can always process it more, but you can't go backward.

Bacon Jam

Makes about 1½ cups

Make today, enjoy immediately

- 1 **pound thick-cut smoked bacon, cut into 1-inch pieces**
- 1 **large onion, halved and sliced thin**
- 1 **shallot, minced**
- 5 **garlic cloves, minced**
- ¾ **cup brewed coffee**
- ½ **cup water**
- ⅓ **cup cider vinegar**
- ⅓ **cup maple syrup**
- 2 **tablespoons packed brown sugar**
- 1 **tablespoon honey**
- 1 **teaspoon ground allspice**
- 1 **teaspoon chili powder**

1. Add bacon to Dutch oven and cook over medium-high heat, stirring occasionally, until crisp, about 20 minutes. Using slotted spoon, transfer bacon to paper towel–lined plate, leaving rendered fat in pot.

2. Return pot to medium heat, add onion, shallot, and garlic, and cook, stirring occasionally, until onion is softened, about 10 minutes. Return bacon to pot, then stir in coffee, water, vinegar, maple syrup, sugar, honey, allspice, and chili powder. Bring to simmer and cook, stirring occasionally to prevent scorching, until mixture thickens and rubber spatula or wooden spoon leaves distinct trail when dragged across bottom of pot, 1 to 1½ hours.

3. Remove from heat and let bacon mixture cool for 15 minutes. Using slotted spoon, transfer mixture to food processor, leaving excess fat behind. Discard excess fat. Pulse bacon mixture until finely chopped, about 5 pulses, or until mixture has reached desired consistency. Transfer jam to jar with tight-fitting lid. Jam can be refrigerated for up to 2 weeks. Bring jam to room temperature before using.

Red Pepper Jelly

PECTIN

Available in both liquid and dry form, commercial pectin can be found in the baking aisle at the supermarket. Be aware the two forms are not interchangeable; we found the liquid to be a little more foolproof.

✔ **WHY THIS RECIPE WORKS:** Whether it's lace curtains, water aerobics, or Alan Alda's best performance, chances are good I'd have something to chat about with your grandma. That list also includes pepper jelly, a Southern classic enjoyed by pearl-wearing grand dames. Draped over cream cheese and slathered on water crackers, pepper jelly is punchy-hot (not slap-you-in-the-face hot) and devilishly sweet. My pepper jelly, I decided, would be ruby red—the same color as the most famous shoes ever.

The basic procedure for my recipe is as follows: Chop red peppers and habaneros (red, red, red!), break them down further using the food processor, boil with white vinegar and sugar, add pectin, and boil until it hits the magic temperature where the jam sets.

While the vinegar, sugar, and pepper amounts were easy enough to suss out, there was one ingredient I had some trouble with: the pectin. Pectin is a naturally occurring substance in many fruits that acts as a gelling agent. For jellies and jams calling for low-pectin fruit or veggies (as is the case here), another solution has to come into play—be it a second, higher-pectin ingredient (green apple or citrus peel are common) or commercial pectin, which can be purchased at most supermarkets or online. The recipe I was working with (my grandmother's, of course) called for liquid pectin, so that's where I started. It took several tests to determine that I was using too much of the stuff—my jelly was way too stiff. Cutting it in half and cooking the jelly beyond the temperature on the pectin package gave me jelly that set perfectly every time without being gloppy. I may have tweaked my grandmother's recipe a bit, but this is a red pepper jelly that I know would make her proud.

—KATE HARTKE, Associate Editor, Books

Pepper prep: After cutting off the tops of the bell peppers and removing the stems, seeds, and ribs, slice down the side of each and open it up like a book. Cut the peppers lengthwise into strips, then crosswise into small pieces. Before moving on to the habaneros, I highly recommend putting on latex gloves, since their seeds and ribs release oils that burn. Prep the habaneros just as you did the bells. I like my jelly without the habanero seeds, but if a spicier jelly is what you're after, hold on to them.

Chop and squeeze: Transfer the peppers to the food processor and pulse until they are broken down into tiny pieces and have released their juice. The processor is faster and does the job more evenly than is possible by hand, and it's better at drawing out the peppers' liquid, which needs to be drained off. Dump the processed peppers into a kitchen towel set over a bowl and gather the corners and squeeze several times to drain all the liquid from the peppers.

Pour on the sugar: Dump the contents of the towel into a large Dutch oven (I'd suggest washing your hands right here to rinse away the oils from the peppers. Or just wear latex gloves for the bundle-squeezing step too.) Add the vinegar and sugar to the pot, stir well, and bring the pot to a boil. At this stage, you want to make sure all the sugar dissolves and the peppers begin to break down.

Watch it like a hawk: Once the mixture is vigorously boiling, stir in 3 ounces liquid pectin. I found I had to cook this mixture a fair bit longer than indicated on the pectin packaging for my jelly to set properly (which has to do with the proportion of sugar to water). Keep the heat to high or medium-high and the contents at a very hard boil. Watch closely because it can easily and quickly boil over. You also need to keep close tabs on the rising temperature. When it hits 221 degrees on an instant-read or candy thermometer, which takes 10 to 15 minutes, you're golden.

Let it set, then put it to work:
Using a canning funnel, ladle the jelly into clean 1-cup jars. The jelly won't quite look like jelly yet, but it won't be as liquidy as when you started. After some time in the fridge, it will be just right. I think its perfect match is cream cheese. With a few jars always on hand, it makes for an easy appetizer with a homemade touch.

Red Pepper Jelly

Makes about five 1-cup jars

Make today, enjoy tomorrow

3 **large red bell peppers (8 ounces each), stemmed, seeded, and chopped coarse**

2 **habanero chiles, stemmed, seeds reserved, and chopped coarse**

5 **cups sugar**

2 **cups distilled white vinegar**

1 **(3-ounce) envelope liquid pectin**

1. Pulse bell peppers, habaneros, and reserved habanero seeds (if desired) in food processor until finely minced, 12 to 15 pulses, scraping down bowl as necessary. Transfer pepper mixture to clean kitchen towel set over bowl and squeeze to remove excess liquid.

2. Combine drained peppers, sugar, and vinegar in Dutch oven and bring to vigorous boil over medium-high heat. Add pectin and return to vigorous boil, stirring frequently, until temperature registers 221 degrees, 10 to 15 minutes. Using large spoon, skim foam from top of jelly.

3. Transfer jam to jars with tight-fitting lids, let cool to room temperature, then cover and refrigerate. Let jelly set in refrigerator for 12 to 24 hours. Jelly can be refrigerated for at least 2 months.

TO PROCESS FOR LONG-TERM STORAGE: In step 3, transfer jelly, while still hot, to hot, sterilized 1-cup jars, leaving ¼ inch of headspace at top, and process following Canning 101 steps on page 71. Processing times depend on your altitude: 5 minutes for up to 1,000 feet, 10 minutes for 1,001 to 6,000 feet, and 15 minutes for above 6,000 feet. Store in cool, dark place for up to 1 year.

Wine Jelly

WHY THIS RECIPE WORKS: I don't know if the American Psychiatric Association has a list of personality traits for first-born children, but if they do, I'm sure "entitled" would be near the top. My "what's yours is mine" instinct has led me to appropriate a Miss Piggy doll from my sister, bracelets from my mom, a toothbrush from a college roommate (not my proudest moment), and anything on my husband's plate or in his glass. My commandeering knows no bounds. Case in point: The canning set my father-in-law received for his birthday last year now resides in my kitchen closet.

Truth be told, he gave it to me after I spent hours in his kitchen pickling vegetables, sealing sour cherries in liqueur, and infusing batches of strawberry jam with lavender. You know you have a canning addiction when you hope that an oncoming hurricane will knock out your power, just so you'll have an excuse to spend a day putting things in jars.

Spring and summer are the prime seasons for canners, but I've figured out how to get my fix during the off-months with recipes like wine jelly. It only requires the most basic ingredients: sugar, pectin, lemon juice, and wine. Making wine jelly is also a great way to turn a cheap bottle (I prefer Merlot) into a luxuriant treat. (Of course if you are willing to sacrifice a nicer bottle, it will only improve the jelly's taste.) It brings an elegant yet personal touch to any cheese board.

My next few jars of wine jelly are earmarked as "sorry I stole your Muppet," "sorry I raided your jewelry box," "sorry I used your toothbrush," and "sorry I continue to violate your personal table space." Even if Hallmark had turned those sentiments into cards, something tells me wine jelly says it better.

—SHANNON HATCH, Assistant Editor, America's Test Kitchen

> *"Spring and summer are the prime seasons for canners, but I've figured out how to get my fix during the off-months with recipes like wine jelly. It only requires the most basic ingredients: sugar, pectin, lemon juice, and wine."*

Red wine reductions aren't just for steak: Most wine jelly recipes have you empty the entire bottle straight into a pot, add sugar, and start cooking. However, I have found that reducing a portion of the bottle going into the jelly intensifies the wine's flavor while cutting the booziness. Reducing 1¼ cups down to ⅓ cup can take 20 minutes, so it's best to get it going first, even though the reduced wine won't go in until the end.

Hitting the sweet spot: Sugar plays an important role in jelly making: it helps preserve, set, and flavor the final product. Thinking of cutting back on sweetness? Think again. Dialing it back too much will prevent your jelly from congealing. I started testing by dissolving 3½ cups sugar in the remaining wine on the stovetop. But I felt the sweetness was a bit too much, so I started cutting it back. I was only able to lose ¼ cup sugar before my jelly lost its jiggle. Nevertheless, it was a change that definitely helped.

Pectin and butter: Some purists shy away from commercial pectin, but since this recipe starts with bottle of wine, not a plethora of pectin-rich fruit, it seemed like a hassle to do anything other than rip open a pouch of the liquid stuff. Along with it, I stir in a little lemon juice (for flavor) and a dot of butter. The butter seems weird, but there's a reason. As the mixture boils, air bubbles rising to the surface create foam. Most recipes require skimming foam (it can cause problems when canning, plus it doesn't look great), but I found the fat from a little butter allows the bubbles to surface, then disappear.

Bring on the reinforcements: Lastly, I add the reduced wine to give the jelly a final punch of flavor. The jelly will still be quite fluid at this point, but don't worry, it will set up perfectly after a little time (you may notice it thickening on the sides of the saucepan or on your spoon).

Let set overnight: Transfer your finished wine jelly to jars. Just remember that sometimes it takes up to 24 hours for the wine mixture to gel and really look like jelly. You just gotta be patient. Once it's set, I serve the jelly with a wide range of cheeses, from soft goat to pungent blue, or even smoky Idiazabal.

Wine Jelly

Makes about four 1-cup jars
Make today, enjoy tomorrow

1	**(750-ml) bottle red wine**
3¼	**cups sugar**
1	**(3-ounce) envelope liquid pectin**
3	**tablespoons lemon juice**
⅛	**teaspoon butter**

1. Bring 1¼ cups wine to boil in small saucepan over medium-high heat, and cook until reduced to ⅓ cup, 15 to 20 minutes; set aside.

2. Bring remaining wine and sugar to boil in large saucepan, stirring frequently. Stir in pectin, lemon juice, and butter, and return to vigorous boil, stirring constantly, for 1 minute. Remove from heat and stir in reserved reduced wine.

3. Transfer jelly to jars with tight-fitting lids, let cool to room temperature, then cover and refrigerate. Let jelly set for 12 to 24 hours. Jelly can be refrigerated for at least 2 months.

TO PROCESS FOR LONG-TERM STORAGE: Transfer jelly, while still hot, to hot, sterilized 1-cup jars, leaving ¼ inch of headspace at top, and process following Canning 101 steps on page 71. Processing times depend on your altitude: 5 minutes for up to 1,000 feet, 10 minutes for 1,001 to 6,000 feet, and 15 minutes for above 6,000 feet. Store in cool, dark place for up to 1 year.

Mango Chutney

✓ **WHY THIS RECIPE WORKS:** For most Americans, the staple condiment is ketchup. My family goes for something more exotic: chutney. Chutneys have been a staple in Indian households for centuries, and no wonder. With their sweet-savory, tart-spicy balance, chutneys add intrigue to most any dish. I went with classic mango, which complements the fruit's grassy sweetness with brown sugar, vinegar, and warm spices. It's perfect for jazzing up roasts, fish, and cheese plates. Who needs ketchup? I'd even put this chutney on a burger. Because of its low acidity, this chutney cannot be water-bath processed; store it in the refrigerator and use within three weeks.

—BRYAN ROOF, Senior Editor, *Cook's Country*

A spicy start: The best mango chutneys strike a balance between warm spices, sweet mango, sugar, and tangy vinegar. I quickly settled on dry mustard, cinnamon, cayenne, and cloves for the spices. To take advantage of their natural oils, I start by blooming them in oil to coax out as much flavor as possible. Then I add a minced red onion for some savory depth and sauté it until softened. Some minced garlic and grated ginger go in next for a burst of heat.

Mango time: After adding several diced mangos and brown sugar (which I prefer to granulated for its caramel flavor), I let the fruit cook down until its juice releases and the mixture begins to thicken. I like to make mango chutney in the summer when mangos are ripest, but fret not if it's January and there is no ripe fruit; the flavor will be great regardless. (Most traditional recipes actually call for unripe mangos.) In these off-season cases, you can add a little extra brown sugar to taste at the end. After 10 to 15 minutes of cooking, it's time to add the water, vinegar, and raisins.

Simmer down: Once everything's in the pan, turn the heat up to medium-high to bring it to a simmer. Let the chutney simmer away until it has cooked down into a thicker consistency. After about 30 minutes, you should be able to see a film beginning to stick to the bottom of the pan. At that point, you could transfer it to a jar for storage or, if you were in my house, you would more likely put it straight to use.

Mango Chutney

Makes about four 1-cup jars
Make today, enjoy immediately

- 2 **tablespoons vegetable oil**
- 1 **teaspoon dry mustard**
- ½ **teaspoon ground cinnamon**
- ⅛ **teaspoon cayenne pepper**
  Pinch ground cloves
- 1 **red onion, minced**
  Salt and pepper
- 4 **garlic cloves, minced**
- 1½ **tablespoons grated fresh ginger**
- 4 **mangos, peeled, pitted, and cut into ¼-inch pieces (6 cups)**
- ½ **cup packed light brown sugar, plus extra as needed**
- 2 **cups water**
- ½ **cup raisins**
- ¼ **cup white wine vinegar**

1. Heat oil in large saucepan over medium heat until shimmering. Stir in mustard, cinnamon, cayenne, and cloves and cook until fragrant, about 10 seconds. Add onion and 1 teaspoon salt and cook until softened, 5 to 7 minutes. Stir in garlic and ginger and cook until fragrant, about 30 seconds. Add mangos and sugar and cook, stirring occasionally, until mangos release their liquid, 10 to 15 minutes.

2. Stir in water, raisins, and vinegar and increase heat to medium-high. Vigorously simmer, stirring occasionally, until mixture is thickened and begins to stick to bottom of pan, 30 to 40 minutes. Season with salt, pepper, and sugar to taste.

3. Transfer chutney to jars with tight-fitting lids, let cool to room temperature, then cover and refrigerate. Chutney can be refrigerated for up to 3 weeks (do not water-bath process this recipe).

Green Tomato Chutney

✓ **WHY THIS RECIPE WORKS:** There comes a time every summer when fall breezes keep tomatoes, content to stay green, on the vine. While these rock-hard fruits may seem a waste to some, I think they're an opportunity. Sure, you can fry 'em, but I prefer to make chutney. Accented with the citrusy warmth of coriander, heat from red pepper flakes, plus sugar, vinegar, and lemon juice, this lip-smacking-good condiment is also a breeze to make. No peeling or seeding tomatoes; just chop, combine everything, and simmer. Serve it with roast meats, with a creamy, mild cheese, or if you want to show 'em who's boss, dollop it over those fried green tomatoes.

—BRYAN ROOF, Senior Editor, *Cook's Country*

It's easy being green: The unripe exterior of green tomatoes hides a plethora of sweet-tart flavor ready for the harvesting. (Even if your tomatoes are turning ever so slightly pink, they'll taste just the same in the chutney as the exclusively green ones.) Much of the flavor is bound up in the juice, seeds, and peel of the tomatoes, so we certainly don't want to toss any of that out. There's no peeling, juicing, or seeding here. All you need to do is cut out the cores of the tomatoes, then chop them into rustic 1-inch chunks.

All in the pot: Green tomatoes are naturally a little bit sweet and a little bit tart, so my recipe plays off these flavors. I brought in a hint of citrus with coriander seeds and lemon juice, cranked up the heat with red pepper flakes, and used equal parts granulated sugar and white vinegar to round it out. Toss all these ingredients in a Dutch oven, mix well, and bring it to a simmer. It can simmer rapidly at first, but as the liquid cooks off, turn down the heat and stir frequently to prevent scorching.

Green goodness: You know the chutney is ready when the tomatoes have broken down, the vinegar has evaporated, and you're left with thick, sticky preserves in the pot. I stir in the lemon juice after cooking to preserve its bright flavor. Then just transfer the chutney to four 1-cup jars and either process the jars for long-term storage, or let the mixture cool before transferring it to the fridge. If I have a plethora of tomatoes, I double the batch and end up with a bounty of canned gifts for my friends.

Green Tomato Chutney

Makes about four 1-cup jars
Make today, enjoy immediately

4	**pounds green tomatoes, cored and cut into 1-inch pieces**
1½	**cups sugar**
1½	**cups distilled white vinegar**
2	**teaspoons coriander seeds**
2	**teaspoons salt**
½	**teaspoon red pepper flakes**
4	**teaspoons lemon juice**

1. Bring tomatoes, sugar, vinegar, coriander, salt, and pepper flakes to boil in Dutch oven over medium-high heat. Reduce heat to medium-low and simmer, stirring occasionally, until mixture thickens to jamlike consistency and rubber spatula or wooden spoon leaves distinct trail when dragged across bottom of pot, about 2 hours. Stir in lemon juice.

2. Transfer chutney to jars with tight-fitting lids and let cool to room temperature before refrigerating. Chutney can be refrigerated for up to 1 month.

TO DOUBLE: Double ingredients and simmer tomato mixture for 3 to 3½ hours in step 1.

TO PROCESS FOR LONG-TERM STORAGE: In step 2, transfer chutney, while still hot, to hot, sterilized 1-cup jars, leaving ½ inch of headspace at top, and process following Canning 101 steps on page 71. Processing times depend on your altitude: 10 minutes for up to 1,000 feet, 15 minutes for 1,001 to 6,000 feet, and 20 minutes for above 6,000 feet. Store in cool, dark place for up to 1 year.

Peach Mostarda

"Between the kick from dry mustard and mustard seeds, warmth from a mix of spices, and sweet-tart hit from cider vinegar, sugar, and orange juice, my simple version of mostarda packs a flavorful, warm-and-spicy, sweet-and-savory punch…"

✔ WHY THIS RECIPE WORKS: As a kid I always carried around a Swiss army knife. It was a symbol that I was ready to "MacGyver" a solution for whatever situation might arise. Today, that ready-for-anything attitude still holds, especially when it comes to cooking. Now I stock my fridge with "multipurpose" foods. I'm armed at all times with condiments, jams, pickles, and preserved meats that can be used in a multitude of ways at a moment's notice. With these tools, I can elevate a meal from ordinary to spectacular.

One of my favorite multipurpose foodstuffs is *mostarda,* a traditional sweet and hot Italian condiment consisting of various candied whole or halved fruits preserved in a syrup that's been boosted with the piquant heat of mustard oil and seeds. It can play well with everything from roast meats to desserts. But candying fruit isn't fast or easy, and mustard oil is hard to find (even worse, it's not approved for consumption by the FDA). My version of this condiment is simpler. It skips the candying and instead preserves cooked halved peaches (slightly underripe ones work best) in a mustardy sugar syrup. It also relies on easier-to-get ingredients. Still, between the kick from dry mustard and mustard seeds, warmth from a mix of spices, and sweet-tart hit from cider vinegar, sugar, and orange juice, my simple version of mostarda packs a flavorful, warm-and-spicy, sweet-and-savory punch that is very much like the traditional version—and equally addictive.

I serve this simple mostarda alongside roasted pork or chicken, chopped into a relish and spooned over seared fish, as a finishing touch to a pan sauce, as a garnish on a cheese plate, or even warmed up and served over homemade ice cream. I suggest you try it first with roast pork, then see what you can MacGyver up on your own.

—CHRIS O'CONNOR, Associate Editor, America's Test Kitchen

Let it macerate: My peach mostarda begins with a few easy-to-obtain ingredients: peaches, sugar, spices, and seasonings. The first step is drawing some of the liquid out of the peaches to make a spice-infused cooking syrup. Combine your peeled peaches with sugar, orange juice, salt, cloves, star anise, bay leaves, and cinnamon, and stir until all of the sugar is moistened. At this point, the peaches need to be covered and refrigerated for 24 hours. The acid in the orange juice as well as the sugar and salt will help draw the liquid out of the peaches.

A juicy flavor infusion: By the next day, the peaches will have released quite a bit of liquid, creating a syrup that's infused with the flavors of the spices. Depending on the juiciness of the peaches, some of the sugar may not have fully dissolved; we'll take care of that next.

Dissolve the sugar: To make sure the peach halves stay intact, I remove them from the liquid and set them aside for this step. Use a slotted spoon to remove the fruit from the syrup-spice mixture and put them in another bowl for now, then transfer the sugary syrup and spices left behind in the bowl to a saucepan. Simmer that syrup mixture until all of the sugar is fully dissolved.

Into the syrup: Now it's time to cook the peaches through. Carefully place them in the syrup and bring it back up to a very gentle simmer.

...and back out of the syrup:
Simmer the peaches until they are just tender. Depending on how ripe they were to begin with, it will take between 10 and 15 minutes. They are done when a paring knife can easily pierce them. When they get to this point, use a slotted spoon to carefully transfer the cooked peaches to a jar with a tight-fitting lid.

Reduce the syrup, then give it a mustardy punch: With the peaches set aside, increase the heat to medium and reduce the syrup to 1½ cups, which generally takes about five minutes. Don't let it go too far or you might not have enough syrup left to cover the peaches (it's fine to have extra, but it's a problem to not have enough). Once the syrup is reduced, whisk together the dry mustard, whole-grain mustard, and cider vinegar, then stir that mixture into the syrup.

Swimming in spicy sweetness:
Next, carefully pour the hot, mustardy syrup over the cooked peaches (you might have some extra syrup, which you can just pitch). At this point, most of the hands-on work is done and it's time to sit back and let the peaches' flavorful syrup do its job.

Waiting time: The jarred mostarda should be covered and refrigerated for at least two weeks. During this time the peaches will preserve and take on the full flavor of the mustard and spices. You'll be surprised at how many different uses you can come up with for this condiment. Be creative!

Peach Mostarda

Makes about 1 quart
Start today, enjoy in 2 weeks

2	**pounds peaches, peeled, halved, and pitted**
2¼	**cups sugar**
½	**cup orange juice**
½	**teaspoon salt**
5	**whole cloves**
3	**star anise pods**
3	**bay leaves**
1	**cinnamon stick**
¼	**cup dry mustard**
¼	**cup whole-grain mustard**
3	**tablespoons cider vinegar**

1. Combine peaches, sugar, orange juice, salt, cloves, star anise, bay leaves, and cinnamon in large bowl. Cover and refrigerate for 24 hours.

2. Using slotted spoon, gently transfer peaches to separate bowl and set aside. Pour sugar syrup and spices from bowl into large saucepan. Cook syrup and spices over medium heat until sugar is completely dissolved, about 3 minutes. Carefully add peaches to syrup and bring to boil. Reduce heat to low and simmer until peaches are just tender and tip of knife inserted into peach meets with very little resistance, 10 to 15 minutes.

3. Using slotted spoon, transfer peaches to 1-quart jar with tight-fitting lid. Increase heat to medium, and return syrup to boil. Cook until syrup reduces to 1½ cups, about 5 minutes.

4. In small bowl, whisk dry mustard, whole-grain mustard, and vinegar together; then whisk mixture into reduced syrup. Pour hot syrup over peaches to cover, discarding any remaining syrup, and let cool to room temperature. Refrigerate peach mostarda for 2 weeks to preserve before using. Mostarda can be refrigerated for up to 3 months.

Apple Butter

"I wanted to take all the things I loved about my mother's applesauce and intensify them into an unctuous, sweet butter that needed no embellishments. Like a modern-day Johnny Appleseed, I was on a mission to spread my apple gospel to the masses."

✔ **WHY THIS RECIPE WORKS:** My mother makes the world's best applesauce. Period. You can try to debate me on that, but you'll lose, and I don't want to make you cry. Now, I'll admit to a certain nostalgia when it comes to the aroma of autumn's apples bubbling on the stovetop in my childhood home, but somehow my mother's applesauce tasted more, well, apple-y than any others I have tasted—homemade or store-bought. She didn't do anything fancy, just cooked down apples with some sugar and a hint of cinnamon, but whether it was her choice of apples, the perfect amount of sugar, or the chunky texture, the combination was sublime: a sweet bowl of apple goodness, best eaten warm right out of the saucepan.

Given my love for the sauce, I thought apple butter would be a sweet treat right up my alley. I mean, what could be better than even more apple flavor, this time spreadable on toast? Imagine my disappointment, then, when I tasted my first overspiced spoonful of the dark spread. Instead of intense apple, all I tasted was an overabundance of cinnamon, nutmeg, and cloves. Where did the apples go?

Since apple butter is essentially applesauce cooked long enough for the apples to caramelize into a dark paste while the liquid evaporates, I saw no reason to add a surfeit of seasonings and make my fresh apples taste like a dusty spice rack. Instead, I wanted to take all the things I loved about my mother's applesauce and intensify them into an unctuous, sweet butter that needed no embellishments. Like a modern-day Johnny Appleseed, I was on a mission to spread my apple gospel to the masses—and convince the nutmeg-loving naysayers to channel their energies into mulled cider and pumpkin pie.

—CHRISTIE MORRISON, Associate Editor, Books

Go apple picking: Nothing says autumn like McIntosh apples; their sweet flavor provides my recipe's backbone, while slightly tart Fujis add complexity. Some might argue that peeling the apples before cooking is best because it's easier to not deal with the skins when it's time to mash them. They are right, it is easier—but not necessarily better. I want to get every bit of apple essence, so cooking the apples with their flavorful skins is essential. I core them, then cut the McIntosh apples into 2-inch pieces. Since Fujis take longer to cook, I cut them into 1-inch pieces to even the cooking time.

Amp up the apple: The apples need some liquid in which to cook. Many recipes use a small amount of water, but that just sounds like a quick way to dilute the flavor to me. I start with apple cider, then, since I hold with the culinary school of thought that says most things taste better with a bit of spirit, I also add some deep, pungent Calvados. Bring the apples, cider, and Calvados to a boil in a Dutch oven, reduce the heat, and leave the apples to simmer, covered (peeking in to check and stir once or twice).

Oh, soften up: After about 30 minutes, your kitchen will smell better than a Yankee Candle. At this point, the apples should be soft and pliable—the perfect texture for the next step: the food mill.

A time to mill: Remember how we left the skins on to extract all that flavor? Well, now we have to remove them so they don't mess up the texture. It just so happens that in addition to providing you with a great upper-body workout, a food mill is also good for removing the skins from apples. Working in batches, transfer the apples to the mill and start to mill . . . and mill . . . and mill. While this isn't my favorite way to spend 10 minutes, it gets the job done, leaving the skins in the mill and pushing the now-smooth apples into a waiting bowl.

A sweet combination: Next, return the puree to the Dutch oven. To sweeten the apples, I had initially added 1½ cups of plain old granulated sugar. But, always looking for ways to enhance flavor, I ended up replacing ½ cup with brown sugar for some extra depth and subtle molasses flavor.

Add some punch: To keep the apple flavor bright and fresh, lemon juice provides a hit of acid, while salt balances the sweetness and acidity. Give it all a stir, set the Dutch oven on the back burner, and let heat, sugar, and time work their magic (with a few stirs to prevent scorching).

The telltale trail: It takes about an hour and a half for the butter to cook down; you will know it's ready when it has darkened to a rich brown color and thickened enough to leave a solid trail behind the path of the spoon or spatula. If you're not sure whether it has reduced enough (it's often hard to tell when it's hot), chill a small plate in the freezer, then drop a spoonful of butter on the plate and see how easily it spreads. If it's the consistency of a very thick but spreadable jam, you've got apple butter, my friend!

Apple butter bliss: Apple butter is delicious spread on toast or scones. My favorite way to eat it (other than with a spoon straight from the jar), however, is atop a bowl of cottage cheese. There's something about the thick apple goodness set against the creamy, slightly tangy curds that makes me smile. I think my mother would approve.

Apple Butter

Makes about 3 cups

Make today, enjoy immediately

- **2 pounds McIntosh apples, cored, quartered, and cut into 2-inch pieces**
- **2 pounds Fuji apples, cored, quartered, and cut into 1-inch pieces**
- **1 cup apple cider**
- **1 cup Calvados or applejack**
- **1 cup granulated sugar**
- **½ cup packed light brown sugar**
- **3 tablespoons lemon juice**
- **¼ teaspoon salt**

1. Combine apples, cider, and Calvados in large Dutch oven, and bring to boil over medium-high heat. Reduce heat to medium-low, cover, and simmer, stirring occasionally, until apples are very soft, about 30 minutes.

2. Working in batches, transfer apples to food mill and process. Discard skins and transfer puree to now-empty Dutch oven. Stir in granulated sugar, brown sugar, lemon juice, and salt. Simmer over low heat, stirring occasionally, until mixture is browned and thickened and rubber spatula or wooden spoon leaves distinct trail when dragged across bottom of pot, 1 to 1½ hours. Transfer apple butter to jar with tight-fitting lid and let cool to room temperature before refrigerating. Apple butter can be refrigerated for up to 1 month.

Marmelada (Quince Paste)

QUICK QUINCE LESSON

This firm, fragrant, yellow fruit is available from autumn to early winter. Quince have a slightly gritty, pearlike texture when cooked; they're very tart and astringent when raw.

✔ WHY THIS RECIPE WORKS: Friends have hinted that, when it comes to international travel, my priorities are out of whack. As soon as I arrive in a new, exotic locale, I make a beeline for the place that is sure to fascinate me for hours: the neighborhood supermarket. I contend that if you really want to learn about a culture, a visit to the grocery store is far more enlightening than a museum. Are the locals suspicious and brusque, or are they welcoming and patient? Are they proud of their traditions? Do they value their health and well-being? The answers await you in aisle 2.

So it was that I found myself in the Supermercado Modelo in Albufeira, Portugal, several years ago. I wandered the enormous supermarket, collecting local specialties as I meandered: olives, sheep's milk cheese, red wine, dried fish, cured sausage, almonds, and a sticky, red-brown brick of something called *marmelada*. A fellow shopper kindly advised me that it was meant to be sliced thin and served with cheese. So that's what I did when I got back to my rented apartment. The sweet, not-quite-smooth, slightly astringent gel provided a perfect counterpoint to the salty, crumbly cheese. It was my favorite discovery of that trip.

Marmelada is essentially quince (*marmelo* in Portuguese) jam that has been cooked down to create a thick, sliceable paste. It is known by several other names: quince paste, quince cheese, and in Spain, *membrillo*. In Latin America, it is often cut into cubes, coated in sugar, and eaten as candy.

While it does take some time, it's easy to make, and my version's ingredient list couldn't be much simpler. Some cooks add vanilla or spice, but I think that's gilding the lily. Quince paste rounds out an impromptu cheese board nicely, and it makes a thoughtful hostess gift.

—ANDREA GEARY, Associate Editor, *Cook's Illustrated*

Curious about quince?: The quince might not be all that familiar to you; maybe you've just passed them by, thinking they are odd-looking pears. They appear in markets from about September through December and taste like something between a pear and an apple, but they're very tart and astringent—far better for cooking than eating raw. Even in their uncut state, they have an amazing fruity-floral aroma. And since they contain a lot of pectin, they are great for recipes such as this.

Keeping down a floating fruit: Start by placing the cored and quartered fruit in a Dutch oven or large heavy saucepan, then cover it with water. Because the fruit floats when it's raw, I put a circle of parchment on the surface of the water, just to keep everything submerged. Bring the water to a boil, then reduce the heat until the fruit is just simmering. Cover the pot and let the fruit cook gently until it is very soft, which takes about an hour and a half. I know they're ready when a paring knife pierces the fruit with no resistance.

Super juice: Next I drain the fruit, and I save the cooking liquid since it has a lot of flavor and pectin that can be put to good use. Cooking that reserved liquid down a bit concentrates the flavor and cooks off water.

Smooth it out: I run the drained quince in the food processor and puree it until smooth. And actually, the puree only looks smooth; the processor doesn't manage to take it quite far enough. So I pass it through a fine-mesh strainer before returning it to the pot where the reduced cooking liquid is waiting.

A safe finish: Add the sugar and lemon juice, stir, then bring it to a boil. Reduce the heat and simmer until the mixture starts to turn red and sputter and "bloop" like the boiling mud pits at Yellowstone. It's almost dangerously bloopy, so I let it finish in the oven to avoid incidental burns.

Seriously thick: Once it's in the oven, make sure to stir every so often, and scrape down the sides each time. I know it's done when it's a dark red-brown and so thick a spatula leaves a clean trail. It's critical for it to get very thick; otherwise it won't set up properly. It should be starting to caramelize a bit at the edges.

Block out: Once it's there, I scrape it into a parchment-lined pan and let it cool to room temperature before putting it into the fridge. Leave it there for at least four hours so it can get really solid. After it has had time to set, I turn the firm paste out onto a cutting board and cut it into blocks. Because the paste is so sticky, I like to wrap the cut portions in parchment, which is a little easier to work with, and then plastic wrap so they'll last several months in the fridge.

Marmelada (Quince Paste)

Makes about 3 pounds (one 8 by 8-inch block)

Make today, enjoy immediately

3½   **pounds quinces, cored and quartered**
8   **cups water**
4   **cups sugar**
¼   **cup lemon juice (2 lemons)**

1. Combine quinces and water in Dutch oven and place parchment paper round (cut to fit) over surface to keep fruit submerged. Bring to boil over high heat. Cover, reduce heat to medium-low, and simmer until quinces are very soft and can be easily pierced with knife, about 1½ hours. Drain quinces through colander set in large bowl, reserving liquid (it should measure about 5 cups).

2. Pour reserved liquid into now-empty Dutch oven and bring to boil over medium-high heat. Boil until liquid is reduced to 3 cups, 12 to 15 minutes. Meanwhile, process quinces in food processor until very smooth, about 45 seconds, scraping down bowl as needed. Working in small batches, pass puree through fine-mesh strainer set over medium bowl; discard solids (you should have about 4 cups puree).

3. Adjust oven rack to middle position and heat oven to 350 degrees. Grease 8-inch square baking pan, line with parchment, and set aside. Add quince puree to reduced liquid in Dutch oven. Stir in sugar and lemon juice and bring to boil. Reduce heat to medium-low and simmer, stirring occasionally, until puree darkens, becomes very thick, and begins to spatter and "bloop," about 30 minutes.

4. Transfer to oven and cook until puree turns dark rusty brown and is thickened, and rubber spatula leaves distinct trail when dragged across bottom of pot, 1 to 1½ hours, stirring and scraping sides of pot every 15 minutes. Scrape into prepared pan, smooth top, and let cool to room temperature. Refrigerate for at least 4 hours until set and firm.

5. Invert baking pan onto cutting board. Remove parchment and cut quince paste into desired portions. Wrap each piece in parchment, then plastic wrap. Quince paste can be refrigerated for up to 6 months.

Pickle It:
From Cucumbers
to Kimchi

104   Sour Dill Pickles

108   Bread-and-Butter Pickles

111   Pickle Relish

114   Dilly Beans

116   Pickled Watermelon Rind

119   Pickled Beets

122   Giardiniera

124   Sauerkraut

127   Kimchi

Sour Dill Pickles

NOT YOUR COMMON CUKE

Kirby, or pickling, cucumbers are not the common cukes you see in supermarkets year-round. Pickling cukes are stubby, usually have a bumpy exterior, and have thinner, lighter skin and smaller seeds than the familiar dark green, long cucumbers. Their thin skin, small size, and lesser amount of watery seeds make them well-suited to pickling. You'll find them cropping up in summer months in some super-markets and farmers' markets.

✔ **WHY THIS RECIPE WORKS:** At my very first job, between scribbling down orders and scooping ice cream, I was often found in the walk-in fridge gobbling down a juicy dill pickle from a giant bucket (sorry, Friendly's). Briny, garlicky, and crisp, a full-sour dill pickle satiated my wicked salt cravings—and still does. After all these years, I finally realized that if I just made my own, I could have a never-ending stash.

First, I had to decide whether I wanted a quick-vinegar or fermented dill pickle. Quick pickles are steeped in a salty vinegar solution and are ready in as little as a few hours. They're good in a pinch, but the sour bite is really just skin deep, as they rely on the vinegar for flavor. With fermented pickles, a saltwater brine is poured over whole cucumbers and they are left to sit. Natural fermentation takes over and the cucumber transforms—all the way to its very center—into a true sour pickle. (A little vinegar is added at the beginning, but it's only enough to keep things food-safe until fermentation kicks in.) This type of pickle can take some time to cure, but the reward is a pickle with a genuine sour bite that's not for wimps. To get the full flavor of a tangy deli-style kosher dill pickle, I was willing to wait for fermentation to do its thing. You should, too.

Be aware that if your garlic is very fresh, it will likely turn blue. Don't worry; it's just reacting to the acid. Note that when fermenting, cleanliness of both the ingredients and your utensils is critical.

—YVONNE RUPERTI, Associate Editor, America's Test Kitchen

The best brine: The first step is to make the saltwater brine. The amount of salt is critical: Salt keeps the bad bacteria at bay (my first batch turned moldy because the salt concentration was too low), but using too much can slow fermentation to a halt. With more than half a cup of kosher salt to 8 cups of water, my brine is fairly salty. I also add vinegar, just enough to keep it food-safe until fermentation kicks in. Dissolve the salt in half of the water over medium-high heat, then stir in the rest of the water and vinegar. Let the brine cool to room temp before pouring it over the cucumbers.

Superlative sours: My pickles took just 10 days to get the flavor that I wanted, but it could take longer. They can sit at room temperature for up to 21 days. When the flavor is where you want it, transfer them to the refrigerator. They'll keep on fermenting in there (at a much slower pace than they do at room temperature). Of course in my house, these babies never last long enough to get the chance!

Sour Dill Pickles

Makes 10 to 12 pickles
Start today, enjoy in 10 to 21 days

8	cups water
½	cup plus 1 tablespoon Diamond Crystal kosher salt (see page 70)
¼	cup distilled white vinegar
10–12	small (3 to 4 ounces each) pickling cucumbers, rinsed well
20	sprigs fresh dill
20	garlic cloves, peeled and smashed
1	tablespoon dill seeds
1½	teaspoons whole peppercorns

1. Bring 4 cups water and salt to boil in large saucepan over high heat. Off heat, whisk in remaining 4 cups water and vinegar. Let cool to room temperature.

2. Using sterilized tongs, tightly pack cucumbers, dill, garlic, and spices into sterilized 3- to 4-quart jar or crock with tight-fitting lid, leaving 2-inch space at top of jar. Fill jar with brine, leaving 1-inch space at top of jar, making sure all pickles are submerged. (Reserve remaining brine in refrigerator.) Press piece of parchment paper against surface of brine, then weight with small plate or bowl. Cover jar with triple layer of cheesecloth and secure with rubber band; store at room temperature in relatively cool place and away from direct sunlight.

3. Check pickles daily, skimming off any residue on surface of brine, and topping off with reserved brine, as needed, to keep pickles submerged. Taste pickles after 10 days to gauge level of fermentation; pickles should be yellow-green in color and sour in flavor. For more sour pickle flavor, continue to ferment at room temperature (in cool place) for up to 11 days longer. Remove cheesecloth, cover, and refrigerate pickles for up to 1 month.

Bread-and-Butter Pickles

"Their sweet-salty flavor and remarkable crispness got me hooked. I remember eating the pickles every which way, including my mom's specialty: cream cheese, ham, and pickle sandwiches served on English muffins. After that summer, it became the one and only cucumber pickle I craved."

✓ **WHY THIS RECIPE WORKS:** I'll never forget the day I came home from lifeguarding one summer to see my mother elbow-deep in a bowl filled with 5 pounds of thinly sliced cucumbers, muttering about sugar, salt, and the sanity (or lack thereof) of my grandmother. Spurred on by the abundance of cucumbers in our garden, she had decided to tackle her mother's recipe for making an enormous batch of bread-and-butter pickles.

At that point in my adolescence, I couldn't fathom the idea of making pickles at home. Even if I could have, I was a full-fledged dill pickle devotee at that time, known to steal many a wedge from an unsuspecting family member's hamburger platter. I turned up my nose at anything other than a lip-puckering spear. But my grandmother's bread-and-butters opened up a whole new world of pickles to me. The cucumbers were accented with thinly sliced onions and red bell peppers, and seasoned with warm, savory spices (mustard and celery seeds, turmeric, and ground cloves). A strong hand with the sugar gave them a sweet backbone, but the vinegar-based brine brought them back in balance. Their sweet-salty flavor and remarkable crispness got me hooked. I remember eating the pickles every which way, including my mom's specialty: cream cheese, ham, and pickle sandwiches served on English muffins. After that summer, it became the one and only cucumber pickle I craved.

When I sat down to remake the recipe in my own kitchen, I thought I'd want to give the whole recipe a makeover. But after some testing, I realized only a couple tweaks were needed. The original was near-perfect as written.

—KATE WILLIAMS, Test Cook, Books

Pick less than a peck:
I knew I wanted to scale my grandmother's recipe to work with a more manageable 2 pounds of cucumbers; I use kirby, aka pickling, cucumbers (see page 104 for more info). The thinly sliced onion and red bell pepper in the original recipe were keepers, lending variety and color. Granulated sugar and water make up the bulk of the brine, but instead of using white vinegar like my grandmother, I call for cider vinegar, which adds a fruity sweetness. Then I flavor the whole caboodle with traditional B&B spices: mustard seeds, turmeric, celery seeds, and ground cloves.

Slice 'em thin: I like to thinly slice all of the vegetables for these pickles (anything to help pile lots of layers of pickles onto my sandwiches!), but I don't do it by hand. A mandoline comes in handy here. Not only does it give my knives a break, but it also ensures even slices and thus even pickling. Slice the cucumbers, onion, and red pepper all ⅛ inch thick.

Ice down: Next I toss all the sliced vegetables together in a bowl with ¼ cup kosher salt. The salt draws water out of the vegetables, helping to leave them crisp and well-seasoned. I cover the salted vegetables with a layer of ice before sticking the bowl in the fridge to ensure they chill as quickly as possible. After three hours in the fridge, the vegetables will have let off much of their liquid, and the onions and peppers will have wilted ever so slightly. Drain and rinse the vegetables.

Boil and bubble: Next, stir the cider vinegar, sugar, water, mustard seeds, turmeric, celery seeds, and cloves together in a Dutch oven until the sugar dissolves, and bring the whole mixture to a boil. This is your brine. Next, carefully add the drained salted vegetables, bring the mixture once again to a boil, and then immediately remove it from the heat. This short cooking time is just enough to start the pickling process.

All jarred up: Divide the pickles and brine evenly among your glass jars (making sure an even amount of spices falls into each jar), let cool, and then transfer them to the fridge. The pickles will be ready to eat in a couple of days, and will keep for about two months, once opened, in the fridge. Most of the time I like to eat my bread-and-butters straight up out of the jar. They are also killer on burgers, grilled cheese, and, of course, my mom's specialty: cream cheese and ham sandwiches.

Bread-and-Butter Pickles

Makes four 1-pint jars
Make today, enjoy in 2 days

- 2 **pounds pickling cucumbers, sliced ⅛ inch thick**
- 1 **onion, halved and sliced through root end into ⅛-inch-thick pieces**
- 1 **red bell pepper, stemmed, seeded, and cut into ⅛-inch-wide strips**
- ¼ **cup Diamond Crystal kosher salt (see page 70)**
- 5–7 **cups ice cubes**
- 2 **cups cider vinegar**
- 2 **cups sugar**
- 1½ **cups water**
- 1 **tablespoon yellow mustard seeds**
- ¾ **teaspoon turmeric**
- ½ **teaspoon celery seeds**
- ¼ **teaspoon ground cloves**

1. Toss cucumbers, onion, bell pepper, and salt together in large bowl. Cover with single layer of ice cubes and refrigerate for 3 hours. Discard ice, then rinse and drain vegetables well.

2. Bring vinegar, sugar, water, mustard seeds, turmeric, celery seeds, and cloves to boil in Dutch oven over medium-high heat. Add rinsed vegetables, return to boil, and immediately remove from heat.

3. Using slotted spoon, transfer pickles to jars with tight-fitting lids. Pour hot brine over pickles, evenly distributing spices, let cool to room temperature, then cover and refrigerate for 2 days before eating. Pickles can be refrigerated for up to 2 months.

TO PROCESS FOR LONG-TERM STORAGE: Transfer pickles and brine, while still hot, to hot, sterilized 1-pint jars, leaving ½ inch of headspace at top, and process following Canning 101 steps on page 71. Processing times depend on your altitude: 10 minutes for up to 1,000 feet, 15 minutes for 1,001 to 6,000 feet, and 20 minutes for above 6,000 feet. Store in cool, dark place for up to 1 year.

Pickle Relish

✓ WHY THIS RECIPE WORKS: When we buy a hot dog at a baseball game or from a street-cart vendor, it's pretty hard to pass up pumping on a good pile of yellow mustard and bright-green sweet pickle relish. It feels like the right thing to do and hey, in the moment it tastes pretty good. But employ a squirt of squeeze-bottle relish on a dog or burger off your home grill and somehow all the flaws seem more clear. The relish is gloppy, too sugary, and a strangely unnatural color. So we came up with a from-scratch version that balances sweet and tart, and it is as fresh tasting and crispy-crunchy as a summer cucumber relish should be.

—THE TEST KITCHEN

Chop chop: The first step in making relish is to get the texture just right, which means doing a good job when it comes to the chopping and mincing. We prefer to leave this task to the food processor. In addition to the cucumbers (use kirby, aka pickling cukes; see page 104 for more info), we also add green bell peppers and onion for balanced sweetness. Chop all the vegetables by hand into 1-inch chunks that the processor can manage, then give each veg a few pulses in the processor so they're minced just right.

Ice cold: To avoid a watered-down relish, we salt the vegetables, then let them sit for a few hours in the refrigerator. Covering the minced vegetables with ice for this stage ensures they chill quickly.

A good squeeze: After releasing their juices, the bowl of salted vegetables will look pretty soupy. Not to worry. Discard the ice, then transfer the vegetable mixture to the center of a clean kitchen towel. Gather the corners up and wring it out until you can't get another drop of juice to be released. Now it's ready for a briny bath.

Brine time: Pickling the vegetables in a brine made with white vinegar, granulated sugar, mustard seeds, and celery seeds creates a relish with a clean, sweet-tart flavor and a little kick. Bring the brine ingredients to a boil, then add the drained vegetable mixture. Simmer until the cucumbers and onions turn translucent, 10 to 15 minutes. The color of the vegetables does dull a bit, but not to worry, what matters is that the flavor is right on the mark.

Top dog: Transfer the relish to jars, and once it's cool, it's ready to be put to use. This homemade relish adds just the right summery bite to tartar sauce, potato salad, and, of course, burgers and dogs.

Pickle Relish

Makes four 1-cup jars

Make today, enjoy immediately

2	**pounds pickling cucumbers, cut into 1-inch pieces**
2	**green bell peppers, stemmed, seeded, and cut into 1-inch pieces**
1	**onion, chopped coarse**
2	**tablespoons kosher salt**
5–7	**cups ice cubes**
2	**cups distilled white vinegar**
1½	**cups sugar**
4	**teaspoons yellow mustard seeds**
2	**teaspoons celery seeds**

1. In 2 batches, pulse cucumbers in food processor to coarse mixture (chopped fine into ⅛- to ¼-inch pieces), about 6 pulses; transfer to large bowl. Pulse peppers in food processor to coarse mixture (chopped fine into ⅛- to ¼-inch pieces), about 6 pulses; transfer to bowl with cucumbers. Pulse onion in food processor to coarse mixture (chopped fine into ⅛- to ¼-inch pieces), about 10 pulses; transfer to bowl with cucumbers and peppers. Stir in salt until well combined. Cover vegetables with single layer of ice cubes and refrigerate for 3 hours. Discard ice, transfer vegetable mixture to clean kitchen towel, and squeeze to remove excess liquid until almost dry.

2. Bring vinegar, sugar, mustard seeds, and celery seeds to boil in Dutch oven over medium-high heat. Add vegetables, reduce heat to medium, and simmer until cucumbers and onions have turned translucent and mixture has thickened slightly, 10 to 15 minutes.

3. Transfer relish to jars with tight-fitting lids, let cool to room temperature, then cover and refrigerate. Relish can be refrigerated for up to 2 months.

TO PROCESS FOR LONG-TERM STORAGE: Transfer relish, while still hot, to hot, sterilized 1-cup jars, leaving ½ inch of headspace at top, and process following Canning 101 steps on page 71. Processing times depend on your altitude: 10 minutes for up to 1,000 feet, 15 minutes for 1,001 to 6,000 feet, and 20 minutes for above 6,000 feet. Store in cool, dark place for up to 1 year.

Dilly Beans

WHY THIS RECIPE WORKS: As a child, I could tell time by the garden yield. Late June into July the green beans came in with a roar. We'd eat beans for days before Mom would say it was time to pickle. We packed beans in jars with lots of dill, poured over the brine, and a week later— we had pickles! Since then I've made a few tweaks, blanching the beans and making a dill-infused brine. But some things didn't change. After packing the beans with fresh garlic, pepper, and red pepper flakes, I pour over the hot brine—just like Mom did.

—BRIDGET LANCASTER, Executive Food Editor, New Media, Television, and Radio

Pack 'em in: First, it's important to trim the beans to fit your jars; they should come up a little less than ¾ inch from the jar's top. The beans fit best in wide-mouth 1-pint jars; if you use regular-mouth jars, you may have extra beans. I found that dilly beans packed into jars raw had a distracting fibrous texture. So I blanch them first, which results in perfectly crisp-tender beans. Once they're drained and cooled, pack them into the jars along with the garlic, peppercorns, and red pepper flakes. It's easiest to fit everything in the jars if you start with the garlic and spices, and then pack in the beans.

Dill flavor infusion: While most traditional dilly bean recipes pack fresh dill into the jars along with the beans and spices, I discovered that the dill weed becomes sludgy and unappealing over time when added this way. Instead of resorting to dried dill (which has a flat flavor) or dill seeds (too medicinal), I infuse the brine with tons of dilliness by adding a sachet of fresh dill to the pot with the salt, water, vinegar, and sugar. After bringing the brine to a boil, let it steep for a full 10 minutes, then remove the sachet.

Hot soak: Next, bring the dill-infused brine back to a boil, then pour it into the jars with the beans. Pouring it over the beans while hot jump-starts the pickling process (and is a must if you are going to process the jars for storage). Now the work is done; they just need to sit for one week before they're good and pickled. When they're ready, these dilly beans are tender, with a crisp snap at their very center. Be aware that if your garlic is very fresh, it will likely turn blue. Don't worry; it's just reacting to the acid.

Dilly Beans

Makes four 1-pint jars

Make today, enjoy in 1 week

- **2** **pounds green beans, trimmed and cut into 4-inch lengths**
- ½ **cup Diamond Crystal kosher salt (see page 70)**
- **4** **garlic cloves, peeled and quartered**
- **1** **tablespoon whole peppercorns**
- ¼ **teaspoon red pepper flakes**
- **2** **cups fresh dill, stems and leaves chopped coarse**
- **3** **cups distilled white vinegar**
- **3** **cups water**
- **6** **tablespoons sugar**

1. Fill large bowl with ice water. Bring 6 quarts water to boil in large pot over high heat. Add green beans and 2 tablespoons salt and cook until beans are crisp-tender but still crunchy at core, about 1 minute. Transfer immediately to bowl of ice water and let sit until completely cool, about 2 minutes. Drain beans well. Evenly distribute garlic, peppercorns, and pepper flakes between jars with tight-fitting lids, then pack beans tightly into jars (make sure there is ¾ inch between top of beans and jar rim).

2. Bundle dill in cheesecloth and tie with kitchen twine to secure. Combine dill sachet, vinegar, water, sugar, and remaining 6 tablespoons salt in large saucepan and bring to boil over medium-high heat. Cover, remove from heat, and let steep for 10 minutes. Discard dill sachet, then return brine to boil.

3. Pour brine over beans to cover, let cool to room temperature, then cover and refrigerate. Let beans sit in refrigerator for 1 week before eating. Beans can be refrigerated for up to 1 month.

TO PROCESS FOR LONG-TERM STORAGE: After blanching and draining beans in step 1, set beans aside. Wait to pack jars with garlic, peppercorns, and pepper flakes until after preparing brine. Prepare brine as directed, then pack seasonings and blanched beans into hot, sterilized 1-pint jars. Pour hot brine over beans to cover, leaving ½ inch of headspace at top, and process jars following Canning 101 steps on page 71. Processing times depend on your altitude: 5 minutes for up to 1,000 feet, 10 minutes for 1,001 to 6,000 feet, and 15 minutes for above 6,000 feet. Store in cool, dark place for up to 1 year.

Pickled Watermelon Rind

✔ **WHY THIS RECIPE WORKS:** I once worked for two farmers who taught me, among other life lessons, to utilize every bit of every thing. One day they were horrified when I almost threw out pounds of watermelon rind. Since I was from the South (where folks pickle everything), the farmers assumed it would be a snap for me to pickle. Truth was, I'd never pickled a thing. Still, I knew pickled watermelon rind. A picnic favorite, cubes of rind are pickled in a slightly spiced, slightly sweet brine. I took on the their challenge with good Southern grit, and I not only came away with a great life lesson, but also with a recipe I still make today.

—REBECCA MORRIS, Test Cook, Books

Peel it: I don't buy a watermelon with the intention of pickling the rind; this recipe always gets pulled out as a bonus when I'm really after the fruit for a picnic or brunch. These pickles make a great addition to such spreads, so I just remember ahead of time to prep my watermelon for pickling the rind, and set aside the flesh to cut up and serve separately. The green skin on the watermelon is inedible, so it has to go. To make peeling safer, I lop off a little bit from both ends of the melon so it will stand upright on the cutting board. Then I use my chef's knife to cut off the green layer from the exterior.

Flesh it out: Next, I quarter the melon and scoop out the flesh with either a knife or a large spoon (and of course set it all aside for that fruit salad or snacking). I like the look of a little pink left on the rind to lend some color to the pickles, but too much will give them a spongy texture. Leaving just ¼ inch of the flesh intact gives the pickles a nice tinge of color without imparting any off-textures. Then cut the rind into 1-inch chunks.

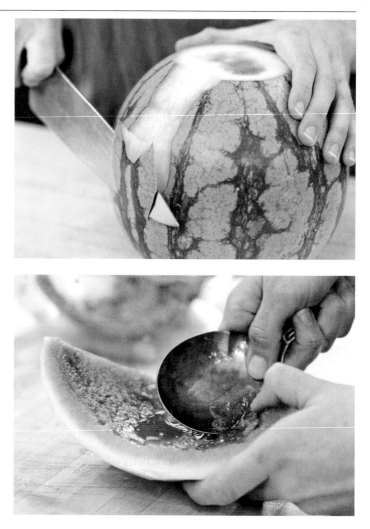

Salt lick: It might be surprising, but just as you would salt cucumbers before pickling them, salting is also a key step when pickling this rind. The salt draws a surprising amount of water out, ensuring crisp pickles and seasoning them at the same time. While pickles made with cucumbers only need to sit in salt for a few hours to release sufficient water, these dense chunks need 8 to 12 hours of draining. A layer of ice on top ensures they become cold as quickly as possible. After their overnight stint salting, the ice will melt, so drain and rinse the rinds, then transfer them to jars, where they'll await their pickling brine.

A clean profile: Most recipes make tooth-achingly sweet pickles with a lot of warm spice like cloves and cinnamon. This may be OK for some, but I wanted something more versatile, pickles I could eat straight, chop and use to top a burger, or even toss into a stir-fry or salad. For a clean profile with a bit of flair, I settled on Asian flavors. Rice vinegar, water, and granulated sugar make up the brine, while lemon grass, ginger, peppercorns, and cardamom lend the seasoning.

Let it steep: To infuse the brine with a delicate flavor that isn't overwhelming, I make a spice sachet and simply steep the spices in the brine. Combine the vinegar, sugar, and water in a large saucepan, then drop in the spice sachet. Bring the brine up to a boil, then pull it from the heat, cover it, and let it steep for 10 minutes. At this point, it's nicely infused, so remove the sachet and bring the brine back up to a boil.

No softies here: A soft pickle should be a punishable offense in my book, so instead of simmering the rinds in the brine "until tender" (read: mushy)—which is what the majority of older recipes have you do—I keep them crunchy by raw packing them. That means I pour the hot brine over the cold, raw rinds, then transfer them to the fridge to pickle. It takes a full 10 days before they are ready (not surprising given watermelon rind's tough nature), but they are definitely worth the wait.

Pickled Watermelon Rind

Makes four 1-pint jars

Make today, enjoy in 10 days

1	**(5- to 6-pound) watermelon**
¼	**cup Diamond Crystal kosher salt (see page 70)**
5-7	**cups ice cubes**
2	**teaspoons cardamom pods**
1	**teaspoon whole peppercorns**
1	**(2-inch) piece ginger, peeled and sliced into ¼-inch-thick rounds**
1	**lemon grass stalk, trimmed to bottom 6 inches and cut into 1-inch pieces**
2	**cups rice vinegar**
2	**cups water**
¾	**cup sugar**

1. Cut off both ends of watermelon and stand upright. Using sharp chef's knife, trim layer of green skin away from rind, then quarter watermelon. Using knife or large spoon, scoop all but ¼ inch of flesh from rind. Cut rind into 1-inch pieces and place in large bowl (you should have 8 cups). Add salt and toss to combine. Cover rind pieces with single layer of ice cubes, cover, and refrigerate for 8 to 12 hours. Discard ice, then rinse and drain rind pieces well. Transfer to jars with tight-fitting lids.

2. Bundle cardamom, peppercorns, ginger, and lemon grass in cheesecloth and tie with kitchen twine to secure. Combine spice sachet, vinegar, water, and sugar in large saucepan and bring to boil over high heat. Remove from heat, cover, and let steep for 10 minutes. Discard spice sachet. Return brine to boil.

3. Pour brine evenly over rind pieces to cover, let cool to room temperature, then cover and refrigerate for 10 days before eating. Pickles can be refrigerated for up to 2 months.

TO PROCESS FOR LONG-TERM STORAGE: After draining watermelon rinds in step 1, set aside; don't pack jars with rind pieces. Prepare brine as directed. In step 3, transfer rinds to hot, sterilized 1-pint jars. Pour hot brine evenly over rinds, leaving ½ inch of headspace at top, and process following Canning 101 steps on page 71. Processing times depend on your altitude: 10 minutes for up to 1,000 feet, 15 minutes for 1,001 to 6,000 feet, and 20 minutes for above 6,000 feet. Store in cool, dark place for up to 1 year.

Pickled Beets

WHY THIS RECIPE WORKS: I spent virtually every weekend of my childhood at my grandparents' rural Pennsylvania home, where the Pennsylvania Dutch influence was strong and the description of most items on the pantry shelf began with "pickled." At the time, of course, nothing appealed to me less than a jarred, briny vegetable…unless it was a beet (briny, sweet, sour, or otherwise). Tasting of dirt and sure to stain anything I was wearing, beets were also the reason I eschewed hard-boiled eggs for years (memories of pickled eggs bobbing in a purple beet-infused brine like a Halloween prank still give me shivers). I was finally shamed into eating a roasted beet in culinary school (childhood phobias don't carry much weight in the kitchen); I experienced my first true culinary epiphany. What was this garnet jewel I tasted? Sweet, with no earthy residue, that beet was a game changer. Shredded raw in a salad? Now I'm all over it. Roasted and sprinkled with goat cheese? Heaven. Pickled in that purple liquid, which makes my childhood seem very close, my grandparents very near, and that now-enviable pantry very, very full? Sigh. Yes, please.

To guarantee I can always snag a bite of beet when the craving hits, I buy a few bunches and get to pickling. Since it's still my preferred method for cooking them, I roast the lot. Then I peel and slice them and toss them in a brine. While more traditional recipes call for cinnamon and allspice, I like to use spicy fresh ginger, licorice-scented star anise, and whole black peppercorns to add dimension without making the beets taste like a spice cake. It's a far cry from my grandmother's recipe, but I have a feeling she wouldn't mind—she'd just be happy that I came around in the end.

—CHRISTIE MORRISON, Associate Editor, Books

"I was finally shamed into eating a roasted beet in culinary school (childhood phobias don't carry much weight in the kitchen); I experienced my first true culinary epiphany. What was this garnet jewel I tasted? Sweet, with no earthy residue, that beet was a game changer."

Clean and roast: Since beets are harvested both in spring and fall, they are a great choice for preserving when other options are few and far between. I prefer to precook them before pickling; roasting is my method of choice since it brings out the beets' sweetness, plus they're easy to peel once roasted. I like beets that weigh 4 ounces or less; larger specimens will work, but they'll need a little extra roasting time (up to an hour and a half, versus an hour for the smaller ones). To speed up the cooking process, wrap each beet in its own foil packet, then place them in a 400-degree oven.

Skewer test, then peel: After about an hour to an hour and a half of roasting, test the beets to see if they're done. They're cooked through when a skewer can pierce them with ease. Be sure to roast the beets until completely cooked; otherwise, the pickles will be too crunchy. Then open up the foil packets and let the beets cool for about 10 minutes before peeling. The skins will come off with just a nudge. I think the easiest way to peel them is to use a few paper towels for grip, but your fingers will work just as well (it's just messier).

The right slice: Quarter the peeled beets, then slice each wedge crosswise into thin, pie-shaped pieces. The pie shape is simply my personal preference; you can cut them into whatever shape you like. However, to ensure even pickling it's important that all the slices are the same thickness. Also, the thicker the slice, the longer the beets will take to soak up the brine. I prefer to slice my wedges pretty thin (between ⅛ and ¼ inch thick) so that they pickle relatively quickly but still retain their structure.

Heat things up: Once the beets are sliced and ready to go, it is time to prepare the brine. For spices, I like a combination of ginger, star anise, and peppercorns, which I tie up in a cheesecloth bundle (so they're easy to fish out later) before adding it to the Dutch oven with white wine vinegar, water, sugar, and salt. Bring this whole mixture to a boil, add the beet slices, and then once again bring the mixture back to a boil. Take the pot off the heat and get ready to put your pickles into jars.

Let it brine: Divide the beets and brine evenly between four 1-pint jars, let them cool to room temperature, and then stick them in the fridge. I like these pickles best after they've been brining for a week; they'll last for six weeks from the time you put them in the fridge. Pickled beets are great on their own as a snack or served on a cured meat and cheese platter. I also like to use them to give a beet and goat cheese salad a sweet-tart twist.

Pickled Beets

Makes four 1-pint jars

Make today, enjoy in 1 week

3	**pounds beets, trimmed**
2	**cups white wine vinegar**
1½	**cups water**
1½	**cups sugar**
1	**teaspoon kosher salt**
1	**(2-inch) piece fresh ginger, peeled and sliced into ¼-inch-thick rounds**
1	**star anise pod**
½	**teaspoon whole peppercorns**

1. Adjust oven rack to middle position and heat oven to 400 degrees. Wrap beets individually in aluminum foil and place on baking sheet. Roast until skewer slips easily into beets, 1 to 1½ hours. Open foil packets, let cool for 10 minutes, then remove skins using paper towels. Quarter beets through root end, then slice thin crosswise.

2. Combine vinegar, water, sugar, and salt in Dutch oven. Bundle ginger, star anise, and peppercorns in cheesecloth, tie with kitchen twine to secure, and submerge in vinegar mixture. Bring vinegar mixture to boil over medium-high heat. Carefully add beets and return to boil. Remove from heat and discard spice sachet.

3. Using slotted spoon, transfer pickles to jars with tight-fitting lids. Pour hot brine over pickles, let cool to room temperature, then cover and refrigerate for 1 week before eating. Pickles can be refrigerated for up to 6 weeks.

TO PROCESS FOR LONG-TERM STORAGE: Transfer pickles and brine, while still hot, to hot, sterilized 1-pint jars, leaving ½ inch of headspace at top, and process following Canning 101 steps on page 71. Processing times depend on your altitude: 30 minutes for up to 1,000 feet, 35 minutes for 1,001 to 6,000 feet, and 40 minutes for above 6,000 feet. Store in cool, dark place for up to 1 year.

Giardiniera

✓ WHY THIS RECIPE WORKS: I first discovered giardiniera, a mix of pickled vegetables with Italian roots, when I was visiting friends in Chicago. They served it simply, in a bowl on the table alongside pasta and salad. Although humble looking, this dish was surprisingly good: crunchy, with a vinegary bite, and almost dangerously hot. It was clear why Italians and Chicagoans alike keep it in their arsenal at all times. Since that trip, giardiniera has served me well tossed with pasta, on sandwiches, and just eaten straight out of the jar. With a little TLC, I hoped to fix what plagues most supermarket brands (harsh brines, flat flavors). It was well worth the effort.

—JULIA COLLIN DAVISON, Executive Food Editor, Books

The perfect mix: I stuck with the traditional giardiniera mix of vegetables since they all hold up well once pickled. Cauliflower florets and celery lend an earthy crunch, red bell pepper and carrots add sweetness, serrano peppers deliver that kick of heat that makes these pickles so addictive, and a little sliced garlic adds depth. After chopping all the vegetables into bite-size pieces, toss them together in a bowl to ensure even distribution, then pack them into your jars. I don't blanch or precook them to make sure they retain their crunch, even if they're processed for storage.

Flavor infusion: I use white wine vinegar instead of the usual distilled white vinegar to give the brine a more mellow, rounded flavor. Water, along with sugar and salt, balances out the harshness and heat. As for flavorings, I love the grassy, anise flavor of fresh dill, but after a couple of weeks in the brine it will turn slimy. Since I don't want to completely lose the dill's flavor, I put it in a sachet and steep it in the hot pickling liquid for 10 minutes.

Distribute: Once the brine has finished steeping, toss the sachet and return the brine to a boil before pouring it evenly into the jars. Fill the jars up until the vegetables are covered (if I am going to process them in a hot water bath, I leave only ½ inch of headspace). You could eat these pickles tomorrow, but it's far better to wait a week, which gives the vegetables a chance to become just a little bit tender. You'll discover all sorts of uses: snacking, adding zing to sandwiches, or tossing in pastas. Get creative—you'll be surprised at all you can come up with. Note that the acid might turn the garlic blue; it's still perfectly safe.

Giardiniera

Makes four 1-pint jars
Make today, enjoy in 1 week

- ½ head cauliflower (1 pound), cored and cut into ½-inch florets
- 3 carrots, peeled and sliced ¼ inch thick on bias
- 3 celery ribs, cut crosswise into ½-inch pieces
- 1 red bell pepper, stemmed, seeded, and cut into ½-inch-wide strips
- 2 serrano chiles, stemmed and sliced thin
- 4 garlic cloves, sliced thin
- 1 cup chopped fresh dill
- 2¾ cups white wine vinegar
- 2¼ cups water
- ¼ cup sugar
- ¼ cup Diamond Crystal kosher salt (see page 70)

1. Toss cauliflower, carrots, celery, bell pepper, serranos, and garlic together in large bowl until combined. Transfer vegetables to jars with tight-fitting lids.

2. Bundle dill in cheesecloth and tie with kitchen twine to secure. Combine dill sachet, vinegar, water, sugar, and salt in large saucepan. Bring to boil over medium-high heat. Cover, remove from heat, and let steep for 10 minutes. Discard dill sachet. Return brine to boil.

3. Pour brine evenly over vegetables. Let cool to room temperature, then cover and refrigerate for 7 days before eating. Pickles can be refrigerated for up to 1 month.

TO PROCESS FOR LONG-TERM STORAGE: In step 1, don't pack jars with vegetables. Prepare brine as directed in step 2, then transfer vegetables to hot, sterilized 1-pint jars. Pour brine, while still hot, evenly over vegetables, leaving ½ inch of headspace at top, and process following Canning 101 steps on page 71. Processing times depend on your altitude: 10 minutes for up to 1,000 feet, 15 minutes for 1,001 to 6,000 feet, and 20 minutes for above 6,000 feet. Store in cool, dark place for up to 1 year.

Sauerkraut

✓ **WHY THIS RECIPE WORKS:** A classic pairing with brats, Reubens, or just about any meat, sauerkraut packs a big punch, yet it's little more than shredded cabbage and salt that have been left to ferment. Naturally occurring bacteria devour sugars in the cabbage, producing lactic acid. The acidity along with the salt keep bad bacteria at bay and lend that trademark sour, funky flavor. Sauerkraut is a snap to make, practically foolproof, and leaves lots of room for flavor experimentation. If mold (which is harmless) appears on the brine, remove as much as you can with a spoon. When fermenting, cleanliness of both the ingredients and your utensils is critical.

—ANDREW JANJIGIAN, Associate Editor, *Cook's Illustrated*

Shred it: After discarding any soft or discolored outer leaves, cut the cabbage into quarters. I like it sliced as thin as possible. How you slice it is entirely up to you: thick or thin, long or short, it'll work fine. Transfer half the cabbage to a bowl, sprinkle 1½ tablespoons kosher salt over it, then top with the rest of the cabbage and another dose of salt. Salting in steps helps to distribute the salt evenly and jump-starts drawing out water. Now knead the heck out of it until it softens and really starts to shed water. It'll take a few minutes to get to this point.

Knead until it hurts: Now add your spices to the bowl, tossing the mixture to combine. Being a gin lover, I'm partial to a juniper berry–flavored kraut myself, but the sky's the limit when it comes to spice or herb add-ins, so long as you don't use too heavy a hand (a tablespoon or so total per 5 pounds of cabbage is good). Transfer the cabbage, a handful at a time, to a clean 1-gallon crock and tamp it down firmly with your fist (make sure your hands are clean; a clean flat-headed potato masher would work as well). This removes any air pockets and ensures that the cabbage is fully submerged in the brine.

Weigh it down: Once you've tamped it down, pour any brine remaining in the bowl over the cabbage. To keep the cabbage covered with brine, place a clean, small plate on top of it. You want to use one that is large enough to cover the kraut well, but not so big that it can't be removed easily. Then top the plate with something heavy. (I dug up a rock from my garden, then ran it through the dishwasher. You could also use a zipper-lock bag filled with water or a quart-size Mason jar filled with water, you'll just need a little extra cheesecloth to drape over it, which is the next step.)

Wait it out: Cover the crock with cheesecloth, and after two hours, push down on the plate to make sure the cabbage is submerged. Do this again at the four-hour and the six-hour marks. At that point, it should be fully submerged in brine; if not, keep checking every two hours until it is. From here, check the cabbage every 48 hours. If it's not submerged, add more brine. Allow the cabbage to ferment at room temperature, somewhere between 65 and 75 degrees; at higher temperatures, fermentation will proceed more rapidly and, while it will be edible, the sauerkraut will soften excessively.

Taste, and taste again: One of the great things about sauerkraut is that it is "ready" to eat almost as soon as it starts to ferment (usually about five days in). How far you take it is up to you; some prefer the crisp, mildly acidic flavor and texture of a young kraut, while others prefer the mouth-puckering acidity and slightly softer texture of a 10-day fermentation. When it's where you like it, move it to the fridge. If you start a new batch of sauerkraut before the last one is fully consumed, you can use some of the brine from the current batch to top off the next one, which will jump-start the fermentation.

Make it your own: I like to serve sauerkraut with a sprinkle of smoked paprika for a dash of color and heat. You could also use red cabbage and experiment with the spices. A combined tablespoon of any of the following spices would work: caraway, dill seeds, celery seeds, red pepper flakes, juniper berries, black peppercorns, or chopped herbs. And don't neglect the "juice" at the bottom of the crock—it's delicious on its own, and makes for a mean "dirty" martini when mixed with gin.

Sauerkraut

Makes about 3 quarts

Make today, enjoy in 5 to 10 days

- **5 pounds green cabbage, quartered, cored, and sliced lengthwise ⅛ inch thick**
- **3 tablespoons Diamond Crystal kosher salt (see page 70)**
- **1 tablespoon juniper berries**

1. Combine half of cabbage and half of salt in large bowl. Forcefully knead salt into cabbage until cabbage just begins to soften, about 3 minutes. Add remaining cabbage and salt and continue kneading until all cabbage has softened and begins to give off moisture, about 3 minutes. Stir in juniper berries.

2. Transfer cabbage and any accumulated liquid to sterilized 1-gallon ceramic crock, pressing down firmly with clean fist or sterilized flat-headed potato masher to eliminate air pockets. Top cabbage with clean plate just small enough to fit inside crock and weigh plate down with clean rock or quart jar filled with water. Cover with triple layer of cheesecloth, securing in place with rubber band. Let ferment at room temperature, 65 to 75 degrees, for 2 hours.

3. Remove cheesecloth and weight, and press plate firmly onto cabbage. Replace weight and cheesecloth and let ferment 2 more hours. Repeat process twice more, or until cabbage is fully submerged under brine. (If brine doesn't completely submerge cabbage within 24 hours, cover cabbage with mixture of 1 cup water and 1 teaspoon salt).

4. Check cabbage every 2 days, pressing down cabbage to keep it submerged (top off with additional brine, made following instructions in step 3, as needed). Let ferment until sauerkraut has reached desired level of fermentation, 5 to 10 days. Transfer sauerkraut and brine to glass jars with tight-fitting lids and refrigerate. Sauerkraut can be refrigerated for up to 2 months.

Kimchi

✔ WHY THIS RECIPE WORKS: My first encounter with kimchi was just plain offensive. My mother used to crack open a jar at the dinner table, and it was only a matter of seconds before my brother and I had our noses buried in our shirts. Eventually, after much coercing, I, too, dipped into the jar, and then I kept on dipping. I was only too happy to now be the one offending my younger brother's senses.

Kimchi at its most basic is a selection of pickled, often fermented, vegetables. The most common variety, at least here in the States, is built around napa cabbage and scallions, and sometimes leeks, radishes, and carrots. It usually includes a hefty amount of garlic, as well as a spicy Korean chili paste that gives it a nice kick. The fermentation process gives kimchi its trademark effervescence and sour, tangy flavor, but many varieties are eaten fresh, or unfermented. Some form of kimchi graces nearly every Korean dinner table. In my home, I usually enjoy it with a bowl of rice, or as an easy side dish to grilled meat, but it can really partner with just about anything.

Korean markets sometimes have, tucked away at the very back of the store, someone—usually a tiny Korean grandmother—elbows deep in a trough of house-made kimchi. If you're lucky enough to happen into one of these stores, leave the name brands on the shelf. But even better, I've found that this spicy–crunchy condiment, steeped equally in tradition and fish sauce, is as easy to make as mixing the ingredients and packing them into jars. Note that when fermenting, the cleanliness of both the ingredients and your utensils is critical.

—BRYAN ROOF, Senior Editor, *Cook's Country*

THE KEYS TO MAKING KIMCHI

The chili paste in this recipe gives the kimchi a distinctive salty, spicy flavor, but you do have to purchase some unusual ingredients to make it. Korean chili powder (*kochukaru*), often labeled "red pepper powder," provides heat as well as hints of smoke and sweetness; don't try substituting for it. Salted shrimp (*saewoojeot*) are simply salted fermented shrimp. Both of these ingredients can be purchased in many Asian markets and online. If you can't find salted shrimp, an equal amount of dried shrimp or 2 teaspoons of shrimp paste may be substituted.

Worth its salt: The first step is salting, which is key for removing excess water from the cabbage. Without first salting the cabbage, the bulk of its water would be released during fermentation and dilute the flavor of the chili paste. Salt one large head of napa cabbage with 5 teaspoons of kosher salt for a minimum of an hour; I really prefer to do it for at least 24 hours, which will allow it to release upwards of ½ cup of water. I then give the cabbage a firm squeeze with my hands to rid it of any remaining water and transfer it to a large bowl.

Garlic power: Anyone who has ever been within 5 feet of someone consuming kimchi can tell you that garlic is a main ingredient. A mere 20 cloves for my batch does the trick. Ginger is used much more sparingly. After all, we wouldn't want to overdo it here. About an ounce of ginger adds a nice peppery freshness.

That's one potent paste: The next step is to turn Korean chili powder (no, this is not the same stuff you put into your Texas bowl of red), sugar, fish sauce, soy sauce, salted shrimp, garlic, and ginger into a paste. Given the ingredients, it's pretty obvious that this paste is going to add a whole lot of complex flavor to your kimchi: salty, fishy, spicy. A purist, itching to go old-school with it, might reach for the mortar and pestle. For me, 20 seconds in the food processor does a fine job. The finished puree will still be somewhat coarse.

Julienne more: With the chili paste at the ready, it's time to prep the scallions, leek, and carrot and add them to the salted cabbage. I cut them all into about 2-inch-long matchsticks. You can cut them however you like, but it helps to cut them all relatively the same size so they pickle at the same rate.

Let 'er sit: Next, add the chili paste to the vegetables and toss to combine. Transfer the kimchi to a couple of sterilized quart-size glass jars and cover with lids. The kimchi will fully ferment in the refrigerator in about two weeks and will develop a mild effervescence. However, it can be eaten "fresh" in as few as four hours. You'll find kimchi has a place at nearly every meal, whether with rice, in soup, as a side to meats, or with scrambled eggs at breakfast.

Kimchi

Makes two 1-quart jars

Make today, enjoy in 4 hours to 2 weeks

1	**large head napa cabbage (2½ pounds), cored and cut into 2-inch pieces**
5	**teaspoons Diamond Crystal kosher salt (see page 70)**
20	**garlic cloves, peeled**
½	**cup Korean chili powder**
⅓	**cup sugar**
¼	**cup fish sauce**
¼	**cup low-sodium soy sauce**
1	**(1½-inch) piece fresh ginger, peeled and sliced thin**
1	**tablespoon salted shrimp**
16	**scallions, cut into 2-inch pieces**
1	**large leek, white and light green parts only, cut into 2 by ¼-inch strips and washed thoroughly**
1	**carrot, peeled and cut into 2-inch-long matchsticks**

1. Combine cabbage and salt in large bowl. Let sit at room temperature for 1 hour, or cover and refrigerate for up to 24 hours. Transfer cabbage to colander, squeeze to drain excess liquid, and transfer to clean large bowl.

2. Process garlic, chili powder, sugar, fish sauce, soy sauce, ginger, and shrimp in food processor until no large pieces of garlic or ginger remain, about 20 seconds. Add chili mixture, scallions, leek, and carrot to cabbage and toss to combine.

3. Transfer to 2 sterilized 1-quart glass jars with tight-fitting lids, cover, and refrigerate. Let ferment until kimchi has reached desired level of fermentation, at least 4 hours or up to 2 weeks. Kimchi can be refrigerated for up to 2 weeks longer.

Milky Ways: Cheese, Yogurt, and Curds

132	American Cheese
138	Neufchatel Cream Cheese
141	Mozzarella
146	Ricotta Cheese
149	Fresh Goat Cheese
153	Feta Cheese
157	Paneer
161	Fromage Blanc
165	Crème Fraîche
167	Greek-Style Yogurt
170	Cultured Butter
174	Tofu

American Cheese

WHOLE DRY MILK POWDER

This recipe calls for whole dry milk powder; don't mistakenly buy nonfat milk powder, which is the far more common of the two. We purchase whole dry milk powder from King Arthur Flour Company; you can order it at kingarthurflour.com or amazon.com.

✔ **WHY THIS RECIPE WORKS:** I'm not afraid to admit that I love American cheese (yes, like Kraft Singles) by itself, on a grilled cheese sandwich, on a cheeseburger, or even just slapped on a plate and microwaved until it's nice and gooey (a childhood pleasure that I never outgrew).

But what exactly is American cheese? I have to think it's the answer to that exact question that's given the stuff such a bad rap. The American cheese you find in the supermarket refrigerator case isn't cheese made in the traditional way (milk that's formed into curds and pressed). Instead, it's either a blend of cheese and additives, or it's a highly processed mixture of ingredients such as water, milk, milk fat, milk protein, whey, food coloring, flavorings, and emulsifiers. The result is a processed cheese with a mild flavor that melts incredibly well. I wanted to get as close as possible to the taste and texture of American cheese using only pantry ingredients and a food processor. A little tinkering proved I didn't need much; the key was quickly melting together a mix of milk, cheese, and a few other ingredients (including plenty of salt), then giving it a chance to set up with the help of a little gelatin.

By making your own American cheese, you will know exactly what went into it, and you can also include add-ins such as black pepper, roasted red peppers … you name it. As I concocted my version of American cheese in the test kitchen, not only did I draw a crowd of curious onlookers, I caused all of the snooty foodies to run for the hills. But that's okay with me; they can keep their Époisses and Robiola—I'm completely content eating my perfectly melty, toasty grilled cheese with American cheese any day of the week.

—YVONNE RUPERTI, Associate Editor, America's Test Kitchen

A fine choice: For homemade American cheese, I discovered you can basically melt cheese, milk, gelatin, and flavorings together, then put the mixture in a mold to set up. For the cheese, mild Colby fills the bill, both for flavor and because its yellow hue tints the cheese the right sunny color (think Kraft Singles). In a few steps, you are going to melt the cheese with the other ingredients into a smooth mixture, and since that mixture will start to firm up almost as soon as it has started melting, it's important for everything to melt quickly. Because of that, I use a box grater's small holes to grate the cheese.

Smooth operator: Knowing I want a quick-melting, ultra-smooth mixture—and because I don't have a commercial processing machine—I turn to my food processor. (The final mixture is too thick for a blender.) Pulse the shredded Colby to small bits, along with some dry milk powder, a bit of cream of tartar, and salt. The cream of tartar gives the final cheese a slight tang and the dry milk powder adds a rich, milky flavor—only whole dry milk powder will do (nonfat gives it an off-taste). There's a good amount of salt here, but I found American cheese really needs it.

Secrets to cheesy success: Gelatin is one key to my recipe's success; with all of the liquid that's added (which helps it melt really well), gelatin is necessary to hold it all together. Soften the gelatin first (also known as "blooming") by sprinkling it over a little water and letting it sit for about five minutes. The second key is getting the milk hot since the hot liquid will melt the cheese mixture, ensuring smooth results. After heating the milk to a boil, remove it from the heat, add the softened gelatin, whisk until it dissolves, then transfer the milk-gelatin mixture to a liquid measuring cup.

The "process" in the product: Now the fun part. With the processor running, pour the hot milk mixture through the feed tube. After a few seconds, the cheese mixture will begin to clump up. It looks a bit gritty and separated at first, but don't worry. Just scrape the sides of the bowl down and then keep processing. After about a minute, the mixture turns into a beautifully smooth and shiny mass of goodness. Now is a good time to stir or pulse in any add-ins such as cracked black pepper or cayenne.

Pack it in: Next I put it in a mold so it can set up into a sliceable form. A square-edged mold would be ideal for mimicking the store-bought shape, but an aluminum loaf pan works fine. I use a 5 by 4-inch pan and line it with plastic wrap, which helps with unmolding the cheese later. Scrape the cheese into the prepared mold and pack it in firmly to eliminate any large air pockets, then fold the plastic wrap over the surface. The cheese begins to set up pretty quickly, so it's important to work fast.

A time to chill: The cheese needs to chill for about three hours to get nicely sliceable. While I initially wanted to achieve a firm American cheese like what you would find at a deli, I found that to get a firmer cheese I had to use less liquid and thus sacrifice meltability—and that wasn't a tradeoff I was willing to make.

Slice it up: In the end, I wound up somewhere in the middle—with a soft but sliceable cheese that oozes gently when heated.

Ooey, gooey perfection: And now for the real test—because no American cheese is worth making unless you can make it melt. I fried up a buttery grilled cheese and sliced it down the middle. Yum!

American Cheese

Makes 1 pound
Make today, enjoy immediately

- 1½ **teaspoons unflavored gelatin**
- 1 **tablespoon water**
- 12 **ounces Colby cheese, shredded fine (3 cups)**
- 1 **tablespoon whole dry milk powder**
- 1 **teaspoon salt**
- ⅛ **teaspoon cream of tartar**
- ½ **cup plus 2 tablespoons whole milk**

1. Line 5 by 4-inch disposable aluminum loaf pan with plastic wrap, allowing excess to hang over sides.

2. Sprinkle gelatin over water in bowl and let sit until gelatin softens, about 5 minutes. Pulse cheese, milk powder, salt, and cream of tartar in food processor until combined, about 3 pulses.

3. Bring milk to boil in small saucepan. Remove pot from heat and whisk in softened gelatin until dissolved. Transfer mixture to liquid measuring cup. With processor running, slowly add hot milk mixture to cheese mixture until smooth, about 1 minute, scraping down bowl as needed.

4. Immediately transfer cheese to prepared pan; working quickly, pack cheese firmly into loaf pan to remove any air pockets, then smooth top. Fold overhanging plastic tightly against surface of cheese, and refrigerate for at least 3 hours to set. American cheese can be refrigerated for up to 1 month.

Cheese Making 101

Making cheese might sound intimidating, but you'll find the fresh cheeses we walk you through in this chapter are easier than you'd think. There's a lot of science involved in the cheese-making process; here we just touch on the basics. The more you understand, the more successful you'll be—and the more fun you'll have doing it. Just remember, cheese making is an art. It might take a little practice to get some of these recipes just right, but the rewards are well worth the effort.

In a Nutshell: How Does Milk Turn into Cheese?

Milk is made up of water and milk solids, which include proteins, milk fat (aka butterfat), and milk sugar (aka lactose). When you cause the proteins in milk to coagulate, or curdle (with the help of rennet or an acid), they produce curds. With the help of heat, time, and sometimes pressure, these curds release liquid, or whey, and become firmer and firmer. That's your cheese.

Cleanliness Counts

Growing bacteria—what we'll consider the "good" kind—is a key part of cheese making. But milk is also susceptible to growing bacteria that is bad and can spoil the whole batch. As such, it's critical to keep your utensils, hands, and work area immaculate. No need to bleach everything, but all utensils should be cleaned and sterilized in boiling water for five minutes before using, and keep your hands clean throughout the cheese-making process.

Follow the Recipe

Every little detail in cheese making counts. Make sure to stick to the specified time-lines and temperatures to ensure success, and make sure you have a good, accurate thermometer. The amount of stirring is also critical. You don't want to stir at all, or even disturb, the pot of milk while it coagulates because doing so can keep the curds from properly forming and cause loss of milk fat, which you want to stay in the curd. After the milk has set, how much (and how hard) you stir affects how quickly curds release whey—if whey is released too quickly, the curds can lose milk fat as well. This is particularly problematic when making a smooth, creamy cheese, since the milk fat is key to creating that desirable texture.

Water

We use water to dilute rennet (and calcium chloride and citric acid), and because chlorine can keep rennet from doing its job, it's critical to use unchlorinated water. Tap water may or may not be chlorinated, so we've found it's easiest to simply stick with distilled, filtered, or purified water.

Supply Source

These days many home-brewing supply shops and some cheese shops also sell cheese-making supplies, both ingredients and equipment like butter muslin and cheesecloth. However, you can also easily purchase what you need online through websites like cheesemaking.com.

Milk

It goes without saying, use the best-quality, freshest milk you can get. But take note: Even if it's organic, it's not necessarily the best choice for making cheese. The most important factor regarding milk is actually whether or not the milk was ultra-pasteurized or ultra-heat-treated (UHT). All the recipes in this chapter were developed using pasteurized, homogenized dairy. Pasteurized milk has been heated to 145 degrees to kill off harmful bacteria (the process also kills off some of the good bacteria). Milk that has been ultra-pasteurized or ultra-heat-treated has been heated to even higher temperatures, which not only kills all enzymes and bacteria, bad and good, but also affects the protein structure. This makes it difficult to form good, strong curds. Thus neither UHT nor ultra-pasteurized milk is a great choice for making cheese. Many organic milks are ultra-pasteurized, so it's important to check the milk's label. By law, dairies don't have to label their products UHT or ultra-pasteurized. If the sell-by date is more than two weeks away, you are probably safe to assume it has been ultra-pasteurized or ultra-heat-treated and not suitable for cheese making. Cheesemaking.com has a list of good milk sources found around the country.

Cheese Making **101**

Starter Cultures

Starter cultures are just what you might guess: bacterial cultures that jump-start the cheese-making process. These bacteria are important because they convert the lactose in milk into lactic acid, and this acid plays several key cheese-making roles: It allows the rennet (see at right) to do its job, contributes tangy flavor, keeps away bad bacteria, and helps preserve the cheese. Raw milk contains naturally occurring lactic acid, but pasteurization kills these off so starters replace them. When you use a starter culture to increase the acidity of milk, that process is known as "ripening," and the milk is referred to as "ripened" when it reaches the proper acidity level.

Starters were traditionally prepared using the whey from previous cheeses. When they were propagated from one batch to the next, they became known as "mother cultures." These required a lengthy culturing time, but luckily there is now an easier option, known as direct-set cultures. These are added straight to the milk, no prep required. For all the recipes you'll find here, you will need what are called mesophilic starter cultures. Mesophilic cultures are intended for low-temperature cheeses; all the recipes in this chapter fall into that category. For fromage blanc, note that we use a specific fromage blanc culture, which also contains a built-in coagulant so you don't need rennet.

Acids

Acids can serve a few different purposes in cheese making. In our easiest recipes (ricotta and paneer), we coagulate the milk by simply adding vinegar, lemon juice, or buttermilk in lieu of a starter culture and rennet. In our mozzarella recipe, we use citric acid to acidify the milk rather than adding a culture, then add the rennet to set it. This means you don't have to let it sit like you would when using a culture, and it also doesn't add flavors that a culture would.

Rennet

To get cheese from milk, you need the milk to separate into curds and whey. Milk would eventually coagulate on its own; rennet speeds up the process. Rennet is a collection of enzymes that, with the help of the acidic environment the starter culture creates (or that you would find in raw milk), will cause the milk to coagulate. Cheese makers used to extract these enzymes from the stomachs of calves or kids after they were slaughtered. They would clean and salt the stomach and hang it to dry. When it came time to make cheese, they would break off a piece of the dried stomach, soak it in water, then add some of that solution to the milk. Luckily for us, technology has made it easy to standardize rennet. Now you can buy it in liquid, tablet, and powdered form, as animal rennet or vegetable rennet. Vegetable rennet takes advantage of the coagulating properties found in a number of different plants. We use liquid animal rennet since it gave us the most consistent results; if you want a vegetarian cheese, you can experiment with vegetable rennet. To distribute rennet evenly in milk, it is important to dilute it as directed in the recipe before stirring it into the pot.

Calcium Chloride

Because pasteurization decreases the amount of calcium in milk, the milk's ability to clot can be reduced and this can in turn slow down the rennet's performance. Basically, if there isn't enough calcium in your milk, you could end up with a milky mixture that never really separates into curds and whey. Some cheese makers bring pasteurized milk's calcium into balance by adding calcium chloride to it. The addition of calcium chloride isn't always necessary; it becomes important when you want firmer curds, such as when making feta (which is the only recipe in this chapter where we found it a must). While you can find it in pellet and flake form, the most commonly used form of calcium chloride for cheese making, and what we use, is a liquid solution. We dilute calcium chloride in water before adding it to milk to ensure better distribution.

Neufchatel Cream Cheese

BUTTER MUSLIN AND CHEESECLOTH

In this recipe, and many in this chapter, we call for butter muslin or several layers of cheesecloth. Either will work fine. Butter muslin is a little harder to find, but because it has a tighter weave than cheesecloth, you don't have to deal with multiple layers when using it; one layer will do. And it's washable, so you can reuse it. You can buy butter muslin for about $6 through cheesemaking.com.

WHY THIS RECIPE WORKS: I've never been a big dieter, but when you work in the food world, some things have to give. I know, there's little sympathy for one complaining of endless croissant tastings as a job, but it only takes one tight pair of jeans before I'm wondering if I really needed that second "tasting" of Nutella bread pudding.

In spite of (or perhaps because of) the temptations, I've learned quite a lot about healthy cooking here in the test kitchen. You should never assume cutting calories and fat has to mean sacrificing flavor—it just might take a little work to figure out how to have that cake and eat it too. So when I had the chance to make one of my favorite spreads, cream cheese, I couldn't wait to pop the hood. It sure wasn't pretty; regular cream cheese is made with heavy cream and whole milk (which get cultured then drained). I shuddered to think how fast one spoonful could permanently apply itself to my thighs. The mass-market low-fat versions were okay, but obviously not as good as the loaded version. So I got to work making my own.

First, I tried switching the cream-milk combo for just skim milk. This cream cheese had a nice spreadable consistency, but my team agreed the taste wouldn't do—too sharp-tasting and lean. I began adding half-and-half in increments. I found my magic ratio after only a few tries: 4 cups of skim milk to 2 cups of half-and-half. My final cream cheese came in at only 4.5 grams of fat and 80 calories per 1-ounce serving, actually less than the leading brand's lower-fat options (which tally 6 grams of fat per serving). But you would never guess. It is ultra-creamy and wonderfully rich tasting. I had no problem retiring that full-fat, store-bought brick of cream cheese for good. Now about that bread pudding…

—REBECCA MORRIS, Test Cook, Books

Warm up, add culture: The dairy needs to be around 72 degrees to culture properly, so start by warming the milk and half-and-half over low heat. Once the dairy is warmed up, remove the pot from the heat and sprinkle the culture over the milk mixture, stirring gently but not too much. Aerating the milk will cause the culture to be less effective in converting the lactose into lactic acid, and the rennet (which comes next) needs that acid to work. The acid is also what adds the familiar cream cheese tang.

Rennet to set it: Next, add the rennet. However, you don't want to add it straight to the pot. It's important to first dilute the two rennet drops in a small bowl with ¼ cup water. Diluting the rennet first will help it evenly distribute in the dairy mixture, which in turn helps to make sure the curd sets properly. As you stir in your diluted rennet mixture, use a gentle up-and-down, vertical motion at the same time you stir horizontally. This further guarantees thorough distribution.

Wait, then scoop: Now all you have to do is cover the pot and let the mixture sit at room temperature until the curd has the consistency of thick yogurt, which usually takes about 24 hours. Don't disturb or move the pot during this time; moving it can disrupt the curd-setting process. Once the mixture has the consistency of yogurt, I use a large spoon to scoop the curd into a colander lined with butter muslin or a triple layer of cheesecloth.

Hang dry: After bundling up the muslin or cheesecloth into a beggar's purse, I knot it at the top and then tie it to a large spoon set over a deep container. Really any apparatus or setup will work as long as the bag is elevated (and it drains into something so you don't create a mess). Let the cheese hang overnight at room temperature.

Taste the difference: After you've gotten some shut-eye (and if you've timed it right, just in time for breakfast), your cream cheese is ready to be taken down. I find the flavor of this homemade cream cheese so pleasantly tangy that all I add is a little salt, which I whisk in, removing any lumps that might be there at the same time. If you want a change of pace from plain cream cheese, this is where you would add whatever mix-in your heart desires, be it fresh herbs, berries, or chopped smoked salmon.

Neufchatel Cream Cheese

Makes 12 ounces

Start today, enjoy in 2 days

- 4 **cups pasteurized (not ultra-pasteurized or UHT) skim milk (see page 136)**
- 2 **cups pasteurized (not ultra-pasteurized or UHT) half-and-half (see page 136)**
- ½ **teaspoon direct-set mesophilic starter culture**
- 2 **drops liquid animal rennet**
- ¼ **cup cold filtered water**
- ½ **teaspoon salt**

1. Combine milk and half-and-half in Dutch oven. Gently heat milk mixture over low heat, stirring occasionally, until it registers 72 degrees, 10 to 15 minutes. Remove pot from heat.

2. Sprinkle culture over surface of milk mixture, stirring gently to combine. Dilute rennet in water, then stir into milk mixture until well combined. Cover, and let sit undisturbed at room temperature, until curd has consistency of thick yogurt, about 24 hours.

3. Line colander with butter muslin or triple layer of cheesecloth and set in sink. Using large spoon, transfer curd to prepared colander. Bundle curd in muslin, then tie with kitchen twine to secure. Tie curd bundle to large spoon set over deep bowl or container, making sure bundle does not touch bottom of bowl. Let drain at room temperature until whey stops dripping from bag and cheese is firm to touch, 18 to 24 hours; discard whey.

4. Transfer cream cheese to medium bowl. Whisk in salt until well combined and cream cheese is smooth. Cream cheese can be refrigerated in airtight container for up to 2 weeks.

Mozzarella

WHY THIS RECIPE WORKS: As a college sophomore, I convinced my parents to let me study in Florence for the summer. I painted, I went to museums…and I ate. There was the pasta and pizza of course, but it was the fresh mozzarella that stole my heart. Back home, I had to re-create it.

The first key to making good mozzarella is realizing that Italian mozzarella is made with water buffalo milk, which has more fat than cow's milk. So using whole milk plus heavy cream makes it taste more authentic. Second, know what you are getting into. Recipes abound online, all proclaiming, "It's easy! It's fun!" Well, I've got news: They lie. It took immeasurable patience and I don't know how many gallons of milk before I got it right. Perfecting mozzarella is definitely a touch, feel, and learn process. Don't get down when your first try fails. Once you get it right, you'll be handsomely rewarded with delectable cheese. Even when it is a disaster—which can result, as I learned, from making a variety of mistakes, from overcoagulating the milk to letting the curd get too hot to letting the curd get too cold or not removing enough whey—the curds are still delicious.

It's critical to use fresh homogenized and pasteurized milk here; do not use ultra-pasteurized or ultra-heat-treated (UHT or long-life) milk, as the milk will not coagulate properly. Make sure to use a Dutch oven that is at least 6 quarts to ensure all the liquid for stretching will fit. Mozzarella is best eaten fresh. If you don't want to eat the entire batch the day you make it, save and refrigerate half the curds (don't stretch them) for up to three days. When you want to make the second batch, dissolve 3 tablespoons salt in 12 cups hot water and use this as your stretching liquid.

—KELLY PRICE, Test Cook, *Cook's Country*

"Perfecting mozzarella is definitely a touch, feel, and learn process. Don't get down when your first try fails. Once you get it right, you'll be handsomely rewarded with delectable cheese."

Grainy milk is the goal: Add your milk and cream (which I include for richness) to a Dutch oven that is at least 6 quarts. It's critical that neither is ultra-pasteurized, a process that ruins the dairy's proteins for mozzarella making. Before turning on the heat, dissolve your citric acid in ¼ cup water, then add it to the dairy mixture. Stir for at least 30 seconds to ensure it's incorporated, then bring the whole mixture up to 90 degrees over medium heat, stirring frequently to make sure the citric acid stays distributed. It will begin to curdle and look slightly grainy like you see here.

A magical 10 minutes: Dilute your animal rennet in another ¼ cup water, then add it to the milk mixture off the heat. Stir in the rennet for exactly 30 seconds. Then, no more stirring. Cover the pot and let it sit for 10 minutes. No peeking during this time; magic is happening in there.

Break time: When the time is up, remove the lid and check the curd formation. You should be able to gently pull the curd away from the side of the pot to reveal clear whey. This is called a clean break. If you can't make a clean break and your whey still looks milky, re-cover, let the mixture sit for five more minutes, then check again.

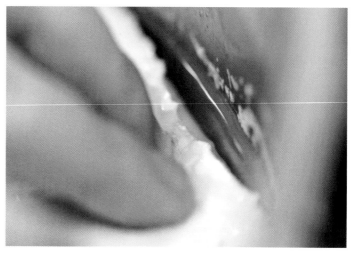

Cut the curd: Using a chef's knife or flat metal spatula, cut the curd into 1-inch blocks. Gently twist the pot using the handles on either side to jostle the curds and release them from the pot's sides, then let it rest for two to three minutes, until the curds start to separate from each other. Then heat the whey to 105 to 107 degrees over low heat, turning and shifting the pot to heat it evenly. It should take at least 10 minutes. Once the whey reaches 105 to 107, let it rest another few minutes, then gently spoon the curds into a colander set inside a large bowl.

The whey out: There's no rushing this step; move slowly. Gently press the curds from the top down. If curds are pressing through the holes in your colander, you're pushing too hard. Swirl and gently press the curds around the colander until they become a cohesive mass and you can no longer see pockets of whey. Toward the end of this step it should look like this.

Cut it up: Place the ball of curds on a cutting board; it should look about like medium-firm tofu and should be firm enough to stay intact in your hand. Cut the curds into 1-inch chunks and place half of them in a deep, large heatproof bowl (working in batches will make the stretching easier). Then, take the drained whey and combine it with the whey left in the pot.

Cleaning the whey: After removing all of the curds, your whey will have some floating bits of curd left behind. You're going to heat this liquid (along with some water and salt) to use for stretching the cheese, and if you leave all those bits, they'll ruin your cheese. So strain the whey into a bowl, give the empty pot a rinse, then return the clean whey to the pot. Add 12 cups water and the kosher salt, then heat the mixture to 180 degrees.

The heat is on: Put on a double layer of kitchen gloves (you'll find out why momentarily). Pour half of the hot whey mixture over the curds you put in the bowl; the whey should cover the curds by at least 4 inches. At this point the curds will be much too hot to touch, so start by using a rubber spatula to gently bring the curds together and press them against the sides of the bowl to begin melting them.

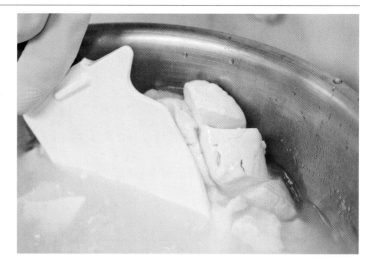

Now stretch. And stretch: As soon as humanly possible, dive in with your hands and gently stretch the curds out then fold the mass back onto itself, repeating until the curds are pliable and stretchy. A few tips: Keep the cheese submerged as much as possible to keep it hot, and work as quickly as possible. Keep the curds all in one mass for efficiency. If the cheese starts breaking apart instead of stretching, let it sit under the hot whey for 30 seconds or so to heat back up. Finally, be sure you're stretching the cheese and not kneading it, or else you will end up with dense, chewy cheese. Think taffy, not bread.

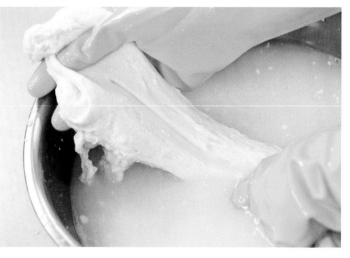

Play ball: Working quickly, form the mozzarella into balls. Take a small piece of cheese off the end of what you just finished stretching and stretch it around your thumb into a smooth, taut ball, then pinch it together at the bottom. Repeat, placing the balls in a clean bowl filled with cold water, until you've gone through all the cheese. Discard the stretching liquid, reheat the remaining whey mixture, and stretch and shape your second batch in the same way. Working in two batches makes the stretching easier since the stretching liquid will stay warm and you have fewer curds to work with.

Mozzarella

Makes about 1½ pounds

Make today, enjoy immediately

2	**teaspoons citric acid**
½	**cup cold filtered water**
1	**gallon pasteurized (not ultra-pasteurized or UHT) whole milk (see page 136)**
½	**cup pasteurized (not ultra-pasteurized or UHT) heavy cream (see page 136)**
¼	**teaspoon liquid animal rennet**
6	**tablespoons Diamond Crystal kosher salt (see page 70)**

1. Dissolve citric acid in ¼ cup water. Place colander over large, deep bowl. Fill second large bowl with cold water and refrigerate until needed. Combine milk and heavy cream in 6-quart (or larger) Dutch oven, and thoroughly stir in citric acid solution for at least 30 seconds. Heat over medium heat, stirring frequently, until mixture registers 90 degrees. Remove pot from heat. Dilute rennet in remaining ¼ cup water and stir into milk mixture for exactly 30 seconds. Cover pot and let sit, undisturbed, for 10 minutes.

2. Remove lid and use your fingers to gently pull curd from sides of pot to check for set. Curd should be slightly firm and custardlike and whey should be clear. (If curd is not set, cover pot and let sit for 5 minutes before retesting set.) Using long flat metal spatula, gently cut curd into 1-inch blocks. Gently twist pot back and forth to release curds from side of pot and let sit until curds separate, 2 to 3 minutes. Return pot to very low heat and slowly bring whey to 105 to 107 degrees, 15 to 20 minutes (check temperature of whey, not curds); as whey comes up to temperature, occasionally twist pot to gently and evenly distribute warming whey. Remove pot from heat and let curds sit for 3 minutes.

3. Using slotted spoon, gently transfer curds to prepared colander. Very gently press down on curds to drain off whey. As curds drain, gently press into a large cake, until curds form a cohesive mass and whey no longer runs out of curds when pressed, 5 to 7 minutes. Reserve whey. Transfer curds to cutting board and cut into 1-inch pieces.

4. Set fine-mesh strainer over bowl. Return reserved whey to pot, then pour all whey through strainer, discarding solids. Return strained whey to clean Dutch oven and stir in 12 cups water and salt. Heat whey to 180 degrees over medium-high heat.

5. Wearing double layer of thick rubber kitchen gloves, transfer half of curd pieces to clean bowl and pour half of hot whey mixture over curds. Using rubber spatula, press curds together against sides of bowl until melted and pliable, about 1 minute. Pull and stretch mozzarella, repeating until curds are stretchy and strands are smooth and shiny, 4 to 5 minutes. If curds begin to break instead of stretch, let curds rest in hot whey for 30 seconds to reheat before stretching again.

6. Pull off small pieces of mozzarella and stretch and form into 2-inch balls. Quickly submerge balls in prepared bowl of cold water to chill and set. Discard stretching liquid, then transfer remaining curd pieces to bowl. Return remaining whey mixture to 180 degrees over medium-high heat and pour over curds. Repeat stretching, shaping, and cooling steps.

Ricotta Cheese

✔️ **WHY THIS RECIPE WORKS:** Creamy, milky, and luxuriously rich, fresh ricotta is a different universe from the grainy, clumpy supermarket stuff. You'll be shocked how easy it is to make at home; all you need is milk, lemon juice, vinegar, a colander, and cheesecloth. It's so fantastic, you'll find yourself sneaking spoonfuls from the fridge. Plus, you can make it to just the texture you want. It works as well in a cheesecake as it does in your favorite lasagna recipe. For the most reliable results, use fresh homogenized and pasteurized milk here; do not use ultra-pasteurized or ultra-heat-treated (UHT or long-life) milk in this recipe, as it will not curdle properly.

—THE TEST KITCHEN

Heat things up: First, heat a mixture of whole milk and salt (for flavor) to a steamy 185 degrees. Why so specific? Heating the milk to 185 degrees rejiggers the proteins, leaving room for the acidifying agent to slip in and curdle the milk. Make sure to stir the milk frequently once it gets past 150 degrees; at this point, it can easily stick to the bottom and scorch (and no one wants to clean up scorched milk).

Have acid, will curdle: Once the milk hits 185 degrees, remove the pot from the heat and stir in lemon juice and vinegar. Most recipes use one or the other, but we felt all lemon made a cheese best for desserts, while only vinegar tasted medicinal. Using a combo creates a nicely balanced, multipurpose cheese. And since the acidity of lemons varies, using vinegar also helps make our recipe more reliable. We found a little over half a cup of acidic ingredients will consistently curdle the milk. Be sure to stir thoroughly to evenly distribute the acid, then let the pot rest, undisturbed, for five to 10 minutes.

Finding the whey (and curds):
The milk should have fully separated into white, billowy curds just below the surface and slightly yellow, translucent whey (it should look like this). But if there is still milky whey in the pot after 10 minutes of sitting, gently stir in additional vinegar, 1 tablespoon at a time, and let sit another two to three minutes, until the curds fully separate.

Drain it: Now all that's left to do is to drain the curds from the whey. Carefully (very carefully; you're dealing with hot, easily splatterable liquid here) pour the entire contents of the pot into a cheesecloth-lined colander set in the sink. We tried gently scooping the curds into the strainer instead of pouring, thinking it would make for more efficient draining since we'd be leaving some whey behind, but we found this tedious and challenging if the curds were on the small side.

Keep it soupy: We like our ricotta moist, perfect for an appetizer or spread, so we only drain the curds for about eight minutes. The edges should be fairly dry, but the center is still pretty soupy. (If you want a firmer cheese to use in cannoli or lasagna, drain for an additional five to 10 minutes.) It is good practice to stop draining just shy of your desired texture since as the cheese chills in the fridge, it will suck up more whey. Transfer the cheese from the cheesecloth to a large bowl, cover, and refrigerate until chilled, about two hours.

Ready to spread: Now that the cheese is cold and has firmed up a bit, give it a stir to even out the curds and redistribute any lingering whey. To highlight the clean, fresh flavor of the cheese, we like to serve ricotta spread on crostini with a little drizzle of olive oil or honey, but it is equally good dolloped on pizza, layered into lasagna, or swirled into custard for ice cream.

Ricotta Cheese

Makes 2 pounds (4 cups)
Make today, enjoy immediately

- ⅓ **cup lemon juice (2 lemons)**
- ¼ **cup distilled white vinegar, plus extra if needed**
- 1 **gallon pasteurized (not ultra-pasteurized or UHT) whole milk (see page 136)**
- 2 **teaspoons salt**

1. Line colander with butter muslin or triple layer of cheesecloth and place in sink. Combine lemon juice and vinegar in liquid measuring cup; set aside. Heat milk and salt in Dutch oven over medium-high heat, stirring frequently with rubber spatula to prevent scorching, until milk registers 185 degrees.

2. Remove pot from heat, slowly stir in lemon juice mixture until fully incorporated and mixture curdles, about 15 seconds. Let sit undisturbed until mixture fully separates into solid curds and translucent whey, 5 to 10 minutes. If curds do not fully separate and there is still milky whey in pot, stir in additional vinegar, 1 tablespoon at a time, and let sit another 2 to 3 minutes, until curds separate.

3. Gently pour mixture into prepared colander. Let drain, undisturbed, until whey has drained from edges of cheese but center is still very moist, about 8 minutes. Working quickly, gently transfer cheese to large bowl, retaining as much whey in center of cheese as possible. Stir well to break up large curds and incorporate whey. Refrigerate ricotta until cold, about 2 hours. Stir cheese before using. Ricotta can be refrigerated in an airtight container for up to 5 days.

Fresh Goat Cheese

☑ **WHY THIS RECIPE WORKS:** Of all the foods I might be able to forgo, I could never deprive myself of cheese. It can be soft, hard, stinky, mild—I love it all. Unfortunately, this means that a "quick stop" at Whole Foods can turn into a serious bender. I've tried averting my eyes when passing the cheese section, but if the sight of wheels of Parm or stacks of aged Gouda can't get me, the smells will. Recently, a wedge of a very fine cheese found its way into my basket, and while it was truly amazing, I had trouble justifying the 28-dollar-a-pound price tag. For the sake of my wallet, I needed to take a stab at making cheese at home.

Cheese making *can* be an incredibly time-consuming and labor-intensive endeavor, requiring specialized equipment and a high level of expertise. But luckily, there are some cheeses that a novice like me (or you) can easily undertake at home. Goat cheese is one of these. Good fresh goat cheese is a beautiful thing. It should be chalky but creamy, tart and bright with an underlying richness, and above all, it should taste like what it is: little more than goat's milk and salt. That being said, you have to appreciate a "goat-y" flavor for this recipe to be worthwhile. If you do, and if you're sick of shelling out seven bucks for a tiny log of the stuff, then give it a whirl. I tried a few different variations on the basic recipe, utilizing different coagulating agents and amounts of culture, but this one was the clear winner.

For the most reliable results, use fresh homogenized and pasteurized milk here; do not use ultra-pasteurized or ultra-heat-treated (UHT or long-life) milk in this recipe or it will not curdle properly.

—REBECCAH MARSTERS, Associate Editor, *Cook's Country*

GOT YOUR GOAT

Goat's milk is sold these days in more places than you might think; just make sure you buy pasteurized, not ultra-pasteurized, for cheese making. For our testing we used goat's milk from Oak Knoll Farm, sold at Whole Foods.

Heat things up: Goat's milk is pricier than cow's milk, but it has its advantages. It's easier to digest, more acidic so it cultures faster, and, because of its structure, it produces a smoother cheese. Warm a half-gallon of goat's milk over low heat, stirring often to prevent scorching. When the milk reaches 90 degrees, take it off the heat. Some recipes add calcium chloride to ensure good curd formation, but I found it wasn't needed and adds a bitter aftertaste. But if you're worried about the quality of your milk, you can add ⅛ teaspoon diluted in 2 tablespoons purified water.

Culture club: Now sprinkle ⅛ teaspoon of culture over the milk and gently stir until combined. The culture will turn the lactose in the milk into lactic acid. The lactic acid is key for several reasons, including giving the cheese tangy flavor and helping the rennet, which comes next, do its job.

Add coagulant: Next comes the rennet, which will make the milk separate into curds and whey. For this step, mix ⅛ teaspoon rennet into 1 tablespoon water, add that to the pot, and give it one final, thorough stir to fully incorporate it.

Wait: This step is as simple as it gets. Cover the pot and let it sit overnight at room temperature to let the milk fully separate. This timing doesn't have to be exact; 12 hours is standard, but it can sit for up to 24 hours.

Keep the curds, lose the whey: In the morning, take a peek inside the pot. The milk mixture should be separated into a raft of curds and liquid whey. Ladle the curds into a colander lined with butter muslin (several layers of cheesecloth will also work). The less you break up the curds the better; whole curds drain more slowly, but they give superior texture. Once they're all in the colander, let the curds drain at room temperature for a few hours. Again, the timing is not crucial here, but somewhere between two and four hours works well. The goal is for the curds to thicken but still be moist.

Salt it, hang it: Tip the partially drained cheese from the colander into a bowl. At this point I mix in 1 teaspoon of coarse sea salt; it's easier to incorporate now than at the end. Then spoon half the cheese into the center of a piece of butter muslin (or a few layers of cheesecloth). Tie it up into a bundle, then repeat with the second half. Hang these bundles from a wooden spoon set over a bowl and let them drain in the fridge. They can drain as little as six hours or up to 24 hours, depending on how soft or firm you want the final cheese to be.

Got your goat: If you let it hang the full 24 hours, the cheese will have a nice, slightly crumbly consistency. I sometimes like to roll it in a mixture of chopped fresh herbs and peppercorns for a nice presentation, but it is just as delicious eaten as is.

Makes about 10 ounces
Start today, enjoy in 1 to 2 days

8 cups pasteurized (not
ultra-pasteurized or UHT)
goat's milk (see page 136)

⅛ teaspoon direct-set
mesophilic starter culture

⅛ teaspoon liquid animal
rennet

1 tablespoon cold filtered
water

1 teaspoon coarse sea salt

1. Slowly heat milk in large saucepan over low heat, stirring often, until milk registers 90 degrees, about 10 minutes. Remove from heat, sprinkle culture over surface of milk and gently stir until combined.

2. Dilute rennet in water, then stir rennet into milk until well combined. Cover and let sit, undisturbed, at room temperature until mixture fully separates into solid curds and translucent whey, 12 to 24 hours.

3. Line colander with butter muslin or triple layer of cheesecloth and set in sink. Ladle curds into prepared colander and let drain at room temperature for 2 to 4 hours, until whey no longer runs freely from colander, and curds are thickened but still moist.

4. Transfer partially drained cheese to medium bowl, stir in salt, and divide cheese in half. Working with one half at a time, bundle cheese in butter muslin or triple layer of cheesecloth, then tie with kitchen twine to secure.

5. Tie cheese bundles to large spoon set over deep bowl or container, making sure bundles do not touch bottom of bowl, and refrigerate for 6 to 24 hours (depending on desired consistency). Goat cheese can be wrapped tightly in plastic wrap and refrigerated for up to 1 week.

Feta Cheese

✔ **WHY THIS RECIPE WORKS:** Salty, creamy, crumbly, and tangy, feta is divine sprinkled on almost anything, or served simply in cubes alongside Marcona almonds and a bowl of olives. Recently, my habitual feta purchases got me wondering, how hard would it be to make myself? This was my first foray into making a firmer cheese, and creating my own recipe turned out to be more difficult than expected. After going through a truckload of goat's milk and an awful lot of my patience, I figured out the tricks. So did all the work end up being worth it? The hard work is done, so let's discuss over a very fine spread of olives, almonds, and homemade feta.

—REBECCA MORRIS, Test Cook, Books

Get things started: Goat's milk is not the most traditional choice for feta, but unless you have a few sheep out back, it comes closest to the real thing. I add calcium chloride to the milk to ensure it will form firm curds, then heat it up to 86 degrees. Now add your culture and give it an hour to acidify the milk. When the hour is up, it's time to dilute the rennet and add it to the pot. To ensure that the rennet distributes evenly and the curd coagulates properly, I like to stir both horizontally and with an up-and-down motion.

Curd is the word: Now cover the pot and leave it alone for an hour. When the time is up, test it for a clean break. Placing a thin metal spatula in the curd at a 45-degree angle, put a little pressure on the curd. If it separates cleanly, leaving a little pool of clear whey in the crevice, then you are free to proceed. If the curd feels really wobbly and mushes up when you do this, let it sit for another 15 minutes before checking again.

Slice and dice: Cutting the curd increases surface area, which in turn lets the whey separate more easily. I cut down through the curd as well as crosswise, and I discovered that a whisk, because of the shape of its tines, does a great job of simplifying this process. Put a long, large whisk into the pot on one side, go all the way to the bottom, then make straight cuts about ½ inch apart, moving from one side of the pot clear across to the other. Then turn the pot 90 degrees and do the same thing to create ½-inch cubes throughout the entire mixture.

Get out the whey: Once cut, let the curds sit undisturbed for about 10 minutes to firm up. Then, using a slotted spoon, ever so gently fold the curds in the pot for about 10 seconds. This step allows more whey to be expelled, but you don't want to really stir it or your curds will break up too much and lose not just whey but also fat (and that's not good unless you want a chalky, dry cheese). I let them sit for a bit, then fold again, and repeat a few times. If you see any big pieces while you are doing this you can cut them down to size.

Two-stage drain: To begin the draining process, scoop out the curds and place them in a cheesecloth- or butter muslin–lined colander. At this point, you also want to reserve about 2 cups of whey from the pot to use for the brine later (just put it in the refrigerator). Let the curds sit in the colander for about 30 minutes for an initial drain, then gather up the cheesecloth's edges, tie a knot around the top using a long piece of twine, and hang the ball from a wooden spoon set over a deep container. A stockpot or soup pot, or even a wide-mouth vase would work.

Flip out: In the beginning phases of testing, I just let the ball of curds hang overnight. Low maintenance, yes. But I realized that unless I wanted my finished cheese to look like an uneven crater (and risk whey pooling in the middle), I would need to flip it over after an hour or two of hanging, just when it began to thicken and take shape (it will have the texture of firm cream cheese). So after a short stint, take the bundle down, untie the string, flip the cake, then rehang the bundle. Now it really is hands off for the next 24 hours.

Salt and sit: This next step is what sets feta apart. Salting the cheese not only adds flavor but also draws out even more whey, giving it an even firmer texture. Cut it in half, then into 1-inch planks, then transfer the planks to a shallow dish. Sprinkle both sides with kosher salt and let it sit at room temperature for two to three days to develop flavor, flipping the pieces over every day and draining off the excess whey. Leaving the cheese out is perfectly safe; the salt and the cheese's acidity will inhibit bad bacteria growth.

Brine time: Dice the feta into 1-inch pieces and place them in a large jar, then whisk 3 tablespoons salt into your reserved whey to make a brine. The whey works well since it has a subtle goat flavor and contains calcium, which will prevent the feta from turning to mush. (If your feta has a lot of small, even holes and feels spongy rather than firm, it means the batch has been contaminated and has to be tossed. But I found if I kept everything clean, the cheese turned out fine.) Don't feel rushed to eat your feta; the longer it sits in the brine, the creamier and better tasting it will become.

Feta Cheese

Makes about 1 pound
Start today, enjoy in 4 days

- **1 gallon pasteurized (not ultra-pasteurized or UHT) goat's milk (see page 136)**
- **¼ teaspoon liquid calcium chloride**
- **½ cup cold filtered water**
- **¼ teaspoon direct-set mesophilic starter culture**
- **½ teaspoon liquid animal rennet**
- **5 tablespoons Diamond Crystal kosher salt (see page 70)**

1. Pour milk into Dutch oven. Dilute calcium chloride in ¼ cup water, then gently stir into milk. Slowly heat milk over low heat, stirring occasionally, until milk registers 86 to 88 degrees, 10 to 15 minutes. Remove pot from heat and sprinkle culture evenly over surface of milk, stirring gently to combine. Cover pot and let sit undisturbed at room temperature for 1 hour.

2. Dilute rennet in remaining ¼ cup water, then gently stir into milk until well combined. Cover pot and let milk mixture sit undisturbed, at room temperature, until curd fully separates from whey and a clean line of separation is formed when cut with flat metal spatula, about 1 hour. If curd does not separate cleanly (it will look wobbly and cut unevenly), wait 15 minutes and test again.

3. Working from far side of pot, repeatedly plunge long, large whisk into curd and drag it toward you, cutting curd into a series of rows. Turn pot 90 degrees and repeat to make cross-hatch pattern in curd. Let cut curd sit undisturbed for 10 minutes. Using large slotted spoon, gently stir curds using a folding motion to break up any large chunks, about 10 seconds; let curds sit for 5 minutes. Gently stir again and let rest another 5 minutes; repeat this gentle stirring and resting process 2 more times, until curds are evenly broken into ½-inch pieces or slightly smaller.

4. Line colander with butter muslin or triple layer of cheesecloth and set in sink. Using skimmer or large slotted spoon, transfer curds to prepared colander and let drain for 30 minutes. Reserve 2 cups whey from pot, and refrigerate; discard any remaining whey. Bundle curds in muslin, then tie with kitchen twine to secure. Tie bundle to large spoon set over deep bowl or container, making sure bundle does not touch bottom of bowl. Let drain at room temperature until feta feels firm, 1 to 2 hours. Untie bundle and gently flip feta over; then retie and rehang bundle until curds form a solid mass and are firm to the touch, about 24 hours.

5. Cut feta round in half, then slice each half into 1-inch-thick slabs. Gently transfer slabs to 13 by 9-inch baking dish. Sprinkle 1 tablespoon salt evenly over each side of feta slabs. Cover and let sit at room temperature until feta is very firm to touch and has stopped exuding whey, 2 to 3 days, flipping slabs over and draining off excess whey once a day. Dice feta into 1-inch cubes and transfer to 1-quart jar with tight fitting lid. In medium bowl, whisk reserved 2 cups whey with remaining 3 tablespoons salt until completely dissolved. Pour brine over feta and refrigerate. Feta can be refrigerated for up to 6 weeks.

Paneer

✔️ **WHY THIS RECIPE WORKS:** There are few North Indian dishes as universally appreciated as *saag paneer*, with its cubes of firm, mild cheese (that's the paneer) simmered in a rich sauce of pureed spinach (that's the saag) and intoxicating warm spices. With its yin-yang of familiarity and exoticism, it's the sort of dish many of us love to go out to enjoy. So why not make it at home? For most folks, it comes down to the paneer. The idea of making cheese at home can be flat-out intimidating. I'm here to tell you in this case it's easy. Plus, paneer's role can go far beyond its well-known pairing with saag; this fresh cheese is great in curries or sautéed and tossed with dal, roasted vegetables, or salads.

The method for preparing paneer, which is a lot like a farmer's cheese, varies little from recipe to recipe; scald milk, curdle it with an acid, strain it, then press the curds into a "cake." This simplicity meant for my own recipe, I would focus on the few variables: the quality and fat content of the milk and the type of acid used to curdle it. After making batches with everything from skim to whole, I can tell you, fresh, pasteurized whole milk produces the creamiest, fullest-flavored cheese. As for the acid, vinegar, lemon juice, and buttermilk are the three common choices; I found that buttermilk packed just the right balancing tang. When it came to forming the "cake," pressing the bundled curds under a Dutch oven, although not traditional, was easy. In 30 minutes, I had paneer at least as good as any I'd had at a restaurant, if not better. Tonight, I'm having Indian at home.

For the most reliable results, use fresh homogenized and pasteurized milk here; do not use ultra-pasteurized or ultra-heat-treated (UHT or long-life) milk in this recipe, as it will not curdle properly.

—MATTHEW CARD, Contributing Editor, *Cook's Illustrated*

"The idea of making cheese at home can be flat-out intimidating. I'm here to tell you in this case it's easy. Plus, paneer's role can go far beyond its well-known pairing with saag."

Curdle with culture: First, heat up the milk (along with some salt) to a rapid simmer, about 200 degrees. Once it's steaming and bubbling, it's time to take it off the heat and stir in the acidifying agent. In my recipe, I use buttermilk. Unlike lemon juice and vinegar, the other two common choices, cultured buttermilk is relatively low in acidity (about 1 percent compared to up to 6 percent in lemon juice), which means in order for the milk to curdle properly, you need a fair bit of buttermilk. I ended up at a 1:4 ratio of buttermilk to milk, which was fine with me since it gives my paneer an appealing tang.

Complete separation: It only takes about 15 seconds for the milk to start to curdle, but let it sit for one full minute to be sure the curds and whey have fully separated. Paneer curds made using buttermilk are usually on the small side, so don't fret if they don't form large, pillowlike curds.

Drain game: Now pour it all into a cheesecloth- or butter muslin–lined colander and allow the curds to drain for 10 minutes. As they drain, the curds will clump together at the bottom of the colander and basically plug it up and stop the whey from getting through. So tilt the colander and pull up on the cheesecloth to jostle the curds. This will allow whey to drain off evenly and entirely, not just from the sides but also from the center. If you try to form the cheese while there's still whey in there, the whey will end up stuck in the middle of the cake of cheese, making it impossible to form a firm block.

Soft and dry: After 10 minutes, the curds will have shed much of their whey and there shouldn't be any pockets of it left in the curds, but the curds should still be slightly moist. At this point, the curds will be warm but not scorching hot.

Squeeze your heart out: Carefully pull the edges of the cheesecloth together and twist them to form a pouch. Twist the bag tighter and tighter until the whey no longer drains freely from the curds. This step not only helps with draining but also creates the taut pouch that you'll use to help the curds form into a cake during pressing.

A full Dutch-oven press: Now it's time to turn these curds into a solid cake of cheese. Place the taut, twisted cheese pouch between two plates, then weigh down the top plate with a Dutch oven or another wide-bottomed pot filled with something heavy like 28-ounce canned goods. Let the cheese sit at room temperature until firm enough to slice (just give it a good poke to check). This will take about 30 minutes.

Slice 'n go: Once it's pressed, I usually cut the cheese into cubes and then sauté it in butter for a snack, or slip it into a curry or sauce for saag paneer. If I'm not quite ready to use it, I wrap the whole cake in plastic wrap. It will keep in the refrigerator for up to three days.

Paneer

Makes 12 ounces
Make today, enjoy immediately

3 **quarts pasteurized (not ultra-pasteurized or UHT) whole milk (see page 136)**
2½ **teaspoons salt**
3 **cups buttermilk**

1. Line colander with butter muslin or triple layer of cheesecloth and place in sink. Bring milk and salt to rapid simmer (about 200 degrees) in Dutch oven over medium-high heat, stirring frequently with rubber spatula to prevent scorching.

2. Remove pot from heat. Slowly stir in buttermilk until fully incorporated and mixture curdles, about 15 seconds. Let sit undisturbed for 1 minute.

3. Pour mixture into prepared colander. Let drain until whey no longer runs freely from colander, about 10 minutes, tilting colander and lifting corners of cheesecloth occasionally to allow whey to drain evenly. Pull edges of cheesecloth together to form pouch. Twist edges of cheesecloth together, firmly squeezing curds until whey no longer runs freely from pouch.

4. Place taut, twisted cheese pouch between 2 large plates and weigh down top plate with heavy Dutch oven or pot filled with weights. Let sit at room temperature until cheese is firm and set, about 30 minutes. Remove cheesecloth, wrap tightly in plastic wrap, and refrigerate. Paneer can be refrigerated for up to 3 days.

Fromage Blanc

✔️ **WHY THIS RECIPE WORKS:** Tangy, creamy, and a bit under the radar, fromage blanc is a European-style fresh cheese hovering somewhere in the vast expanse of the cultured-dairy universe. It comes in many styles, its texture resembling anything from sour cream (ideal for using over fruit or granola, which is the most classic version) to cream cheese to fresh goat cheese. It's an incredibly flexible cheese, since you can customize the texture to fit whatever you're in the mood for. Plus the idea of making a cultured fresh cheese from plain ol' cow's milk is pretty appealing. Making fromage blanc at home also makes sense since it is still a rarity in supermarkets.

Legit fromage blanc is made with milk of varied fat levels plus cultures, a drop of rennet, and salt (yes, there are recipes that use buttermilk or lemon juice, but these are shortcut versions). I was thinking about going beyond the sour-cream-esque style. I found recipes that gave it a firmer consistency by draining and pressing the curds. Others created a creamy, fresh goat cheese–like spread, while some pressed almost all of the liquid out to produce something akin to paneer. I tested several draining and pressing methods. I found that the cheeses pressed with heavy weights were unpleasantly dry, and the cheeses that were simply drained were still too much like sour cream. I ended up with a drain-then-press process: This gave me a cheese that was creamy and spreadable like goat cheese, but it had a cleaner flavor. Plus, I didn't have to deal with tracking down goat's milk. I spread it on crackers with a bit of fig jam and was in heaven.

For the most reliable results, use fresh homogenized and pasteurized milk here; do not use ultra-pasteurized or ultra-heat-treated (UHT or long-life) milk in this recipe, as it will not curdle properly.

—KATE WILLIAMS, Test Cook, Books

Good milk, low heat: To begin, measure 2 quarts of milk. I wholeheartedly endorse using whole milk for the best flavor and texture (it's possible to make the cheese using lower-fat dairy but I did all my testing with whole). Whatever you choose, you need to use milk that has not been ultra-pasteurized. Add the milk to a large saucepan and heat it slowly over low heat until it just hits 80 degrees. This temperature provides the optimum incubation environment for the fromage blanc culture.

A dash of culture, then say good night: Next, add ¼ teaspoon of fromage blanc starter culture and give it all a good stir. I decided to order a culture specifically for fromage blanc because it already has the rennet, which will cause the milk to form curds, included. Remove the pot from the heat, cover it with a snug lid, and let the whole thing rest at room temperature overnight. This step gives the culture time to grow and develop, which will give the cheese its tangy flavor, and the rennet time to coagulate the milk.

A clean break: I know my curds are set and my cheese is ready to drain when I can insert a metal spatula into the pot and see a clean line of separation. This is called the clean break test. If the curds are not fully separated, just set the lid back on the pot, let it sit for another hour, then retest.

Scoop the curds: For the draining stage, set a colander inside a large bowl, then line the colander with butter muslin (a triple layer of cheesecloth will also work). Now grab a skimmer or a large slotted spoon and scoop the curds (they should come out in pretty large chunks) from the pot and transfer them to the muslin-lined colander, leaving the whey behind.

Let it drain: After transferring all of the curds to the colander, fold the muslin over the curds and cover the bowl tightly with plastic wrap. Place it in the refrigerator and let the cheese drain for about four hours.

Now weight: Your curds are well drained if they look like ricotta cheese. At this point, sprinkle ½ teaspoon salt evenly over the cheese, then re-cover it with the muslin. Now it's time to weight it. I don't have a cheese press, so I jury-rigged one. Top the cheese with a plate, pressing firmly to make sure it evenly touches the surface of the curds. Then place a large container of pie weights (a jar of pennies, cans of tomatoes, or even more plates would work too) on top of the plate and cover with plastic wrap. Now it goes back in the fridge for about another hour.

With jam and bread (or crackers): When the cheese is finished, you'll be left with a nice big bowlful of whey (which I like to use in homemade bread instead of water to add protein). My final product looks a lot like goat cheese, but it has a milder flavor. I like this style of fromage blanc best with jam and crackers or bread, but it is also delicious as a *queso fresco* substitute for tacos or enchiladas.

Fromage Blanc

Makes 1 pound
Start today, enjoy tomorrow

- **8 cups pasteurized (not ultra-pasteurized or UHT) whole milk (see page 136)**
- **¼ teaspoon direct-set fromage blanc starter culture**
- **½ teaspoon salt**

1. Slowly heat milk in large saucepan over low heat until milk registers 80 degrees. Remove from heat, sprinkle culture over surface of milk, and gently stir until combined. Cover saucepan and let milk mixture sit, undisturbed, at room temperature until curd fully separates from whey and a clean line of separation is formed when cut with flat metal spatula, 12 to 18 hours.

2. Line colander with butter muslin or triple layer of cheesecloth and set inside large, deep bowl. Using a skimmer or a large slotted spoon, gently transfer curd to prepared colander, and fold excess muslin over top of curd. Cover with plastic wrap, refrigerate, and let drain until curd is very thick and ricotta-like, about 4 hours.

3. Sprinkle cheese with salt, re-cover with muslin, and place plate on top of curd. Place container of pie weights (or a 28-ounce can) on plate and cover with plastic wrap. Refrigerate and let drain until cheese is very thick and has the consistency of goat cheese, 1 to 2 hours. Gently fold with rubber spatula to incorporate salt. Fromage blanc can be refrigerated in an airtight container for up to 1 week.

TO MAKE FROMAGE BLANC WITH MESOPHILIC STARTER AND ANIMAL RENNET: If you already have mesophilic starter culture and animal rennet on hand, you can use them instead of the fromage blanc starter: In step 1, Sprinkle ¼ teaspoon direct-set mesophilic starter culture over the warmed milk and stir to combine. Then, dilute 1 drop of rennet in 2 tablespoons cold purified or distilled water and stir it into the milk.

Crème Fraîche

✔ **WHY THIS RECIPE WORKS:** When I first heard the term "crème fraîche," way before the word "foodie" was commonplace and all the haute foods associated with it were considered cool, I scoffed. On paper, it sounds so fussy, so fancy, so…French. What do you even need crème fraîche for when you have sour cream and yogurt?

But once I finally got around to tasting the stuff, I shut up. Tangy and rich in all the right ways, crème fraîche made a perfect addition to my growing collection of homemade refrigerator staples. And as a bonus, it is just about the easiest "fancy" food on the planet to make.

All we're talking about here is cultured (that is, good-bacteria-filled) cream—proto-butter, if you will. Back when raw, unpasteurized milk was the norm, old-school crème fraîche recipes (if you could even call them recipes) simply directed you to place milk or cream in a warm place for a day or two, and let the natural bacteria take over. Unfortunately, unless you live on a farm or have really awesome connections, it is crazy difficult to find raw milk (legally) in America. In this post-Pasteur world, then, it's necessary to reintroduce a little bacteria into the cream. You can do this in a couple of ways, but the easiest, totally foolproof method—the one I use regularly—is to use buttermilk as a starter culture. In a day or less, the cream will thicken up to just the right spoonable consistency. It's good on sweet foods like fruit and chocolate, on savory foods like soups and tacos, and even straight up, licked off a spoon. Just remember, the better the cream that you start with, the better the crème fraîche. For the most reliable results, use fresh homogenized and pasteurized milk here.

—KATE WILLIAMS, Test Cook, Books

"Tangy and rich in all the right ways, crème fraîche made a perfect addition to my growing collection of homemade refrigerator staples. And as a bonus, it is just about the easiest 'fancy' food on the planet to make."

Source it, start it, stir it: I used pasteurized cream throughout my testing because it works best; ultra-pasteurized is heated to a higher temperature and therefore contains fewer helpful bacteria for making crème fraîche. The cream should be around 75 degrees (a high room temperature) before culturing, or it will take much longer to develop that tangy flavor. To make 1 cup crème fraîche, measure out 1 cup cream and then add 2 tablespoons buttermilk and stir it together.

Stash it: Pour the cream into a glass jar, cover it with cheesecloth or butter muslin, then put it in a warm place. It can go anywhere: on top of a toaster oven, in a sunny window, or inside an oven with the oven light on. Ideally, you want a high room temp. It still works at lower temperatures but can take up to 36 hours to reach the proper consistency. Assuming you've found the warmer temp, leave the mixture undisturbed for 12 to 24 hours (the exact timing varies depending on temperature and cream used), until it is thickened but still pourable.

Eat it: If I'm out of patience, or am just in the mood for a thinner, drizzle-able product, I just give the crème fraîche a good stir at this point and eat it as is. Sometimes, though, I want something thicker to dollop on soups or spread on cinnamon graham crackers. In that case, I put the crème fraîche in the refrigerator overnight to firm up. Either way, it's an easy win.

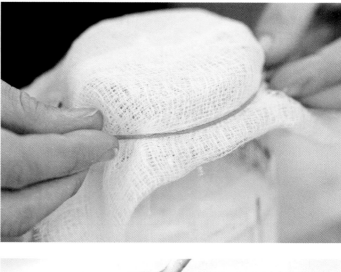

Crème Fraîche

Makes 1 cup
Make today, enjoy tomorrow

1 **cup pasteurized (not ultra-pasteurized or UHT) heavy cream, room temperature (see page 136)**
2 **tablespoons buttermilk, room temperature**

Stir cream and buttermilk together until combined and pour into 1-pint jar. Cover with butter muslin or triple layer of cheesecloth, securing in place with rubber band. Place in warm place, about 75 degrees, until crème fraîche is noticeably thickened but still pourable, 12 to 24 hours. Stir to recombine, then cover jar with lid. Crème fraîche can be refrigerated for up to 1 month.

Greek-Style Yogurt

✔ **WHY THIS RECIPE WORKS:** My devotion to all forms of dairy began at an early age, a given since I grew up in Vermont. Today, making yogurt is a favorite ritual for me. There are good reasons to make your own. It's easy, and quality pints don't run cheap. But perhaps most important, many brands take shortcuts, like using gelatin, pectin, or inulin (a flavorless dietary fiber) to make a thicker product, which saves money and time but degrades flavor. Instead of worrying about additives, off-textures, or sour flavors, just make your own. Use the best-quality homogenized, pasteurized milk and "starter" yogurt (with live active cultures) that you can find.

—JENNIFER LALIME, Test Cook, Books

Pour it in, heat it up: I always start with the best-quality milk I can find. I use low-fat milk, but you can use whole or skim. Heat the milk in a saucepan to 185 degrees. Resist the urge to stir since stirring will lead to small lumps in the final yogurt. At 185, the milk's proteins reconfigure and create a creamy, viscous texture once cultured (which will happen in a few steps), rather than separating into curds and whey. Off the heat, gently stir in dry milk powder, which will help thicken the yogurt. I find that the yogurt sets more reliably if I let the milk cool for about 10 minutes, or until it reaches 160 degrees.

Quick cool: Once the milk has cooled to 160, you can speed up the process a bit. The milk needs to be between 110 and 112 degrees to create a friendly environment for the culture and to prevent curdling. To reach this temperature quickly, strain the mixture into a bowl set over an ice bath. Not many yogurt recipes call for straining, but I find it wise since it removes any stray lumps from the bottom of the pot or clumps of dry milk that didn't dissolve. When the milk is cooled to about 112 degrees, it will feel warm, but not hot, to the touch (similar to water when proofing yeast).

Get your starter: Making yogurt from milk requires adding a starter with live cultures. Freeze-dried starters such as Yógourmet work, but the flavor is too tangy for me. I buy a small container of yogurt (make sure it contains live active cultures) as a starter. To make it easier to incorporate, I thin it first by stirring a little of the cooled milk into the yogurt until smooth. Then add the starter to the bowl with the milk and stir to combine. Cover the bowl with plastic wrap and pierce several holes in the top to allow the yogurt to breathe.

Find a warm place: The bacteria prosper around 100 to 110 degrees. Any lower and the culturing will take days; any higher and the milk will curdle. I tested keeping the bowl in the oven with the light on, or, if your oven goes low enough, set it to 100 degrees. It will take five to seven hours to transform into yogurt; start checking it at the five-hour mark. (Yogurt doesn't like to be disturbed, so try not to jiggle the bowl too much.) When it's ready, the yogurt will appear thickened, creamy, and set. Sometimes there is a little liquid in the bowl. It's simply separated whey, which you can stir back in.

Go Greek: Since I like a thicker texture and richer flavor, I strain my yogurt to mimic Greek-style. But first, let it cool completely in the fridge (it will firm up a bit). Then set a fine-mesh strainer over a large liquid measuring cup or bowl and line it with a couple of coffee filters or a double layer of cheesecloth. After pouring the yogurt into the strainer, cover it with plastic wrap and refrigerate until 2 cups of whey drain from the yogurt, which will take seven to eight hours. For thinner yogurt shorten the time or just skip draining altogether.

Breakfast is served: After the seven or eight hours of straining, you'll have about 2 cups of delightfully rich and creamy yogurt. (If you used skim milk and nonfat yogurt, your final yogurt will be a little bit thinner but you can always drain it longer.) Honey is my go-to sweetener for yogurt, with raw sugar coming in a close second. Top the yogurt with a handful of fresh berries, and I'm ready to start my day.

Greek-Style Yogurt

Makes 2 cups

Make today, enjoy tomorrow

- **4 cups 2 percent pasteurized (not ultra-pasteurized or UHT) low-fat milk (see page 136)**
- **¼ cup nonfat dry milk powder**
- **¼ cup plain 2 percent Greek yogurt**

1. Adjust oven rack to middle position. Place fine-mesh strainer over large glass bowl, then set bowl in larger bowl filled with ice water. Heat milk in large saucepan over medium-low heat (do not stir while heating), until milk registers 185 degrees. Remove pot from heat, gently stir in milk powder, and let cool to 160 degrees, 7 to 10 minutes. Strain milk through prepared strainer and let cool, gently stirring occasionally, until milk registers 110 to 112 degrees; remove from ice bath.

2. In small bowl, gently stir ½ cup warm milk into yogurt until smooth. Stir yogurt mixture back into milk. Cover tightly with plastic wrap and poke several holes in plastic. Place bowl in oven and turn on oven light, creating a warm environment of 100 to 110 degrees. Let yogurt sit undisturbed until thickened and set, 5 to 7 hours. Transfer to refrigerator until completely chilled, about 3 hours.

3. Set clean fine-mesh strainer over large measuring cup and line with double layer of coffee filters. Transfer yogurt to prepared strainer, cover with plastic, and refrigerate until about 2 cups of liquid have drained into measuring cup, 7 to 8 hours. Transfer strained yogurt to jar with tight fitting lid, discarding drained liquid. Yogurt can be refrigerated for up to 1 week.

TO MAKE LACTOSE-FREE GREEK-STYLE YOGURT: Dry milk powder helps thicken this yogurt, but it contains so much lactose the cultures can't consume it all. Omit the dry milk powder for a lactose-free version. The draining step may take as few as 4 to 5 hours.

Cultured Butter

"And while I love it for sautéing and baking, a good butter—I mean a really good butter— can stand on its own. We're not talking Land O'Lakes here, but the European-style cultured stuff."

WHY THIS RECIPE WORKS: When other kids in preschool were eating peanut butter and jelly, I was munching on butter sandwiches. Our family had a separate freezer when I was growing up just for butter—my mother bought 75 pounds every time it went on sale. So it's not surprising that today I'm regularly pouring brown butter sauces over fish, churning up butter ice cream, and baking brioche. And while I love it for sautéing and baking, a good butter—I mean a really good butter—can stand on its own. We're not talking Land O'Lakes here, but the European-style cultured stuff.

Making butter, even cultured butter, isn't that hard. Take 48 hours plus about 30 minutes of hands-on time, and presto. All you have to do is add some live cultures to heavy cream and leave it to sit for a day or two. Then use your stand mixer to whip your cream until it separates into butter and buttermilk, go through a few simple steps to wash the butter, and that's it.

Maybe I don't need to state the obvious, but better cream gives you better butter. Butter made from generic store-brand cream gave me pale, uninteresting stuff that honestly wasn't worth the trouble, while the cream from a local dairy gave me rich, golden-hued butter. But don't fret if you can't get cream from the farm; something between the two is still great. And don't overlook the buttermilk you drain off. What you are getting here is the old-fashioned stuff that you've heard your mother and grand-mother go on about. Use it for making waffles, pancakes, pies, or dressing, or drink it as is. Like butter, you can freeze buttermilk; it will lose some of its creaminess, but it's just fine for baking. Frozen buttermilk will look separated once thawed; simply shake to recombine. For the most reliable results, use fresh homogenized and pasteurized milk here.

—LOUISE EMERICK, Senior Editor, Books

Shake it up: The first step is culturing the cream. I didn't want to fuss with tracking down starter culture, and while some people use buttermilk, I didn't want to buy a quart and end up with leftovers when I was about to get a far superior product. Yogurt is easy and affordable. Stonyfield Farm's Plain Cream Top Yogurt, with its six live cultures, worked really well. Use a yogurt without preservatives or gums for best results. Pour the cream and yogurt into a large container with a lid (a 2-quart Mason jar works well), cover, and shake it to thoroughly combine.

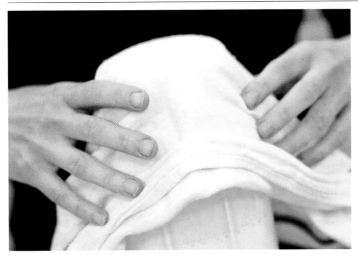

Give it time: Now it just needs time for the cultures in the yogurt to do their thing and culture the cream. So remove the lid and cover the jar with a clean kitchen cloth (or butter muslin or a triple layer of cheesecloth) and secure it with a rubber band. You want to keep it clean from any debris that might try to venture in, but the cream needs some air to culture properly. Put the jar in a warmish (around 75 degrees, if possible) part of your house, and let it sit for at least 18 hours.

Getting it thick: After 18 to 24 hours, your culturing cream might have a foamy "head." Give it a stir and a taste. You are after a thick, silky consistency, a tangy flavor, and a slightly sour smell (think yogurt or buttermilk). If it's not there yet, re-cover and let it sit for up to 24 hours longer. Once the cream is thick, put on the lid and refrigerate it until it reaches around 60 degrees. It churns best when slightly cool. (If you are short on time, you can also leave the jar in the fridge for a few days, then let it sit at room temp until it hits 60 degrees.)

One good churn: I use a stand mixer with the whisk attachment for this step. Transfer the cream to the mixer bowl. Later, when the cream separates into butter and buttermilk, buttermilk will splatter, so I cover the space between the mixer head and workbowl with plastic wrap. Now let 'er rip. If the cream is properly thick, the whole thing takes less than five minutes. First it looks like whipped cream. When you start seeing buttermilk splatters on the plastic, stop. You are finished when you see yellow curds (butter) and glimpses of white liquid (buttermilk).

Strain it, squeeze it: Line a fine-mesh strainer with cheesecloth and set it in a bowl, then grab about 4 cups of ice water. (I like efficiency, so I get this ready before churning.) Transfer the butter and buttermilk to the cheesecloth and let it drain for a minute. Then gather the cheesecloth up around the butter and push the butter down into a ball, then squeeze. Get out as much buttermilk as possible, because, yes, you want it for cooking and drinking, but also, buttermilk left behind will cause the butter to go rancid more quickly.

Washed out: Now you have to wash the butter several times with the ice water to get rid of lurking buttermilk. Place the butter in a large bowl and pour about ⅓ cup ice water over the butter. Start smashing and folding the butter to squeeze out buttermilk, tilting the bowl to cover the butter with more water. Pour off the milky-white liquid (this watered-down stuff isn't worth saving), then repeat until the water stays clear. It should take about six washes. The butter will firm up as you go; earlier washes are best done with a rubber spatula but toward the end it's easier to just get in there with your hands.

Get in shape: After you've drained off the last of the water, give the butter one last squeeze and smash to get rid of any last bits of liquid, sprinkle over the salt (if using) and incorporate it into the butter with the same folding and smashing technique. Portion the butter however you wish (I typically divide it in half), dropping each portion onto the top third of a piece of waxed paper or parchment. If you are feeling crafty, you can also mold the butter into something with a little aesthetic appeal, or simply store it in a ramekin.

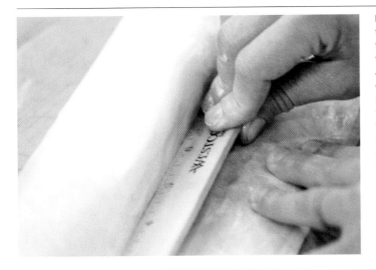

Roll with it: Use your hands to form the mass into a rough log, then fold the paper over. Perfectionist that I am, I use a straight edge (like a ruler) to push into the bottom of the log, then use a downward pushing motion to inch back the top of the paper while holding the bottom in place with my free hand. This will push the butter into a perfectly smooth log. Tape over the edges and put it in the fridge. Or just dig in. My newest—and now favorite—way to enjoy it is on a slice of sourdough or rye soda bread with Maldon salt and Seville Orange Marmalade (page 63). Phenomenal.

Cultured Butter

Makes about 12 ounces butter and 1½ cups buttermilk

Start today, enjoy in 1 to 3 days

- **4 cups pasteurized (not ultra–pasteurized or UHT) heavy cream, room temperature (see page 136)**
- **½ cup plain whole-milk yogurt, room temperature**
- **¼ teaspoon sea salt or kosher salt (optional)**

1. Combine cream and yogurt in 2-quart jar with tight-fitting lid, cover, and shake to combine. Remove lid, cover with clean kitchen towel, butter muslin, or triple layer of cheesecloth, securing in place with rubber band. Place jar in warm place, about 75 degrees, and let sit until thickened to the consistency of yogurt, 18 to 48 hours. (If temperature dips much below 75 degrees, culture may take up to 60 hours.) Once thickened, remove kitchen towel, cover jar with lid, and transfer to refrigerator to cool until mixture registers 60 degrees, about 2 hours.

2. Place 4 cups of ice water in refrigerator. Line fine-mesh strainer with butter muslin or triple layer of cheesecloth and set over large bowl. Using stand mixer fitted with whisk and covered with plastic wrap, whip cream on high speed until cream separates into buttermilk and small clumps of yellow butter, 2 to 5 minutes. Strain butter through prepared strainer for 1 minute. Gather edges of muslin and twist to squeeze butter until buttermilk no longer flows freely from pouch. Remove butter from muslin and transfer to clean large bowl; reserve buttermilk for another use.

3. Pour about ⅓ cup ice water over butter. With butter resting in water, use rubber spatula to fold butter against side of bowl, letting water wash over butter to rinse off any remaining buttermilk. Discard milky liquid, and repeat washing process until water remains clear, about 6 washes. After final wash, discard any water in bowl and continue to fold butter to squeeze out any remaining liquid; discard liquid. Sprinkle butter with salt, if using, and fold into butter. Divide butter in half, transfer to parchment paper, and roll into 2 logs or desired shape. Butter can be refrigerated for up to 1 month or frozen for at least 4 months.

Tofu

WHAT YOU NEED TO MAKE TOFU

Dried soybeans are available at Asian markets, some supermarkets, and online. Liquid nigari can be found online at culturesforhealth.com and at Asian supermarkets. You can find tofu molds at amazon.com, but if you don't want to invest, poke three even holes in the bottom of a quart-size plastic berry container, then cut off the lid and trim it down to just fit inside the container. Line the container with muslin or cheesecloth and scoop the curds into the container just the same as you would with a mold, then cover with the muslin/cheesecloth and place the trimmed plastic lid on top.

WHY THIS RECIPE WORKS: Many of my friends look at me pityingly when I confess to liking tofu. Who could blame them? In the three-plus decades since the natural foods movement helped make tofu a household word here in the United States, many awful things have been done with it. (Tofu meatloaf, anyone?) Then there's the fact that commercial brands of tofu have a chalky taste and, in firmer styles, a spongy texture.

My turnaround came when I moved to Asia after college and learned that tofu wasn't just some amorphous block of soy curd appropriated by '70s vegans as a meat and cheese substitute. Treated properly, tofu is a stunner. And its possibilities are endless. In Japan, tofu is made at dawn, like bread, for early morning distribution. There I sampled chilled silky-smooth blocks adorned with nothing more than a sprinkle of grated ginger. In China I ate tofu tea-smoked and pressed to a dense, meaty texture. In Indonesia, I tasted tofu steamed in banana leaf, redolent of coconut cream and spices. I also learned that, like bread, tofu is best on the day it's made. Once I got back to the States, there was only one way to ensure the freshest tofu with the same clean, delicate taste I'd grown addicted to: Make it myself.

Happily, tofu is no harder to make than yogurt. Whether your end product is silky, firm, or extra-firm, the process is the same: Curdle hot soy milk with a mineral salt called nigari, then press out the whey to create the desired texture. It's best to make your own soy milk from dried beans or the tofu might not coagulate properly, unless you can get your hands on genuinely fresh soy milk from an Asian market. This recipe won't work with supermarket soy milks such as Silk and WestSoy.

—AMANDA AGEE, Executive Editor, *Cook's Illustrated*

Soak your beans to make milk:
Tofu is simply curdled soy milk, but not any soy milk will do. Mainstream supermarket brands contain additives or have been heat-treated, which prevents them from curdling properly. The fresh soy milk made with just water and soybeans that's sold in Asian markets is a viable starting point, but I like the control of making my own—which is not only easy but inexpensive. Start by soaking 8 ounces of dried beans overnight in enough water to cover by a couple of inches. The next day, the beans will have more than doubled in size and turned from beige to pale yellow.

Blend and simmer: Next, the soaked beans are run through the blender. I work in batches, adding 3 cups of water for every 1 cup of beans and blending until the mixture is milky and mostly smooth (the texture will be grainy, but we'll sort that out), then transferring each blended batch to a Dutch oven. Next I bring the blended beans up to a boil and simmer them for about 10 minutes, which gives the soy milk a richer consistency and makes the raw beans more digestible. Heating the soy milk turns it foamy and prone to boiling over, so keep an eye on it and stir occasionally.

Pulp? No problem: To remove the fibrous bits of soybean that are still left in the milk, next you need to strain the soy milk through a butter muslin–lined colander, squeezing the pulp to extract as much liquid as possible. After straining, you should have about 8 cups of smooth, silky soy milk; return it to your Dutch oven. The pulp that remains is called *okara* and is rich in fiber, calcium, and protein. Many cooks save the okara and add it to quick breads, stir-fries, or cold deli-style salads like tuna or chicken salad.

Now the nigari: For a coagulant, I use nigari, a salt from seawater. I prefer liquid over flaked since it reliably delivers fluffy curds and tofu with a nice neutral flavor. Adding the nigari (which I dilute first) in stages ensures the whey isn't expressed too quickly so you'll get a better yield and fluffier curds. Bring the soy milk to a boil, stir it in a figure-eight motion to get it churning (to ensure even distribution), then pour in half the nigari mixture off the heat. Let the milk sit for two minutes. The curds should be starting to form; gently stir in the remaining nigari, trying not to break up too many curds.

Mold it: Put the lid on the pot and let it sit. After 20 minutes, there should be white, fluffy, well-defined curds surrounded by clear yellow whey. Scoop the curds into a butter muslin–lined tofu mold. I use a tofu mold that I ordered online, but I've also had success using a plastic quart-size strawberry container, which I poke with three holes in the bottom for even drainage.

Weight it: At this point, the tofu is a loose mass of curds, but with a little well-applied pressure, it will turn into a firm block. For a weight, I found a box of chicken broth fits well into the constructs of the mold. Put the box lid on top of the tofu, then top with your box of broth. If you are using a strawberry container, cut the lid off the container, then place it on top of the tofu and top with the box of broth. Depending on how you like your tofu (soft, medium, firm), you can press the curds anywhere from 20 to 50 minutes. I like medium tofu most often, so I press the curds for about 30 minutes.

Make it sturdy: After my tofu has reached its perfect texture, I gently lift it out of its mold, place it in a shallow dish, and fill the dish with cold water. The cold water will help firm up the block of tofu so it will be more sturdy and sliceable. It only needs 10 minutes before it's ready to be put to use. Or store it, refrigerated and submerged in water, for up to 1 week. Just make sure to change the water daily to keep the tofu as fresh as possible.

Tofu

Makes 14 ounces
Start today, enjoy tomorrow

- **8 ounces (1¼ cups) dried soybeans, picked over and rinsed**
- **9½ cups water, plus extra for soaking beans**
- **2 teaspoons liquid nigari**

1. Place beans in large bowl or container and add enough water to cover by 2 inches. Soak until beans are pale yellow and split apart when rubbed between fingertips, 12 to 18 hours.

2. Drain and rinse beans (you should have about 3 cups beans). Working in batches, process 1 cup soaked soybeans and 3 cups water in blender until mostly smooth, about 3 minutes. Transfer mixture to Dutch oven and repeat twice more with remaining 2 cups soybeans and 6 cups water.

3. Line colander with butter muslin or triple layer of cheesecloth and set over large bowl. Bring soy milk mixture to boil over medium-high heat, stirring frequently with rubber spatula to prevent scorching and boiling over. Reduce heat to medium-low and simmer, stirring frequently, until slightly thickened, about 10 minutes.

4. Pour soybean mixture into prepared colander to strain. Being careful of hot soy milk, pull edges of muslin together to form pouch, and twist edges of muslin together. Using tongs, firmly squeeze soybean pulp to extract as much liquid as possible. You should have about 8 cups of soy milk; discard soybean pulp or reserve for another use. Transfer soy milk back to clean Dutch oven and bring to boil over medium-high heat, stirring occasionally to prevent scorching. Remove pot from heat. Combine remaining ½ cup water and nigari in measuring cup.

5. Begin stirring soy milk in fast, figure-eight motion with rubber spatula, about 6 stirs. While still stirring, add ¼ cup prepared nigari mixture. Stop stirring and wait until soy milk stops moving. Cover pot and let sit undisturbed for 2 minutes. Uncover, sprinkle remaining ¼ cup nigari mixture on surface of milk, and gently stir using figure-eight motion, about 6 stirs. Cover pot and let sit undisturbed until curds form and whey is pooling on top and around sides of pot, about 20 minutes.

6. Line tofu mold with butter muslin or triple layer of cheesecloth and place in colander set over large bowl or sink. Using skimmer or large slotted spoon, gently transfer soy milk curds to prepared mold, trying not to break up too much of their natural structure. Cover top of curds with excess muslin and place top of press in place. Weight with 2-pound weight. Press tofu until desired firmness is reached: 20 minutes for soft; 30 minutes for medium; 40 to 50 minutes for firm. Gently remove tofu from mold and place in pie plate or baking dish. Fill with cold water to cover and let sit until tofu is slightly firmer, about 10 minutes. Tofu can be refrigerated in airtight container filled with water for up to 1 week; change water daily.

Cured, Smoked, and Terrined: Preserving Meat and Fish

180   Bacon

184   Pancetta

187   Guanciale

190   Duck Prosciutto

194   Gravlax

197   Merguez

201   Mexican Chorizo

204   Mortadella

208   Duck Confit

211   Mousseline

214   Country-Style Pâté

218   Pork Rillettes

222   Beef Jerky

Bacon

PINK SALT

Curing salt goes by many names, including DQ Curing Salt and Insta Cure #1, but it's most commonly labeled pink salt, so that's the term we use in the test kitchen. Curing salt is important for curing meats because it contains nitrites, which prevent bacterial growth, boost the meaty flavor, and preserve the red color. You can find curing salt in specialty food stores or through online retailers such as butcher-packer.com. (Do not substitute Morton's Tender Quick or Insta Cure #2.)

MAPLE SUGAR

Maple sugar, which is made from maple syrup, is available in many grocery stores and online from kingarthurflour.com and various Vermont maple farms.

WHY THIS RECIPE WORKS: My name is Bryan, and I'm addicted to bacon. Maybe it's the smoky maple scent that wafts from the skillet. Or the crispy bits of fat intertwined with the chewy streaks of meat. Or the irresistible flavor it imparts to everything it comes into contact with. Bacon is just plain good. I've recently taken to making my own in bulk. In the driver's seat, I can start with a relatively inexpensive slab of pork belly and create my own personal blend of salt, sugar, and seasonings to flavor it with. Plus, homemade bacon easily beats anything you'll be tearing from a package bleary-eyed on Sunday morning.

I developed this recipe using a smoker, which delivers the best results because it's the ideal source for moderate, indirect heat that allows the bacon to cook slowly and evenly. But for those who don't own a smoker, I also found a way to make my bacon using a charcoal grill. This method is a great option if you own a charcoal grill and aren't ready to make the leap toward buying a smoker. Just keep in mind that bacon cooked on a charcoal grill will render a bit more and pick up some extra smoky flavor and color because it is much closer to the heat source—but that's not necessarily a bad thing.

This recipe calls for pink salt to preserve the meat's pink color and add flavor. Pink salt is not just for seasoning; it also contains nitrites, so be sure to stick to the quantity listed.

—BRYAN ROOF, Senior Editor, *Cook's Country*

Remove the skin, leave the fat: When you buy pork belly, the skin is usually left intact; you'll need to remove it before proceeding. Start by separating the skin from the fat layer at one corner. Then, holding the knife almost parallel to the belly with one hand and the corner of skin with your other hand, make short horizontal cuts, pulling the skin back as you move across the belly. Take your time to ensure you leave as much of the thick layer of fat intact as possible. After all, fat absorbs flavor, so once you've cured and smoked the belly, you'll be glad you left it all on there.

Give it a rub down: Curing the pork belly adds flavor and firms it up. I use a 13 by 9-inch dish, though a 2-gallon zipper-lock bag would work. I like maple sugar as my rub's base; it gives the bacon a sweetness that perfectly complements the meatiness. The pink salt, which contains nitrites, prevents bacterial growth, boosts flavor, and preserves the meat's red color. I could have tweaked my recipe to work without it, but it's a smart safety measure, plus bacon made without pink salt just doesn't taste as good. When rubbing on the dry cure, be sure to cover the sides and edges of the belly well.

Let it cure: Once you've coated your pork belly with the rub, cover the dish with plastic wrap and put it in the fridge. I flip it every other day, which ensures that as the belly releases liquid, the cure is evenly distributed and stays in direct contact with the meat. After seven to 10 days, the belly will be fully cured, at which point it will feel firm to the touch yet still pliable. After a quick rinse under cold water to remove any excess cure (it will be too salty if you don't), it's ready to smoke.

Keep your cool: While smoking the belly, you want to maintain a moderate heat level. Too much heat and all the fat will render from the bacon; not enough and the bacon won't cook through. By placing lit coals on top of unlit charcoal in your smoker, you can achieve the appropriate temperature (200 to 225 degrees) without having to replenish coals halfway through cooking. The water pan in the smoker also helps to temper the heat. For making bacon on a charcoal grill, I create an indirect heat by arranging unlit and lit coals on one half of the grill and a water pan on the other half.

Smoke break: Next, place the wood chunks on top of the charcoal. It takes about five minutes for them to be ready; just let the initial burst of smoke cook off before putting the meat in the smoker since the first few seconds of smoke can impart a bitter flavor. I find it best to place the pork belly fat side up to allow the rendered fat to baste the meat. If you're using a charcoal grill, make sure to place the belly on the cooler side of grill, over the water-filled pan.

A real beauty: After about 1½ hours in the smoker, the bacon will register 150 degrees and have a deep amber hue. At this point you might be tempted to just stand and stare at how amazing your homemade bacon looks, but I suggest removing it instead. It tastes even better than it looks.

Have a slice...or five: Since the bacon is smoked until it registers 150 degrees, it is fully cooked once you take it out of the smoker. Frying it is just an extra step and not completely necessary. Sometimes I slice it paper-thin and serve it cold, garnished with some Green Tomato Chutney (page 88). When served cold like this, the smoke flavor is much more forward. Pan-frying the bacon tames its smokiness. Whichever way you slice it, this bacon is delicious.

Bacon

Makes about 3½ pounds
Start today, enjoy in 1 week

1	**cup maple sugar**
½	**cup Diamond Crystal kosher salt (see page 70)**
1	**tablespoon peppercorns, cracked**
2	**teaspoons minced fresh thyme**
¾	**teaspoon pink salt (see page 180)**
1	**bay leaf, crumbled**
1	**(4-pound) pork belly, skin removed**
4	**medium hickory wood chunks, soaked in water for 1 hour**

1. Combine sugar, salt, peppercorns, thyme, pink salt, and bay leaf in small bowl. Place pork belly in 13 by 9-inch glass baking dish and rub all sides and edges of pork belly with dry cure mixture. Cover dish tightly with plastic wrap and refrigerate until pork feels firm yet still pliable, 7 to 10 days, flipping meat every other day.

2. Thoroughly rinse pork with cold water and pat dry with paper towels.

3. Open bottom vent of smoker completely. Arrange 1½ quarts unlit charcoal briquettes in center of smoker in even layer. Light large chimney starter three-quarters filled with charcoal briquettes (4½ quarts). When top coals are partially covered with ash, pour evenly over unlit coals. Place wood chunks on coals. Assemble smoker and fill water pan with water according to manufacturer's instructions. Cover smoker and open lid vent completely. Heat smoker until hot and wood chunks are smoking, about 5 minutes.

4. Clean and oil smoking grate. Place pork belly meat side down in center of smoker. Cover (positioning lid vent over pork) and smoke until pork registers 150 degrees, 1½ to 2 hours.

5. Remove bacon from smoker and let cool to room temperature before slicing. Bacon can be wrapped tightly with plastic and refrigerated for up to 1 month or frozen for up to 2 months.

TO MAKE BACON ON A CHARCOAL GRILL: For step 3, open bottom vent of charcoal grill halfway and place large disposable roasting pan filled with 2 cups water on 1 side of grill. Arrange 1 quart unlit charcoal briquettes evenly over half of grill opposite roasting pan. Light large chimney starter one-third filled with charcoal briquettes (2 quarts). When top coals are partially covered with ash, pour evenly over unlit coals. Place wood chunks on coals. Set cooking grate in place, cover, and open lid vent halfway. Heat grill until hot and wood chunks are smoking, about 5 minutes. Clean and oil cooking grate. Place pork belly meat side down on cooler side of grill over water-filled pan and smoke as directed in step 4.

Pancetta

✔ **WHY THIS RECIPE WORKS:** I've been eager to try making charcuterie for a while, and when I decided to give it a go, I settled on pancetta. It's ideal for a beginner. Like bacon, it is cured and thus has a salty, rich pork flavor, but it skips the smoke in favor of a more easily attainable bold seasoning profile—herbs and spices are simply added to the curing mix. Curing is simple, the shopping and equipment list relatively short, and there's little hands-on time. Best of all, the results are impressive. This recipe calls for pink salt to preserve the meat's pink color and add flavor. Pink salt contains nitrites, so be sure to stick to the quantity listed.

—DAN ZUCCARELLO, Associate Editor, Books

A quick trim: Pancetta starts with pork belly. You want to pay close attention while selecting your piece of pork; make sure to choose a belly that has a fresh, clean smell, light-pink skin, and deep-red meat. Begin by removing the skin (see how on page 180), then flip the belly over, trim it to a uniform thickness, and square off the sides. This helps the belly roll evenly.

Add the cure: The dry cure imparts most of the flavor here, so I include plenty of herbs and spices along with salt. I also add 1 teaspoon pink salt, which contains nitrites, key here for both preserving the color and helping to prevent bacterial growth (see page 180 for more on pink salt). The proportion of pink salt to protein is important so be sure to stick to 1 teaspoon pink salt per 5 pounds of belly. Put the belly in a baking dish, then rub the cure all over the meat. Red wine also adds flavor; use just a sprinkling to prevent the cure from washing away.

Rollin': Now refrigerate the belly until its texture changes from soft to firm but still pliable. Over the course of seven to 10 days, flip the belly every other day. Once cured, the pancetta could be rinsed and cooked as is, but I take it a step further, rolling and drying it to develop a firmer texture and deeper flavor. Arrange the rinsed pancetta meaty side up, long side facing you. Sprinkle it with some coarsely ground pepper, then, starting with the side closest to you, roll the pancetta as tightly as possible. You want to avoid air pockets in the center (the ends may stay slightly open even if the center is tight).

Tie it tight: Starting with the center and ends, tie the cylinder with twine—the tighter, the better. Work your way along the length from center to ends, tying at ½-inch intervals. Once it's completely tied, trim excess twine. For a foolproof approach to drying, I place my pancetta in the fridge on a wire rack. After you've made a few batches, you could give the traditional method, hanging at room temperature, a shot. It can be finicky and might not always work, but it allows for more even air circulation. Form a loop at one end with twine and hang in a cool, humid place away from sunlight.

Cut and cook: After two or three weeks, the pancetta should be very firm but not hard. Since it's not meant to be eaten raw, I usually slice it thin and crisp it in a skillet or cube it for soups and stews. If you eventually decide to try the hang-drying method, just remember even if you do everything right, things can still go wrong because of environmental factors out of your control. If you see white mold, just wipe it off with a little vinegar. And if the exterior of the pancetta seems hard or conditions become less ideal, at any time you can move it to the refrigerator, where you're guaranteed success.

Makes about 3 pounds
Start today, enjoy in about
3 weeks

DRY CURE

- ¼ cup Diamond Crystal kosher salt (see page 70)
- 3 tablespoons coarsely ground pepper
- 2 tablespoons packed dark brown sugar
- 2 tablespoons minced fresh rosemary
- 2 tablespoons juniper berries, cracked
- 4 garlic cloves, minced
- 4 bay leaves, crumbled
- 1 tablespoon red pepper flakes
- 1 tablespoon minced fresh thyme
- 1 teaspoon pink salt (see page 180)
- 1 teaspoon ground nutmeg

PORK BELLY

- 1 (5-pound) pork belly, skin removed, belly trimmed to uniform thickness and shape
- ¼ cup dry red wine
- 2 tablespoons coarsely ground pepper

1. FOR THE DRY CURE: Combine all ingredients in small bowl.

2. FOR THE PORK BELLY: Place pork belly in 13 by 9-inch glass baking dish. Rub all sides and edges of pork belly with dry-cure mixture. Sprinkle with wine, being careful to not wash away any cure. Cover dish tightly with plastic wrap and refrigerate until belly feels firm yet pliable, 7 to 10 days, flipping every other day.

3. Thoroughly rinse pancetta with cold water and pat dry with paper towels. Transfer to cutting board meaty side up, with long side facing you. Sprinkle meaty side with pepper, then roll into tight cylinder and tie very tightly at ½-inch intervals with kitchen twine.

4. Place pancetta on wire rack set in rimmed baking sheet and refrigerate, uncovered, until very firm but not hard, 2 to 3 weeks. (Alternatively, use additional kitchen twine to form loop at one end of pancetta and hang pancetta in cool, humid place, around 60 degrees with 60 percent humidity, away from sunlight.) Dried pancetta can be wrapped tightly in plastic and refrigerated for up to 2 weeks or frozen for up to 2 months.

Guanciale

✔ **WHY THIS RECIPE WORKS:** If you like bacon, pancetta, and pork products in general, let me introduce you to *guanciale*, pancetta's under-utilized Italian cousin. The name comes from *guancia*, Italian for "cheek," logical since guanciale is made from a pig jowl. After the pig jowl is cured with salt and seasonings and dried, it becomes firm and dark, with rich, silky fat. Guanciale's fat is sweeter than what you get with pancetta (or bacon), and the meat has a porkier, yet more delicate flavor. Guanciale is great simply pan-fried and eaten as is or incorporated into soups, stews, and, of course, pasta sauces (it's the classic choice for pasta *all'amatriciana*).

But guanciale is not always easy to find, even if you have a great Italian market nearby. So I decided to develop a recipe that was doable even in my modest kitchen yet still was as authentic as what you'd get from a professional Italian kitchen. True, it was a little work to hunt down the jowl itself, but I found I could get it from a farm not too far away, and it's also something you can get, affordably, by mail order.

The method for curing pork jowl is quite simple—you just cure it and dry it. After only a few tests, I found I could turn out guanciale that even an Italian meat-curing master would be proud of.

—DANIEL CELLUCCI, Assistant Test Cook, America's Test Kitchen

PORK JOWLS

While pork belly has become more widely available and you can usually spy it in the butcher's case, pig jowls are not commonly stocked. However, they shouldn't be that hard to get. Ask your local specialty butcher to procure one for you, or mail-order jowls from Savenor's Market by calling 617-723-6328.

Very cheeky: First you need to prep the jowl by removing the salivary glands, which can spoil and have an unappealing texture once cured. I also make sure to remove any fatty tissue around these glands because it can have an off-texture as well. Finding the glands is relatively easy. They are typically raised above the surface and are light brown in contrast to the bright red color of the meat. Using a sharp knife makes easy work of removing them.

Keep it simple: Pork jowl already has a lot of rich flavor, so when it comes time to cure it, I keep the flavorings simple: salt, sugar, cracked peppercorns, and thyme, though I have also used juniper berries, bay leaves, and chopped garlic. Feel free to play around with spices as you like; just grind any larger spices beforehand. Place the jowl in a glass baking dish and rub it well with the cure, cover it, and place it in the refrigerator (a zipper-lock bag would also work here). Flipping the jowl every other day helps keep the cure evenly distributed.

Rinse and dry: After five to seven days the jowl will feel firm yet still pliable, signaling that it's ready to be hung and dried. At this point, rinse the cure off of the jowl with cold water; leaving the salt on would make the guanciale far too salty. Then blot the jowl dry using paper towels.

Hole in one: Since finding the ideal heat and humidity for drying the jowl can be hard, I recommend the refrigerator. It's easy to hang in the fridge since it's thin and doesn't need much room, although you could dry it on a wire rack. I prefer hanging since it's traditional and allows for even air circulation (also the meat won't touch anything). To hang, loop a piece of twine through the guanciale by poking a hole through the corner of the jowl, then threading twine through the hole and tying the ends together. Don't make the hole too close to the edge or the twine will break through the meat as it dries and shrinks.

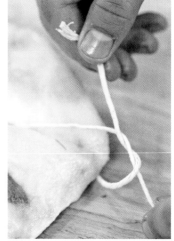

Hang tight: To hang the jowl, tie the loose end of the twine around anything with some weight. Make sure the jowl isn't touching anything else; it will depend on your fridge whether you can hang it down the middle, back, or front. (Of course, if you go the wire rack route, just put it wherever you've got room.) It takes about three weeks for the guanciale to achieve proper firmness. Fried up on its own or cooked into your favorite pasta sauce, this guanciale will give you some of the deepest, richest pork flavor you've ever tasted.

Guanciale

Makes about 1 pound
Start today, enjoy in 1 month

- ½ **cup Diamond Crystal kosher salt (see page 70)**
- ½ **cup sugar**
- ¼ **teaspoon peppercorns, cracked**
- 8 **sprigs fresh thyme**
- 1 **(1½- to 2-pound) pork jowl, trimmed and glands removed**

1. Combine salt, sugar, peppercorns, and thyme in small bowl. Place pork jowl in 13 by 9-inch glass baking dish and rub all sides and edges of pork jowl with salt mixture. Cover dish tightly with plastic wrap and refrigerate until jowl feels firm yet still pliable, 5 to 7 days, flipping every other day. (If after 7 days, jowl still feels soft, continue refrigerating for additional 1 to 2 days until firm yet still pliable.)

2. Thoroughly rinse jowl with cold water and pat dry with paper towels. Use sharp knife to poke hole through corner of jowl, then form loop through hole with kitchen twine. Hang jowl in refrigerator until very firm but not hard, about 3 weeks. (Alternatively, place jowl on wire rack set in baking sheet to refrigerate.) Dried guanciale can be wrapped tightly in plastic and refrigerated for up to 2 weeks or frozen for up to 2 months.

Duck Prosciutto

"Given the huge price savings and the minimal labor required, not to mention the equally delicious if not superior results, this D.I.Y. project is a win in more ways than one."

✔ **WHY THIS RECIPE WORKS:** With its firm texture, salty, meaty flavor, and lines of rich fat running throughout, prosciutto is perhaps the quintessential cured meat, the classic choice for topping a pizza or serving on an antipasto platter. Traditionally, prosciutto is made by salting and drying a whole pig's leg. The hanging time alone can take months and sometimes years. Given the timeline, and the fact that finding such a huge, fully intact cut is a serious challenge, traditional pork prosciutto isn't exactly on my short list for a home curing project.

Duck breast is a more D.I.Y.-friendly option than a whole pig's leg. It is very flavorful and has plenty of fat, plus duck breast isn't hard to find and will easily fit in my refrigerator. Duck prosciutto isn't unheard of—D'Artagnan and Hudson Valley Foie Gras both offer it—but at about $2 per ounce, it's a luxury. Meanwhile, consider the fact that duck breasts only cost about $11 per pound. Given the huge price savings and the minimal labor required, not to mention the equally delicious if not superior results, this D.I.Y. project is a win in more ways than one.

I use Moulard duck breasts here; Muscovy will work, but the final drying time may be shorter.

—REBECCAH MARSTERS, Associate Editor, *Cook's Country*

Cut the fat: Most recipes I found for duck prosciutto call for Muscovy breasts, which weigh in at about 8 ounces each. My thinking is that bigger is better, so instead I opt for Moulard, which are almost twice the size and have a seductive, buttery crown of fat. To ensure the cure penetrates all that amazing fat and meat, I score the skin and fat cap in a crosshatch pattern before curing.

Toast your spices: The curing period is the only opportunity to infuse the duck with flavor, and since duck meat is pretty robust, it can stand up to some substantial seasoning. I like using juniper berries, fennel seeds, peppercorns, bay leaves, and coriander seeds, all of which contribute aromatic and woodsy notes. Toasting the spices is key because it helps to release their flavorful oils. Then a quick whirl in the spice grinder ensures they will mix evenly with the sugar and salt.

Cover up: While some meats cure with only a fine layer of dry cure spread onto them, duck breast does best when surrounded by the cure, maximizing the extraction of moisture from the meat. Start by selecting a vessel that is large enough to hold the duck breast and still leaves room on the sides so the cure can completely surround it; an 8½ by 4½-inch glass loaf pan works well. Spread a layer of cure over the bottom of the dish, place the duck breast on top, and cover it with the remaining cure. Because you need to cover the breast, volume of salt is what counts here; use 3 cups of whatever brand you have on hand.

Completely cured: After four days in the refrigerator, the duck breast will be fully cured. After emerging from its salt cocoon, it will be firm but still pliable, slightly withered, and deep crimson-colored on its underside. Rinse it thoroughly with water, dry it well, then sprinkle it with some black pepper.

That's a wrap: For the drying stage, a cloak of cheesecloth and a sash of twine make for a neat satchel to hang the duck breast. No need to break out the fancy knots here, you just need to tie it well enough to secure the cheesecloth and give yourself a loop at the end for hanging. Hanging is my preference since it's traditional and allows for even air circulation. But if you don't want to manage the hanging setup, you can also dry it on a wire rack set in a baking sheet.

Hang time: While I could search out a place in my home that has the ideal drying conditions, I prefer to use the refrigerator; I've always gotten good results. If you go the hanging route, just tie the loose end of the twine around something like a wine or beer bottle, anything with some weight, then hang it down into a spot in the refrigerator where it will get good circulation. You want it to become very firm, but not hard. This should take about three weeks, but don't be afraid to hang it longer if it still feels too soft.

A perfect slice: I find it best to place the breast fat side up on the cutting board and slice it as thin as possible. As with any cured meat, this duck prosciutto is as versatile as it is delicious, and—if it lasts past the first day—can be stored in the refrigerator tightly wrapped in plastic wrap for a couple of weeks. My favorite way to enjoy it is with figs and arugula, but any combination of fruit, cheese, bread, and greens is sure to be delectable.

Duck Prosciutto

Makes 8 to 10 ounces
Start today, enjoy in 1 month

1 **(12- to 14-ounce) boneless Moulard duck breast, trimmed**
2 **tablespoons juniper berries**
5 **teaspoons fennel seeds**
4 **teaspoons whole white peppercorns**
4 **teaspoons whole black peppercorns, plus ½ teaspoon ground**
7 **bay leaves**
2 **teaspoons coriander seeds**
3 **cups kosher salt**
1 **cup sugar**

1. Using sharp knife, score skin and fat cap of duck breast in ½-inch diagonal crosshatch pattern, being careful not to cut into meat.

2. Toast juniper berries, fennel seeds, white peppercorns, black peppercorns, bay leaves, and coriander seeds in 10-inch skillet over medium-high heat, stirring occasionally, until fragrant, 4 to 6 minutes, reducing heat if spices begin to smoke; let cool to room temperature. Process cooled spices in spice grinder until finely ground, about 20 seconds. Transfer to large bowl and whisk in salt and sugar until combined.

3. Spread ½-inch-thick layer of spice mixture over bottom of 8½ by 4½-inch glass loaf pan, then place duck breast skin side up on top, being careful to keep duck from touching sides of dish so that cure can completely surround it. Pour remaining cure over duck breast to completely surround. Cover tightly with plastic wrap and refrigerate for 4 days.

4. Remove breast from cure, thoroughly rinse with cold water, and pat dry with paper towels. Sprinkle both sides evenly with ground pepper.

5. Wrap breast in double layer of cheesecloth and tie with kitchen twine. Use additional twine to form loop at 1 end of breast and hang breast in refrigerator until very firm, about 3 weeks. (Alternatively, place breast on wire rack set in rimmed baking sheet to refrigerate.) Dried duck breast can be wrapped tightly in plastic and refrigerated for up to 2 weeks.

Gravlax

"As my mother-in-law taught me, the virtues of gravlax are several, but one is that it is so simple to prepare."

WHY THIS RECIPE WORKS: I am probably not the only person to have lumped gravlax into the same category as smoked salmon, lox, and nova (as in Nova Scotia, not the PBS science show). To me, they were all just preserved salmon that topped a cream cheese–slathered bagel or slice of rye.

But last November, when my mother-in-law visited for the Thanksgiving holiday, I learned that I was wrong. Easily our most popular Thanksgiving-day appetizer, her thinly sliced, salt-and-sugar-cured gravlax disappeared in less than five minutes.

So here's the difference. To make smoked salmon, lox, or nova, the salmon is smoked, and it is usually brined before the smoking step. As my mother-in-law taught me, the virtues of gravlax are several, but one is that it is so simple to prepare. The word "gravlax" comes from *gravad lax*, which is Swedish for "buried salmon." Most recipes follow the same, ridiculously effortless procedure: Salmon fillets are hit with a splash of booze, coated with sugar and salt, and blanketed with a thick layer of dill. The salmon is then pressed under the weight of a few cans and refrigerated for about three days, during which time it releases moisture and is cured and flavored by the salt (the sugar, dill, and liquor lend a hand, too). Once a day, the salmon is basted with the released liquid. Finally, on the last day, the toppings are brushed away and the tender, compact fillet is sliced thin and enjoyed on its own or with cream cheese, shallot, or other accoutrements. You can serve it however you like, but I suspect you will end up following the same protocol I use—a piece for me, a piece for the plate.

—KATE HARTKE, Associate Editor, Books

Begin with brandy: Salmon is an easy fish to cure, so while many recipes call for salting a whole 4-pound side of salmon, I don't think you have to go quite so all out. I like to stick with a much more manageable 1-pound fillet. The whole process only takes three days, so you can make a second batch if your craving isn't satisfied by the first. Place your salmon in a glass baking dish and drizzle it with 3 tablespoons of brandy. If necessary, spoon up any brandy in the dish and drizzle over any spots you missed; the goal is to hit every part of the fillet with some moisture so the salt cure will adhere.

The sweet spot: Most gravlax recipes use granulated sugar in the cure, but instead I opt for brown sugar, which adds a deeper, richer flavor that amplifies the salmon's richness and sweet undertones. Combine your salt and sugar in a bowl, then use your hands to cover the salmon, both top and sides, with the mixture—you want to really pack it on.

Dill dump: Top it off with a good, thick layer of chopped dill, then loosely cover the salmon with plastic wrap. Don't make it too taut; you're going to put another dish with weights on top of it. Just make sure the fish is covered completely.

Weight it, then bring on the basting: Place a smaller baking dish on top of the plastic wrap–covered fillet and place some weights (heavy canned goods are perfect) in the smaller dish. Move the whole thing to the refrigerator. Each day, remove the weights, dish, and plastic wrap and baste the salmon with the exuded liquid. Make sure to hit every part of the dill with the basting liquid so it looks thoroughly moistened. If any of the dill swims off, put it back in place before re-assembling and returning it all to the fridge.

Clean sweep: Three days later, it's time to slice and eat. Swipe off the dill, sugar, and salt. A butter knife works well for pushing back the dill without cutting into the fish. After transferring the cleaned fillet to a cutting board, slice the salmon as thin as you can, on the bias, using a long sharp knife. Don't cut through the skin underneath; this flap can be folded over the remaining gravlax to help keep it fresh and moist. I like to serve the gravlax on rye toasts, with thin strips of red onion or shallot on top, and a little schmear of cream cheese underneath.

Gravlax

Makes about 1 pound
Start today, enjoy in 3 days

⅓ **cup packed light brown sugar**
¼ **cup Diamond Crystal kosher salt (see page 70)**
1 **(1-pound) skin-on salmon fillet**
3 **tablespoons brandy**
1 **cup coarsely chopped fresh dill**

1. Combine sugar and salt. Place salmon, skin side down, in 13 by 9-inch glass baking dish. Drizzle with brandy, making sure to cover entire surface. Rub salmon evenly with sugar mixture, pressing firmly on mixture to adhere. Cover with dill, pressing firmly to adhere.

2. Cover salmon loosely with plastic wrap, top with square baking dish or pie plate, and weight with several large heavy cans. Refrigerate until salmon feels firm, about 3 days, basting salmon with liquid released into baking dish once a day.

3. Scrape dill off salmon. Remove fillet from dish and pat dry with paper towels before slicing. Gravlax can be wrapped tightly in plastic and refrigerated for up to 1 week; it should be left whole and sliced just before serving.

Merguez

✔ WHY THIS RECIPE WORKS: When I was a freshman in culinary school, making sausage was intimidating. What did I—a Florida girl who had grown up eating turkey products manipulated into the shape of bacon—know about making great sausage? No, this craft was better left in the hands of my instructor, a seventh-generation Austrian butcher who could slaughter and break down a pig faster than you could say Oscar Mayer.

It wasn't until after college, when I apprenticed on a biodynamic meat farm, that I saw sausage making for what it was: a simple technique for using up and preserving scraps of meat. And, if the sausage maker employs a little extra know-how, this food isn't just practical but also delicious. Since then, I have made a whole range of different types of links, but there is one particular variety I think stands above the rest: *merguez.*

A spicy fresh sausage typically made from lamb, merguez hails from North Africa. I've adapted a recipe created by the sous chef I worked for in Maine at the restaurant Hugo's. I tinkered a little with the seasoning but maintained its traditional mix of warm spices, plus dried oregano and garlic. I also held on to a couple of the more unorthodox ingredients. Roasted red peppers are not part of a traditional merguez, but I love how their sweet, smoky flavor complements the spices and lamb. Pork fat is also a little controversial for this recipe, since merguez originated in a country whose main religion forbids consumption of pork products. You could use lamb fat, but I prefer pork fat because of its milder flavor and accessibility.

You'll need a meat grinder for this recipe as well as a sausage stuffer if you want to make links. Make sure to use fresh, unsalted fatback, not salt pork (which is salt-cured) in this recipe.

—REBECCA MORRIS, Test Cook, Books

CASINGS AND STUFFERS

Sausage casings are derived from the inner lining of animal intestines or produced artificially; we use natural casings for all our recipes. They come in a range of sizes, from smaller lamb casings to larger hog or cattle casings, allowing for a variety of sausage shapes. Most casings can be bought through a specialty butcher or through online retailers such as butcher-packer.com. As for stuffers, we prefer manual-style sausage stuffers to electric, which are likely to overheat the meat mixture. You can find manual stuffers reasonably priced on amazon.com.

Mix it, chill it: Merguez is known for its aromatic and bold seasonings, and this recipe is no exception. Once the lamb, pork fat, peppers, and spices are in the bowl, give everything a good toss to ensure all the meat is coated with the spices. Then place the mixture in the freezer for about 35 minutes. Temperature plays a large role in the success of sausage making and if things get too warm, the meat and fat will get pulverized through the grinding plate, leaving you with a messy paste. It also helps to freeze the grinder attachments.

Grind in stages: Once the sausage mixture is partially frozen, it's time to grind. I prefer to grind the meat fine for this type of sausage, grinding in stages to avoid overworking and overheating the meat. To do this, start with a coarse die (¼ inch) then transition to a fine one (⅛ inch). I also make sure to grind the meat into a bowl set over ice to keep the meat as cold as possible.

Just beat it: Ground meat doesn't naturally stick together—think of how you need to work ground beef to form it into a patty. So to ensure the sausage mixture sticks together and isn't dry and crumbly once cooked, it is important to mix it well. A stand mixer does a great job of this, though you could also do it by hand (it will just take a bit longer). I also add some dry red wine (any table wine will do) and water for flavor and to help the meat stick together.

Stuffer setup: At this point, you have loose sausage that would work in any recipe calling for ground meat. It's incredibly versatile—it can be fried up with some potatoes for breakfast or rolled in a pita for a quick gyro. Forming the sausage into links is also an option. I like to use lamb casings, which are smaller in diameter than those from hog or cattle. Start by filling the sausage stuffer (a manual-style stuffer works best) with the sausage, then slip the prepared casing onto the stuffing tube, leaving about 6 inches off the end of the tube.

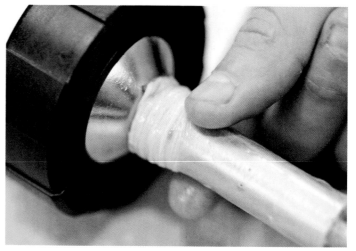

Keep it coiled: As the stuffer begins to push the meat forward and out of the tube, the first thing to come out is air, which is why I leave that bit of untied casing hanging off the tube. Once the meat starts coming out, use one hand to support the casing and control how firmly it is packed. You want the sausage to be slightly loose within the casing at this point because it will become firmer and pack more tightly once you begin to form it into links. Coil the sausage as it gets longer to keep it condensed.

Twist for links: Once finished, tie off one of the ends with a double knot. Starting at the knotted end of the sausage, use both hands to pinch off a five-inch-long section, then twist the link several times away from you. Move on to the next section of sausage and pinch again, but this time twist the link toward you. Pinch the remaining sausage into links, alternating twisting directions, until you reach the end, then tie it off with a double knot.

Remove bubbles: If there are any air bubbles trapped in the links, simply prick them with a pin or small toothpick; just be careful not to create any large holes in the casings. At this point you may be tempted to taste the results of your work, but you have to resist. The links need to refrigerate uncovered for 12 hours or so to give the casing time to set. When it does come time to cook the sausage, just cut the links apart at the twists.

Merguez

Makes about 2½ pounds

Make today, enjoy immediately

- **4**   **teaspoons kosher salt**
- **3**   **garlic cloves, minced**
- **1**   **tablespoon minced fresh oregano**
- **1½**   **teaspoons pepper**
- **1**   **teaspoon ground cumin**
- **½**   **teaspoon red pepper flakes**
- **½**   **teaspoon ground cinnamon**
- **½**   **teaspoon ground cloves**
- **½**   **teaspoon ground nutmeg**
- **¼**   **teaspoon cayenne pepper**
- **2**   **pounds boneless lamb shoulder or leg of lamb, cut into ½-inch pieces**
- **8**   **ounces pork fatback, cut into ½-inch pieces**
- **1**   **cup jarred roasted red bell peppers, patted dry and cut into ½-inch pieces**
- **2**   **tablespoons dry red wine, chilled**
- **2**   **tablespoons ice water**
- **12**   **feet lamb casing, soaked in room-temperature water for 30 minutes and rinsed (optional)**

1. Place meat grinder attachments in freezer. Line rimmed baking sheet with parchment paper. Combine salt, garlic, oregano, pepper, cumin, pepper flakes, cinnamon, cloves, nutmeg, and cayenne in large bowl. Add lamb, fatback, and peppers and toss to coat. Spread lamb mixture evenly on prepared pan and freeze, uncovered, until meat is very firm and starting to harden around edges but still pliable, about 35 minutes.

2. Using meat grinder fitted with coarse die (¼ inch), grind chilled lamb mixture into bowl set over ice. Fit meat grinder with fine die (⅛ inch) and grind mixture again into bowl set over ice. Transfer mixture to stand mixer fitted with paddle and add chilled wine and ice water. Mix on medium speed until combined and sausage looks sticky, about 1 minute.

3. Store merguez in bulk or formed into patties, wrapped tightly in plastic wrap. Merguez can be refrigerated for up to 5 days or frozen for up to 2 months.

TO MAKE MERGUEZ LINKS: Follow recipe through step 3. To form links, load sausage stuffer with sausage and slip casing onto nozzle, leaving about 6 inches of casing hanging off end. Slowly stuff sausage into casing, using 1 hand to support casing and ensure it is packed uniformly, coiling packed sausage as you go. Once casing has been filled, remove from nozzle and tie double knot on 1 end. Measure, pinch, and twist sausage into tight 5-inch links. Tie double knot on other end and trim any excess casing. Prick any air bubbles in sausage casing with pin or small toothpick and refrigerate, uncovered, until casing is set, about 12 hours. Wrap links tightly in plastic and store as directed.

Mexican Chorizo

✔ **WHY THIS RECIPE WORKS:** When I was very young my family lived in the border city of Ciudad Juarez, and every morning my mother would wake us up before dawn to go to school across the border in El Paso. The line to cross the border in the morning could take hours, so we usually had our breakfast in the car: a burrito filled with scrambled eggs, chorizo, and beans (refried with chorizo). To this day the smell of chorizo frying in a pan brings me back to those sleepy mornings. It wasn't until I moved to New England that I realized there were other kinds of chorizo, and these didn't resemble the heavily spiced fresh sausage I grew up with at all. Since I couldn't find Mexican chorizo, I would have to make my own.

Luckily, chorizo is easier to make than many sausages because it is fresh and doesn't require curing. The biggest challenge is getting the right mix of spices. I found a recipe with a flavor profile similar to what I was looking for, but most of the ingredients were preground spices that gave the chorizo a stale, dusty texture. I cut the ingredients to mostly pantry staples, and I added complexity and improved texture by toasting and grinding the chiles and spices myself. For the chiles, I wanted a blend of sweet, smoky, a hint of bitterness, and heat. Availability was also a factor; I eventually came up with a mix of chiles you can find in most grocery stores.

Although chorizo is often sold in links, the casing is usually removed so the sausage can be crumbled and incorporated into a dish. I usually just freeze it in bulk, though you can make links if you like. A few of my favorite ways to use homemade chorizo: scrambled with eggs, mixed in with melted cheese for a dip, and fried up with potatoes. You'll need a meat grinder for this recipe as well as a sausage stuffer if you want to make links.

—TAIZETH SIERRA, Assistant Editor, America's Test Kitchen

DRIED CHILES

This recipe calls for a variety of dried chiles: New Mexican (earthy, flavorful, with a little heat and a nice red color), guajillo (bright, slightly tangy, with a hint of spice), ancho (smoky-sweet), and arbol (fairly hot). You should be able to find most of these at supermarkets, as well as spice stores, Mexican markets, or online at marxfoods.com.

D.I.Y. chili powder: Mexican chorizo is well known for its heavy dose of bold spice and smoky chiles. But the faded, flat flavor and grittiness of store-bought chili powder doesn't come close to the freshly made variety. Making chili powder from scratch is simple. Start by toasting a bunch of chiles (I use ancho for smokiness and hint of sweetness; guajillos are bright and slightly tangy; and New Mexican chiles lend good color). Add a few spices, like cumin, coriander, cinnamon, and hot paprika, then grind the mix in a spice grinder. I also add arbol chiles, untoasted since toasting can make them bitter.

Grind and mix: Pork butt serves as the meat component in my chorizo, plus some fatback for richness and to keep the sausage from being too dry. Make sure that the pork mixture is really cold before you start to grind (freeze the grinder parts too). This ensures that the fat does not overheat and end up separating once you cook the sausage (if you skip the freezing, the mixture will be mushy). Once ground, transfer the mixture to a stand mixer and beat it until it starts to look sticky.

Store it: Since Mexican chorizo is most commonly cooked as bulk sausage for dishes such as tacos or queso fundido, I usually don't mess with forming it into links and just freeze it as is. But you can go the links route if you prefer (to do this, follow the steps on pages 198–199).

Put it to work: Chorizo, potato, and eggs make a great breakfast taco or burrito (with homemade tortillas of course; see page 240). This sausage is also great with skillet potatoes or stirred into melted cheese for a dip, and it will give a spicy kick to savory bread stuffings.

Makes about 2½ pounds
Make today, enjoy immediately

1½	**ounces dried New Mexican chiles, stemmed, seeded, and torn into 1-inch pieces**
1½	**ounces dried guajillo chiles, stemmed, seeded, and torn into 1-inch pieces**
1½	**ounces dried ancho chiles, stemmed, seeded, and torn into 1-inch pieces**
½	**stick cinnamon**
1	**teaspoon cumin seeds**
½	**teaspoon coriander seeds**
1	**clove**
10	**garlic cloves, unpeeled**
2	**dried arbol chiles, stemmed**
2	**tablespoons hot paprika**
2	**tablespoons kosher salt**
1½	**teaspoons pepper**
1½	**teaspoons dried oregano**
¾	**teaspoon ground nutmeg**
½	**teaspoon grated fresh ginger**
2	**pounds boneless pork butt roast, cut into ½-inch pieces**
8	**ounces pork fatback, cut into ½-inch pieces**
2	**tablespoons cider vinegar, chilled**
12	**feet pork casing, soaked in room-temperature water for 30 minutes and rinsed (optional)**

1. Place meat grinder attachments in freezer. Line rimmed baking sheet with parchment paper. Working in 2 batches, toast New Mexican chiles, guajillos, anchos, cinnamon, cumin seeds, coriander seeds, and clove in 12-inch skillet over medium-high heat, stirring frequently, until fragrant, 4 to 6 minutes, reducing heat if chiles begin to smoke. Transfer pepper mixture to bowl and let cool to room temperature.

2. Add garlic to now-empty skillet and toast over medium heat until softened and spotty brown, about 8 minutes. When cool, remove skins and chop coarse.

3. Working in batches, process cooled chile mixture and arbols in spice grinder until finely ground, about 20 seconds; transfer to large bowl. Stir in chopped garlic, paprika, salt, pepper, oregano, nutmeg, and ginger. Add pork and fatback and toss to coat. Spread pork mixture evenly on prepared pan and freeze, uncovered, until meat is very firm and starting to harden around edges but still pliable, about 35 minutes.

4. Using meat grinder fitted with coarse die (¼ inch), grind chilled pork mixture into bowl set over ice. Transfer mixture to stand mixer fitted with paddle and add chilled vinegar. Mix on medium speed until combined and sausage looks sticky, about 1 minute.

5. Store chorizo in bulk or formed into patties, wrapped tightly in plastic wrap. Chorizo can be refrigerated for up to 5 days or frozen for up to 2 months.

TO MAKE CHORIZO LINKS: Follow recipe through step 5. To form links, load sausage stuffer with sausage and slip casing onto nozzle, leaving about 6 inches of casing hanging off end. Slowly stuff sausage into casing, using 1 hand to support casing and ensure it is packed uniformly, coiling packed sausage as you go. Once casing has been filled, remove from nozzle and tie double knot on 1 end. Measure, pinch, and twist sausage into tight 5-inch links. Tie double knot on other end and trim any excess casing. Prick any air bubbles in sausage with pin or small toothpick and refrigerate, uncovered, until casing is set, about 12 hours. Wrap links tightly in plastic and store as directed.

Mortadella

I NEED A WHAT CAP?

This recipe calls for a beef bung cap, which comes from the cow's appendix. Beef bung caps are fairly big, about 4 to 5 inches in diameter and about a foot and a half long. They are typically used for stuffing large bologna, headcheese, capicola, and mortadella. You can order them from butcher-packer.com.

✔ WHY THIS RECIPE WORKS: For years I have been playing around with charcuterie. The results of chopping, grinding, seasoning, and curing meat are truly rewarding. And recently, I've become particularly fascinated with emulsified sausages, like bologna, hot dogs, and mortadella. We all grew up hearing horror stories about what exactly might be in commercial hot dogs and bologna. I recall an episode of *The Simpsons* where Lisa envisions a hot dog as a combination of raccoon, rat, pigeon, and a shoe. Perhaps extreme, but it's that line of thinking that shaped my aversion to hot dogs and bologna as a kid, and that disdain stuck with me over the years. But recently, I decided it might be time to give these meats a fresh look.

I decided to start with mortadella as my guinea pig (don't worry; I wouldn't actually include any of the little furry guys in the recipe). As a close but slightly more complex cousin of bologna, it seemed like an approachable, interesting place to start. The emulsification process isn't hard, but the results can vary considerably if you don't watch the details. And you may have a few failures; they only make the successes taste better.

Remember to have a good thermometer handy; it's crucial. I also suggest reading up a bit on this process first. You'll find it's a lot of fun to try and even more rewarding to eat. I use pink salt primarily to preserve the meat's color. Pink salt isn't just for seasoning; it also contains nitrites, so be sure to stick to the quantity listed. Make sure to have plenty of ice on hand. You will need a meat grinder for this recipe. Use either a manual-style stuffer or a pastry bag to stuff the casing; do not use a motorized stuffer for this recipe because it will overheat the meat mixture.

—CHRIS O'CONNOR, Associate Editor, America's Test Kitchen

Freeze first: Finding the right protein-to-fat ratio is one key to making mortadella. Even if you are using the same cut from recipe to recipe, it's hard to control the amount of fat in each one. So I trim the pork butt of all visible fat, then add 7 ounces of fatback. This gives me 100 percent control over the ratio. To ensure a clean, even grind, freeze the meat until it is very firm but still pliable (you should freeze the grinder attachments as well). This will prevent it from overheating while grinding and help promote a smooth texture.

It's all in the grind: I find that grinding in stages helps to prevent the grinder from overworking and overheating the meat. Begin with a coarse die then transition to a fine one. If you are grinding the meat properly, it should extrude easily and look like really nice ground beef.

What makes it mortadella: Mortadella is an emulsified sausage, which means the ground meat and fat are whipped until the fat is evenly distributed. I process the ground pork and seasonings, then add the ground fatback and process until very smooth. To keep it from overheating, I also include ice in the bowl (the amount is critical, so go by weight rather than volume). I simply crush the cubes in the processor before adding the meat. As the ice melts, it also helps the mixture emulsify. Dry milk powder likewise helps with emulsification. Once fully processed, the pork mixture should register 58 degrees.

Flavor (and texture) boost: Classic mortadella has additional pieces of poached pork fatback folded in before it is cooked. The fact that this fat is poached, not raw, is important. When fat cooks, it shrinks, so if raw fat were folded into the sausage mixture, it would shrink while the sausage cooked, leaving behind large, empty holes. Cooking it in boiling water for a minute is sufficient. When I fold in the poached fat, I also add pistachios—another classic addition—and some cracked peppercorns.

The good stuff: To achieve the impressive size expected of mortadella, you need a large casing. I use a beef bung cap. Slip the open end onto the nozzle of the stuffer and slowly fill it, using one hand to support the bung cap and ensure it's firmly packed. A manual-style stuffer is essential here; a motorized stuffer can overheat the mixture and cause it to separate while cooking (a pastry bag would also work). Or if you don't want a casing, you can form the mixture into a log and wrap it in plastic wrap for the next step, poaching the meat.

Poach perfect: Unlike link sausage, which is typically cooked by pan-frying or grilling, a sausage of mortadella's stature does best when poached. Place the sausage in a large pot filled with water, cover with a small plate to submerge, and bring the water up to 176 degrees. Once that temperature is reached, reduce the heat to low and cook the sausage until it registers 161 degrees. Why so specific? It turns out 161 degrees is the optimal temperature for obtaining the perfect pink color. At this point, transfer the mortadella to an ice bath to stop the cooking, then refrigerate it until completely chilled.

The best cold cut you've ever tasted: It's true that making mortadella is an involved process, but aren't all great things worth a little extra effort? When it comes time to enjoy, I like to slice the mortadella thin and enjoy it with some mustard, or I build myself a mean cold cut sandwich.

Mortadella

Makes about 2½ pounds
Make today, enjoy tomorrow

3 **pounds boneless pork butt roast**

11 **ounces pork fatback (7 ounces cut into ½-inch pieces, 4 ounces cut into ¼-inch pieces)**

10½ **ounces ice**

¼ **cup dry red wine, chilled**

2 **tablespoons kosher salt**

¾ **teaspoon ground coriander**

¾ **teaspoon ground white pepper**

¾ **teaspoon sugar**

⅝ **teaspoon garlic powder**

½ **teaspoon ground mace**

¼ **teaspoon pink salt (see page 180)**

⅛ **teaspoon cayenne pepper**

2 **tablespoons nonfat dry milk powder**

¼ **cup shelled pistachios**

1¼ **teaspoons peppercorns, cracked**

1 **(18-inch) beef bung cap, soaked in room-temperature water for 30 minutes and rinsed**

1. Place meat grinder attachments in freezer. Pull pork roast apart at seams and trim it of all visible fat; discard fat. Weigh out 1½ pounds of pork and cut it into ½-inch pieces; save remaining pork for another use. Spread pork and ½-inch fatback pieces in single layer, on separate sides, of parchment-lined rimmed baking sheet. Freeze until very firm and starting to harden around edges but still pliable, about 35 minutes.

2. Meanwhile, bring 4 cups water to simmer in medium saucepan. Add ¼-inch fatback pieces and cook for 1 minute. Transfer fatback to bowl of ice water and let sit for 5 minutes until completely chilled. Transfer to paper towel–lined plate, cover, and refrigerate. Using meat grinder fitted with coarse die (¼ inch), grind chilled ½-inch fatback into bowl set over ice; cover and refrigerate. Using coarse die, grind chilled pork into separate bowl set over ice. Fit meat grinder with fine die (⅛ inch) and grind pork again into bowl set over ice; cover and refrigerate.

3. Process 10½ ounces ice in food processor until finely ground, about 30 seconds, scraping down bowl as needed. Add ground pork, wine, salt, coriander, white pepper, sugar, garlic powder, mace, pink salt, and cayenne and process until mixture registers 40 degrees, 6 to 12 minutes, scraping down bowl often. Add ground fatback and continue to process until pork mixture registers 50 degrees, about 2 minutes. Add milk powder and continue to process until mixture registers 58 degrees, about 1 minute. Transfer mixture to bowl and fold in blanched fatback pieces, pistachios, and peppercorns; cover and refrigerate while assembling sausage stuffer.

4. Load sausage stuffer with pork mixture and slip open end of beef bung cap onto nozzle. Slowly stuff pork mixture into cap, using 1 hand to support cap and ensure it is packed firmly. Once cap has been filled, remove from nozzle and tie other end closed with kitchen twine. Trim excess twine and trim end of cap, leaving about 1 inch still attached. Alternatively, form pork mixture into 10 by 6-inch log on large sheet of plastic wrap. Tightly roll pork mixture in plastic and twist ends to firmly compact sausage into tight cylinder. Tie double knot in ends of plastic to seal.

5. Fill large pot with 5 quarts water. Place mortadella in water and set small plate on top to submerge. Bring water to 176 degrees over medium-high heat, then reduce heat to low. Cook mortadella until it registers 161 degrees, 1½ to 2 hours, adjusting burner, if necessary, to maintain water temperature at 176 degrees. Transfer mortadella to bowl of ice water and let cool for 20 minutes. Pat dry and refrigerate until completely chilled, at least 8 hours. Mortadella can be wrapped tightly in plastic and refrigerated for up to 2 weeks or frozen for up to 2 months.

Duck Confit

☑ **WHY THIS RECIPE WORKS:** The literal translation of the French word *confit* might be "preserved," but I've always said it means "delicious." In my mind, anything salted, then slowly cooked in its own fat until supremely tender and rich can't be anything other than amazing. You can use almost any meat to make confit, but duck is most common. The process is incredibly simple: Cure duck legs in a salt rub, then gently simmer them in fat. It's easily adapted to suit your taste by varying seasonings. Duck confit is fantastic served with roasted potatoes, or shredded in an elegant salad, and of course in the classic French white bean stew, cassoulet.

—DAN ZUCCARELLO, Associate Editor, Books

FINDING DUCK FAT

You can order duck fat through an online retailer, such as dartagnan.com. The fat can be reused several times (it's great for French fries).

Trim the fat (and skin): It seems a little counterintuitive since the recipe relies so heavily on duck fat, but you still should trim off any excess skin (which is where all the fat is) from the legs. This ensures that once the legs are made into confit, they are ready to serve, use in a recipe, or store, with no further prep needed. Kitchen shears make easy work of removing the large pieces of skin and fat from around the edges and back side of the legs.

Worth their salt: One of the key steps to making great duck confit is allowing the legs to spend time in a salt rub, which enhances their flavor and texture. This is the time to tailor the flavor of the legs to your own tastes. I typically keep things basic, using pepper, thyme, and bay leaves, but you could try other aromatics such as garlic, ginger, star anise, cinnamon, or cloves. Once the duck legs are coated in the salt mixture, transfer them to a zipper-lock bag and let them sit for at least 12 hours.

Get ready for the slow simmer: If you cooked the duck legs as is, you'd end up with a salt lick, so you should thoroughly rinse them and pat them dry before you move on to the cooking phase. Since the duck legs need to be completely submerged in fat while they cook, I use the largest pot in my kitchen—a Dutch oven—for the simmering stage. After melting the fat in the pot, arrange the legs evenly in the fat, then bring everything to a simmer.

Opt for the oven: It takes about six hours of simmering for the duck legs to become completely tender. To give myself a bit more freedom from the kitchen, I move the pot from the stovetop to the oven after it has come to a simmer. Set at 225 degrees, the oven is perfect for keeping the fat at just the right temperature.

Falling off the bone: After six hours in the oven, the legs should be fall-apart tender. You can tell that they are done when you are able to easily twist the leg bones away from meat. When they hit that stage, carefully transfer the pot to a wire rack and let the legs cool in the fat. This gives the duck legs plenty of time to finish cooking through gently, plus it makes handling the fat for storage more manageable.

Better with time: The duck legs can be simply seared to crisp up their skin (my favorite) or used in a recipe (try it shredded over frisée for an elegant salad or incorporated into cassoulet). If possible, allow the legs to chill in their fat for a few days, even a week. They will taste even better. When it's time to remove the legs from the fat, just be sure to allow the fat to soften; otherwise you may tear the meat from the legs. You can strain the fat and reuse it to make more confit or for use in other recipes (like frying potatoes).

Duck Confit

Makes 6 preserved duck legs
Start today, enjoy tomorrow

¼ **cup Diamond Crystal kosher salt (see page 70)**
2 **tablespoons peppercorns, cracked**
2 **tablespoons minced fresh thyme**
4 **bay leaves, crumbled**
6 **(12- to 14-ounce) whole duck legs, trimmed**
8 **cups rendered duck fat**

1. Combine salt, pepper, thyme, and bay leaves. Rub duck legs evenly with salt mixture and place in 1-gallon zipper-lock bag. Press out air, seal bag, and refrigerate for 12 to 24 hours.

2. Adjust oven rack to lower-middle position and heat oven to 225 degrees. Thoroughly rinse duck legs with cold water and pat dry with paper towels. Melt duck fat in Dutch oven over medium heat until completely transparent. Add duck legs, making sure they are completely submerged under fat, and bring to simmer. Cover pot, transfer to oven, and cook until meat is very tender and leg bones twist easily away from meat, about 6 hours.

3. Being very careful of hot fat, transfer pot to wire rack and let duck legs cool completely, in fat, about 2 hours. Carefully transfer legs to 13 by 9-inch baking dish and cover completely with cooled fat. Refrigerate until fat is hardened, about 1 hour, then wrap in plastic wrap. Sealed duck confit can be refrigerated for up to 1 month.

Mousseline

WHY THIS RECIPE WORKS: I like to think I have an adventurous palate, game to order anything on a menu that's unfamiliar or strikingly creative. But there are a few foods that give me instant tunnel vision—once I spy them on a menu I can't think of eating anything else, even if I just had it. Anything in the pâté family is a great example.

Rich and decadent, pâté is a slow-down, relish-every-bite sort of food. For the most part, I live my life going 100 miles a minute. So some time spent leisurely with a pâté board is a chance for me to put my feet up (figuratively, of course; I wouldn't actually do that in a restaurant). Pâté boards usually include smooth and country pâté as well as rillettes. I love all three, but there's a fourth type that I see far less often: mousseline. As a result, I've learned to make it at home.

Mousseline is a close cousin to smooth pâté; you start by sautéing livers with aromatics and cognac, then puree with butter until smooth. But then comes the difference: You fold whipped cream into that dense pâté mixture. The cream adds lightness and counterbalances the livery flavor. It's easy to spread and really easy to eat. The key to a good mousseline is getting just the right amount of whipped cream into the mix: Too much and the liver flavor is lost, too little and what's the point of adding it in the first place?

Mousseline is ideal for parties since it's easy to prepare, can be whipped up ahead of time, and is surprisingly affordable yet still feels celebratory. It also makes a fantastic dinner for one or two, served with a hunk of baguette, a simple salad, and some good wine. And you know what is really great about having mousseline at home? You can actually put your feet up.

—LOUISE EMERICK, Senior Editor, Books

"The key to a good mousseline is getting just the right amount of whipped cream into the mix: Too much and the liver flavor is lost, too little and what's the point of adding it in the first place?"

Get prepped: Because this recipe moves quickly, it's important to have all the ingredients prepped first. Chop your thyme and shallots and measure out the cognac and heavy cream. As for the butter, you'll need 2 tablespoons for sautéing, and 4 more for processing. After rinsing off the livers to remove any dark spots (you may need to use your fingers or a paper towel to help), cut the larger livers in half so they are all roughly the same size. Pat the livers dry and season them with salt and pepper.

Brown in butter: Start by melting 2 tablespoons of butter in the skillet over medium-high heat. Add the livers and thyme sprigs and let it cook until the livers are lightly browned on the first side. Avoid the temptation to stir the livers—it will only cause them to release excess moisture and steam rather than brown. Then flip them over, add the shallots, and cook until the livers are browned on the second side (again, no stirring). Off the heat, add the cognac, and then allow the residual heat in the pan to reduce the cognac to about a tablespoon.

Process with more butter: Remove the thyme sprigs and transfer the liver mixture to the food processor. Process the livers until smooth. Then, with the machine running, add the chilled butter, 1 tablespoon at a time, processing until thoroughly incorporated after each addition. I really love butter and always have plenty in the fridge so it's my default fat of choice, but I suspect duck fat would make an excellent substitute. At this point, it's smooth but not perfect. Transfer the puree to a fine-mesh strainer set over a bowl.

Use a little elbow grease: Press the puree through the strainer using the back of a ladle or spatula. It takes some elbow grease (and patience), but the ultra-smooth outcome is worth it. Next, fold in the whipped cream, which balances the liver flavor and adds a silky richness. It's such a small amount, I just whip it by hand (no need to drag out another appliance), then fold it in with minced thyme, salt, and pepper. Transfer the mousseline to ramekins, cover with plastic wrap, and refrigerate for an hour to set.

Enjoy the results: If the mousseline has been in the fridge for a while, let it sit out at room temperature for 45 minutes, then gently rewhip (a butter knife works fine) for that trademark fluffy texture before serving. It doesn't need much, just a baguette or crostini.

Mousseline

Makes 1½ cups
Make today, enjoy immediately

12 **ounces chicken livers, rinsed, patted dry, trimmed, and halved if large**
     Salt and pepper
2   **tablespoons unsalted butter, plus 4 tablespoons cut into 4 pieces and chilled**
2   **sprigs fresh thyme, plus ¼ teaspoon minced**
1   **shallot, minced**
3   **tablespoons cognac**
¼   **cup heavy cream**

1. Pat chicken livers dry with paper towels and season with salt and pepper. Melt 2 tablespoons butter in 12-inch nonstick skillet over medium-high heat. Add livers and thyme sprigs to skillet and cook, without stirring, until livers are lightly browned, about 2 minutes. Flip livers, add shallot, and cook until livers are lightly browned on second side and shallot is just beginning to soften, about 2 minutes. Off heat, add cognac and allow residual heat in skillet to reduce cognac to 1 tablespoon, about 1 minute. Discard thyme sprigs.

2. Process liver mixture in food processor until smooth, about 30 seconds. With processor running, add remaining 4 tablespoons butter, 1 piece at a time, until incorporated, about 1 minute, scraping down bowl as needed. Transfer mixture to fine-mesh strainer set over bowl. Using back of ladle or rubber spatula, press liver mixture through strainer.

3. Whip heavy cream in separate bowl until stiff peaks form. Fold whipped cream and minced thyme into strained liver mixture until fully incorporated. Season with salt and pepper to taste.

4. Spoon mousseline into two 6-ounce ramekins and smooth tops. Press plastic wrap against surface of mousseline and refrigerate until completely chilled and set, about 1 hour. Bring to room temperature before serving. Mousseline can be wrapped tightly in plastic and refrigerated for up to 3 days or frozen for up to 1 month.

Country-Style Pâté

BRIGHT SPICY KICK

Spicy green peppercorns are underripe peppercorn berries packed in brine; look for them near the capers at the supermarket.

✔ **WHY THIS RECIPE WORKS:** Full disclosure: I was an off-again, on-again vegetarian during my college years, mostly subsisting on dishes like bean-and-cashew chili and spicy tofu. But, alas, times have changed and so have I. A post-graduation trip to Paris awakened my palate to meaty foods that are simply too good to ignore, and I have never looked back. At the top of my list is pâté. I'm talking about a pull-out-all-the-stops masterpiece chock-full of meat. And fat. And delight.

Ground pork and fat (lard or bacon) typically serve as the base for pâté, and "country-style" signifies a rustic texture. Although some cooks pass pork butt through a meat grinder, I have gotten terrific results using preground meat. I like to combine 2 pounds of ground pork with finely chopped bacon (chosen for its smokiness), and plenty of it: My recipe calls for 1½ pounds. That's not a typo—good pâté requires lots of fat for richness and the proper dense texture.

If that doesn't get your heart racing, consider this: If you can mix up a simple meatloaf, then you have the culinary chops to make a pâté to rival that of the finest charcuterie.

—REBECCA HAYS, Managing Editor, *Cook's Illustrated*

Mix it up: Ground pork and finely chopped bacon serve as the base for my pâté. From here, I could mix in any number of meats, offal, or poultry. My choice: chicken livers. I have it bad for their rich flavor and velvety smooth texture—they're an absolute must in my pâté. Once all the meats are in the bowl, I like to dive right in with my hands and mix them together until uniformly combined. Don't forget to also set aside 12 slices of whole bacon— you'll get to them later.

Make a binder: All of that meat needs to be bound together. I start by mixing together eggs and heavy cream—ideal ingredients for the job. Then it's time to break out the good stuff: cognac. Don't be shy. It's important to add enough so that it can be tasted once the pâté is cooked. Next I add a good dose of garlic, thyme, and salt, along with quatre épices, a French spice blend. While quatre épices is available in some supermarkets, I prefer to make my own by simply adding black pepper, freshly grated nutmeg, ground cloves, and ground ginger to my binder mixture. Pour this tasty concoction over the meat.

Get your hands dirty: Lastly, add green peppercorns for their bright flavor and chopped pistachios, which contribute color and crunch, to the bowl with the meat and binder. Now get your hands in there again and mix it up.

A bed of bacon: All that's left to do is prepare the pan. A terrine mold is completely unnecessary; I use an everyday 8½ by 4½-inch loaf pan. I like to arrange three fresh bay leaves, shiny side down, in the pan (just omit them if you can't find them; dried won't look good once baked). They will scent the pâté as it cooks and also beautify the finished product. Next, line the pan with the 12 slices of reserved bacon. Lay six slices all the way down the length of the pan to line the bottom. Then drape three slices over each short end, and just let the excess hang over.

Pile it in: Scrape the pâté mixture into the lined pan. Don't panic when it nearly overflows. There is a lot of fat in the mixture, and as it melts during baking, the pâté will shrink and settle into the pan. Use your hands to really pack the meat tightly, then fold over the bacon slices and cover the pan with foil.

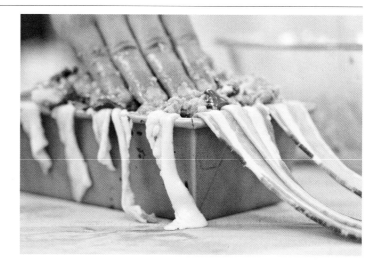

Bake, then weight: Place the pan in a baking dish, transfer the assembly to the oven, and pour boiling water into the baking dish to come halfway up the sides of the pan. This setup, called a bain-marie, will help the pâté cook through gently and evenly. After about 2½ hours, the pate should register 165 degrees. Transfer the loaf pan to a rimmed baking sheet. To ensure a compact texture, place a heavy skillet on top of the pâté (liquid will seep out; that's okay) and let it cool at room temperature for one hour. Then transfer it to the refrigerator, where it needs to chill for at least eight hours to completely set.

Serving time: To unmold the pâté, place it in a baking dish full of hot water for about one minute. Then, using a paring knife, loosen the edges from the pan. Place a cutting board on top of the pâté and invert the loaf pan. At this point the pâté can be brought to room temperature before serving, or it can be wrapped back up and refrigerated for up to a week. I like to cut the pâté into thick slices and serve it with the traditional accompaniments of crusty French bread, cornichons, and Dijon mustard.

Country-Style Pâté

Makes about 3 pounds, one
8½ by 4½-inch loaf

Make today, enjoy tomorrow

2	tablespoons unsalted butter
4	large shallots, minced
2	pounds ground pork
1½	pounds bacon (12 slices left whole, remaining bacon chopped fine)
8	ounces chicken livers, rinsed, patted dry, trimmed, and cut into ½-inch pieces
2	large eggs
½	cup cognac
⅓	cup heavy cream
1½	tablespoons minced fresh thyme
3	garlic cloves, minced
2½	teaspoons salt
1	teaspoon pepper
⅛	teaspoon ground nutmeg
⅛	teaspoon ground cloves
⅛	teaspoon ground ginger
¾	cup shelled pistachios, toasted and chopped coarse
1	tablespoon jarred green peppercorns, rinsed
3	fresh bay leaves

1. Adjust oven rack to lowest position and heat oven to 350 degrees. Bring kettle of water to boil.

2. Melt butter in 10-inch skillet over medium heat. Add shallots and cook until softened, about 5 minutes. Remove from heat and let cool to room temperature.

3. Mix pork, chopped bacon, and chicken livers together in large bowl until thoroughly combined. In separate bowl, beat eggs, cognac, and cream together with fork until combined, then stir in thyme, garlic, salt, pepper, nutmeg, cloves, and ginger. Add egg mixture, softened shallots, pistachios, and peppercorns to meat mixture and mix with your hands until thoroughly combined.

4. Arrange bay leaves, bright green side down, in 8½ by 4½-inch loaf pan. Line pan with bacon slices, arranging 6 slices across width of pan and draping 3 slices over each short side of pan. Transfer pâté mixture to bacon-lined pan, using hands to press mixture firmly into pan (pan will be very full). Fold bacon slices over mixture and cover tightly with aluminum foil.

5. Place pan in 13 by 9-inch baking dish and transfer to oven. Pour boiling water into baking dish until it comes halfway up sides of pan. Bake pâté until it registers 165 degrees, about 2½ hours.

6. Remove pan from baking dish and transfer to rimmed baking sheet. Place heavy skillet or small baking dish filled with heavy cans on top of pâté to weigh down. Let cool at room temperature for 1 hour. Remove skillet and refrigerate pâté until completely chilled and set, about 8 hours.

7. Fill baking dish with hot water. Place pâté (still in loaf pan) in baking dish for 1 minute. Remove foil. Using paring knife, loosen edges of pâté from pan, then invert pan onto cutting board. Pâté can be wrapped tightly in plastic wrap and refrigerated for up to 1 week or frozen for up to 1 month; it should be left whole and not sliced until ready to serve. Bring to room temperature before serving.

Pork Rillettes

WHY THIS RECIPE WORKS: My brother's wedding in L.A. was memorable for a lot of reasons. Chiefly, of course, he was marrying someone fantastic. Second, the days prior were complete and utter chaos, with Ali and Bryan running to and fro into the wee hours, me preparing desserts in their tiny kitchen, and the backyard getting transformed overnight from a pile of dirt into a landscaped paradise for the evening reception. And third, the food.

Ali fits right into our family because she loves food as much as we do, and being from Argentina, she considers meat (beef or otherwise) a priority. So when the wedding-day lunch started with a spread of charcuterie and potted meats, aka rillettes, we were all in, well, hog heaven. At the end of the day, the pork rillettes really stole the show. Classic rillettes (pronounced ree-yehts) are made by braising meat (or fish) until the meat is tender and easily shreddable, then beating that tender meat with fat to turn it into a spread. Along the lines of pâté, rillettes are a meaty, rich treat. What Bryan and Ali served certainly was that, but somehow this potted pork was lighter than the more staid French restaurant versions I've had. It was like luscious whipped pâté meets Southern-style pulled pork, with a slew of fresh herbs mixed in. What's not to love?

The restaurant that held their wedding-day lunch closed recently, so I thought the least I could do was take a stab at re-creating that famous potted pork so it wasn't lost forever. I'm not sure this recipe is exactly the same, but it's rich, meaty, spreadable, and packed with parsley, thyme, and chives. If you ask me, it's definitely hog heaven.

—LOUISE EMERICK, Senior Editor, Books

Prep the pork: Rillettes are basically tender, flavorful bits of shredded meat mixed with fat, and while a variety of proteins could be used, I start with fatty, rich pork. Cut a 2-pound boneless pork butt into small, even chunks. Since the meat is salted overnight, the smaller chunks allow for better distribution of seasonings; and when it comes time for braising, their size also helps to cut down on the cooking time.

Salt and let sit: Shortcut rillettes recipes skip this salting step, but I think it makes a huge difference in terms of flavor and texture, and it only requires time, not much effort, so just plan ahead. At this point, I also like to add some pepper and thyme. Toss the pork in the salt mixture, cover the bowl, and let it sit in the refrigerator for at least 12 hours, or up to a day.

Take stock: Some recipes braise the meat in fat while others opt for a seasoned stock. I had a hunch the rillettes from my brother's wedding were the latter, so I went that route. Start by softening some onion and celery, add a cup of white wine, simmer until it's reduced, then add chicken broth and bring it back to a simmer. Pat the pork dry to remove any excess salt and add it to the pot along with a couple of bay leaves. Two hours in a 325-degree oven is all it takes to turn the pork supremely tender.

Liquid gold: Once the pork is done, transfer it to a large plate to cool (we'll get to shredding it in a bit). What's left in the pot is a flavorful braising liquid, so I reserve some to add to the rillettes. Strain the liquid into a fat separator (to remove the aromatics), then measure out ¼ cup of liquid.

Mix it up: Instead of shredding the pork by hand, I use a stand mixer to get the job done quickly. This also allows me to easily mix in some shallots (which I sauté in butter while the pork is braising), another whole stick of melted butter (I have never been one to short the butter), the reserved braising liquid, and chives and parsley. You could probably also do this step by hand.

Seal the deal: Spoon the rillettes into ramekins and put them in the refrigerator for about an hour to set. Then you need to seal each portion with melted butter. This helps them keep in the refrigerator for a few weeks, but even if you are serving the rillettes in the near future, this additional butter adds yet more richness and makes the rillettes very spreadable. Make sure to plan a little ahead and let any refrigerated servings come to room temperature before serving.

Pork Rillettes

Makes 3 cups
Start today, enjoy tomorrow

5   teaspoons minced fresh
     thyme
     Kosher salt and pepper
2   pounds boneless pork
     butt roast, pulled apart at
     seams, trimmed, and cut
     into 1-inch pieces
2   tablespoons unsalted
     butter, plus 16 tablespoons
     melted and cooled
1   onion, chopped
2   celery ribs, chopped
1   cup dry white wine
2   cups low-sodium chicken
     broth
2   bay leaves
2   shallots, minced
2   tablespoons minced fresh
     chives
2   tablespoons minced fresh
     parsley

1. Combine 1 tablespoon thyme, 2 teaspoons salt, and 2 teaspoons pepper in large bowl. Add pork and toss to coat. Cover and refrigerate for 12 to 24 hours.

2. Adjust oven rack to lower-middle position and heat oven to 325 degrees. Melt 1 tablespoon butter in Dutch oven over medium heat. Add onion and celery and cook until softened and lightly browned, 5 to 7 minutes. Stir in wine, bring to simmer, and cook until almost completely evaporated, 6 to 8 minutes. Stir in broth and bring to simmer.

3. Pat pork dry with paper towels. Add pork and bay leaves to Dutch oven and return to simmer. Cover, transfer pot to oven, and cook until pork is tender and falls apart when prodded with fork, about 2 hours. Transfer pork to large plate and let cool to room temperature, about 30 minutes. Strain braising liquid through fine-mesh strainer into fat separator. Measure out and reserve ¼ cup of liquid from fat separator; discard remaining liquid and fat.

4. Meanwhile, melt 1 tablespoon butter in 10-inch skillet over medium heat. Add shallots and cook until softened, about 5 minutes. Stir in remaining 2 teaspoons thyme and cook until fragrant, about 30 seconds. Let cool to room temperature.

5. Using stand mixer fitted with paddle, mix cooled pork, reserved braising liquid, cooled shallot mixture, 8 tablespoons melted butter, chives, and parsley on low speed until meat shreds and mixture is cohesive, 1 to 2 minutes. Season with salt and pepper to taste.

6. Spoon rillettes into four 8-ounce ramekins and smooth tops. Refrigerate until completely chilled and set, about 1 hour. Top chilled ramekins evenly with remaining 8 tablespoons melted butter to seal and return to refrigerator to set, about 1 hour. Bring to room temperature and stir in butter cap before serving. Sealed pork rillettes can be wrapped tightly and refrigerated for up to 2 weeks.

Beef Jerky

WHY THIS RECIPE WORKS: Sure, beef jerky seems a little bit primitive, but at the same time it's totally retro-cool. At its simplest, jerky involves nothing more than leaving thinly sliced meat outside to let the sun and air do their work. There's something about this simple process—no fancy ingredients or equipment required—that has always appealed to me. For some reason, I'd never gotten around to making it. That is, until now.

Beyond exposure to air and sun, traditional drying methods for making jerky include smoking and freeze-drying. And before being dried, the meat is almost always first rubbed with salt (and sometimes seasonings), which aid in preservation as well as flavoring. In modern jerky-making practice, this step is achieved by soaking the meat in a salty liquid (called "wet-cure," it's essentially a marinade). Nearly every homemade jerky recipe I found opted for this latter approach, but I decided to go retro with the dry-rub method, followed by a stint in the oven. The reasons for my methodology were twofold: First, I think the wet-cure has a tendency to dilute the meat's flavor and break down its texture. I wanted a jerky that was well seasoned but still had the texture and taste of beef. On top of that there was the time consideration: Why add moisture to something you ultimately intend to dry? With a clear objective, homemade beef jerky was quickly becoming within my reach.

Fair warning; I like my jerky spicy. If you want, you can toss the steak with the spice mixture incrementally in step 4 and test the seasoning by cooking a small piece of the beef in the microwave. Also, if your oven has a convection setting, use it, and do not prop open the oven door in step 5. You'll need two rimmed baking sheets and wire racks for this recipe.

—ADDY PARKER, Associate Editor, Books

Steak strips: Any lean cut of beef is a candidate for jerky; I use flank steak because it's so flavorful. It's also a good choice because the steaks' rectangular shape requires little butchery to slice into consistently sized pieces—an important factor for even drying—and its thick muscle fibers ensure the slices hold together. To make cutting easier, I freeze the meat for an hour to firm it up, then slice it into ¼-inch-thick strips. Chewy jerky is a must in my mind, and it's easy to achieve by slicing the meat with the grain (that is, lengthwise); if you like more tender jerky, slice the meat across the grain.

Spice things up: You could use any seasoning you like for your dry rub, but I like it hot, so I start by toasting chiles and Sichuan peppercorns, then pulverize the chiles and some of the peppercorns in a spice grinder. I crush the remaining peppercorns with a meat pounder, which adds a little textural contrast to the final jerky.

Adding the right balance: Sweet and smoked paprika and ground coriander also make the list for my spice rub. For sweetness, Demerara sugar is ideal; the coarse grains are easy to distribute and form a good crust. Ditto for kosher salt.

Got it covered: Once I have my spice rub ready to go, I toss it with the strips of meat. I use my hands to get a thorough coating on each piece, then arrange the strips on wire racks. An overnight stay in the refrigerator seasons the meat and draws out moisture.

Time to dry out: You want to dry the jerky at as low a temperature as your oven will allow. The oven produces hot air, but it's also dry air, and it is this quality that we are making use of. My oven at home doesn't have a temperature setting below 225 degrees, so I worked with that, but if your oven goes lower, go with it. Prop open the oven door with a wooden spoon to allow air to circulate and moisture to escape. Other than flipping the strips and rotating the baking sheets halfway through, all the work is done.

Perfect jerky: The finished jerky should be dark, somewhat dry, and firm to the touch but still flexible. Drying time can vary slightly depending on the thickness of the meat and the oven temperature you use, but I find I am able to achieve the ideal texture in three to four hours. After all that waiting, feel free to snag a strip now, but leave the rest to cool to room temperature and finish firming up to the proper texture.

Beef Jerky

Makes about 1 pound

Start today, enjoy tomorrow

- 1 (2½-pound) flank steak, trimmed
- ¼ ounce dried red Thai chiles
- ¼ cup whole Sichuan peppercorns
- 2 tablespoons kosher salt
- 5 teaspoons Demerara or turbinado sugar
- 1 tablespoon paprika
- 1 teaspoon smoked paprika
- 1 teaspoon ground coriander

1. Pat steak dry with paper towels. Place steak on parchment paper–lined rimmed baking sheet and freeze, uncovered, until meat is very firm and starting to harden around edges but still pliable, about 1 hour.

2. Meanwhile, toast chiles in 8-inch skillet over medium-high heat, stirring frequently, until fragrant, about 4 minutes, reducing heat if chiles begin to smoke. Let chiles cool to room temperature, then break into small pieces, discarding seeds and stems. Add peppercorns to now-empty skillet and toast over medium-high heat, stirring occasionally, until dark and fragrant, about 1 minute, reducing heat if peppercorns begin to smoke; transfer to separate bowl and let cool to room temperature.

3. Process chile pieces and 2 tablespoons toasted peppercorns in spice grinder until finely ground, about 20 seconds; transfer to large bowl. Spread remaining peppercorns in zipper-lock bag and pound with meat pounder or rolling pin until crushed; transfer to bowl with chile mixture. Stir in salt, sugar, paprika, smoked paprika, and coriander; set aside.

4. Spray 2 wire racks with vegetable oil spray and set in 2 rimmed baking sheets. Cut chilled steak in half against grain, then cut each half into ¼-inch-thick strips with grain. Add steak to spice mixture and toss until evenly coated. Arrange steak strips on prepared wire racks, spaced about ¼ inch apart, and refrigerate, uncovered, for at least 12 hours and up to 24 hours. Remove steak from refrigerator about 30 minutes before baking.

5. Adjust oven racks to upper-middle and lower-middle positions and heat oven to 225 degrees. Pat steak dry with paper towels and place in oven, propping door open with handle of wooden spoon (for air circulation). Bake until steak is dark, somewhat dry, and firm to touch but still pliable, 3 to 4 hours, flipping strips of steak and switching and rotating baking sheets halfway through baking. Pat jerky dry with paper towels and let cool to room temperature. Beef jerky can be refrigerated in airtight container for up to 1 month.

Snacks from Scratch: Everyday Favorites and Gourmet Goodies

228   Granola

230   Granola Bars

233   Corn Chips

237   Kettle Chips

240   Corn Tortillas

243   Lavash Crackers

246   Grissini

249   Rich Butter Crackers

253   Graham Crackers

       Cinnamon Graham Crackers

Granola

✓ **WHY THIS RECIPE WORKS:** Not to be a grump about it, but packaged granola really irks me. It's expensive (one brand costs $9.95 for 12 ounces), and the texture usually resembles loose driveway gravel. I figured that making my own would be a better route to the crisp, substantial clumps of toasty oats and nuts that should make granola such a simple pleasure. And it was, once I stopped following the advice of most recipes to stir, stir, stir. Eventually I went to the opposite extreme, packing the mixture into the pan and leaving it be, to achieve hefty, satisfying clusters that are beautifully browned and have a nice, crisp texture, too.

—ADAM RIED, Contributing Editor, America's Test Kitchen

Bye-bye binders: Most granola recipes include a liquid fat for crispness and sometimes an additional binder (such as dry milk powder). I found a simple mixture of vegetable oil with mild but viscous maple syrup (honey was a bully) and some brown sugar provided all the binding I needed. Old-fashioned rolled oats add hearty, crisp texture (forget instant, quick, or steel-cut). For the nuts, I like chopped almonds, but 2 cups of almost any type contribute rich, toasty flavor. Add the oats and nuts to the liquid mixture and stir to coat every little bit.

Cease stirring: Many granola recipes recommend frequent stirring during baking so that everything will brown evenly, but I think this works against cluster formation. Instead, use a sturdy spatula to tamp the mixture into the pan, bake it gently at 325 degrees, and skip the stirring altogether. This produces granola "bark" that you can break into beautiful chunks.

Break up the bark: After the granola has cooled to room temperature, break it up as much (or as little) as you'd like. All it needs now is some dried fruit, which I add at the very end so it will stay plump (it tends to turn leathery in the oven). I prefer relatively moist dried fruits like raisins, cranberries, apples, pears, and mangos, but you can use anything that strikes your fancy. Experimentation is heartily encouraged!

Granola with Dried Fruit

Makes about 12 cups
Make today, enjoy immediately

⅓ **cup maple syrup**
⅓ **cup packed (2⅓ ounces) light brown sugar**
4 **teaspoons vanilla extract**
½ **teaspoon salt**
½ **cup vegetable oil**
5 **cups (15 ounces) old-fashioned rolled oats**
2 **cups (10 ounces) raw whole almonds or other nuts, chopped coarse**
2 **cups raisins or other dried fruit, chopped if large**

1. Adjust oven rack to upper-middle position and heat oven to 325 degrees. Line rimmed baking sheet with parchment paper. Spray stiff metal spatula with vegetable oil spray.

2. Whisk maple syrup, sugar, vanilla, and salt together in large bowl. Whisk in oil. Fold in oats and almonds until thoroughly coated.

3. Transfer oat mixture to prepared baking sheet and spread across sheet into thin, even layer (about ⅜ inch thick). Using prepared spatula, compress oat mixture until very compact. Bake until lightly browned, 40 to 45 minutes, rotating baking sheet halfway through baking. Remove granola from oven and let cool on wire rack to room temperature, about 1 hour. Break cooled granola into pieces of desired size. Stir in raisins. Granola can be stored at room temperature in airtight container for up to 1 month.

Granola Bars

✅ **WHY THIS RECIPE WORKS:** This recipe was born out of necessity. Granola in its loose form has long been a staple for me, and it didn't take long for my family—and especially my 2-year-old daughter—to get hooked on it too. The problem? She would try to eat it by the fistful, and most of it would end up on the floor. My goal was to take the flavor profile of the only store-bought granola I'm a fan of and turn it into bars. It's the perfect marriage of salty and sweet, accomplished with the help of extra-virgin olive oil, maple syrup, and sea salt baked up with oats, nuts, coconut, and seeds. In bar form, it's something even my 2-year-old can handle.

—SUZANNAH MCFERRAN, Senior Editor, Books

Granola goodies: These bars are based on a granola called Farmhand's Choice by Early Bird Foods & Co. It includes pecans, pumpkin and sunflower seeds, and big pieces of flaked coconut, along with rolled oats. I use maple syrup and brown sugar for sweetness and as binders. Olive oil provides pleasant savory notes as well as a crisp texture. Coarse flake sea salt adds a great salty element you just won't find in most granolas. (If you opt to use table salt, you won't need as much; probably a rounded ¼ teaspoon would do it.) You could make nut-free bars by adding ½ cup more oats instead of pecans.

(Oat) flour power: Most granola bar recipes rely on large amounts of sugar to bind the bars. Since I didn't want a sticky-sweet bar, I tried a couple of different techniques for binding without excess sweetness. After testing cornstarch, a maple syrup reduction, and even soaked oats as binders, I finally landed on the answer: oat flour. The key is processing some of the oats already in the recipe until they turn into a coarse powder. Combine that flour with modest amounts of sugar, maple syrup, and oil and you have a "glue" that will hold the bars together.

Well-coated: After making the oat flour, everything else is a breeze. Add the dry ingredients (old-fashioned rolled oats, pecans, pepitas, sunflower seeds, and coconut) to the sugar–oat flour mixture and stir, stir, stir. Since there is a relatively small amount of liquid, you want to stir thoroughly to make sure each and every oat and nut is completely coated.

Press and pack: I like my granola bars on the thin-and-crisp side, so I spread the mixture out in a 13 by 9-inch cake pan. Lining the pan first with a well-greased foil sling keeps the bars from sticking and makes for easy removal. For cohesive bars, I found the best trick is to press the mixture into the pan as firmly as possible. I use a large metal spatula for the job, but the bottom of a dry measuring cup works as well; just be sure to grease it well with vegetable oil spray first.

Precut perfection: Bake the granola mixture in a 300-degree oven until it turns a deep golden brown (this takes about 45 minutes), then let the pan cool just a bit (about 15 minutes) before cutting. Cutting the block into bars while it's still slightly warm makes it easy to cut clean lines—if you wait until it's completely cool it will just shatter. Keeping them in the pan for this cutting step gives the bars a little bit of support and helps them hold their shape until completely cool.

Slice 'n' snack: After about another hour, the bars will finally be cool— the wait is over. Transfer the bars to a cutting board using the sling. They sort of glue themselves back together along the cut lines, so you'll need to recut them following your original cuts, but at this point it's easy. The bars will keep for up to a week, although in my house they never last that long.

Granola Bars

Makes 16 bars

Make today, enjoy immediately

- ⅓ **cup maple syrup**
- ¼ **cup (1¾ ounces) packed light brown sugar**
- ¾ **teaspoon flake sea salt**
- ⅓ **cup extra-virgin olive oil**
- 2 **cups (6 ounces) old-fashioned rolled oats**
- ½ **cup pecans, chopped fine**
- ½ **cup raw pepitas**
- ½ **cup raw sunflower seeds**
- ½ **cup (1 ounce) unsweetened flaked coconut**

1. Adjust oven rack to middle position and heat oven to 300 degrees. Make foil sling for 13 by 9-inch baking pan by folding 2 long sheets of aluminum foil; first sheet should be 13 inches wide and second sheet should be 9 inches wide. Lay sheets of foil in pan perpendicular to each other, with extra foil hanging over edges of pan. Push foil into corners and up sides of pan, smoothing foil flush to pan. Spray with vegetable oil spray. Generously spray large metal spatula with oil spray.

2. Whisk maple syrup, sugar, and salt together in large bowl. Whisk in oil.

3. Process ½ cup oats in food processor until finely ground, 30 to 40 seconds. Transfer to bowl with maple syrup mixture and stir in remaining 1½ cups oats, pecans, pepitas, sunflower seeds, and coconut, until all dry ingredients are thoroughly coated.

4. Transfer oat mixture to prepared pan and spread into thin, even layer. Using prepared spatula, firmly compress oat mixture until very compact. Bake granola bars until deeply golden, about 45 minutes, rotating pan halfway through baking.

5. Let granola bars cool on wire rack in pan for 15 minutes, then cut, still in pan, into 16 bars. Let cool to room temperature, about 1 hour. Using foil sling, remove bars and transfer to cutting board. Using sharp knife, carefully recut bars following original cuts. Granola bars can be stored at room temperature in airtight container for up to 1 week.

Corn Chips

✓ **WHY THIS RECIPE WORKS:** Ah…the power of advertising. As a kid, I remember singing the "muncha-buncha, muncha-buncha, Fritos go with lunch" jingle every time my mother and I went grocery shopping. Annoying? Yes. But it worked, and I'd get a heaping pile of super-crunchy, corny Fritos served with my peanut butter sandwich later that day. Later on in life, when I experienced my first "Frito pie," my love of Fritos only grew. For the uninitiated, that's where you scoop chili, cheese, and other fixings into a small bag of Fritos. Grab a spoon and eat it right out of the bag. It's heaven (especially if you're at a Texas Rangers ballgame).

But I had to wonder, was there a way to create my own homemade corn chips, with all of the hearty, corny grit and crunch of a real Frito? I started my testing by making a corn tortilla dough, but this dough—made from water and *masa harina* (a flour made from hominy)—lacked the right crunch and grit. The next time I was at the store, I spotted a bag of *masarepa*. I decided to give this corn flour a try, and the resulting chips were crunchier and cornier. For even more texture and crunch, I worked in some stone-ground cornmeal, plus corn oil and salt for just the right taste.

After rolling and cutting the dough into strips, I slid the strips in batches into hot oil (I use corn oil but you could use canola in a pinch). I have to say, seasoned with a little more salt, these corn chips were better than anything I'd get out of a bag. Now to make some chili…

For an accurate measurement of boiling water, bring a full kettle of water to a boil, then measure out the desired amount. Do not use coarse stone-ground cornmeal in this recipe.

—BRIDGET LANCASTER, Executive Food Editor,
New Media, Television, and Radio

A CORNY CRUNCH

For the best texture, use Goya yellow corn masarepa flour. You can find it in the international aisle of larger grocery stores (sold in bags) or online through goya.com or sites like amazon.com. I like to use fine or medium stone-ground cornmeal here; it has a cornier flavor than regular cornmeal and adds the right texture to the chips (regular cornmeal would work in a pinch). Don't use coarse stone-ground cornmeal; the dough won't hold together.

Cornering the components: My goal was a chip that was rustic, fairly thick, plenty corny, and salty—just like Fritos. The hardest part was finding the right cornmeal. Masa harina, a flour made from hominy that's used to make tortillas, is readily available, but it created chips with too fine a texture and without much corn flavor. Masarepa, a corn flour used for making thick corncakes called arepas, has a slightly coarser texture and subtle popcorn flavor that works much better and is still pretty easy to find. A little stone-ground cornmeal added to the dough really gives the chips the right Frito-like grit.

Getting the dough right: After whisking the cornmeals and salt together, stir in boiling water and a bit of corn oil (for extra corn flavor, of course). Start by pouring in about 1⅓ cups water and 4 teaspoons oil to hydrate the dry ingredients. Depending on the brand of masarepa and cornmeal you use, you might need slightly more hot water. The final texture of the dough should be like what you see here (far right): just wet enough to be malleable and hold together.

Get it thin: To keep the dough from sticking to the counter or my rolling pin (and to prevent the need for using flour), I roll the dough out between two pieces of parchment. Working with about one quarter of the dough at a time (keep the remainder covered with plastic wrap), roll it out into a rough rectangle as thin as possible (I aim for 1⁄16 inch, which is about the thickness of a nickel). The thinner the dough, the less the strips will puff up in the hot oil (which you don't want).

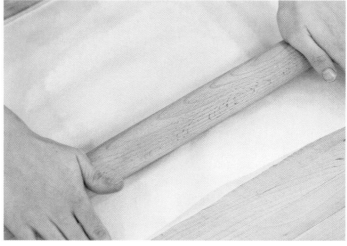

Slice into strips: To cut the dough into strips, I use a pizza wheel. Start by trimming off any ragged edges and save them to reroll. Cut the dough into long ¾-inch-wide strips. Then turn the sheet of dough 90 degrees and slice crosswise into 2-inch-long pieces. Slide the cut strips of dough—while still on the parchment—to a baking sheet and cover with plastic wrap to keep the dough from drying out. Then repeat with the remaining dough and leftover scraps, stacking the sheets of parchment with the cut strips on top of each other on the baking sheet as you go.

Fry 'em: Some homemade Frito recipes bake the chips, but I found the most authentic Frito flavor comes from—no surprise—frying them in corn oil. Heat your oil in a large Dutch oven over medium-high heat until it hits 375 degrees. This temperature ensures the chips will crisp and brown quickly. At lower temperatures, the chips soak up too much oil and turn greasy, so I fry in batches to prevent the oil temperature from dipping too low. It's easiest to add them to the pot by sliding a portion right off the parchment into the oil.

Muncha buncha: You'll know the chips are done once they've turned golden brown and have stopped bubbling in the oil. (The bubbles signal water being released from the dough, and once all of the water has been released, it means they're crisp.) Transfer the chips to a paper towel–lined baking sheet and season them with salt. It takes some willpower, but try to let the chips cool to room temperature before digging in.

Snack time: A batch of these homemade corn chips is ideal for cookouts, Super Bowl parties, or when you are craving my favorite snack, corn chips topped with a scoop of chili, shredded cheese, and all the fixings.

Makes about 9 cups
Make today, enjoy immediately

- 1½ **cups (7½ ounces) masarepa**
- ½ **cup (2½ ounces) fine or medium stone-ground cornmeal**
  Salt
- 1½ **cups boiling water**
- 4 **teaspoons plus 2 quarts corn oil**

1. Whisk masarepa, cornmeal, and 2 teaspoons salt together in medium bowl. Using rubber spatula or wooden spoon, stir in 1⅓ cups boiling water and 4 teaspoons oil until smooth. Dough should be thick, malleable, and just hold together; if dough is still dry, add more water, 1 tablespoon at a time, until dough holds together.

2. Divide dough into 4 equal pieces and wrap 3 pieces in plastic wrap. Roll unwrapped piece of dough between 2 sheets of parchment paper into ⅟₁₆-inch-thick rectangle (about 12 by 9 inches). Trim edges, reserving scraps. Using pizza cutter or sharp knife, cut dough into 2 by ¾-inch pieces. Slide cut dough, still on parchment, onto baking sheet, and cover with plastic. Repeat with remaining pieces of dough, stacking sheets of cut dough on top on each other and keeping stack covered with plastic. Gather scraps, gently reroll ⅟₁₆ inch thick, and cut into pieces.

3. Heat remaining 2 quarts oil in Dutch oven over medium-high heat to 375 degrees, and line rimmed baking sheet with triple layer of paper towels. Carefully slide 1 sheet of corn strips off parchment into hot oil. Fry, stirring occasionally with wire skimmer or slotted spoon, until oil stops bubbling and strips are golden brown, 3 to 5 minutes. Adjust burner, if necessary, to maintain oil temperature around 375 degrees. Using wire skimmer or slotted spoon, transfer chips to prepared baking sheet and season with salt.

4. Return oil to 375 degrees and repeat with remaining strips in 3 more batches. Let cool to room temperature before serving. Corn chips can be stored at room temperature in airtight container for up to 1 week.

Kettle Chips

✔ **WHY THIS RECIPE WORKS:** Whether thick cut, crinkle, plain, or flavored, potato chips are one of America's most beloved snack foods. Our favorite is the small-batch, kettle-style chip. These chips have good potato flavor and a crisp, light texture. Though seemingly simple, perfecting a homemade version proved to be a challenge. Frying at too low a temperature made them soggy and greasy, but if we increased the heat, they burned. Targeting the potatoes' starch as the source of our troubles, we finally landed on a method of rinsing, parboiling, then frying. It was a bit of work, but the reward of fresh, golden homemade potato chips was well worth it.

—THE TEST KITCHEN

Get 'em thin: The first trick to kettle-chip perfection is to slice the potatoes to just the right thickness. We tested potatoes cut in increments from near-translucent and whisper-thin up to ⅛ inch thick. Thicker chips never got properly crisp, while those that were too thin fried up as light as confetti. We found the sweet spot at 1⁄16 inch for thin but substantial, crisp chips. A mandoline makes easy work of this potentially tedious task (just make sure it's extra sharp).

No starch, please: Yukon Golds deliver the best potato flavor, but they also contain a fair bit of starch. So the next step is to agitate the potato slices in a bowl of cold water. This removes exterior starch, which, if left on, would result in chips that brown (or burn) before they crisp, plus they would taste slightly bitter. After swirling the potato slices for a short time in the bowl, drain them and repeat the process until the water in the bowl no longer turns cloudy. (This should take about 5 rinses.) This method (versus simply rinsing them in a colander) makes it easy to tell when the exterior starch has been rinsed off.

Parboil first: Rinsing removes exterior starch; alone it's not enough. A quick parboil before frying jump-starts the cooking and reduces the amount of starch in the potatoes. Gently boil the potatoes in a saucepan until they just start to soften, which should take two to three minutes. The slices should gently bend. Drain the parboiled potatoes thoroughly, then transfer them to a kitchen towel–lined baking sheet. You want the potatoes to be as dry as possible before frying, so make sure to pat them dry.

Best in batches: While you are taking care of the parboiling step, start heating up 2 quarts of vegetable oil in a large Dutch oven. We found 325 degrees to be the optimal chip-frying temperature; it's enough heat to ensure the potatoes cook through but don't burn. Once the oil is hot and your parboiled potatoes are nice and dry, carefully add a small portion of the slices to the pot. Frying in very small batches ensures even cooking and prevents the oil temperature from dropping too much.

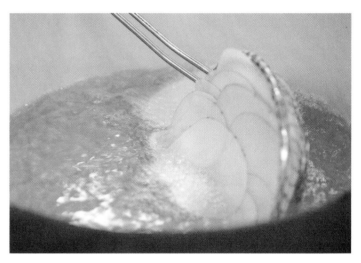

Watch the bubbles: Fry the chips, stirring frequently, just until they turn golden brown and stop bubbling in the oil. When the oil stops bubbling, this means that all of the water has cooked out of potatoes, the signal they are cooked through and crisp. Some chips may cook faster than others, so as soon as chips are done, begin transferring them to a paper towel–lined wire rack set in a baking sheet.

Salt them while they're hot:
We like to season the chips with fine sea salt for greater depth of flavor, but table salt will work as well. Just be sure to salt the chips immediately after they come out of the oil so that the salt adheres.

Kettle Chips

Makes about 6 cups

Make today, enjoy immediately

1 **pound medium Yukon Gold potatoes, sliced ¹⁄₁₆ inch thick on mandoline**
2 **quarts vegetable oil**
 Fine sea salt

1. Line rimmed baking sheet with clean kitchen towel, and set wire rack in second rimmed baking sheet and line with triple layer of paper towels; set both aside. Place potato slices in large bowl and cover with cold water. Gently swirl potatoes to release starch. Drain potatoes and return to bowl. Repeat rinsing step until water no longer turns cloudy, about 5 rinses.

2. Bring 2 quarts water to boil in large saucepan over high heat. Add potatoes, return to gentle boil, and cook until just beginning to soften, 2 to 3 minutes. Drain potatoes well, then spread out over kitchen towel–lined sheet and thoroughly pat dry.

3. Meanwhile, heat oil in Dutch oven over medium-high heat to 325 degrees. Carefully place one-quarter of potato slices in oil. Fry, stirring frequently with wire skimmer or slotted spoon, until oil stops bubbling and chips turn golden and crisp, 3 to 4 minutes. Adjust burner, if necessary, to maintain oil temperature around 325 degrees. As soon as chips finish frying (some chips may cook slightly faster than others), transfer to prepared wire rack using skimmer or slotted spoon. Season with salt to taste.

4. Return oil to 325 degrees and repeat with remaining potato slices in 3 more batches. Let cool to room temperature before serving. Kettle chips are best enjoyed the day they are made.

Corn Tortillas

TORTILLERIA AT HOME

You can find masa harina in the international aisle of grocery stores or near the flour; we used Maseca brand for our testing. Bob's Red Mill makes a non-GMO masa harina (made with corn that's not genetically modified), which you can buy in some stores and online at bobsredmill.com. Do not substitute cornmeal or other corn flour, such as masarepa or Harina P.A.N. Tortilla presses (we use an 8-inch press) are available online from sites such as amazon.com for less than $20.

WHY THIS RECIPE WORKS: Growing up in Mexico, I knew freshly made tortillas would always be on the table. There was a *tortilleria* in every neighborhood; this one food is so integral to the Mexican diet that there were protests when the cost of a kilo of tortillas went up 2 pesos. Even when we moved to Texas, if we wanted good tortillas we'd get them from across the border.

But I no longer live just 15 minutes from the border, and the supermarket bagged tortillas are closer to Frisbees than real, fresh tortillas. Luckily, making them at home is far easier than people realize. It's a short ingredient list and an easy-to-make, very forgiving dough, and for equipment you just need a tortilla press and a griddle (a cast-iron or nonstick skillet will also work).

Tortillas are also easy to troubleshoot: If your first tortilla has cracked edges, add a bit more water to the dough. If your first one sticks to the griddle, you can let the dough sit uncovered for a minute to let it dry out a bit. But the real trick for soft, pliable tortillas is to let the tortillas steam inside the cloth once they come off the griddle. And my last tip: The best fresh tortilla is the one at the bottom of the stack.

—TAIZETH SIERRA, Assistant Editor, America's Test Kitchen

Get prepped: Things move quickly once you're cooking, so get set up. For the press, cut open a small zipper-lock bag along the two sides, but not the bottom, so that it hinges open, then place the bag inside your press with the hinge facing the back. The bag will keep the dough from sticking. Line a large plate with a clean kitchen towel and dampen a few paper towels to put over the bowl of dough to keep the dough from drying out. Finally, start heating the griddle over medium-high heat (cast iron is the classic choice, but any griddle will do).

Measure carefully: Tortillas have a very basic ingredient list: masa harina, warm water, and a little salt. Because of their simplicity, the key is getting the proportions right. I like to use 1 cup water and ¼ teaspoon salt for each cup of masa. This combination should give you a dough with the texture of Play-Doh. Sometimes the humidity (or lack thereof) can affect the dough; if the first tortilla you cook cracks around the edges and is dry, work a tablespoon of water into the remaining dough. Or if the tortilla sticks to the griddle, leave the dough uncovered for a few minutes to dry out.

Make it smooth, then press and peel: For perfect taco-size tortillas, I break off about an ounce of dough (if you want a slightly bigger tortilla, increase the amount of dough to 1½ or 2 ounces). Roll it into a smooth ball (it'll be about the size of a walnut) and transfer it to the lined tortilla press. The smoother the ball, the more even your tortilla will be, so roll with care. Press the tortilla gently and evenly until it is about ¹⁄₁₆ inch thick and 5 inches in diameter. Gently peel back the top layer of the bag and transfer the tortilla to your hand.

Char and flip: Now gently peel off the other side of the bag and place the tortilla on the hot griddle. You know the tortilla is ready to flip to the second side when the edges curl up enough to grasp them with your fingertips and the bottom is spotty brown. If you're nervous about grabbing a hot tortilla with your bare hands, you can use a spatula to flip it. (You'll just look like less of a seasoned tortilleria pro.) If you've heated your griddle properly, your tortillas should cook in about three minutes total, 90 seconds per side.

Bundle them up: The griddle step actually only cooks the outside of the tortilla. To finish cooking and soften the tortillas, as soon as they come off the griddle, transfer them to your kitchen towel–lined plate and cover them up. The heat from the growing stack of tortillas will gently steam them until they are soft and pliable. If you're patient, let the whole stack rest wrapped in the towel for at least three minutes after you've finished griddling. If you're not, simply grab from the bottom.

Corn Tortillas

Makes 12 tortillas

Make today, enjoy immediately

1	**cup (5 ounces) masa harina**
¼	**teaspoon salt**
1	**cup warm water**

1. Cut sides of sandwich-size zipper-lock bag but leave bottom intact so that bag folds open completely, and line tortilla press with open bag. Line large plate with clean kitchen towel. Heat griddle over medium-high heat for 5 minutes.

2. Mix masa harina and salt together in medium bowl. Using your hands, mix in water until well incorporated (dough should feel like Play-Doh). Pinch off 1-ounce piece of dough and roll into 1¼-inch ball. Cover remaining dough with damp paper towel. Place ball in center of press on open bag, and fold top side of bag over dough. Press ball gently into ¹⁄₁₆-inch-thick tortilla (about 5 inches in diameter). Working quickly, gently peel plastic away from tortilla and carefully place tortilla on hot griddle.

3. Cook tortilla without moving until sides of tortilla curl up, about 90 seconds. Flip, and continue to cook until lightly charred, about 90 seconds. Transfer to prepared plate and wrap in kitchen towel.

4. Meanwhile, continue to press tortillas, transferring each to griddle and cooking as they are pressed. Stack cooked tortillas on top of one another on plate, keeping tortillas covered by towel. Once all tortillas are cooked, let steam inside towel for at least 3 minutes before serving. Tortillas are best eaten the day they are made.

Lavash Crackers

✓ **WHY THIS RECIPE WORKS:** For one of my first events as a caterer, I decided to bake lavash crackers for the appetizer spread. These crackers are made by mixing together three kinds of flour with water and oil. The dough is formed into little balls that are rolled out and baked quickly on a pizza stone. They're a little bit nutty, a little bit sweet, and have a crisp and airy texture, perfect when topped with a bit of goat cheese or eaten as is. Unfortunately, I got carried away turning out batch upon batch of lavash when I should have been roasting chickens and braising kale. But luckily, they were a hit. Ever since, they've been a regular in my repertoire.

—KATE WILLIAMS, Test Cook, Books

Balance the flours: Since these crackers are made solely of flour, water, and oil, it's important to choose the ingredients carefully. I use a high proportion of semolina flour since it's high in gluten and makes the dough easy to roll out, plus it lends a subtle sweetness. Whole-wheat flour adds nuttiness, while all-purpose flour balances the whole wheat and keeps the crackers from being too heavy. Finally, I add ¾ teaspoon salt for seasoning. Using a stand mixer fitted with the dough hook makes preparing the dough simple; the first step is adding these dry ingredients to the bowl.

Knead away: As far as liquid ingredients go, crackers made with just water tend to bake up dry and tough. You do have to add some water for a binder, but I also add extra-virgin olive oil, which makes the crackers crisp and adds savory notes. Set the mixer to medium speed, gradually add the water and oil, then knead until the dough is smooth and very elastic, which takes less than 10 minutes.

Divide the dough, then oil and rest: Since these crackers are unleavened, they don't need time to rise, but they will roll out more easily if you let the dough rest and hydrate for about an hour before baking. I like to divide the dough into four pieces (since I'll be making four cracker sheets) before letting it rest. Be sure to coat each piece with olive oil and cover with plastic wrap to keep the dough from drying out while it sits.

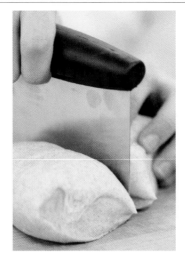

Think easy, think thin: When I first made these crackers, I rolled them out on the counter, carefully transferred each rolled sheet to a pizza peel, then moved them to a pizza stone in the oven. To make things easier, now I just roll and stretch the crackers out directly on an inverted 18 by 13-inch rimmed baking sheet or a cookie sheet (as long as there are no edges to get in the way of the rolling pin). Roll and stretch the dough until it is very thin and reaches the edges of the baking sheet.

Dock, wash, season: Before baking, it's important to dock the dough with a fork about every 2 inches to prevent the crackers from forming bubbles in the oven. The first few times I made these, I simply brushed them with olive oil before sprinkling on salt, pepper, and sesame seeds. While the oil certainly added nice flavor, it didn't do much in terms of holding the seasoning in place. An egg wash works much better at firmly holding on to the toppings and (bonus!) gives the crackers a beautiful golden sheen.

The breakup: Once the cracker sheets are baked and cooled, break them into large, rustic pieces. You'll probably end up with some small scrap pieces (which are conveniently snack-size). Once you've mastered this basic version, you can experiment with your favorite spices and seeds for toppings. I've tried caraway seeds, cumin seeds, and fennel seeds, just to name a few, but anything small and flavorful works well.

Lavash Crackers

Makes about 1 pound
Make today, enjoy immediately

1½ cups (8⅝ ounces)
    semolina flour
¾   cup (4⅛ ounces)
    whole-wheat flour
¾   cup (3¾ ounces)
    all-purpose flour
¾   teaspoon salt
1   cup warm water
⅓   cup extra-virgin olive oil,
    plus extra for brushing
1   large egg, lightly beaten
2   tablespoons sesame seeds
2   teaspoons flake sea salt
1   teaspoon coarsely ground
    pepper

1. Using stand mixer fitted with dough hook, mix flours and salt on low speed. Gradually add water and oil and knead until smooth and elastic, 7 to 9 minutes. Turn dough out onto lightly floured counter and knead by hand to form smooth, round ball. Divide dough into 4 equal pieces, brush with oil, and cover with plastic wrap. Let rest at room temperature for 1 hour.

2. Adjust oven racks to upper-middle and lower-middle positions and heat oven to 425 degrees. Lightly coat two 18 by 13-inch inverted (or rimless) baking sheets with vegetable oil spray.

3. Press 1 piece of dough (keep remaining dough covered with plastic), into small rectangle, then transfer to one of prepared sheets. Using rolling pin and hands, roll and stretch dough evenly to edges of sheet. Using fork, poke holes in dough at 2-inch intervals. Repeat with second piece of dough on second prepared sheet.

4. Brush rolled-out dough with beaten egg, sprinkle with sesame seeds, sea salt, and pepper, then gently press seasonings into dough. Bake crackers until deeply golden brown, 15 to 18 minutes, switching and rotating sheets halfway through baking. Transfer crackers to wire rack and let cool completely. Repeat rolling, seasoning, and baking with remaining 2 pieces of dough, making sure baking sheets are completely cool before rolling out dough.

5. Break cooled lavash crackers into large pieces. Lavash can be stored at room temperature in airtight container for up to 2 weeks.

Grissini

✓ **WHY THIS RECIPE WORKS:** A major chain of faux-Italian restaurants entices diners with "all-you-can-eat breadsticks." Fat and soft as dinner rolls, their breadsticks don't come close to the real thing, called grissini. Wrapped up in waxed-paper packages and placed on authentic Italian dinner tables or sold at corner delis, grissini are as thin and leggy as runway models, have a texture that's ultra-crisp, and taste purely of browned wheat, olive oil, and salt. They are the perfect foil to any boldly flavored Italian meal. Despite their humble ingredients, I discovered I had to pull out a few tricks to get just the right crispness and fresh, not stale, flavor for grissini at home.

—MATTHEW CARD, Contributing Editor, *Cook's Illustrated*

Keep it simple: After a little digging into Italian baking books, I realized that grissini dough is a pretty simple affair, not too different from pizza dough. All-purpose flour lends the dough just enough strength to be stretched without turning tough, yeast gives it lift, and water and oil make it slack enough to roll easily. While it's common to knead doughs in a stand mixer, I like to use a food processor to bring this dough together. The processor builds gluten quickly; it takes less than a minute to turn flour and water into perfectly kneaded dough.

Let it rise, punch it down: After processing, put the dough in an oiled bowl and leave it in a warm environment for about two hours to rise. It could take a little more or less time, but you want the dough to be doubled in size. Once it's reached that point, press the dough down to deflate it.

Start with strips: Grissini offer charm in their rustic, hand-shaped form. Most recipes I found provided only vague instructions for shaping, so I experimented until I found the easiest method that also delivered perfectly golden, crispy sticks. I divide the dough in half for easier handling. Roll each half into a rectangle about 12 by 8 inches, then slice that into ¾-inch strips. The breadsticks were less likely to break when rolling if I doubled up the strips, so I fold each strip in half onto itself, then give these a quick roll to make the halves adhere. Let the dough rest for about five minutes.

Roll long and thin: On a barely moistened surface (the moisture helps the dough grip the counter and form a more taut log), roll each log into a long snake that's about 20 inches long. Make the snakes a little bit longer than your baking sheet (they'll contract a little when you transfer them to the sheet).

Brushed and spiced: Traditionally, grissini flavorings are kept simple: salt, pepper, and maybe a spice or two. I like the rougher texture of kosher salt and coarsely ground pepper, plus fennel seed for a touch of anise flavor. Brushing the grissini with olive oil before seasoning adds an extra layer of flavor and helps the seasoning adhere.

Gentle heat does the job: Pizzas cook best at a blistering heat, and even though this grissini dough is a lot like pizza dough, the breadsticks burned to a crisp when cooked at 500 degrees. A 350-degree oven delivers perfectly crisp grissini that are lightly browned from tip to tip. I also found that a little extra cooling and drying time (about two hours) helps to ensure that if there are thicker spots on the breadsticks (which is likely, given the fact you're shaping them by hand), they become totally dry.

Grissini

Makes 30 breadsticks

Make today, enjoy immediately

- 1 **cup water, heated to 110 degrees**
- 1 **tablespoon extra-virgin olive oil, plus extra for brushing**
- 2 **cups (10 ounces) all-purpose flour**
- 1 **teaspoon instant or rapid-rise yeast**
- ¾ **teaspoon salt**
- 1½ **teaspoons kosher salt**
- 1 **teaspoon coarsely ground pepper**
- ½ **teaspoon fennel seeds, chopped fine**

1. Combine water and oil in 2-cup liquid measuring cup. Lightly coat large bowl with vegetable oil spray. Process flour, yeast, and salt in food processor until combined, about 3 seconds. With processor running, slowly add ¾ cup water mixture and process until dough forms ball, about 10 seconds. If dough doesn't readily form ball, add remaining liquid, 1 tablespoon at a time, continuing to process until ball forms, about 3 seconds. Continue to process until dough is smooth and elastic, about 30 seconds. Transfer dough to oiled bowl and cover with plastic wrap. Let rise until doubled in size, 1½ to 2 hours. Press dough to deflate.

2. Adjust oven racks to upper-middle and lower-middle positions and heat oven to 350 degrees. Line 2 rimmed baking sheets with parchment paper. Combine kosher salt, pepper, and fennel in small bowl.

3. Divide dough in half. Working with 1 piece of dough at a time (keep remaining piece covered in plastic), roll dough on lightly floured counter to 12 by 8-inch rectangle. Cut rectangle widthwise into ¾-inch-wide strips (about 15 strips). Fold each piece in half and gently roll to form 4-inch-long log. Let logs rest, covered in plastic wrap, for about 5 minutes.

4. On slightly damp counter, roll each log into thin breadstick, about 20 inches long, and transfer to prepared baking sheet. Brush breadsticks with oil and sprinkle with seasoning mixture. Bake until golden brown, 25 to 30 minutes, switching and rotating sheets halfway through baking. Slide breadsticks, still on parchment, onto wire racks; let dry completely, about 2 hours, before serving. Grissini can be stored at room temperature in airtight container or wrapped in plastic wrap for up to 2 weeks.

Rich Butter Crackers

✓ **WHY THIS RECIPE WORKS:** Ritz crackers are one of those retro-chic foods we all can't help but love. They've been around since the 1930s, a staple on generations of party platters. And we love them because they're so rich and buttery, right? Well, lo and behold, Ritz don't contain butter (they do, however, contain several ingredients we can't pronounce). Knowing that puts them in a whole other light, but they're awfully hard to give up. It was time to make our own. Starting with an all-butter pie dough recipe, we tweaked it until we had a rich, buttery cracker made only with familiar pantry ingredients—and, of course, plenty of butter.

—THE TEST KITCHEN

Cake flour for crackers: This dough comes together just like pie dough in the food processor, though we made a few changes to turn crust into crackers. First, we mix a little cake flour in with the all-purpose to create a bit more tenderness and a slightly crumbly crumb. Next, we add leavener in the form of baking powder for extra lift. Upping the salt turns the dough from sweet to savory.

Chill and pulse: While Ritz crackers are made with shortening, oils, and "natural flavor," we wanted to get rich butter flavor from the source. An all-butter cracker, however, baked up tough and not quite as flaky as we wanted. To add flakiness without sacrificing butter flavor, we used a 2:1 ratio of butter to shortening. Be sure to keep both of these fats chilled so they can be worked into the dry mixture without melting. Process the shortening with the dry ingredients for about 10 seconds, then pulse in the butter until the mixture looks like coarse cornmeal.

The pinch test: To bind the dough, pulse in an egg yolk (it also adds color and flavor and increases tenderness) and ice water. Add just enough water (probably somewhere between 6 and 8 tablespoons) to start to bind the dough; you should be able to pinch crumbs together between your fingertips, but the dough should not have formed into a cohesive ball. At this point, adding more liquid would bring the dough together like you want, but it would also make for leaden crackers. So we stop here and use an alternative method.

Smear campaign: Next, we turn to the French technique *fraisage*. It makes the dough cohesive while keeping the bits of fat intact, which are key for making a flaky cracker. It may sound fancy, but it's easy to do: Fraisage basically means smearing the dough. Pour the crumbs out onto the counter into a rectangle. Starting from the far end of the rectangle and, using the heel of your hand, press and smear crumbs in small portions (about the size of an egg) away from you, about a foot or so. Continue until you've gone through the pile. Then gently form the crumbs into a rectangle again, and repeat the process.

Form two disks and let them rest: Now the dough should hold together in a cohesive ball that's soft and malleable. Because we find it's easier to roll out thin crackers when we're working with a relatively small amount of dough, we divide the dough in half and form each half into a 4-inch disk. Before you roll it out, however, let the dough rest for about an hour in the fridge (just wrap the disks in plastic wrap). This resting time will help the flour hydrate and make the dough easier to roll.

Even-steven: When the hour is up, place one disk on a floured counter and roll the dough to an even ⅛-inch thickness. It's important to get this right; if you are a little off here or there it can have a big effect on the end result and the cooking will be uneven. Bust out the ruler and measure all around the dough if you need to. Next, stamp out the crackers with a 2-inch scalloped biscuit cutter and transfer them to a parchment-lined baking sheet. Gather and gently reroll the scraps to form a few extra crackers before tossing the last scraps.

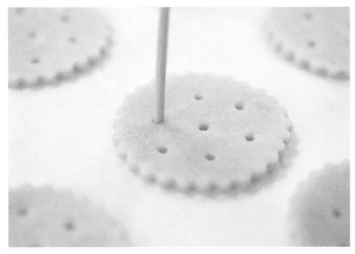

All for show: Now all these crackers need is a little sprucing up. Dock the crackers in a Ritz-like pattern (six holes in a circle, and one in the middle) using the end of a wooden skewer, then brush them with egg wash for extra color and shine. It means a little extra time, but we think baking one sheet at a time makes a difference here in terms of even cooking. Baking the crackers in a hot, 450-degree oven gives them lift and a deeply golden exterior.

Butter up: For ultimate butter flavor and the best coloring, we brush the crackers, hot out of the oven, with melted butter. The final touch? A sprinkling of salt on top. Whether eaten on their own or paired with a dip, spread, or cheese, these rich, buttery crackers really live up to their name.

Rich Butter Crackers

Makes about 50 crackers
Make today, enjoy immediately

1½	cups (7½ ounces) all-purpose flour
½	cup (2 ounces) cake flour
2½	tablespoons sugar
1½	teaspoons salt
1	teaspoon baking powder
2	tablespoons vegetable shortening, cut into ½-inch pieces and chilled
4	tablespoons butter, cut into ¼-inch pieces and chilled, plus 4 tablespoons melted and cooled
1	large egg yolk, plus 1 large egg, lightly beaten
6–8	tablespoons ice water Kosher salt

1. Process all-purpose flour, cake flour, sugar, salt, and baking powder in food processor until combined, 3 to 5 seconds. Scatter shortening over top and process until mixture resembles coarse cornmeal, about 10 seconds. Scatter chilled butter pieces over top and pulse until mixture resembles coarse cornmeal, about 8 pulses. Continue to pulse, adding egg yolk and then water, 1 tablespoon at a time, until the dough begins to form small curds that hold together when pinched with your fingers (the dough will be crumbly), about 10 pulses.

2. Turn dough crumbs onto lightly floured counter and gather into rectangular pile. Starting at farthest end, use heel of your hand to smear small amount of dough against counter. Continue to smear dough until all crumbs have been worked. Gather smeared crumbs together in another rectangular pile and repeat process. Divide dough in half. Place each piece of dough on sheet of plastic wrap and flatten each into 4-inch disk. Wrap each piece tightly in plastic, and refrigerate for 1 hour.

3. Adjust oven rack to middle position and heat oven to 450 degrees. Line 2 rimmed baking sheets with parchment paper. Working with 1 piece of dough at a time, remove from refrigerator, and, on lightly floured counter, roll dough into ⅛-inch-thick circle (about 12 inches in diameter). Using 2-inch scalloped biscuit cutter, cut dough into rounds and transfer to prepared sheet, spaced about ½ inch apart. Gently reroll scraps ⅛ inch thick, cut into rounds, and transfer to prepared sheet.

4. Using back end of wooden skewer, poke 7 decorative holes in dough rounds. Brush tops of dough with beaten egg. Bake crackers, 1 sheet at a time, until deep golden brown, 10 to 12 minutes, rotating sheet halfway through baking.

5. Brush 2 coats of melted butter over hot crackers immediately after removing from oven. Sprinkle with kosher salt. Let cool to room temperature before serving. Crackers can be stored at room temperature in airtight container for up to 1 week.

Graham Crackers

✓ **WHY THIS RECIPE WORKS:** There are few things I consider myself good at doing, but among them is cooking. So when I was helping out my daughter's class and saw her teacher lean over and say, "I know which snack you want, Lola!" as she gave her a pile of graham crackers from a cardboard box, I thought: (1) "Why does that woman know my daughter's snack preferences better than me?" and (2) "I will make them better!" (I'm good at being competitive, too.) Graham crackers' flavor traditionally comes from graham flour, yet the supermarket crackers contain mostly all-purpose. This added one more goal; I would bring the graham back to the cracker.

—SARAH WILSON, Associate Editor, *Cook's Country*

GETTING GRAHAM FLOUR

Graham flour is sold at health food stores and Whole Foods. Labeling may vary: Both Bob's Red Mill Whole Wheat Graham Flour and Arrowhead Mills Stone-Ground Whole Wheat Flour work.

Easy as pie dough: Graham crackers get their distinct wheat flavor from graham flour, a coarsely ground whole-wheat flour. However, many store-bought graham crackers these days contain far more white flour than wheat. For my version, I wanted a graham-forward cracker with hearty texture, so I use twice as much graham as all-purpose. Granulated sugar complements the wheat's sweetness and helps the crackers crisp. Pulse the dry ingredients in a food processor to combine them, then add chilled cubes of butter, pulsing until the butter is well incorporated and the mixture looks like coarse cornmeal.

A touch of the sweet stuff: Next, add all of the liquid ingredients to the food processor and process the mixture until it comes together in a cohesive dough. Molasses gives the crackers a toasty, caramel flavor that goes well with the whole-wheat flour. I found I needed about ½ cup of liquid to bring this dough together, but crackers made solely with molasses were too intensely flavored. A couple tablespoons of molasses plus 5 tablespoons of water make crackers with just the right balance, and a little vanilla extract rounds it all out.

For an even roll: The first time I tried rolling out this dough, it stuck to the counter like cement. To make things easier, roll it out between two pieces of parchment (this is also handy because you can use the bottom piece to move the prepped crackers right onto a baking sheet). It's easiest to roll crackers to a uniform thickness if you divide the dough into quarters and roll each one out into a small rectangle that's about ⅛ inch thick. It means baking two batches of crackers (two baking sheets at a time), but the oven time is so short it's not a big deal.

For good measure: Once you have the dough rolled out into rough rectangles, pull off the top pieces of parchment. Trim the edges of the dough to form a 10 by 7½-inch rectangle, then score the dough into 2½-inch squares (you can use a sharp knife, or if you have a fluted pastry cutter, that will give them an old-fashioned edge). Be sure to cut all the way through the dough, then dock each cracker a few times with a fork to keep the crackers from puffing too much in the oven.

Browned and crisp: Transfer two of the rolled-and-scored sheets of dough to their own baking sheets, then transfer the baking sheets to the oven. The crackers need to bake until they are fully crisp, but not so long that they turn dry and crumbly. In a 375-degree oven, this takes about 15 minutes, but check the crackers as they bake. You'll know they're done when they are golden and firm around the edges.

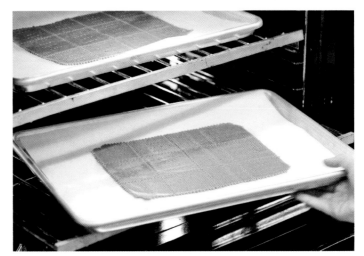

Cut and enjoy: Let the crackers cool on the parchment paper, then transfer the whole thing to a cutting board. Cut the crackers apart along the scored lines, then repeat with the second batch. These graham crackers are great for making s'mores (with homemade marshmallows, page 282, of course) or pie crusts, or for just plain snacking.

Graham Crackers

Makes 48 crackers

Make today, enjoy immediately

- 1½ **cups (8¼ ounces) graham flour**
- ¾ **cup (3¾ ounces) all-purpose flour**
- ½ **cup (3½ ounces) sugar**
- 1 **teaspoon baking powder**
- 1 **teaspoon baking soda**
- ½ **teaspoon salt**
- ¼ **teaspoon ground cinnamon**
- 8 **tablespoons unsalted butter, cut into ½-inch pieces and chilled**
- 5 **tablespoons water**
- 2 **tablespoons molasses**
- 1 **teaspoon vanilla extract**

1. Adjust oven racks to upper-middle and lower-middle positions and heat oven to 375 degrees. Process graham flour, all-purpose flour, sugar, baking powder, baking soda, salt, and cinnamon in food processor until combined, about 3 seconds. Add butter and process until mixture resembles coarse cornmeal, about 15 seconds. Add water, molasses, and vanilla and process until dough comes together, about 20 seconds.

2. Divide dough into quarters. Working with 1 piece of dough at a time (keep remaining pieces covered with plastic wrap), roll dough out between 2 pieces of parchment paper into 11 by 8-inch rectangle, ⅛ inch thick. Remove top piece of parchment and trim dough into tidy 10 by 7½-inch rectangle with knife, and then score rectangle of dough into twelve 2½-inch squares. Prick each square several times with fork.

3. Slide 2 pieces of rolled-out and scored dough, still on parchment, onto separate baking sheets. Bake crackers until golden brown and edges are firm, about 15 minutes, switching and rotating sheets halfway through baking. Slide baked crackers, still on parchment, onto wire rack and let cool completely. Repeat with remaining 2 pieces of rolled-out dough.

4. Transfer cooled crackers, still on parchment, to cutting board and carefully cut apart along scored lines. Graham crackers can be stored at room temperature in airtight container for up to 2 weeks.

TO MAKE CINNAMON GRAHAM CRACKERS: Increase amount of cinnamon in dough to ½ teaspoon. Toss ¼ cup sugar with 1 teaspoon ground cinnamon, then sprinkle mixture over scored crackers just before baking.

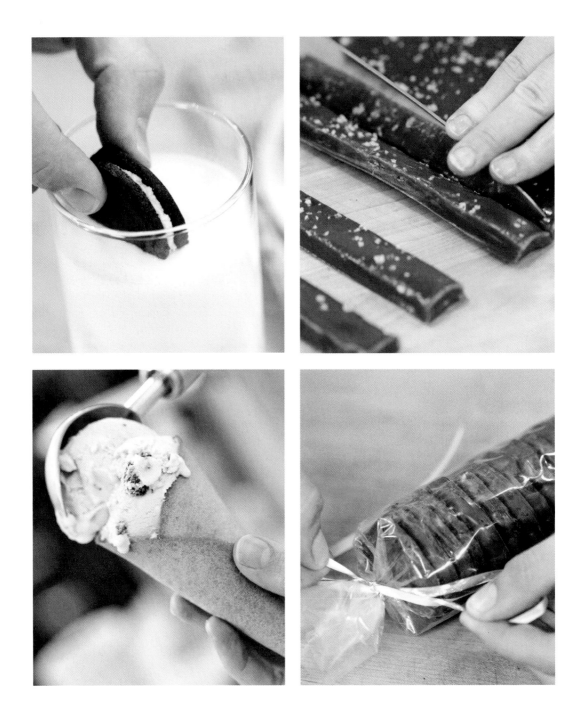

The Sweet Kitchen: Cookies, Candies, and Dessert Sauces

258   **Chocolate Sandwich Cookies**

262   **Peanut Butter Sandwich Cookies**

265   **Thin Chocolate-Mint Cookies**

       Thin Chocolate-Mint Cookies with Easy Chocolate Coating

269   **Chocolate-Toffee Bark**

272   **Brigadeiros**

274   **Salted Caramels**

278   **Almond Torrone**

       Pistachio-Orange Torrone

282   **Marshmallows**

285   **Orange Jelly Slices**

289   **Sugar Cones**

293   **Chocolate Ice Cream Shell**

295   **Cajeta**

297   **Maple Cream**

Chocolate Sandwich Cookies

✔ WHY THIS RECIPE WORKS: Given its tag line "milk's favorite cookie," it's no surprise Oreos unfailingly appeal to the kid in everyone, myself included. But at the risk of offending diehard Oreo fans, I have to admit that while the nostalgic draw remains pretty high for me, recently I've finally faced facts: The flavor of Oreos is pretty wan.

Re-creating the famed sandwich cookie—but with a bolder chocolate flavor and a richer filling—felt like a manageable task out of the gate, but it didn't take me long to realize that creating a homemade Oreo recipe was actually a serious challenge. The dark cookies were easy to overbake (their color obscures browned edges) and the filling seemed to turn out either bland and forgettable or supremely saccharine. But once I figured out the secrets, making these cookies proved pretty straightforward. I found that for the right deep chocolate cookie that wasn't too sweet, black cocoa powder, plus a little regular cocoa powder and espresso powder, were the keys. For the filling, using both butter and shortening created a winning texture and flavor.

They do require a little attention to detail in terms of slicing evenly sized cookies, plus some time in terms of assembly. But whether you are a dunker or prefer to twist and lick, you'll find these cookies have a supreme flavor and texture that make the effort worthwhile.

—DAN ZUCCARELLO, Associate Editor, Books

The dark secret: Since building serious chocolate flavor was one of my main objectives, I started my testing with black cocoa powder. This cocoa has an intense flavor and gives the cookies the right dark color. Using too much, however, produces cookies with an overly assertive flavor. I found the key is tempering it with some regular Dutch-processed cocoa and a little espresso powder. Combining the cocoas and espresso powder with melted butter helps their flavors bloom and allows them to blend with the other cookie ingredients quickly.

Sweet key to crispness: Making the dough is pretty basic. Start by beating the cocoa mixture, more butter, sugar, and salt together until fluffy, then beat in an egg yolk and vanilla for extra richness and flavor. One of the keys to a crisp cookie is using the right type of sugar. Granulated does the trick, giving these cookies structure and a good snap. With the butter-sugar mixture combined, it's finally time for the flour. Add it in small batches to incorporate it without overworking the dough.

Roll 'em: The easiest way to achieve thin and uniformly round cookies is to roll the dough into logs, then slice the logs into disks. Start by dividing the dough in half, then roll each half into a 6-inch-long log. (If the dough is sticky and hard to roll, just chill it for a few minutes.) Wrap each log of dough in plastic wrap and twist the ends to help the dough keep a uniform shape. Chill the dough in the refrigerator until it's firm.

Cut them thin and win: Once the dough is firm, use a sharp knife to trim off the ends of each log, then slice off ⅛-inch-thick rounds. The proper thickness is important here for even cooking, so before slicing, I find marking the trimmed logs every 1 inch gives me a good guide to help stay on target. Also, to ensure the log doesn't become flattened and misshapen on one side from the weight of the knife, roll the dough log a quarter turn every couple of slices.

Dented = Done: The cookies don't spread much while baking, so you can fit all 80 slices on two baking sheets. Because these cookies are so dark, it can be difficult to know when to pull them from the oven. The most reliable indicator is touch; the cookies are ready when the edges feel firm and gently pressing in the center of a cookie only leaves a slight indentation. Once they're baked, let the cookies cool on the baking sheets for a few minutes, then transfer them to a wire rack to cool completely.

The filling of success: Now it's time for the sweet filling that glues the chocolate cookies together. A filling made by whipping together shortening, confectioners' sugar, and vanilla extract produces the pure white color just like you find in Oreos, but it makes for a tasteless and unremarkable center. At the other extreme, all butter is simply too rich. The key is simply using a combination of the two for a filling that's white, perfectly sweet, and just rich enough. A rounded half teaspoon is just the right amount of filling per sandwich cookie. I find it most efficient to top half of the cookies with filling in one go.

To assemble the cookies: Finally, top the filling off with another cookie and gently squeeze them together until the filling is evenly distributed. These homemade sandwich cookies are crisp without being hard, and they'll hold up to dunking and twisting as well as the store-bought version does. One taste and I think you'll decide your milk just found a new favorite cookie.

Chocolate Sandwich Cookies

Makes about 40 cookies
Make today, enjoy immediately

COOKIES

- 3 tablespoons unsalted butter, melted and cooled, plus 5 tablespoons softened
- ¼ cup (¾ ounce) black cocoa
- 2 tablespoons Dutch-processed cocoa
- ½ teaspoon instant espresso powder
- ½ cup (3½ ounces) sugar
- ¼ teaspoon salt
- 1 large egg yolk
- 1½ teaspoons vanilla extract
- 1 cup (5 ounces) all-purpose flour

FILLING

- 2 tablespoons unsalted butter, softened
- 2 tablespoons vegetable shortening
- 1 cup (4 ounces) confectioners' sugar
- ½ teaspoon vanilla extract
  Pinch salt

1. FOR THE COOKIES: Stir melted butter, black cocoa, Dutch-processed cocoa, and espresso powder together in bowl until combined and smooth.

2. Using stand mixer fitted with paddle, beat cocoa mixture, remaining 5 tablespoons butter, sugar, and salt together on medium-high speed until combined and fluffy, about 2 minutes, scraping down bowl as needed. Beat in egg yolk and vanilla until combined, about 30 seconds. Reduce speed to low and slowly add flour in 3 batches, beating well after each addition and scraping down bowl as needed. Continue to beat until dough forms cohesive ball, about 30 seconds.

3. Divide dough in half and roll each piece into 6-inch log, about 1½ inches thick. Tightly roll logs in plastic wrap and twist ends to firmly compact dough into tight cylinder. Refrigerate until firm, about 1 hour.

4. Adjust oven racks to upper-middle and lower-middle positions and heat oven to 325 degrees. Line 2 baking sheets with parchment paper. Using sharp knife, trim ends of dough logs, then slice into ⅛-inch-thick rounds, rolling dough slightly forward or backward so that it won't become misshapen from weight of knife. Arrange cookies ½ inch apart on prepared baking sheets.

5. Bake until cookies are firm and reveal slight indentation when pressed with finger, 14 to 16 minutes, switching and rotating baking sheets halfway through baking. Let cookies cool on sheets for 5 minutes. Transfer cookies to wire rack and let cool completely, about 30 minutes.

6. FOR THE FILLING: Using dry, clean bowl and paddle attachment, mix butter, shortening, sugar, vanilla, and salt together on medium-low speed until combined, about 1 minute. Increase speed to medium-high and beat until filling is light and fluffy, about 2 minutes.

7. TO ASSEMBLE: Place 40 cookies upside down on work surface. Place rounded ½ teaspoon filling in center of each cookie. Place second cookie on top of filling, right side up, and squeeze gently until filling is evenly distributed. Cookies can be stored at room temperature in airtight container for up to 1 week.

Peanut Butter Sandwich Cookies

✔ **WHY THIS RECIPE WORKS:** When I was a kid, I loved Nutter Butters. I'm not sure if the draw was the crunchy peanut-shaped cookies or the creamy-yet-solid filling sandwiched between them. Either way, I was sorely disappointed when I recently tasted them again and found them overly sweet, stale, and utterly lacking in peanut flavor. Maybe the formulation has changed, or maybe my palate has grown more discerning. Either way, I knew I could do better.

—ANDREA GEARY, Associate Editor, *Cook's Illustrated*

Peanut power: In addition to using peanut butter in this cookie dough, I also work in plenty of actual peanuts. I like the bumpy and crunchy texture that chopped nuts give the cookies (I simply throw them into the food processor), and adding 1¼ cups means these cookies have a seriously crunchy, super nutty flavor. If you use raw peanuts, make sure to toast (and cool) them first. Dry-roasted, unsalted peanuts also work; you only have to toast them a few minutes, just to give them some color. Cocktail peanuts (which are salted and oil-roasted) won't work here.

Simple and thin: I wanted to keep the process of mixing this dough simple: no chilling, no slicing, no rolling, no stamping. Just a couple of bowls and some whisking (and stirring). Because these cookies have to bake up thin and flat (so you can eat two plus filling) as well as crunchy, I evaluated each of the dough's ingredients carefully. To start, I limited the eggs to one, which helped keep the cookies from being cakey. Whisk the egg with some creamy peanut butter, milk, melted butter, and both granulated and brown sugar (just half a cup of each keeps the cookies from being overly sweet).

Only a little flour power: In another bowl I whisk together my flour, salt, and baking soda. Using just ¾ cup flour (versus the 2-plus cups you might find in a typical peanut butter cookie) is a good step toward keeping the cookies thin, and a full teaspoon of baking soda helps them spread and makes them dry and crunchy. I combine my egg mixture with the flour mixture, then stir in the peanuts.

Cookie press: I portion the dough with a #60 scoop for simplicity, but a tablespoon would also work. Either way, just make sure each mound is uniform in shape and size. Twelve cookies will fit on a baking sheet, which means two batches of two baking sheets each, but the best things in life require a little extra effort, peanut butter cookies included. After scooping the dough onto the baking sheets, I find hands-on force is the best (and easiest) approach for ensuring thin cookies. I just wet my hand a bit to prevent stickiness, then press each mound into a 2-inch round.

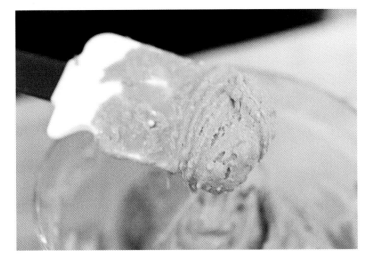

Fill 'er up: A good sandwich cookie is all about balanced flavors and textures, so my filling had to complement the cookie (and vice versa). A lot of recipes call for blending peanut butter and confectioners' sugar with a dairy element, such as butter, cream cheese, or heavy cream. I settled on butter since it provides the silkiest consistency and allows for the purest peanut butter flavor. A full 1 cup of confectioners' sugar makes the filling thick enough to stay put and not squirt out the sides, which means this filling is sweet, but the not-too-sweet cookies ensure it all works together.

Scoop it warm, squish it gently:
After a few failed attempts at
assembling these cookies, I realized
success is all about timing. If
I prepared the filling after the
cookies were cooled and right
before assembly, the warm filling
could be easily scooped and
squished between the cookies, no
painstaking spreading necessary.
It's easier if you fill just six cookies
at a time because if you dawdle, the
filling on each cookie cools and sets
up, making it hard to squish.

Peanut Butter Sandwich Cookies

Makes 24 cookies

Make today, enjoy immediately

COOKIES

1¼	cups (6¼ ounces) unsalted raw or dry-roasted peanuts, toasted and cooled
¾	cup (3¾ ounces) all-purpose flour
1	teaspoon baking soda
½	teaspoon salt
3	tablespoons unsalted butter, melted
½	cup creamy peanut butter
½	cup (3½ ounces) granulated sugar
½	cup (3½ ounces) light brown sugar
3	tablespoons whole milk
1	large egg

FILLING

¾	cup creamy peanut butter
3	tablespoons unsalted butter
1	cup (4 ounces) confectioners' sugar

1. FOR THE COOKIES: Adjust oven racks to upper-middle and lower-middle positions and heat oven to 350 degrees. Line 2 baking sheets with parchment paper. Pulse peanuts in food processor until finely chopped, about 8 pulses. Whisk flour, baking soda, and salt together in bowl. Whisk butter, peanut butter, granulated sugar, brown sugar, milk, and egg together in second bowl. Stir flour mixture into peanut butter mixture with rubber spatula until combined. Stir in chopped peanuts until evenly distributed.

2. Using #60 scoop or tablespoon measure, place 12 mounds, evenly spaced, on each prepared baking sheet. Using damp hand, flatten mounds until 2 inches in diameter.

3. Bake until deep golden brown and firm to touch, 15 to 18 minutes, switching and rotating sheets halfway through baking. Let cookies cool on sheets for 5 minutes. Transfer cookies to wire rack and let cool completely, about 30 minutes. Repeat portioning and baking with remaining dough.

4. FOR THE FILLING: Microwave peanut butter and butter until butter is melted and warm, about 40 seconds. Using rubber spatula, stir in sugar until combined.

5. TO ASSEMBLE: Place 24 cookies upside down on work surface. Place 1 level tablespoon (or #60 scoop) warm filling in center of each cookie. Place second cookie on top of filling, right side up, pressing gently until filling spreads to edges. Allow filling to set for 1 hour. Assembled cookies can be stored at room temperature in airtight container for up to 3 days.

Thin Chocolate-Mint Cookies

✔ WHY THIS RECIPE WORKS: I have great memories about my days as a Girl Scout, most revolving around the brief yet intense cookie season. I pounded the pavement each season for three years, armed with dimples, a bowl cut, and a dream: to convince my neighbors that they should buy their cookies from me. While some cookie flavors always took a little sales–manship, there was never any need to talk my customers into buying Thin Mints in bulk. Always my best-selling cookie, they were also a personal favorite. Even when I take a bite today, I am immediately transported to those sweltering summer days in Florida, where the only relief from the hot, humid air came from a cool, crisp Thin Mint (eaten right out of the freezer, of course).

When I recently began mentioning to friends and colleagues that I was working on a recipe for a homemade version of Thin Mints, it was no surprise that I was greeted with plenty of excitement and anticipation— as well as numerous volunteers for tasters. But, while that tenacious little girl with the bowl cut and the leadership badges still exists somewhere deep in my psyche, I realized early in my testing that my palate had grown up. I wanted cookies with a more complex, chocolaty flavor. Luckily, I found a way to mature this cult favorite to produce a thin, crisp, and light chocolate cookie surrounded in just the right amount of chocolaty, slightly minty coating. And best of all, I no longer need to count the days until the fleeting cookie season arrives. This more sophisticated spin lives up to all the Thin Mint expectations—and then exceeds them. You won't be disappointed, scout's honor.

—REBECCA MORRIS, Test Cook, Books

COUVERTURE CHOCOLATE

This professional-quality coating chocolate is high in fat due to added cocoa butter, which allows it to create a perfectly thin coating. Couverture is available in bar form and wafers (also referred to as feves or callets); we prefer the wafers since they eliminate the need for chopping. You can buy Guittard couverture chocolate wafers at Sur La Table and Williams-Sonoma. Some higher-end grocery stores also sell them. Note that some brands, such as Valrhona and Callebaut, sell feves and callets that are couverture but not specifically labeled as such. You can also order it online at kingarthurflour.com.

Butter isn't better: I was after a crisp, short cookie, so I started with a wafer-style dough, which begins by creaming sugar and butter. However, the water in the butter caused the cookies to come out like hockey pucks. Thin Mints, I realized, include palm kernel oil. Using an oil, which contains no water, would solve my problem, but I wasn't about to go the same route (palm kernel oil is extracted using a gasoline-like solvent and relies on unsustainable production methods). Coconut oil, which is in the same family as palm, did the trick. Chilling the oil ensures it stays solidified, making it easy to work with.

Mix it up: After beating the oil and sugar together, I add the liquid ingredients. An egg and milk lend richness and structure; vanilla adds a flavor boost. (The mixture will look curdled; that's okay.) Next, add the dry ingredients: flour, cocoa powder, baking powder, baking soda, and salt. You might be surprised, but I held back on adding any peppermint flavor here. There is a fine line between nice, subtle mint flavor and feeling like you just took a swig of mouthwash, so I reserve it for the chocolate coating.

Keep them thin: Turn the dough out onto the counter, shape it into two disks, and refrigerate the disks until they're firm. After about 45 minutes, roll one of the disks between parchment until it's ⅛ inch thick. Thin cookies are crucial so they bake evenly and crisp properly. Stamp out the cookies with a 1¾-inch round or fluted cookie cutter and bake them in a 350-degree oven for 16 to 18 minutes, until the edges and centers are very firm to the touch. Baking the cookies until they are thoroughly dry ensures the proper crunch. Let them cool completely before coating them in chocolate.

Wafers are winners: For the chocolate coating, I found standard chocolate created a coating that was far too thick, not to mention messy looking. I use wafers of couverture chocolate here because, due to added cocoa butter, it is easier to work with and creates just the right thin coating (cocoa butter is what makes a chocolate thin out when melted, making it optimal for dipping). I also discovered, after numerous tests, that for a coating that hardened properly and also looked appealing, I would have to temper the chocolate.

Temper tantrum: Tempering requires heating chocolate, cooling it down while agitating it, then heating it back up for dipping. This changes the structure of the chocolate so that it sets up into a glossy, hard coating. Yes, it's a little fussy, but the standards for Thin Mints are high, so I think the effort is completely acceptable. Start by melting two-thirds of your chocolate along with ⅛ teaspoon of peppermint oil (you can add more or less but remember a little goes a long way). It's easy to overheat the chocolate; go slow and stir often. Once the mixture reaches 118 degrees, take it off the heat.

Plant the seeds: Now add, or "seed," the remaining chocolate into the melted chocolate, stirring constantly until the chocolate has cooled to 82 degrees. This will take 15 to 30 minutes (you'll finish seeding early in the process). It will look pretty thick. To get it in dipping shape, now you want to take it on and off the heat every 15 seconds until it hits 90 degrees. If it goes over that temp (even to 91 degrees), you will break up the structure and need to re-temper. If it happens, bring the whole batch of chocolate back up to 118 degrees, then let it cool to 82 and bring it back up to 90 as directed.

Go for a dip: To test for temper, dip a knife's tip in the chocolate and let it sit on a plate for 10 minutes. If the chocolate hardens and looks glossy, you're good. For a thin coating, just dunking the cookies in the chocolate won't cut it. I put a cookie on a fork and dip it into the chocolate to cover the bottom. Then, using an offset spatula, I pour a little chocolate on top and spread it all over to create a thin coating. I did come up with an easier coating option that doesn't require tempering. Both versions are good, but I think you'll find the perfectly thin tempered coating really gives Thin Mints a run for their money.

Thin Chocolate-Mint Cookies

Makes about 70 cookies
Make today, enjoy immediately

COOKIES

- 1½ **cups (7½ ounces) all-purpose flour**
- ½ **cup (1½ ounces) cocoa**
- ½ **teaspoon salt**
- ¼ **teaspoon baking powder**
- ¼ **teaspoon baking soda**
- ¾ **cup (5¼ ounces) sugar**
- ½ **cup refined coconut oil, chilled**
- 2 **tablespoons milk**
- 1 **large egg**
- 1 **teaspoon vanilla extract**

CHOCOLATE COATING

- 1 **pound semisweet couverture chocolate wafers**
- ⅛ **teaspoon peppermint oil**

1. FOR THE COOKIES: Whisk flour, cocoa, salt, baking powder, and baking soda together in medium bowl; set aside. Using stand mixer fitted with paddle, beat sugar and oil on medium-high speed until fluffy, about 2 minutes. Reduce speed to low, add milk, egg, and vanilla, and beat until combined, about 30 seconds. Slowly add flour mixture and beat until just combined, about 1 minute, scraping down bowl as needed. Divide dough in half. Place each piece of dough on sheet of plastic wrap and flatten each into 4-inch disk. Wrap each piece tightly in plastic and refrigerate until firm but still malleable, about 45 minutes.

2. Adjust oven racks to upper-middle and lower-middle positions and heat oven to 350 degrees. Line 2 baking sheets with parchment paper. Working with 1 piece of dough at a time, roll dough between 2 large sheets of lightly floured parchment paper into even ⅛-inch-thick circle (about 11 inches). Using 1¾-inch round cookie cutter, stamp out cookies and transfer to prepared sheets, spaced about ½ inch apart. Gently reroll scraps ⅛ inch thick, cut into rounds, and transfer to prepared sheet. Bake cookies until very firm, 16 to 18 minutes, switching and rotating sheets halfway through baking. Let cookies cool on sheets for 5 minutes. Transfer cookies to wire rack and let cool completely, about 30 minutes.

3. FOR THE CHOCOLATE COATING: Line 2 baking sheets with clean parchment paper. Melt two-thirds of chocolate with oil in medium metal heatproof bowl set over small saucepan filled with 1 inch of barely simmering water, stirring often, until chocolate registers 118 degrees. Remove bowl from heat and slowly add remaining chocolate, stirring constantly until chocolate registers 82 degrees, 15 to 30 minutes. Briefly return bowl to saucepan and heat, stirring often, until mixture reaches 90 degrees, moving bowl on and off the heat every 15 seconds to prevent overheating.

4. To test for temper, dip tip of butter knife in chocolate and let sit for 10 minutes. Chocolate should harden and be glossy. Working with 1 cookie at a time, place cookie on fork and dip bottom of cookie in chocolate. Use spatula to spread chocolate over top of cookie, creating thin coating. Transfer cookie to prepared baking sheet and repeat with remaining cookies. Let cookies sit until chocolate is hardened, about 10 minutes. Cookies can be stored in airtight container for up to 2 weeks.

TO MAKE COOKIES WITH EASY CHOCOLATE COATING: For step 3, melt all couverture chocolate and oil in heatproof bowl set over small saucepan filled with 1 inch of barely simmering water, stirring often. Coat cookies as directed in step 4, and refrigerate until set, about 10 minutes. Cookies can be refrigerated in airtight container for up to 2 weeks.

Chocolate-Toffee Bark

✔ WHY THIS RECIPE WORKS: This bark is a Christmas tradition in my family. For years, a good friend dropped off a huge tin of it. The tin stayed on the kitchen counter and we'd eat it nonstop, taking a little nibble every time we walked by. Eventually, I asked her to write down the recipe. She gave me a copy from a cookbook and there were a few notes in the margins. She told me she had taken liberties with the recipe, so I didn't feel guilty when I made my own changes, making the toffee flavor deeper, and the chocolate richer and darker. You will need a candy thermometer or another thermometer that registers high temperatures for this recipe.

—JULIA COLLIN DAVISON, Executive Food Editor, Books

Avoiding a sticky situation:
Although the goal is irregular chunks of delicious chocolate-covered toffee, you can't make this recipe free-form because the hot toffee mixture needs to set up to a decent thickness (about ¼ inch). I pour it into a 13 by 9-inch baking pan. The only issue: Getting the toffee out of the pan can be a challenge. The best way to avoid any problems is to line the pan with an aluminum foil "sling" that you coat with vegetable oil. It's best to go ahead and make your sling and grease it first, before you start cooking.

Making the toffee: Making the toffee doesn't require much, just butter, water, sugar, and salt, which you heat to 325 degrees. But the mixture can be finicky; just follow a few rules. First, when adding the sugar, pour it into the center of the pan. If sugar hits the sides, it will stick and not dissolve, eventually causing crystals to form. Second, don't agitate the mixture for the first stage. It is during the initial boil that the sugar is most likely to crystallize, and agitation is one of the main causes. And third, reduce the heat once you begin to see a faint golden color (shown here) since toffee cooks quickly.

Coating with chocolate, side 1:
Once the toffee hits 325 degrees, stir in some nuts, pour the toffee into the pan, and smooth it into an even layer. Refrigerate it until it's hardened, then it's ready for the first chocolate coating. I find microwaving the chocolate is the easiest way to melt it, and by using the 50 percent power setting, you'll avoid scorching. Pour the chocolate onto the toffee, then evenly spread it out. Sprinkle on some additional nuts, then back into the fridge it goes to harden.

Coating with chocolate, side 2:
To coat the second side with chocolate, use that trusty foil sling to lift the toffee out of the pan and flip it onto a parchment paper–lined baking sheet; remove the foil. Working in the same fashion as for the first side, melt more chocolate, pour the chocolate onto the toffee and spread it into an even layer, and finally sprinkle over more nuts. Now it just needs one last round in the fridge to set the chocolate before it's ready to break up.

Taking a toffee break: Don't bother with cutting the bark into neat squares, just get your hands in there and break it into rough pieces. The toffee's fantastic for gifts or simply to have on hand during the holidays.

Chocolate-Toffee Bark

Makes about 1½ pounds
Make today, enjoy immediately

8	**tablespoons unsalted butter**
½	**cup water**
1	**cup (7 ounces) sugar**
¼	**teaspoon salt**
1½	**cups (6 ounces) pecans or walnuts, toasted and chopped**
8	**ounces semisweet chocolate, chopped coarse**

1. Make foil sling for 13 by 9-inch baking pan by folding 2 long sheets of aluminum foil; first sheet should be 13 inches wide and second sheet should be 9 inches wide. Lay sheets of foil in pan perpendicular to one another, with extra foil hanging over edges of pan. Push foil into corners and up sides of pan, smoothing foil flush to pan. Spray with vegetable oil spray.

2. Heat butter and water in medium saucepan over medium-high heat until butter is melted. Pour sugar and salt into center of pan (do not let sugar hit pan sides). Bring to boil and cook, without stirring, until sugar has dissolved completely and syrup has faint golden color and registers 300 degrees, about 10 minutes.

3. Reduce heat to medium-low and continue to cook, gently swirling pan, until toffee is amber colored and registers 325 degrees, 1 to 3 minutes. Off heat, stir in ½ cup pecans, then pour toffee into prepared pan and smooth into even layer with spatula. Refrigerate, uncovered, until toffee has hardened, about 15 minutes.

4. Microwave 4 ounces chocolate in bowl at 50 percent power, stirring occasionally, until melted, about 2 minutes. Pour chocolate over hardened toffee and smooth with spatula to cover completely. Sprinkle with ½ cup pecans and press lightly to adhere. Refrigerate, uncovered, until chocolate has hardened, about 15 minutes.

5. Line rimmed baking sheet with parchment paper. Use foil sling to invert bark onto prepared baking sheet. Peel away and discard foil. Microwave remaining 4 ounces chocolate in bowl at 50 percent power, stirring occasionally, until melted, about 2 minutes. Pour chocolate over toffee and smooth with spatula to cover completely. Sprinkle with remaining ½ cup pecans and press lightly to adhere. Refrigerate, uncovered, until chocolate has hardened, about 15 minutes. Break bark into rough squares. Bark can be stored at room temperature in airtight container for up to 2 weeks.

Brigadeiros

✔ WHY THIS RECIPE WORKS: It was a colorful, glamorous photo that brought *brigadeiros*—the gooey, chocolaty, caramel-y Brazilian candy treat—to my attention. They were irresistibly cute, all decked out in brightly colored sprinkles. And I was happy to discover the recipe couldn't be easier. Sweetened condensed milk, cocoa powder, and butter are cooked until thick, then poured into a dish and chilled before being rolled into truffle-size nuggets and coated in any number of fun toppings. They require no thermometer and involve only one cooking technique: stirring.

—KELLY PRICE, Test Cook, *Cook's Country*

Stir it already: Combine a can of sweetened condensed milk, ½ cup Dutch-processed cocoa, and 2 tablespoons butter in a saucepan. Over time I've adjusted my recipe to emphasize the chocolate. It deviates from many authentic recipes, but I love the extra hit of chocolate flavor. Cook the mixture over low heat, stirring frequently, until it's very thick. This should take 20 to 25 minutes. If you don't stir the chocolate frequently while it cooks, it's going to burn, and don't be tempted to up the heat. The chocolate should get so thick you can run a spatula through it and see a trail.

Pour it: Pour this thick mixture into a greased 8-inch square pan and refrigerate it until chilled, at least 30 minutes, though it's fine in the fridge, covered, for up to 24 hours. I like to work with the chocolate when it is really cold and feels as firm as a Tootsie Roll, which makes it easier to roll and decorate.

Pinch it: After it's fully chilled, the chocolate will be very stretchy and pliable, perfect for rolling into those cute little balls. Pinch off roughly tablespoon-size (no need to get too technical) pieces of chocolate, then roll them into 1-inch balls. If they stick to your hands, spray your hands with a bit of vegetable oil spray.

Prettify it: Now the fun part: decorating! Gently roll each brigadeiro in the coating of your choice. Chocolate sprinkles, colored sprinkles, nonpareils, blinged-out gold and silver sugars…really, it's whatever makes you happy. Pouring the décor in little bowls first makes the coating process easier. Just make sure to store your treats in the refrigerator; they'll keep for 2 weeks—unless of course you eat them all up first. And while a lot of tasters likened them to a Tootsie Roll, I can safely say brigadeiros taste much better.

Brigadeiros

Makes about 30 candies
Make today, enjoy immediately

- 1 **(14-ounce) can sweetened condensed milk**
- ½ **cup (1½ ounces) Dutch-processed cocoa**
- 2 **tablespoons unsalted butter**
  Sprinkles, colored sugar, or nonpareils for coating

1. Grease 8-inch square baking dish. Combine condensed milk, cocoa, and butter in medium saucepan. Cook over low heat, stirring frequently, until mixture is very thick and rubber spatula leaves distinct trail when dragged across bottom of saucepan, 20 to 25 minutes.

2. Pour mixture into prepared baking dish and refrigerate until cool, at least 30 minutes or up to 24 hours (cover if leaving overnight). Pinch chocolate into approximately 1 tablespoon–size pieces and roll into 1-inch balls. Place desired coatings in small bowls and roll each chocolate until covered. Brigadeiros can be refrigerated in airtight container for up to 2 weeks.

Salted Caramels

✓ **WHY THIS RECIPE WORKS:** I like chocolate as much as the next person, but when it comes to my sweet tooth, I'm a sucker for caramel. Cake, ice cream, cookies—if it has a streak of caramel in it, I'm a goner. As a child, I could be enticed to do just about anything for the hydrogenated goodness of a Caramel Cream (aka Bulls-Eye). So what if you could poke the cream center out in a solid chunk? I was no critic; I was in love.

With the passage of time, my tastes matured, and I slowly outgrew my obsession with Caramel Creams and other early loves (yes, I'm talking about you, Emilio Estevez) and replaced them with gourmet caramels studded with sea salt or laced with espresso. It wasn't until I began making my own caramels from scratch, however, that I felt like a true caramel sophisticate. I'll admit, part of the allure of making caramels was the challenge they presented. Sugar is a fickle friend, taking forever to caramelize and then going from golden amber to dark mahogany to burnt-beyond-recognition before you can say "St. Elmo's Fire." It took a little trial and error to reach the right color and chew, but I was happier than my preteen self with a new copy of *Tiger Beat* when I figured out a go-to recipe that meant I could have chewy, delightfully sticky caramels whenever I had a craving.

The thing to remember about working with caramel is that you can never turn your back on it. You can stand and watch sugar syrup bubble for what seems like hours without even the slightest color change, but walk away to answer the phone and your caramel will burn before you have the receiver to your ear. It *knows*. Trust me on this.

You will need a candy thermometer or another thermometer that registers high temperatures for this recipe.

—CHRISTIE MORRISON, Associate Editor, Books

Make it rich: First, you'll need to infuse a mixture of heavy cream and unsalted butter with the seeds from a vanilla bean and a teaspoon of salt. This mixture adds richness and flavor to the caramel, but it also helps keeps the caramels soft and chewy. Bring the mixture to a boil, then turn off the burner and let the flavors meld for at least 10 minutes. If you feel like taking care of a few chores before starting the caramel, no problem—just let the cream mixture steep a while longer. The longer it sits, the more vanilla flavor it will develop.

The caramel showdown: I suggest you use a large, high-sided saucepan to make the caramel. You might think a smaller vessel would work, but the caramel will foam up when you add the cream mixture, and you don't want a sweet version of Mount Vesuvius erupting all over your stovetop. Combine the corn syrup, water, and sugar in the saucepan. One of the dangers in making caramel is crystallization. To safeguard against this, I pour the sugar into the middle of the pan to prevent any granules from getting stuck on the pan's sides.

Golden moment: Now heat the mixture up until the sugar dissolves (don't stir). Then, gently swirl the pan periodically as you continue to cook the mixture, and wait for the color to change to amber. You can also watch the bubbles: Early on they are separate and boil vigorously; over time, they become smaller and more delicate, almost foamy. Of course, using a candy thermometer (or any thermometer with a high upper limit) is pretty fail-safe; when the mixture reaches 350 degrees, it's done. I turn the heat down in the latter stages for more control and to guard against burning.

Add the cream, heat it up: Carefully remove your saucepan full of *very hot* (just want to hammer that point home) caramel from the heat. Carefully stir in the cream mixture, watch it foam, and breathe a sigh of relief that you listened to me and went with the high-sided saucepan. Now return the pan to the heat and cook the caramel until it reaches 248 degrees. Now that the cream mixture has been added, it's not only safe but also imperative to stir the caramel so it doesn't burn. This step should only take about five minutes, so you won't be stirring long.

Into the pan: Remember the temperature of that caramel when you're tempted to stick your finger in to taste the buttery mixture you've just made. Also keep it in mind as you're pouring the caramel into the pan—caramel burns are no fun. Since caramel is sticky by nature, it's a good idea to use a pan lined with parchment. I also spray the parchment with vegetable oil spray for added insurance. I suggest you prepare the pan ahead of time (because you sure won't have time to when you're holding a pan of foaming hot caramel).

The final touch: Once it's in the pan, smooth the surface of the caramel and let it cool for 10 minutes. Then add the best part: *fleur de sel*. It adds great flavor and crunch to these caramels. If you're slightly more daring (and of course you are), try substituting smoked sea salt. But hold on, you can't cut into them quite yet. To ensure the caramels cut into nice clean squares, let the pan cool to room temperature for 1 hour, then pop it in the fridge for another hour.

Making the cut: When it's finally cool, lift the sling to remove the caramel square from the pan and peel the parchment away. Use a sharp knife to cut the caramel into ¾-inch squares. Since the caramels tend to stick together, it's best to individually wrap them in pieces of waxed paper. A handful of caramels in a little jar, tin, or cellophane bag makes a great gift. Just remember, the caramels will get too soft if left at room temp, so it's best to store them in the refrigerator.

Salted Caramels

Makes about 50 caramels
Make today, enjoy immediately

- **1 vanilla bean**
- **1 cup heavy cream**
- **5 tablespoons unsalted butter, cut into ¼-inch pieces**
- **1½ teaspoons fleur de sel or flake sea salt**
- **¼ cup light corn syrup**
- **¼ cup water**
- **1⅓ cups (9⅓ ounces) sugar**

1. Cut vanilla bean in half lengthwise. Using tip of paring knife, scrape out seeds. Combine vanilla bean seeds, cream, butter, and 1 teaspoon fleur de sel in small saucepan over medium heat. Bring to boil, cover, remove from heat, and let steep for 10 minutes.

2. Meanwhile, make parchment sling for 8-inch square baking pan by folding 2 long sheets of parchment paper so each is 8 inches wide. Lay sheets of parchment in greased pan perpendicular to each other, with extra parchment hanging over edges of pan. Push parchment into corners and up sides of pan, smoothing parchment flush to pan. Grease parchment; set aside.

3. Combine corn syrup and water in large saucepan. Pour sugar into center of pan (do not let sugar hit pan sides). Bring to boil over medium-high heat, and cook, without stirring, until sugar has dissolved completely and syrup has faint golden color and registers 300 degrees, 7 to 9 minutes. Reduce heat to medium-low and continue to cook, gently swirling pan, until mixture is amber colored and registers 350 degrees, 2 to 3 minutes.

4. Off heat, carefully stir in cream mixture (mixture will foam up). Return mixture to medium-high heat, and cook, stirring frequently, until caramel reaches 248 degrees, about 5 minutes.

5. Carefully transfer caramel to prepared baking pan. Using greased rubber spatula, smooth surface of caramel, and let cool for 10 minutes. Sprinkle with remaining ½ teaspoon fleur de sel and then let cool to room temperature, about 1 hour. Transfer to refrigerator and chill until caramel is completely solid and cold to touch, about 1 hour.

6. Lift parchment sling out of baking pan and place on cutting board. Peel parchment away from caramel. Cut caramel into ¾-inch-wide strips and then crosswise into ¾-inch pieces. Individually wrap pieces in waxed-paper squares, twisting ends of paper to close. Caramels can be refrigerated for up to 3 weeks.

Torrone

WHY THIS RECIPE WORKS: I love all things Italian. The food. The culture. The architecture. The language. The people. You get the idea. My favorite part of an Italian day is late afternoon into early evening. All the shops are open and the streets are crowded with locals out for a *passeggiata*. Italian-English dictionaries sometimes translate this word as "walk," but I think "stroll" is more accurate. At the end of the afternoon, in pretty much every Italian city and town, the narrow streets are clogged with people strolling past shop windows. I spent last Christmas in Venice and found myself making a passeggiata past the same candy shop every afternoon. The window was filled with brightly colored torrone, a nougat candy made with egg whites, honey, sugar, and nuts. The versions made with pink, green, and yellow food colorings were visually appealing, but every afternoon I was drawn to the classic taupe torrone and bought several pieces.

There are two distinct styles of torrone: really hard (think jawbreakers) and firm with a touch of chew (think taffy). I much prefer the latter. I like almonds in my torrone, but pistachios and skinned hazelnuts are traditional choices, too. You can add chopped dried or candied fruit or even crystallized ginger, but I usually stick with a little vanilla extract or citrus zest. And don't forget the salt, which keeps the sweetness in check.

You will need a candy thermometer or another thermometer that registers high temperatures. This recipe also requires precise timing as well as some multitasking: Start whipping the egg whites a few minutes before the honey mixture reaches its final temperature, and put the nuts in the oven as soon as the honey mixture has been added to the mixer. It's critical to make torrone on a dry day; don't attempt this recipe when it's humid.

—JACK BISHOP, Editorial Director, America's Test Kitchen

Paper you can eat: Torrone is best made in a mold that will give form to the molten mass of candy. I use an 8-inch square baking pan, but I've seen recipes that call for larger pans or loaf pans. The important thing is to grease the pan and then line the bottom and sides with edible wafer paper, trimmed as necessary to fit. The paper melts into the surface of the candy and keeps it from sticking to the pan.

Hands off: To keep the sugar from crystallizing on the sides of the pan, I pour the honey into the saucepan first, then add the sugar, piling it up in the middle. Add a pinch of salt, then turn on the burner. Just leave the pan alone; the sugar around the edges will start to melt on its own. Once the honey is boiling, gently swirl the pan to wash over any undissolved sugar. Use a candy thermometer or an instant-read thermometer that registers high temperatures to monitor the progress of the sugar syrup. Just make sure that the tip of the probe is not touching the pan bottom.

Take whites to soft peaks: Once the sugar reaches 270 degrees, start whipping the egg whites. It's important to separate the eggs before you start making the sugar syrup so you aren't fussing with the eggs while the sugar mixture continues to cook on the stovetop. A little cream of tartar increases the volume of the whipped whites and stabilizes them. Once the whites reach soft, billowy peaks, they're done. Don't take them to stiff peaks because the torrone will have a spongy texture.

Dark amber is best: Italian recipes call for heating the honey mixture to a wide range of temperatures, but I found the candy was too soft when the syrup was not cooked enough. I cook the syrup to 320 degrees; it will have a dark amber color. Turn your mixer to low and carefully pour in the syrup, avoiding the sides of the bowl and the whisk attachment. Once the syrup has been incorporated, increase the speed and beat the mixture until it's just warm to the touch and is pale and thick. Scrape down the sides of the bowl with a greased rubber spatula twice to incorporate any stray bits of syrup.

Add warmed nuts: As soon as you start beating the candy mixture, put the nuts in a 350-degree oven for five minutes. Blanched are preferable, but skins-on whole almonds work fine. The goal is to warm them so they don't cool down the candy mixture and cause it to harden before you get it scraped into the pan. You will still be beating the candy mixture when the nuts are done; just leave them on the baking sheet to stay warm. When the candy mixture is ready, reduce the mixer speed to low and fold in the warm nuts and vanilla extract.

Work quickly: Use a greased rubber spatula to scrape the candy into the prepared pan. Don't dawdle. As the mixture cools, it becomes increasingly difficult to work with. As soon as the mixture is in the pan, place another piece of edible wafer paper, trimmed to an 8-inch square, on top. Lightly press the paper into the candy, then place a large piece of parchment on top. Use a second pan (a wide metal spatula would also work) and some brute force to compact the torrone. Press down firmly on the top pan and bang it with your fist until the candy has a perfectly flat top. Then let the torrone cool for one hour.

Chill, slice, store: I hurry along the firming process by putting the cooled torrone in the refrigerator. Once it feels rock solid (about 2 hours later), discard the parchment and trim excess wafer paper. Turn the candy out onto a cutting board, rapping the pan against the board to free the candy, then use a heavy chef's knife to saw the candy into 1-inch-thick slabs. Cut each slab in half and store the torrone in an airtight container lined with parchment. To keep the pieces from sticking to each other, make sure to give each piece of candy some space, and separate each layer in the tin with more parchment.

Almond Torrone

Makes 16 pieces
Make today, enjoy immediately

2–3	edible wafer papers
3	large egg whites
¼	teaspoon cream of tartar
½	cup honey
2	cups (14 ounces) sugar
⅛	teaspoon salt
3	cups (15 ounces) whole almonds, preferably blanched
1	teaspoon vanilla extract

1. Spray 8-inch square baking pan with vegetable oil spray. Line bottom and sides of pan with edible wafer paper, cutting pieces as necessary to fit. Adjust oven rack to middle position and heat oven to 350 degrees. Place egg whites and cream of tartar in bowl of stand mixer fitted with whisk.

2. Place honey in medium saucepan. Pour sugar and salt into center of pan (do not let sugar hit pan sides). Cook mixture, without stirring, over medium heat until honey starts to boil around edges of pan, about 5 minutes. Reduce heat to medium-low and cook, gently swirling pan, until sugar has dissolved and mixture is dark amber colored and registers 320 degrees, 8 to 12 minutes. Remove pan from heat and let bubbles subside, about 30 seconds.

3. Meanwhile, when honey mixture reaches about 270 degrees, turn mixer to medium-low and whip egg whites and cream of tartar until foamy, about 1 minute. Increase speed to medium-high and whip until soft peaks form, 2 to 3 minutes. Reduce speed to low, and carefully add hot honey mixture, avoiding whisk and sides of bowl, and mix until incorporated. Increase speed to medium and whip, scraping down sides of bowl twice, until mixture is pale and very thick and stiff, 10 to 12 minutes.

4. While candy mixture is whipping, spread nuts on rimmed baking sheet and heat until warm and lightly fragrant, about 5 minutes. Remove nuts from oven and keep on baking sheet to keep warm.

5. Reduce mixer speed to low and add warm nuts and vanilla to candy mixture. Working quickly, scrape candy evenly into prepared pan using greased rubber spatula. Cover top surface of candy with single piece of edible wafer paper, trimmed to fit pan. Place parchment paper on top and press very firmly with second 8-inch square baking pan to compact candy and remove air bubbles. Let cool to room temperature, about 1 hour. Refrigerate until very firm, at least 2 hours.

6. Discard parchment. Use paring knife to trim excess bits of edible wafer paper, then turn candy onto cutting board. Cut torrone into 1-inch-thick slabs (applying pressure to push blade through stiff candy), then cut each slab in half. Torrone can be stored at room temperature or refrigerated in airtight container for up to 2 weeks, using parchment to line container and separate layers.

TO MAKE PISTACHIO-ORANGE TORRONE: Replace almonds and vanilla extract with 3 cups shelled pistachios and 1½ teaspoons grated orange zest.

Marshmallows

✓ WHY THIS RECIPE WORKS: One-dimensional candies aren't usually my thing, but make a s'more and I'll come running before your campfire toasting twig has a chance to cool. Yet when I was prepping for a s'mores-making party, I just couldn't pull the trigger on the Jet-Puffed purchase. My awareness of what goes into processed food has grown since my Camp Longhorn days, and I don't want tetrasodium pyrophosphate or Blue 1 in my marshmallows. Homemade aren't just better because they're additive free; they're also fun to make and toast like a dream. You will need a candy thermometer or another thermometer that registers high temperatures.

—LOUISE EMERICK, Senior Editor, Books

Get going with gelatin: Homemade marshmallows don't require much. You heat up a sugar mixture, then beat it with a few packets of unflavored gelatin until the mixture transforms from a translucent liquid into a bowlful of white fluffy goo. You spread this into a pan, let it set up, then cut it into cubes. The gelatin is key for structure. Without it, you'd end up with something like Marshmallow Fluff (yuck). To ensure the gelatin dissolves evenly, start by blooming it in the mixer bowl with some water. Let it sit for at least 15 minutes, during which time you can heat the sugar mixture.

Make your syrup: Combine the water, corn syrup, salt, and sugar in a saucepan. I'm not a huge fan of corn syrup, but there's no getting around it here. Corn syrup-free marshmallows just didn't come out right for me (without turning to obscure ingredients). Plus, this is plain corn syrup, not the high-fructose stuff, so I got over it. Bring it all to a boil and let it go (no stirring) until the syrup reaches 240 degrees. By now, the 15 minutes for the gelatin should be up. Flip the mixer to low and slowly pour in the sugar syrup, doing your best not to hit the side of the bowl or the whisk (to avoid splattering).

Marshmallow magic: Now gradually increase the speed to high. After a few minutes of beating, that steaming, near-translucent (and slightly smelly) liquid will turn opaque white and expand to nearly fill the bowl (like this first picture). You'll think, "Gee, I'd better stop." Don't. It isn't quite firm enough, so keep going. You want to mix for 10 to 12 minutes. The key is to keep going until the bowl feels just barely warm. You don't want it to totally cool off or you'll make a heck of a mess getting it out of the bowl, but push it as far as you can to ensure firm, springy marshmallows. Toward the end, I also add vanilla extract.

A good spread: What happens next should happen fast. Using a spatula you've sprayed with oil, scrape the marshmallow into a baking pan (which you've already lined with foil and sprayed with oil), then smooth the top. This mixture is sticky and stringy and gets harder to work with the cooler it gets, so be speedy. Don't try to scrape every last bit out of the bowl. If you start futzing with that stuff, the blob in the dish is going to firm up into some weird uneven shape. Once it's pretty and even, mix together some cornstarch and confectioners' sugar in a bowl, sift a little over the marshmallow, and save the rest.

Cut, toss, toast: Let the marshmallow set up overnight. The next day, dust a little of the cornstarch mixture on a cutting board and spray a chef's knife with oil. Turn the marshmallow out, peel off the foil, then cut the block into 1-inch-wide strips. Cut these strips into cubes (you could cut them smaller for minis). Roll the marshmallows in the cornstarch mixture. Lastly, I toss them in a strainer to get off excess powder. They keep for a while, but take them to a cookout or a winter party and you won't have any leftovers.

Marshmallows

Makes about 90 marshmallows
Make today, enjoy tomorrow

- ⅔ cup (2⅔ ounces) confectioners' sugar
- ⅓ cup cornstarch
- 1 cup cold water
- 2½ tablespoons unflavored gelatin
- ⅔ cup light corn syrup
- 2 cups (14 ounces) granulated sugar
- ¼ teaspoon salt
- 2 teaspoons vanilla extract

1. Make foil sling for 13 by 9-inch baking pan by folding 2 long sheets of aluminum foil; first sheet should be 13 inches wide and second sheet should be 9 inches wide. Lay sheets of foil in pan perpendicular to each other, with extra foil hanging over edges of pan. Push foil into corners and up sides of pan, smoothing foil flush to pan. Spray pan with vegetable oil spray. Whisk confectioners' sugar and cornstarch in small bowl; set aside.

2. Pour ½ cup water into bowl of stand mixer fitted with whisk. Sprinkle gelatin over water. Let stand until gelatin becomes very firm, about 15 minutes.

3. Meanwhile, combine remaining ½ cup water and corn syrup in medium saucepan. Pour granulated sugar and salt into center of pan (do not let sugar hit pan sides). Bring to boil over medium-high heat, and cook, gently swirling pan, until sugar has dissolved completely and mixture registers 240 degrees, 6 to 8 minutes.

4. Turn mixer speed to low and carefully pour hot syrup into gelatin mixture, avoiding whisk and bowl. Gradually increase speed to high and whip until mixture is very thick and stiff, 10 to 12 minutes, scraping down bowl as needed. Add vanilla and mix until incorporated, about 15 seconds.

5. Working quickly, scrape mixture evenly into prepared pan using greased rubber spatula, smoothing top. Sift 2 tablespoons confectioners' sugar mixture over pan. Cover and let sit overnight at room temperature until firm.

6. Lightly dust cutting board with 2 tablespoons confectioners' sugar mixture, and lightly coat chef's knife with oil spray. Turn marshmallow slab out onto cutting board and peel off foil. Sift 2 tablespoons confectioners' sugar mixture over slab. Cut into 1-inch-wide strips, and then cut crosswise into 1-inch squares. Working with 3 or 4 marshmallows at a time, toss marshmallows in bowl with remaining confectioners' sugar mixture, then toss in fine-mesh strainer to remove excess powder. Marshmallows can be stored in zipper-lock bag or airtight container for up to 2 weeks.

Orange Jelly Slices

✔ **WHY THIS RECIPE WORKS:** Some of my coworkers will tell you that they haven't got much of a sweet tooth. Exactly the opposite is true in my case. As a child, I developed a serious weakness for anything made with sugar, and I place the blame squarely on penny candy stores. There's something about a garish display of brightly colored sweets that has always set my salivary glands to work.

My favorite candies have always been fruit-flavored, and tart more often than not. Fruit jelly slices are a good example. If done well, they're exceptional: tender, sweet and tart, with bright flavors and brighter colors. If not, they're a tough, bland, cellophane-wrapped nightmare best left in gas stations and convenience stores. Since fresh, properly made fruit jelly slices are hard to find (there's a place on Cape Cod that does a great job), I decided to make my own.

I chose to base this recipe on an agar gel, rather than pectin or gelatin, for a few reasons. Agar is a vegetarian thickener made from seaweed that forms a short-textured, tender gel. This gel is nearly transparent and it has good slicing characteristics. Also, unlike pectin or gelatin, agar doesn't gel until brought to a relatively high temperature, and so the chances of premature setting, which would lead to lumps in the final jelly slices, are low.

This recipe is for orange slices, but feel free to experiment with different fruit concentrates. Just be aware that you might have to tinker a bit with the recipe and amount of agar so the jellies set up. The corn syrup in the recipe adds shelf-stability to the final product and stiffens the jellies' texture slightly, so don't omit or replace it. You will need a candy thermometer or another thermometer that registers high temperatures.

—MARCUS WALSER, Systems Administrator, America's Test Kitchen

SHAPING UP JELLY SLICES

We use a round-bottom 14 by 2¼ by 1¾-inch tinned steel terrine mold for this recipe, which you can purchase at jbprince.com. You can also layer the rind and filling in a 13 by 9-inch parchment-lined baking pan, but then you won't get the trademark citrus slice shape. Instead, you'll cut the cooled jelly into squares (if going this route, just be sure to let the rind cool completely before pouring in the filling). You can buy agar, a gelling agent, at Asian supermarkets or through amazon.com. Citric acid is sold by cheese-making resources (see page 137), natural foods stores, and kingarthurflour.com.

Rind part 1: A basic fruit jelly is a combination of fruit juice, sugar, and some sort of thickener to firm everything up; this is what the center of my jelly slices is. The rind portion of the slices is just a creamy version of that same jelly, made by stirring a stiff meringue into a separate batch of jelly. I start with the rind. The meringue is made by simply whipping egg whites and a hot sugar syrup together until thick and glossy. I prefer dry egg white powder here because it's easier to measure than liquid whites. Once you've made the meringue, set it aside so you can make the other rind component, the jelly.

Rind part 2: Next, bring water, powdered agar (a gelling agent), sugar, and corn syrup to a boil and cook it until it hits 223 degrees. Then mix in the orange juice concentrate, meringue, and orange food coloring. And while I use orange juice concentrate here, I've also had success playing around with grape juice and pink lemonade concentrate; feel free to experiment (you might have to adjust the amount of agar you add). Just make sure whatever you use is pulp free.

Let the rules be your guide: Next, trace a 13¾ by 6-inch template onto a piece of parchment for shaping the rind. This shape will fit perfectly in the mold lengthwise, with some extra room on the sides to help remove the jelly log. To keep track of the guides once the jelly is spread out, I extend the lines of the rectangle at the corners. Pour the creamy jelly mixture into the traced guide and smooth it into an even layer until it goes just beyond the outline. Let that set for an hour, then cut the rind and parchment so the edges are even with the traced rectangle.

Make the filling: I use a metal round-bottom terrine mold, measuring 14 by 2¼ inches (it looks like a little trough), which will form the jelly into the familiar citrus-slice shape. So with the rind ready to go, place it parchment side down in the mold. Then, make the jelly filling, which uses the same ingredients and method as the jelly rind, just without the meringue and food coloring. Make your jelly filling and pour it into the mold over the rind. Now let it set up, which takes about two hours.

A quick trim: Once the jelly filling is fully set, use a sharp paring knife to trim away any excess rind so that the rind is even with the filling. Make sure not to cut through the parchment; you will need it to lift the log from the mold.

A jelly log becomes jelly slices: Most jelly slices get a coating of sugar to prevent them from sticking together. I mix a teaspoon of citric acid with the sugar to add a burst of tartness. (For even more sourness, you could add up to 2 teaspoons citric acid here.) Sprinkle the top of your jelly log (still in the mold) with a tablespoon of your sugar/citric acid mixture, then use the parchment to lift the jelly out of the mold and flip it onto a cutting board. Remove the parchment and cut the log into ¼-inch-thick slices. You can toss them in the sugar mixture as you go.

Let them sit before you snack: At this point the slices are fine to eat, but I prefer to wait and let them sit overnight on a wire rack so that the jelly can continue to firm up and the coating has time to fully adhere. These slices are great (and impressive!) as stocking stuffers, party favors, or birthday treats. And since they keep so well, there is nothing wrong with making a batch just to have handy for times when your sweet tooth needs a fix.

Makes about 40 slices

Make today, enjoy tomorrow

RIND

- ¼ cup (¾ ounce) dry egg white powder
- 2 tablespoons warm tap water, plus 6 tablespoons water
- ½ cup plus 1 tablespoon corn syrup
- 1 cup (7 ounces) plus 2 tablespoons sugar
- 2¼ teaspoons powdered agar
- ⅓ cup pulp-free orange juice concentrate, thawed
- ⅛ teaspoon orange food coloring

FILLING

- ½ cup plus 1 tablespoon water
- 2¼ teaspoons powdered agar
- 6 tablespoons corn syrup
- ¾ cup (5¼ ounces) plus 2 tablespoons sugar
- ½ cup pulp-free orange juice concentrate, thawed

COATING

- ½ cup (3½ ounces) sugar
- 1–2 teaspoons citric acid

1. FOR THE RIND: Using stand mixer fitted with whisk, whip egg white powder and 2 tablespoons warm water together on medium speed until combined and smooth, about 2 minutes, scraping down bowl as needed; let sit while making syrup. Pour ¼ cup plus 1 tablespoon corn syrup into small saucepan. Pour ½ cup sugar into center of pan. Bring to boil over medium heat and cook, gently swirling pan, until sugar has dissolved and syrup registers 240 degrees, 2 to 4 minutes. Turn mixer speed to low, and carefully pour hot syrup into egg whites, avoiding whisk and sides of bowl. Increase speed to medium-high and whip until mixture has cooled slightly and is very thick and shiny, about 5 minutes. Reserve ½ cup of meringue; discard remaining meringue.

2. Draw or trace 13¾ by 6-inch rectangle in center of sheet of parchment paper, extending lines to edges of parchment; flip parchment over and place on baking sheet. Lightly spray 14 by 2¼-inch metal round-bottom terrine mold with vegetable oil spray.

3. Whisk remaining 6 tablespoons water and agar together in medium saucepan until agar has dissolved completely. Add remaining ¼ cup corn syrup, then pour remaining ½ cup plus 2 tablespoons sugar into center of pan. Bring to boil over medium heat and cook, stirring occasionally, until sugar has dissolved and syrup is thick and registers 223 degrees, about 6 minutes. Off heat, stir in reserved meringue, orange juice concentrate, and food coloring until combined. Pour mixture in center of rectangle on prepared parchment and smooth into even layer with spatula until it just overhangs all four sides of rectangle. Let sit until firm, about 1 hour.

4. Transfer rind, still on parchment, to cutting board. Using sharp knife, cut rind and parchment evenly along traced rectangle; discard excess. Place rind, parchment side down, into prepared mold; set aside.

5. FOR THE FILLING: Whisk water and agar together in dry, clean medium saucepan until agar has dissolved completely. Add corn syrup, then pour sugar into center of pan. Bring to boil over medium heat and cook, stirring occasionally, until sugar has dissolved and syrup registers 223 degrees, 6 to 8 minutes. Off heat, stir in orange juice concentrate until combined, then pour into lined mold and let sit until jelly is firm, about 2 hours.

6. FOR THE COATING: Combine sugar and citric acid in shallow dish. Trim and discard excess rind from jelly log so that rind is even with filling, leaving parchment intact. Evenly sprinkle 1 tablespoon sugar mixture over top of jelly log. Use edges of parchment to lift log out of mold and flip onto cutting board; remove parchment. Cut log into ¼-inch slices and coat each slice with remaining sugar mixture. Transfer slices to wire rack and let sit, uncovered, for 24 hours to dry. Jelly slices can be stored in airtight container between sheets of parchment for up to 2 weeks.

Sugar Cones

☑ **WHY THIS RECIPE WORKS:** When it comes to ice cream, there are cone people, and there are cup people. I'm a cone person. My mother is a cone person. Her mother was a cone person. My father-in-law passed away not long after my husband and I met, but I like knowing he was a cone person too. Now, I don't dislike cup people (my husband is one, after all, as is my dad), but to me, it's just not the same to eat ice cream from a cup. Ice cream is quintessential summertime, which means it's carefree and messy. Enjoying an ice cream cone makes me as relaxed and happy as getting a massage, and, thankfully, cones are a whole lot cheaper.

And yet, while I'm a steadfast cone advocate, the cones in my life have always been relegated to the occasions when I buy a scoop. I've just never been able to put homemade ice cream on a store-bought cone. So recently, I decided it was time to put the churn aside and focus on perfecting the vessel. There are plenty of waffle cone recipes out there, but I've always considered them overkill since they're such scoop swallowers. And most recipes for sugar cones call for a cone roller and really just have you make *tuiles*, a delicate, shatteringly thin French cookie. After some tinkering, I found the magic formula, no special equipment required. The flavor will remind you of commercial sugar cones but these are far fresher tasting. They're also more delicate, but not too much so. They require a little bit of work, but you only have to make the cone molds once and can save them for the next time around, and the cones themselves keep surprisingly well. Even if you are a cup person, maybe it's time you give cones a try. These cones just might win you over. You will need poster board and a silicone baking mat for this recipe.

—LOUISE EMERICK, Senior Editor, Books

"The cones in my life have always been relegated to the occasions when I buy a scoop. I've just never been able to put homemade ice cream on a store-bought cone. So recently, I decided it was time to put the churn aside and focus on perfecting the vessel."

Make your template: At first I thought making a template for the circles of batter was fussy, but after many rounds of variously sized cones, I realized it added five minutes on the front end but made the process a lot easier. Draw four 5-inch circles on a piece of parchment paper trimmed to fit under a silicone baking mat. I like to cut one circle out of poster board so I can quickly trace the circles onto the parchment. Use a Sharpie to make sure the outlines are visible through the mat. (If you own two mats, you can set up two sheets and spread the batter for a second batch while the first is in the oven.)

Show your crafty side: Making the cone molds takes a little effort, but they're cheap (poster board, tape, scissors, foil), and you can keep them for the next time you make cones. Cut out a 10-inch circle from a sheet of poster board, then cut the circle into quarters. Bring the two straight sides of one quarter-circle together and overlap them slightly to make a cone shape, then tape it shut (Scotch, masking, duct, it doesn't matter). Wrap the outside of the mold with foil, keeping it as smooth as possible. Repeat this to make four molds.

Make the batter: I started testing with a tuile batter (melted butter, flour, an egg white, granulated sugar, vanilla) but found these cones too sweet, and using just the white of the egg made for a very delicate cookie—nice for decorating a dessert plate, but not all that functional for supporting a scoop of ice cream. My preferred brand of store-bought sugar cones uses brown sugar, and I found a near 1:1 ratio of granulated to dark brown sugar gave me cones with the flavor I wanted and that were still crisp. A whole egg plus some milk also helped make my cones sturdier.

Spread and bake: Drop 1½ tablespoons batter into the center of each outlined circle, then fill in the circle using a small offset spatula. The batter should be spread pretty thin; too thick and it won't crisp properly, but any especially thin areas run the risk of overbrowning and becoming too brittle to roll. Take your time and make sure the whole circle is even. Bake the cookies in a 325-degree oven until they are browned around the perimeter and golden toward the center. Don't overbake them because they'll be impossible to mold, but if they're underbaked your cones will be doughy.

Start rolling: Working quickly, place a mold about a third of the way from the edge of a cookie, making sure the tip of the mold is about ¼ inch from the cookie's edge. This will make it easier to roll the tip end tightly (I try to avoid leaky cones, although you can always drop a treat like a chocolate chip in the bottom to close it off if you find it's a little bit open). Use a wide metal spatula (like you use to flip pancakes) to lift the cookie edge onto the mold.

Roll over: Holding the edge of the cookie on the mold, tightly roll the mold over the remaining cookie (or the cookie around the mold, depending how you look at it) to form a cone. Try to make sure the tip end is tightly shut when you first start rolling. Then, press firmly on the seam of the cone to seal. Stand the cones, still on the mold, on a wire rack. Quickly repeat with the remaining cookies. If you find a cone tip is too open or the last cookie has cooled too much, just put the cookie back in the oven (still on the baking sheet or on the mold if already rolled), for one minute to soften.

Cool cones: Once the cones are completely cool, you can remove them from the molds. They might get a little stuck, so just be gentle when loosening the mold. For subsequent batches, make sure to use a clean and cool baking mat and baking sheet (the parchment template can be reused). This ensures that the cookies will set properly and cook evenly. If you have two silicone mats, get two batches going at once to save time. And remember to save your cone molds so you can use them the next time around.

Makes 12 cones

Make today, enjoy immediately

5	**tablespoons (2¼ ounces) granulated sugar**
¼	**cup packed (1¾ ounces) dark brown sugar**
1	**large egg**
¼	**cup whole milk**
2	**tablespoons unsalted butter, melted and cooled**
1	**teaspoon vanilla extract**
½	**cup (2½ ounces) all-purpose flour**

1. Adjust oven rack to middle position and heat oven to 325 degrees. Draw or trace four 5-inch circles on sheet of parchment paper. Line baking sheet with prepared parchment, then top with nonstick silicone baking mat. Cut out 10-inch circle from sheet of poster board, then cut circle into quarters. Bring straight sides of each quarter-circle together and slightly overlap to make cone; tape to secure. Cover each cone with aluminum foil, keeping foil as smooth as possible, and spray with vegetable oil spray.

2. Whisk granulated sugar, brown sugar, and egg together in bowl until smooth. Whisk in milk, melted butter, and vanilla until combined. Whisk in flour until combined and smooth. (Batter can be refrigerated in airtight container for up to 5 days; bring to room temperature before proceeding.)

3. Drop 1½ tablespoons batter into center of each outlined circle on prepared baking sheet. Using small offset spatula, spread batter into 5-inch circle, using stenciled outline as guide. Bake until golden brown, 14 to 16 minutes, rotating sheet halfway through baking.

4. Working quickly, place prepared mold just off center of cookie, making sure tip of mold is about ¼ inch from cookie's edge. Use metal spatula to lift edge of cookie onto mold, then tightly roll cookie around mold to form cone. Press firmly on outside seam of cone to seal. Stand cone, upside down, still on mold, on wire rack. Repeat with remaining 3 cookies. (If cookies become too hard to roll, return to oven for up to 1 minute to soften.) Let cones cool completely, about 10 minutes, before gently removing from molds.

5. Repeat spreading, baking, and shaping on clean and cool baking mat and baking sheet with remaining batter. Cones are best fresh, but can be stored at room temperature in airtight container for up to 2 weeks.

Chocolate Ice Cream Shell

✔ WHY THIS RECIPE WORKS: When you get a letter from a man named Bullets, you feel compelled to respond. Bullets Gillespie of Nashville wrote to *Cook's Illustrated* to ask about Elmer Gold Brick Topping, a chocolate sauce that forms a thin, brittle shell when poured over ice cream. It's hard to find in stores, and Bullets wanted us to develop a recipe for a homemade version. He noted he would not be appeased with some anemic, overly sweet, waxy coating that tasted like it came from the local soft-serve stand.

Now, don't tell Bullets, but I used exactly such a product—Smucker's Magic Shell—as my starting point. The way it immediately sets up when it hits ice cream is downright magical; unfortunately, the chocolate flavor is sorely lacking. Still, I figured that understanding its basic mechanics might be the first step in engineering a sophisticated rendition.

Turns out Magic Shell's magic ingredient is coconut oil, which is liquid at about 74 degrees but solid at 70 degrees. Because of this quick transition, you can pour a fluid mixture of chocolate and coconut oil over ice cream and it will set into a crackly shell in mere seconds. Refined coconut oil plus bittersweet chocolate provided rich flavor and snappy texture, and to ensure the flavor would meet Bullets' exacting standards, I also added a bit of salt, espresso powder, cocoa, and vanilla.

When I anxiously phoned Bullets to offer my recipe, I was delighted to find that he was not at all the fearsome type I had envisioned, but a true Southern gentleman. He inherited his intimidating nickname from a great-grandfather who ran away at age fourteen to fight in the Spanish-American War. I'm hopeful that this tempting recipe might help Bullets persuade current Gillespie generations to stick closer to home.

—ANDREA GEARY, Associate Editor, *Cook's Illustrated*

> *"Turns out Magic Shell's magic ingredient is coconut oil, which is liquid at about 74 degrees but solid at 70 degrees. Because of this quick transition, you can pour a fluid mixture of chocolate and coconut oil over ice cream and it will set into a crackly shell in mere seconds."*

Coconut oil is key: Store-bought Magic Shell's key ingredient is coconut oil. This oil is extremely high in saturated fat, which makes it liquid at 74 degrees and solid at room temp (70 degrees). I found that combining coconut oil in a 2:3 ratio by weight with chocolate produces a sauce that is drizzle-able when just slightly warmed but morphs into a shatteringly thin shell seconds after being poured over ice cream. Melting these two ingredients together in the microwave at 50 percent power is easy and ensures the chocolate doesn't scorch.

More chocolaty, more flavorful:
For an extra boost of chocolate, I whisk some cocoa into the melted chocolate mixture. I also add a little vanilla and espresso to round out the sauce. Diluting the espresso in the vanilla before adding it to the chocolate mixture ensures it gets evenly distributed. And that's all there is to it. Except you also need a little bit of patience because at this point the sauce is too warm to turn into a shell once poured onto ice cream, so let it sit until it cools to room temperature.

The magic moment: Once the sauce is cooled, simply pour it over your favorite ice cream and watch the magic happen. The sauce will keep for quite a while at room temperature, though it will solidify somewhat. I find the best way to bring it back to the right consistency is to scoop out the amount I need and microwave it until it's thin and saucy.

Chocolate Ice Cream Shell

Makes ¾ cup
Make today, enjoy immediately

¼	**teaspoon vanilla extract**
⅛	**teaspoon instant espresso powder**
	Pinch salt
4	**ounces semisweet chocolate, chopped**
⅓	**cup coconut oil**
1	**teaspoon cocoa**

Stir vanilla, espresso powder, and salt together in small bowl until espresso dissolves. Microwave chocolate and coconut oil in medium bowl at 50 percent power, stirring occasionally, until melted, 2 to 4 minutes. Whisk in vanilla mixture and cocoa until combined. Let cool to room temperature, about 30 minutes, before using. Chocolate shell can be stored at room temperature in airtight container for at least 2 months; microwave, stirring occasionally, until melted and smooth, 1 to 2 minutes, before using.

Cajeta

✔ WHY THIS RECIPE WORKS: I first discovered dulce de leche in the mid '60s, when I spent a summer in Uruguay, where I quickly acquired a taste for this caramel-like sauce that people drizzled over ice cream, sandwiched in cookies, and generally used in more ways than I could count. About 25 years later, on a trip to Mexico, I discovered something even better: cajeta, which is basically dulce de leche made with goat's milk. It has a slightly richer, more interesting flavor. These days, you can easily find commercial dulce de leche. But, like most things, it's better if you make it yourself; and it's even better if you make it cajeta. Plus, it's insanely easy.

—JOHN WILLOUGHBY, Editorial Director, Magazines

Just the right spice: This recipe is based on Rick Bayless's version in *Mexico One Plate at a Time*, but it's pretty much exactly the same as you'd find all over Mexico. Since cajeta is basically caramelized goat's milk, start by adding sugar to the milk in a Dutch oven. The sugar sweetens things up but also jump-starts the caramelization process. The traditional proportion of 2 cups sugar to 2 quarts milk works perfectly for my taste buds. To complement the slight tang of the goat's milk, I add just a bit of vanilla, a good pinch of salt, and a cinnamon stick, which is a Mexican innovation.

Simmer down: Bring the milk mixture up to a boil, then take the pot off the heat and add baking soda that you've dissolved in water. The baking soda lowers the milk's pH and will thus keep the milk from coagulating. It also allows the milk solids to brown more readily. The mixture will foam up; after it has calmed, return it to a boil. Now turn the heat down and keep the mixture at a constant simmer, stirring occasionally. After about 45 minutes, it will look somewhat beige. Once it has hit that point, you really need to stir every few minutes to keep it from scorching. It will take another 30 minutes.

Cool and serve: When the mixture is caramel colored and coats the back of a spoon, it's cajeta. Remove the pot from the heat and take out the cinnamon stick. If you want a flawlessly smooth sauce, pour it through a fine-mesh strainer, but you don't have to. The cajeta can be eaten as soon as it's cooled down or refrigerated until ready to use. Drizzle it over ice cream, sandwich it between layers of yellow cake, spoon it over gingerbread, put a teaspoon in your coffee—once you've got some cajeta on hand, you'll find lots of uses.

Cajeta

Makes about 3 cups

Make today, enjoy immediately

8	**cups goat's milk**
2	**cups (14 ounces) sugar**
2	**teaspoons vanilla extract**
¼	**teaspoon kosher salt**
1	**cinnamon stick (optional)**
¾	**teaspoon baking soda dissolved in 1 tablespoon water**

1. Bring milk, sugar, vanilla, salt, and cinnamon stick, if using, to boil in Dutch oven over medium-high heat, stirring occasionally with rubber spatula.

2. Remove pot from heat, then stir in baking soda mixture (milk will start to foam). When foaming subsides, return milk mixture to boil over medium-high heat. Reduce heat to medium-low and simmer rapidly, adjusting heat as necessary to maintain a rapid simmer and stirring occasionally to prevent scorching, until mixture is pale golden-brown, 45 minutes to 1 hour.

3. Continue to cook, stirring frequently, until cajeta is caramel colored and heavily coats back of spoon, about 30 minutes longer. Discard cinnamon stick, if using. If desired, strain cajeta through fine-mesh strainer. Cajeta can be refrigerated in airtight container for up to 2 months.

Maple Cream

✔ **WHY THIS RECIPE WORKS:** I grew up in Boston, so I was steeped in Yankee food traditions from an early age. My family picked blueberries in the summer and apples in the fall, regularly cooked from the *Boston Globe Cookbook*, and ate franks and beans and B&M brown bread for supper almost every Saturday night. Given my New England upbringing, you might expect me to have a militant allegiance to Real Maple Syrup, but the fact is, I'm not a huge fan of the stuff.

Sure, the flavor of bona fide maple syrup is great. But for me, it's just too runny. It doesn't sit on top of your waffles like that glistening pool of syrup in the picture on the Aunt Jemima bottle. Instead, it immediately sinks in, transforming your waffles into limp, sodden sponges. Why bother going to the trouble to make your waffles crisp if you're just going to douse them with something that will instantly sog them out? And worse, because of its thin consistency, maple syrup doesn't linger on the palate, so you have little time to enjoy its wonderful flavor. Enter maple cream.

I first encountered this lovely product (also known as maple butter) at a Vermont sugarhouse I visited one March. As I passed through the little gift shop, I spied a stack of small jars labeled "Maple Cream" next to a plastic tray of soda crackers topped with a humble-looking beige paste. It was an uninspiring display, but—because I am constitutionally incapable of resisting a free sample—I paused for a taste. The sweet spread was deliciously silky, almost buttery, and it packed a powerful maple wallop.

Curious about how much butter and cream this luxurious concoction contained, I checked the ingredients listed on the jar: pure maple syrup. Nothing else. I immediately snatched up three jars and headed for the checkout. The next few weeks found me spreading it on just about every bread-type item I consumed.

Maple cream is just maple syrup, cooked to 235 degrees, cooled to 100 degrees, and then beaten with a spoon until very fine crystals form, turning the syrup into a thick, pale, opaque mass. Making it is simple, but it would be dishonest to describe it as easy. The challenge lies in the beating of the cooled syrup, which requires strong arms, a sturdy grip, a resolute nature, and—if possible—a similarly equipped assistant to share stirring duties when the going gets tough.

Maple cream is a delicious topping for toast, scones, biscuits, and waffles, and it's really good in a peanut butter sandwich. If your batch comes out a bit stiffer than you'd like, you can roll it into small balls and coat them with finely chopped nuts—instant confections, perfect for gift-giving. Or, something I've always wanted to try: Use it as a filling between two cookies. Do not substitute Grade B maple syrup here; it will not crystallize properly once boiled.

—ANDREA GEARY, Associate Editor, *Cook's Illustrated*

"Curious about how much butter and cream this luxurious concoction contained, I checked the ingredients listed on the jar: pure maple syrup. Nothing else. I immediately snatched up three jars and headed for the checkout."

Set up the ice bath: After heating up the maple syrup to the proper temperature (which we will get to momentarily), you will need to quickly transfer the syrup to a clean medium saucepan set in a large bowl of ice. It's wise to keep an eye on the maple syrup once it's boiling (if you get overconfident and walk away, the syrup will certainly take offense and boil over just to teach you a lesson), so I set up the ice bath first. It's not necessary to add water since the ice will begin to melt as soon as you pour the hot syrup into the saucepan.

Heat it up, cool it down: It's time to pour the syrup into a medium saucepan, and, if you like, add ¼ teaspoon vegetable oil and a pinch of salt. The oil will keep the foam down during boiling, while the salt brings a bit of balance. Boil the syrup until the temperature reaches 235 degrees; don't stir or disturb it while this is happening. I usually continue to heat and monitor the temperature for 60 seconds after the thermometer first hits 235 degrees, just to be sure the entire contents of the pan are precisely at my desired temperature. Pour the hot syrup into the saucepan in the ice bath.

Start stirring: Once the syrup has cooled to 100 degrees, remove the saucepan from the ice bath and start stirring the syrup with a wooden spoon. I like to think of this as a marathon, not a sprint; speed isn't as important as maintaining a constant, steady pace. You might think about taking the easy way out and put the syrup in your stand mixer. I strongly recommend against this; not only because I consider stirring by hand a point of honor, but also because there's a chance you'll burn out your mixer's motor— that would be an expensive mistake to make.

Getting close: Over time (anywhere from five to 15 minutes), the syrup starts to lighten in color; this is the crystal structure starting to form. My arm is usually getting a bit tired at this point; the maple cream is about halfway there. When the maple cream starts to lose its shine and takes on the texture of a thick but pourable batter and is the color of tahini, stop stirring. Since this process requires about 30 minutes of stirring start to finish, it's a bonus to have a buddy to jump in to help out, but it is certainly manageable by a single person with the proper focus.

The many uses for maple cream: Working quickly—the maple cream remains pourable for only about 30 seconds—use a rubber spatula to scrape the cream into a clean jar. As it continues to cool, it will take on the texture of peanut butter. It's fantastic on scones, biscuits, toast, and waffles. Or if you feel a little more adventurous, try it in a peanut butter sandwich or between cookies.

Maple Cream

Makes about 2 cups
Make today, enjoy immediately

3 cups grade A maple syrup
¼ teaspoon vegetable oil (optional)
Pinch salt (optional)

1. Set medium saucepan in bowl of ice and scatter more ice around sides of pan. Bring syrup, oil, if using, and salt, if using, to boil in second medium saucepan over medium heat and cook, without stirring, until syrup registers 235 degrees, 16 to 18 minutes. Quickly pour hot syrup into prepared saucepan and let cool, without stirring, until syrup registers 100 degrees, about 15 minutes.

2. Remove saucepan from ice bath and stir syrup vigorously with wooden spoon until it turns thick, pale, and opaque, about 30 minutes. Quickly transfer cream to jar with tight-fitting lid. Maple cream can be stored at room temperature or refrigerated for at least 2 months.

The Beverage Center: Sips, Brews, and Spirits

302   Root Beer

306   Ginger Beer

309   Tonic Water

312   Cold-Brew Coffee

315   Horchata

317   Eggnog

321   Hot Cocoa Mix

323   Coffee Liqueur

325   Sweet Vermouth

329   Cocktail Bitters

333   Citrus-Infused Vodka

339   America's Test Kitchen IPA

Root Beer

✔ **WHY THIS RECIPE WORKS:** When I was growing up, my dad was always brewing something. Most of the time his brew pot was full of brown ale or chocolate stout, but occasionally he would pull the step stool up to the counter and we would brew a batch of root beer together. He kept the recipe short and simple (much like my attention span at the time) by working with a bottle of root beer extract and a basic brewing method: Combine the proper proportions of water, sugar, extract, and yeast; bottle; and ferment. This was a far cry from many of his beer recipes, which took the better part of a day to get started, but the resulting root beer did the trick for my youthful palate—it was my absolute favorite drink.

Now, I wouldn't call myself a root beer fanatic by any means—I certainly don't drink as much of it as I used to—but when I have a craving for a glass, I almost always go for the small-batch brands, which are packed with a lot more spice and rich flavor than those made by the larger cola companies. Maybe that's why, when I finally tasted some of my own root beer, I was disappointed with its relatively boring flavor.

In all honesty, I really shouldn't have expected much from that first batch. After all, I had been relying on a bottle of extract from the grocery store for all the flavor. Curious about producing a bottle of homemade root beer that would be respectable, I started researching. I went in thinking the process would be a challenge, but I quickly realized that making a spicy, richly flavored batch entirely from scratch didn't require much more effort than the shortcut version. It was time to get out the brew pot again.

—DAN ZUCCARELLO, Associate Editor, Books

Establish roots: Typical from-scratch root beer recipes start by steeping sassafras root in hot water, then adding sugar and yeast and allowing the mixture to ferment (and carbonate) in bottles. To further enhance the flavor, additional barks and roots such as sarsaparilla, burdock, and birch might be added. To get started, I settled on sassafras and sarsaparilla. Luckily, you don't have to forage in the woods for these ingredients. You can buy them neatly packaged and ready to use from a local home-brew store or online.

Steep it: Next up, the aromatics. It's not uncommon to find recipes calling for licorice, vanilla, mint, ginger, citrus zest, or cinnamon. For an interesting mix, I use mint, star anise, ginger, and cinnamon for spice, plus a vanilla bean for fragrance. To make about 1 gallon of soda (an amount that's small-kitchen friendly), start with 9 cups of filtered water in a saucepan and add the roots, bark, and aromatics. After bringing the mixture to a boil, cover the pot and allow everything to steep for about 2 hours.

Sanitize in the sink: While the mixture steeps, I sanitize the bottles and equipment (a large pot, a fine-mesh strainer, 8-cup liquid measuring cup, metal spoon, ladle, funnel, and bottle capper). For some, like my dad (who is a chemist by trade), brewing can imitate lab work; for others, dunking equipment in soapy water is sufficient. I take the middle road and combine 1 tablespoon bleach per gallon of hot water in my sink. I soak my bottles and equipment for 2 minutes, then let it all air-dry on a drying rack for at least 30 minutes. For the caps, I simmer them for 5 minutes then let them sit in the pan until bottling.

Strain and finish the base: Once the sanitizing is finished, I turn my attention back to the steeping mixture. At this point, it's more like a concentrate. Strain it, then add the sweeteners (I tested several options and found that 1½ cups brown sugar plus ½ cup molasses lends the right flavor and color) along with the remaining 2 quarts of water. I could have added all of the water for the steeping step, but reserving half to add at the end helps cool the mixture to room temperature (around 75 degrees) more quickly—if it's too hot, you could accidentally kill the yeast, which comes next.

Make it bubbly: Once the mixture has cooled to 75 degrees, add the yeast. Yeast is what carbonates this home brew; as it eats sugars, it releases carbon dioxide gas. Most recipes I found recommend ale yeast because it doesn't impart any flavors, though I also read recipes that called for regular active dry yeast. Since I was already at the home-brew store to pick up sassafras and sarsaparilla, grabbing some ale yeast was convenient so that's what I settled on. Once you add the yeast, allow 15 minutes for proofing before you begin bottling.

Bottle it: Using a funnel and ladle makes bottling easy. To avoid exploding bottles due to pressure buildup, I leave 2 inches of space at the top of each. Place a cap on top of each bottle and crimp it on with a bottle capper (see page 337 for more about this equipment). I always sanitize a few extra caps just in case I mess up. At this point, the bottles need to sit at room temperature in a dark place so the yeast can do its job. It usually takes about two days at room temperature for this root beer to carbonate.

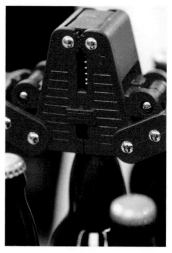

Drink up: Once your soda is carbonated, place the bottles in your refrigerator and wait a couple of days for the flavors to meld. Refrigerating also causes the yeast to go dormant, which restricts the production of carbon dioxide (no explosions on my watch). This root beer is full of unique spice and rich flavor—everything I'm looking for in an old-fashioned homemade root beer. I recommend drinking it within five weeks (I tend to drink mine within five days). Cheers!

Root Beer

Makes ten 12-ounce bottles
Make today, enjoy in 4 to 5 days

1	**vanilla bean**
4	**quarts plus 1 cup filtered water, room temperature**
¼	**cup (½ ounce) dried sassafras root bark**
¼	**cup (¾ ounce) sarsaparilla root**
3	**sprigs fresh mint**
3	**star anise pods**
1	**(1-inch) piece ginger, crushed**
1	**cinnamon stick**
1½	**cups packed brown sugar**
½	**cup mild molasses**
⅛	**teaspoon ale yeast**

1. Cut vanilla bean in half lengthwise. Using tip of paring knife, scrape out seeds. Combine vanilla bean and seeds, 2 quarts plus 1 cup filtered water, sassafras, sarsaparilla, mint, star anise, ginger, and cinnamon in large saucepan and bring to boil over high heat. Remove pot from heat, cover, and let steep for 2 hours.

2. Combine 4 gallons hot water with ¼ cup bleach in sink. Soak large pot, ten 12-ounce bottles, fine-mesh strainer, 8-cup liquid measuring cup, metal spoon, funnel, ladle, and bottle capper in bleach solution for 2 minutes. Remove and let dry completely on drying rack, at least 30 minutes. Place 12 bottle caps and 1 quart water in small saucepan. Bring to simmer over medium heat. Let simmer for 5 minutes, remove from heat, and let sit until bottling.

3. Pour root mixture through strainer set over large pot; discard solids. Add remaining 2 quarts filtered water, sugar, and molasses and stir until sugar and molasses are completely dissolved. Let cool until liquid reaches 75 degrees, stirring occasionally.

4. Stir in yeast and let sit for 15 minutes. Using funnel and ladle, fill each bottle to within 2 inches of top. Place cap over mouth of bottle. Center bottle capper over top of cap and push both handles completely down, applying even pressure around cap. Release bottle capper and twist cap to test for tight fit. If cap is loose or improperly attached, remove and top bottle with new cap. Repeat with remaining bottles. Store bottles in dark place until carbonated, about 48 hours.

5. Place bottles in refrigerator and chill for 2 days to let flavors meld. When serving, open bottles slowly to prevent foaming. Root beer can be refrigerated for up to 5 weeks.

Ginger Beer

ALL BOTTLED UP

Bottles, caps, bottle cappers, and champagne yeast are available at home-brew stores or online at northernbrewer.com or beerbrew.com.

WHY THIS RECIPE WORKS: Ginger beer is on the rise, and it didn't take me long to realize that while it's good on its own, Dark and Stormys are even yummier. And they're just the opening salvo to what ginger beer can do. Ginger beer can, however, be hard to find—especially the high-quality stuff. Fortunately, it's cheap and easy to make at home. Best of all, you can tweak the recipe to suit your particular tastes, adjusting the amounts of ginger or lemon juice as you see fit. Let your ginger beer adventures begin.

—CHRIS DUDLEY, Associate Editor, Special Interest Publications

Spicy-sweet: The first step isn't glamorous: You have to sanitize your bottling equipment in a bleach solution in the sink and simmer your caps. But once that's done, you can move on to the good stuff. The key to making great ginger beer is using lots of ginger. I use a whopping 12 ounces. Peel and roughly chop the ginger, then throw it in the food processor for 30 seconds. Next, use this pulp to build a ginger syrup. Combine 4 cups filtered water with sugar and the grated ginger, heat it until the sugar dissolves, and let it infuse for an hour. I don't like to use too much sugar in my ginger beer; ¾ cup is just enough.

Worth every drop: When the hour of infusing is up, strain the syrup through your fine-mesh strainer into a large measuring cup or bowl (which you've already sanitized). Once most of the liquid has drained through, I press on the ginger using a spoon to extract as much of its juice (and flavor) as possible, and I keep going until it is as dry as possible. It's a slightly sticky situation, but it's worth the work for the ultimate ginger flavor.

The final touches: Now that the ginger syrup is strained, whisk in the final two ingredients: lemon juice and yeast. I like to add just a couple of tablespoons of juice; not so much that you can taste lemon flavor, but enough to balance the sweet and spicy notes of the brew. The yeast is, of course, added to carbonate the ginger beer (this means it'll be slightly fermented, but no, it won't make you tipsy). I like to use champagne yeast because it produces pleasantly petite bubbles and imparts little distinct flavor of its own.

Bottle it: The final step is bottling. Grab your sanitized bottles, funnel, and ladle. Divide your ginger beer mixture between the bottles (about ¾ cup per bottle) with the help of your handy funnel. Then top off each bottle with additional filtered water until the liquid is 2 inches from the bottle's lip. This headspace leaves room for increased pressure during carbonation. Clamp the caps onto the bottles using your capper (these things are really intuitive, don't worry; see pages 304 and 336 for visuals), and then place them in a dark space for two days to carbonate. It doesn't have to be cool; room temp is fine.

Chill out, kick back: After 48 hours have passed, transfer the bottles to the fridge to slow down fermentation. If you wait too long to refrigerate, the beer will continue to carbonate and could potentially force the bottles to explode. Not fun. The beer will continue to carbonate in the fridge, but it will move very slowly (slowly enough that it won't be at risk of exploding before its shelf life is up). Once my ginger beer is chilled, I like to mix up a Dark and Stormy, kick back, and think of all the things my brew can do that regular beer can't.

Ginger Beer

Makes six 12-ounce bottles

Make today, enjoy in 2 days

12	**ounces fresh ginger, peeled and chopped coarse**
8½	**cups filtered water**
¾	**cup sugar**
2	**tablespoons lemon juice**
⅛	**teaspoon champagne yeast**

1. Combine 4 gallons hot water with ¼ cup bleach in sink. Soak six 12-ounce bottles, fine-mesh strainer, 8-cup liquid measuring cup or large bowl, second large liquid measuring cup, metal spoon, whisk, ladle, funnel, and bottle capper in bleach solution for 2 minutes. Remove and let dry completely on drying rack, at least 30 minutes. Place 8 bottle caps and 1 quart water in small saucepan. Bring to simmer over medium heat. Let simmer for 5 minutes, remove from heat, and let sit until bottling.

2. Process ginger in food processor until finely minced, about 30 seconds, scraping down bowl as needed. Transfer to medium saucepan. Stir in 4 cups filtered water and sugar and heat over medium heat until sugar dissolves completely, about 5 minutes. Remove from heat and let steep, uncovered, for 1 hour.

3. Pour infused ginger syrup through strainer set over sanitized 8-cup measuring cup. Let drain for 30 seconds. Press ginger with metal spoon to extract any remaining liquid; discard pulp. (Ginger syrup should measure about 5 cups.) Whisk in lemon juice and yeast until yeast is dissolved.

4. Using funnel and ladle, divide ginger syrup evenly among bottles. Using sanitized large measuring cup, divide remaining 4½ cups filtered water among bottles, filling each bottle to within 2 inches of top. Place cap over mouth of bottle. Center bottle capper over top of cap and push both handles completely down, applying even pressure around cap. Release bottle capper and twist cap to test for tight fit. If cap is loose or improperly attached, remove and top bottle with new cap. Repeat with remaining bottles. Shake gently to combine ingredients.

5. Store bottles in dark place until carbonated, about 48 hours. Transfer to refrigerator and chill. Ginger beer can be refrigerated for up to 2 weeks. When serving, open bottles slowly to prevent foaming.

Tonic Water

WHY THIS RECIPE WORKS: Anyone who's had a really great custom-made gin and tonic knows there's something missing from saccharine, one-dimensional, mass-market tonic water. My own quinine revelation came at a Brookline restaurant called Lineage, where the bar staff creates many of their mixers in-house. While you can make a serviceable tonic water with carbonated water, simple syrup, and cinchona bark, mine is more like a bitter citrus soda, with a stronger flavor profile that also incorporates lemon, lime, and orange, as well as lemon grass. The taste is a complete revelation, and it's so easy to make, you'll never go back to store-bought.

—MARCUS WALSER, Systems Administrator, America's Test Kitchen

CINCHONA AND CITRIC ACID

Cinchona bark can be found at spice shops, natural foods stores, and online at pennherb.com. Citric acid is sold though cheese-making resources (see pages 136–137), and kingarthurflour.com.

Tonic, for what ails you: The defining ingredient in my tonic recipe is bark from the cinchona tree. Cinchona contains quinine, the flavor most recognized in tonic. British colonials used quinine as an antimalarial agent, flavoring it with lime and sugar. Since they couldn't stand to drink the bitter tonic straight, they added gin—and thus gin and tonics were born. Cinchona comes in either powdered or chopped form, but I prefer chopped because it is easier to strain; the powdered version is fine enough to slip through sieves, but large enough to clog coffee filters, making it difficult to work with.

A full-flavored infusion: Start by peeling and juicing an orange, a lemon, and a lime. These add flavorful citrus oils and a sweet-tart brightness to the concentrate. In a medium saucepan, combine all the peels and juice with 4 cups of water, two chopped lemon grass stalks (for fragrance and depth), ½ cup cinchona bark, and a pinch of salt. Simmer it all for about 20 minutes to reduce the mixture slightly and intensify the flavors.

Strain it: Now you have a flavorful infusion that will be the base for a tonic concentrate. Pour the infused liquid through a fine-mesh strainer lined with a triple layer of cheesecloth, which will ensure you catch any and all stray splinters from the bark.

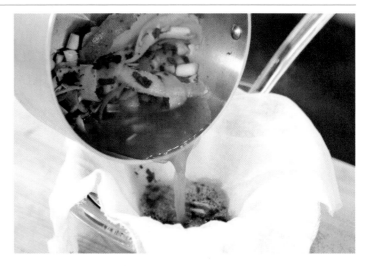

Sweet and sour: Return the liquid to the stove. It's time to add some sweetness. Some recipes I found called for brown sugar or agave syrup, but I like the clean, pure flavor of granulated. Bring the tonic up to a boil, then add the sugar and reduce the heat, simmering to dissolve the sugar and thicken the mixture slightly. What you'll end up with is really an infused simple syrup base for tonic water. Once the sugar is dissolved, remove the saucepan from the heat and stir in the final ingredient, citric acid, which balances the sweet and bitter flavors.

Make it fizzy: Once the tonic concentrate has cooled to room temperature, you are ready to dilute it and add carbonation with the help of seltzer water. I use water I carbonate in a home soda maker, but you can also simply add store-bought seltzer water (I like using lime flavored). In either case, combine equal parts concentrate and seltzer water.

Cheers: From there, you can sip it straight if you so choose, but I prefer it as a mixer. I like it best, of course, paired with gin. I recommend using one that is citrus-forward, like Tanqueray 10 or Hendrick's. I also like this tonic combined with orange juice; it tastes like a bitter Orangina.

Tonic Water Concentrate

Makes about 3 cups, enough for about 6 cups tonic water

Make today, enjoy immediately

1	orange
1	lemon
1	lime
4	cups water
2	lemon grass stalks, trimmed to bottom 6 inches and chopped coarse
½	cup (1 ounce) cut cinchona bark
⅛	teaspoon salt
3	cups sugar
¼	cup citric acid

1. Remove zest in large strips from orange, lemon, and lime (leave white pith behind), then halve and juice fruits. Combine zest, juice, water, lemon grass, cinchona bark, and salt in medium saucepan and bring to boil over high heat. Reduce heat to low and simmer until slightly reduced, about 20 minutes.

2. Line fine-mesh strainer with triple layer of cheesecloth and set over bowl. Strain cinchona mixture through strainer. Return liquid to clean saucepan and bring to boil over medium-high heat.

3. Reduce heat to medium-low, add sugar, and simmer, stirring occasionally, until sugar dissolves completely and mixture thickens slightly, about 5 minutes. Off heat, stir in citric acid until dissolved. Let tonic cool to room temperature, then transfer to jar with tight-fitting lid. Tonic water concentrate can be refrigerated for up to 2 months.

TO DILUTE AND CARBONATE: Dilute tonic concentrate with an equal amount of plain or flavored seltzer water.

Cold-Brew Coffee

"For me, good cold-brew balances hints of dark chocolate, caramel, ripe black fruits, and vanilla with a pleasant viscosity, mild acidity, and pitch-perfect bitterness. If my description sounds florid to you, it's probably because you didn't have cold-brew this morning."

✓ **WHY THIS RECIPE WORKS:** When I was a culinary arts student, there were a handful of commandments that my mentors persistently reinforced (read: screamed). One such precept is that heat equals flavor. Heat browns meat, caramelizes sugar, and extracts body-giving gelatin from bones. It creates aroma and concentrates flavor. So if heat is so great, why am I promoting the practice of combining ground coffee with room-temperature water to make iced coffee? The answer lies in the fact that heat is indiscriminate.

It's true that coffee brewed at 210 degrees will contain more aroma compounds, dissolved solids, and flavor than coffee brewed at 72 degrees. But this is one case where more isn't necessarily better. Heat also extracts the majority of bitterness and astringency found in coffee beans. Cold-brew coffee is significantly less acerbic than its sweltering sibling. For me, good cold-brew balances hints of dark chocolate, caramel, ripe black fruits, and vanilla with a pleasant viscosity, mild acidity, and pitch-perfect bitterness. If my description sounds florid to you, it's probably because you didn't have cold-brew this morning.

Cold-brew critics complain that it lacks the body and complex flavor of a heat-extracted brew. In the hope of achieving the best of both worlds, I've tried a number of out-there techniques, including pressurized brewing in a cream whipping canister, near-continuous agitation, and five-day-long extractions in the fridge. But none of these techniques improved my cup of cold-brew. What they did was turn a simple, satisfying process into a chore.

After reconciling my love of cold-brew with years of heat-focused culinary indoctrination, I am ready to pass along my own cold-brew coffee commandments. I promise not to yell.

—DAN SOUZA, Associate Editor, *Cook's Illustrated*

The right roast: I use medium-roast beans (left), which have been heated to a lower temperature than dark-roast beans (right). In my opinion they taste more like coffee beans and less like the roasting process.

Water plus coffee: Combine room-temperature water (I use filtered, as my tap water doesn't taste great) and your freshly ground coffee in a large French press. The press makes it a snap to separate the concentrate from the grinds after brewing. I use a high ratio of grounds to water so that I end up with an easy-to-store concentrate that can be diluted to suit individual tastes.

Stir it, cover it, let it sit: After about 10 minutes, a solid raft of coffee grounds will form on the surface. It's important to stir this raft into the water to maximize the water's contact with the ground coffee. Then cover the French press with plastic wrap and let it sit at room temperature for 24 hours (give or take an hour in either direction). I've done room-temperature brews as short as 12 hours and as long as 72 hours. Twenty-four hours is consistently the sweet spot.

Make it sediment free: After 24 hours, place the lid on the press and press the plunger down. Pour the concentrate into a coffee filter–lined fine-mesh strainer set over a large measuring cup. Some would say that filtering is optional, but I don't like silt in my cup. I speed up the filtering process by gently clearing the sediment with the back of a ladle or rubber spatula. I also transfer the grounds to a piece of cheesecloth and give it a good squeeze to get the last few bits of concentrate out.

Dilute, add salt, and drink: At last you have your concentrate, which you can dilute with your preferred amount of water before serving with plenty of ice. I like the robust flavor from a 1:1 ratio of cold water to concentrate, though you could also make it lighter by using a 2:1 ratio. Now, instead of reaching for the sugar (which is unnecessary with super-smooth cold-brew) I stir in a pinch of kosher salt. Just trust me on this one.

Cold-Brew Coffee Concentrate

Makes about 1½ cups; enough for 3 cups iced coffee

Start today, enjoy tomorrow

9 ounces medium-roast coffee beans, ground coarse (3½ cups)

3½ cups filtered water, room temperature
Kosher salt (optional)

1. Stir coffee and water together in large (about 2-quart) glass French press. Allow raft of ground coffee to form, about 10 minutes, then stir again to recombine. Cover with plastic wrap and let sit at room temperature for 24 hours.

2. Line fine-mesh strainer with coffee filter and set over large liquid measuring cup. Place lid on press and slowly and evenly press plunger down on grounds to separate them from coffee concentrate. Pour concentrate into prepared strainer. Line large bowl with triple layer of cheesecloth that overhangs edges. Transfer grounds to cheesecloth. Gather edges of cheesecloth together and twist; then, holding pouch over strainer, firmly squeeze grounds until liquid no longer runs freely from pouch; discard grounds.

3. Using back of ladle or rubber spatula, gently stir concentrate to help filter it through strainer. Concentrate can be refrigerated in jar with tight-fitting lid for up to 3 days.

TO MAKE ICED COFFEE: Combine equal parts coffee concentrate and cold water. Add pinch kosher salt, if using, and pour into glass with ice.

Horchata

✓ WHY THIS RECIPE WORKS: The first time I tried cool, refreshing horchata at a local taqueria, I was hooked. This traditional Mexican street drink is typically made by steeping rice, nuts, or seeds in water, then blending the mixture. Recipes vary throughout the Spanish-speaking world: Many are rice based, but horchatas made with tiger nuts (aka chufa, a root with a chestnutlike flavor) or almonds are also popular. Some include dairy, and most are sweetened and have a hint of cinnamon. The perfect complement to spicy Mexican cuisine and fantastic on a warm summer day, horchata, I've learned, isn't hard to make at home.

—LAUREN PERKINS, Marketing Assistant, America's Test Kitchen

BLANCHED ALMONDS

You can find blanched almonds (almonds with their skins removed) at higher-end grocery stores or purchase them online through amazon.com.

Go for a soak, then blend: Many horchata recipes are rice based, but I find incorporating almonds lends great flavor and a creamy feel to the beverage. I use whole blanched almonds, but slivered will also work. Combine your water, almonds, and rice, along with vanilla and cinnamon to perfume the mix, in a bowl. Let the mixture sit overnight or up to 24 hours. The soaking not only softens the nuts and rice to make blending feasible, but it also deepens the flavor. After the soak is done, pour the contents of the bowl into a blender and blend for about 30 seconds, until the rice and almonds are broken down.

Get rid of the grit: Next you need to pour the almond-rice mixture into a fine-mesh strainer lined with a triple layer of cheesecloth. Don't skimp on the cheesecloth or your horchata will be gritty. Once the liquid has passed through the cloth and strainer, gather the edges of the cheesecloth to form a pouch and give it a good squeeze to extract any remaining liquid.

Refreshment time: At this point the mixture only needs a little milk and sugar. I prefer to use evaporated milk because it makes the horchata creamier. I avoid sweetened condensed milk so that I can sweeten the beverage to my liking. Serve your horchata chilled over ice with a little sprinkle of cinnamon on top.

Horchata

Makes about 5 cups

Start today, enjoy tomorrow

4½	**cups water**
1¼	**cups blanched whole almonds or 1⅓ cups slivered almonds (6¼ ounces)**
⅓	**cup long-grain white rice**
1½	**teaspoons vanilla extract**
1	**teaspoon ground cinnamon**
1	**cup evaporated milk**
½	**cup sugar**

1. Combine water, almonds, rice, vanilla, and cinnamon in bowl. Cover and let sit at room temperature for at least 12 hours or up to 24 hours.

2. Line fine-mesh strainer with triple layer of cheesecloth that overhangs edges and set over large bowl. Process almond mixture in blender until very smooth, about 30 seconds. Pour mixture into prepared strainer and let drain until liquid no longer runs freely from strainer, about 5 minutes. Pull edges of cheesecloth together to form pouch. Twist edges of cheesecloth together, firmly squeezing pulp until liquid no longer runs freely from pouch; discard pulp.

3. Stir milk and sugar into almond liquid until sugar is completely dissolved. Refrigerate until completely chilled, about 2 hours. Horchata can be refrigerated in jar with tight-fitting lid for up to 3 days.

Eggnog

WHY THIS RECIPE WORKS: The first seasonal sighting of eggnog in the supermarket brings on a routine dialogue between my husband and me. I exclaim that I'm ready to stock our fridge (and bar), to which he retorts, "Not until after Thanksgiving." If I start indulging in thick, creamy 'nog in September, he points out, my love will be a thing of the past come Christmas, when every holiday party we hit features a boozy bowl.

So every year I cave to his reasoning, because deep down I know he's right. Despite my soft spot for ready-made eggnog, I admit that it's a bit over the top, more dessert than beverage. Perhaps if I developed my own recipe, I could scale back the heaviness without sacrificing the classic flavor. It could be a version I'd never tire of.

Standard homemade eggnog is made by first preparing a cooked-custard base. Just before serving, egg whites and sugar are whipped until stiff and folded into the chilled custard for a light, frothy texture. Though I've eaten plenty of raw cookie dough, I've managed to escape having my salmonella card pulled, and I'd rather not push my luck with a recipe that requires raw egg whites. With the help of a stand mixer and a lighter custard base, I managed to make a light and frothy 'nog with the trademark silky texture—no raw whipped whites needed.

—CALI RICH, Senior Editor, America's Test Kitchen

"Despite my soft spot for ready-made eggnog, I admit that it's a bit over the top, more dessert than beverage. Perhaps if I developed my own recipe, I could scale back the heaviness without sacrificing the classic flavor."

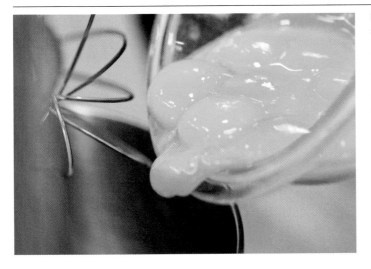

Better by the dozen: Eggnog starts with making a custard, which means you need a lot of yolks. I begin by separating a dozen eggs. And don't throw out those whites. Save them for another recipe, like meringue cookies, angel food cake, frostings, or omelets.

Whip for a frothy 'nog, then slowly sweeten: I whip the yolks in a stand mixer at a fairly high speed. The key to light eggnog is to incorporate enough air into the yolks. You'll know you have fluffed them up enough when they have thickened and become lighter in color. It should take about a minute. Then I slowly add the sugar over the course of a couple of minutes. This gradual addition ensures the yolks won't deflate and that the sugar will completely dissolve.

A perfect drizzle: Once the sugar is fully incorporated, the mixture will be glossy and should hold a ribbonlike outline for several seconds when drizzled back and forth in the bowl. When your mixture is to that point, set it aside and turn your attention to the stovetop.

Mix it: Eggnog's custardy base is typically made with a high proportion of heavy cream. However, I opt instead for a 3:1 ratio of milk to half-and-half to create an eggnog that is lighter yet still silky. Using a whisk for the saucepan's hard-to-reach corners, whisk the dairy mixture over medium heat just until you see a few bubbles appear (like you see here). Transfer this hot dairy to a large liquid measuring cup.

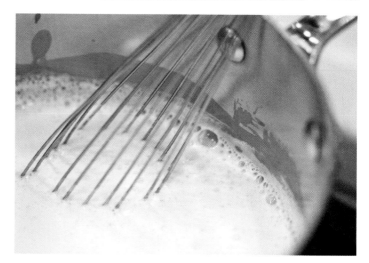

Temper it: With the mixer running, slowly add the dairy to your yolk-sugar mixture. It's important that the motion of the whisk is continuous and that the stream of dairy is gradual to ensure that the egg proteins don't scramble. All of this whipping will add much-needed lightness to the final eggnog since you won't be folding in whipped whites. According to the USDA, eggs should be heated to 160 degrees for safe consumption, and while pouring in the hot dairy nearly gets them there, it's not quite enough. Heating the custard back on the stove for a minute or two is usually sufficient.

Spike, then spice: Once your base hits the 160 mark, it is ready for the booze. Adding the bourbon (my preference) to the custard mixture just before serving the 'nog will leave you breathing fire, while adding it on the heat will dull its smoky burn a bit too much. Stirring it in just off the heat strikes the perfect balance. Much like the bourbon, the nutmeg and vanilla will be too muted when added on the heat, so stir them in after adding the alcohol.

Cool it: Next you need to cool the eggnog down using an ice bath before putting it in the fridge. Fill a large bowl with ice and top with another large bowl. Then add the eggnog to the chilled bowl and, stirring occasionally, let it cool for about 10 minutes. After that, refrigerate it until completely chilled, about 1½ hours.

Garnish it: A final hit of freshly grated nutmeg is the last touch to this "light" eggnog. Can you blame me for wanting to enjoy this year round?

Eggnog

Makes about 7 cups

Make today, enjoy immediately

12	**large egg yolks, room temperature**
1½	**cups sugar**
4½	**cups whole milk**
1½	**cups half-and-half**
1	**cup bourbon**
	Ground nutmeg
1½	**teaspoons vanilla extract**

1. Using stand mixer fitted with whisk, whip egg yolks on medium-high speed until thickened and pale, about 1 minute. Gradually add sugar and whip until mixture is thickened and sugar is completely incorporated, about 2 minutes, scraping down bowl as needed; set aside.

2. Bring milk and half-and-half to bare simmer in large saucepan over medium heat, whisking often, until bubbles begin to appear around edges of pan; transfer to 8-cup liquid measuring cup. Turn mixer to medium-low speed and gradually add hot milk mixture to whipped egg yolks until combined, about 2 minutes. Return mixture to saucepan and cook over medium heat, whisking constantly, until mixture registers 160 degrees, 1 to 2 minutes.

3. Off heat, stir in bourbon, 2 teaspoons nutmeg, and vanilla. Fill large bowl with ice and set second large bowl on top. Transfer eggnog to prepared bowl and let cool over ice bath until lukewarm, about 10 minutes. Refrigerate until well chilled, about 1½ hours. To serve, sprinkle grated nutmeg to taste over individual glasses. Eggnog can be refrigerated for up to 1 week.

Hot Cocoa Mix

✔ WHY THIS RECIPE WORKS: Many of us in the test kitchen grew up with cold New England winters, and we remember how a mug of hot cocoa could turn a snowstorm into sunshine. But now that we're all grown up, watery hot cocoa from a packet just doesn't cut it. We set out to make our own "instant" mix that could be ready whenever a cocoa craving hit.

After some tinkering, we had a decent base, but it didn't taste any better than Swiss Miss. We eventually discovered white chocolate provided an impressively creamy texture and pushed the chocolate flavor to new heights. Now this was a cocoa mix that was worthy of our childhood memories.

—THE TEST KITCHEN

White chocolate is key: Cocoa mix made with the usual suspects (Dutch-processed cocoa powder, sugar, and nonfat dry milk) was okay, but the granulated sugar took a long time to dissolve and the chocolate flavor was faint at best. Using confectioners' sugar instead of granulated fixed one problem. Remedying the wan chocolate flavor was more challenging. After trying unsweetened, milk, and semisweet chocolates, we found our surprising solution in white chocolate chips.

The right process: To best incorporate the white chocolate chips into the mix and grind them to the right small size, we turn to the food processor. About 1 minute of processing the ingredients together is enough. Because of the volume, we found it critical to process the mixture in two batches.

Well-ground: Once the mix is fully processed, you shouldn't have any chocolate pieces larger than a small pea. Transfer the mix to airtight containers for storage (or gift-giving).

Hot and steamy: We like to use ⅓ cup mix for every cup of milk. Heat the milk on the stove or microwave until steaming, then whisk in the mix. All you need now is a dollop of freshly whipped cream or a few marshmallows, and you'll be in cocoa bliss. It makes a great holiday gift, especially when paired with a package of homemade marshmallows (see page 282).

Hot Cocoa Mix

Makes 8 cups; enough for 24 servings of cocoa

Make today, enjoy immediately

3	**cups nonfat dry milk powder**
2	**cups confectioners' sugar**
1½	**cups white chocolate chips**
1½	**cups Dutch-processed cocoa**
¼	**teaspoon salt**

Stir all ingredients together in large bowl until well combined. Working in 2 batches, process mixture in food processor until chocolate chips are ground fine and well incorporated into cocoa mix, about 1 minute. Hot cocoa mix can be stored in airtight container for up to 3 months.

TO MAKE HOT COCOA: Heat 1 cup whole milk in small saucepan over medium heat until steaming, 3 to 5 minutes. Whisk in ⅓ cup mix until dissolved. Pour into mug and top with whipped cream or marshmallows.

Coffee Liqueur

☑ WHY THIS RECIPE WORKS: When my sister started showing up on Christmas Eve with homemade Kahlúa, I was impressed—and grateful. At the time, we had small children, and the assembly of bikes and toys meant we caught only a few hours of sleep. A little of my sister's potent, almost smoky, brandy-spiked coffee liqueur, poured into a strong cup of coffee, got us through the chaos of many a holiday morning. I discovered it was also good poured in a glass over ice or drizzled on ice cream. When she stopped making it for us, I asked for the recipe. Now I make it myself. Best of all, I can double or triple this recipe for gifts.

—ELIZABETH CARDUFF, Editorial Director, Books

Start with simple: To make any style of liqueur, you first need to start with simple syrup (sugar melted into water). I like my simple syrup on the viscous side, so I heat up 1⅓ cups sugar with 1¼ cups water until the sugar dissolves.

Spike it: Many recipes for coffee liqueur call for brewed coffee, but I like to use a one-two punch of espresso powder and cocoa powder, which really brings out the rich, roasted coffee notes. Stir a generous scoop (¼ cup) of espresso powder into the simple syrup, as well as a teaspoon of cocoa powder. Bring this whole mixture to a boil to ensure that everything is dissolved. Finally, add the booze. I like a mixture of vodka (for potency) and brandy (for caramel undertones). Add these off the heat so that none of the alcohol ignites or evaporates.

Infuse it: I like the sweet, floral flavor vanilla brings to the mix. Instead of adding extract, I steep two beans in a quart-size jar of liqueur. To get the most out of the beans, I slice them in half before adding them to the jar. Then I just pour the liqueur mixture over the beans and let it infuse and mellow for one to two months. Once a week, I give the jar a shake to redistribute the solids that settle on the bottom. The liqueur will continue to mellow with age and will be drinkable for at least six months.

From cocktails to breakfast to dessert: For gifts and long-term storage, I like to transfer the liqueur to bottles. A White Russian (a potent elixir of vodka, coffee liqueur, and cream) is probably the most common beverage choice using coffee liqueur, but it is also great on the rocks, drizzled over ice cream, or simply stirred into a cup of coffee for an indulgent pick-me-up.

Coffee Liqueur

Makes 4 cups
Start today, enjoy in 1 to 2 months

1⅓ **cups sugar**
1¼ **cups water**
¼ **cup instant espresso powder**
1 **teaspoon cocoa**
1⅓ **cups vodka**
⅔ **cup brandy**
2 **vanilla beans**

1. Heat sugar and water in medium saucepan over medium heat, stirring occasionally, until sugar dissolves, about 5 minutes. Stir in espresso powder and cocoa, increase heat to medium-high, and bring to boil. Off heat, stir in vodka and brandy.

2. Slice vanilla beans in half lengthwise and place in 1-quart glass jar or bottle with tight-fitting lid. Pour liqueur mixture into jar with beans. Let mixture steep in cool, dark place until mellowed, 1 to 2 months, shaking jar to redistribute mixture once a week. Coffee liqueur can be stored at room temperature for at least 6 months. It will continue to mellow with age.

Sweet Vermouth

✓ **WHY THIS RECIPE WORKS:** These days, a Manhattan is my cocktail of choice. But with only bourbon, sweet vermouth, and bitters in the shaker, it requires top-quality ingredients. Most store-bought sweet vermouths are overly sweet and have none of the complexity of the 18th century original—a medicinal concoction that used up to a hundred roots, herbs, and aromatics. Meanwhile, artisanal brands come at a steep price. After an initial investment for ingredients, homemade vermouth is surprisingly easy to make and offers all the complexity and depth of the original (and not nearly as many ingredients, believe it or not).

—REBECCAH MARSTERS, Associate Editor, *Cook's Country*

STOCKING UP FOR D.I.Y. VERMOUTH

You can buy the more obscure ingredients used in this recipe through mountainroseherbs.com.

Measure ingredients: The ingredient list may seem daunting, but vermouth relies on dozens of herbs and spices for complexity and balance. Most cinnamon sticks sold in the United States are cassia, but it's worth seeking out Ceylon cinnamon for its subtler, less abrasive flavor. And once you've made the initial purchase, you'll be stocked up for making many batches.

Simmer and steep: Simmering most of the ingredients with the base wine begins the infusion process, just like hot water draws flavor out of tea. Pinot Grigio, with its neutral profile, is a must here. I let everything simmer together for 10 minutes, then take it off the heat. Let the infusion rest for at least 24 hours before straining; this is essential to ensure fully developed flavor.

Strain: After 24 hours of steeping, strain the liquid and discard the solids. Lining your strainer with cheesecloth will help remove most of the debris from the mixture. It will still be slightly cloudy, but this is what makes it look homemade! And as the vermouth sits, the particles will sink to the bottom of the container and the mixture will become clearer.

Sweeten, heat it up, and fortify: All vermouth is sweetened and fortified. Before refrigeration, fortification was for preservation purposes; nowadays, it's done to provide balance. Melting the sugar in a little water over heat is crucial to ensure that it integrates into the mixture; turbinado sugar lends a deeper sweetness than regular granulated, and its slight bitter edge works well here. Cognac (or a good brandy) adds body and caramel flavor, and a touch of ruby port rounds out the flavor with bright, fruity notes. After preparing this sugar mixture, add it to the infusion.

Finish: After fortification, the vermouth needs more of the base wine to reach the optimal strength (about 15 percent alcohol by volume). To make 750 milliliters of vermouth (the same volume as a bottle of wine), you'll need an additional 1 to 1¼ cups of wine. The amount will vary depending on how much liquid was lost to evaporation during the simmering process. Now you're ready to enjoy it or store it (in the fridge, to keep it as fresh as possible). Get out that cocktail shaker!

Sweet Vermouth

Makes one 750-ml bottle
Start today, enjoy tomorrow

3–3¼	cups Pinot Grigio
2	tablespoons raisins
1	teaspoon dried bitter orange peel
1	(2½-inch) Ceylon cinnamon stick
1½	teaspoons wormwood
½	teaspoon gentian root
½	teaspoon anise seeds
½	teaspoon angelica root
½	teaspoon ground ginger
½	teaspoon chamomile tea flowers
½	teaspoon ground nutmeg
¼	teaspoon coriander seeds
¼	teaspoon sassafras bark
¼	teaspoon centaury herb
¼	teaspoon dried oregano
¼	teaspoon dried sage leaves (not ground)
¼	teaspoon dried basil
¼	teaspoon dried thyme
⅛	teaspoon fennel seeds
⅛	teaspoon cardamom seeds
⅛	teaspoon orris root
⅛	teaspoon dried rosemary
1½	bay leaves
6	peppercorns, lightly crushed
5	allspice berries, lightly crushed
5	whole cloves
4	juniper berries, lightly crushed
1	star anise
½	cup turbinado sugar
2	tablespoons water
½	cup cognac
4	teaspoons ruby port

1. Combine 2 cups wine and remaining ingredients except sugar, water, cognac, and port, in small saucepan and bring to simmer over medium heat. Reduce heat to medium-low and simmer, uncovered, for 10 minutes, adjusting heat as necessary to maintain gentle simmer. Remove pot from heat, cover, and let sit at room temperature for at least 24 hours or up to 48 hours.

2. Line fine-mesh strainer with triple layer of cheesecloth and set over 4-cup liquid measuring cup; strain infusion through prepared strainer and discard solids.

3. Combine sugar and water in small saucepan and cook over medium heat, swirling occasionally, until sugar is completely dissolved and mixture is bubbling, about 6 minutes. Off heat, stir cognac and port into sugar mixture. Add sugar mixture to infusion; then add enough of remaining 1 to 1¼ cups wine to measure 3 cups total and stir well to combine. Transfer vermouth to bottle with tight-fitting lid. Vermouth can be refrigerated for at least 3 months.

Roots, Barks, and Herbs 101

We use a variety of barks, roots, and herbs in this chapter. They contribute aroma, flavor, complexity, and depth to our Tonic Water, Sweet Vermouth, Root Beer, and Cocktail Bitters. They do require a trip to a natural foods or herb and spice shop, or an online order (we use mountainroseherbs.com and pennherb.com), but the final results will prove they are worth the effort, and one order will last you through numerous recipes.

ANGELICA ROOT Angelica is a flowering plant related to carrots, dill, and fennel. It has an intense yet sweet aroma and carrot-like flavor; the roots are dried and often used to make teas.

CENTAURY HERB Centaury is an annual plant with a stiff stem, pale green leaves, and rose-colored blooms. All parts of the plant are used; it smells of sweet hay and has a bitter flavor.

CINCHONA BARK Native to South America, cinchona trees contain quinine, the flavor most recognized in tonic. Cinchona bark has a menthol aroma and a bitter, astringent flavor.

DANDELION ROOT The common dandelion is actually exceptionally nutritious, containing a variety of vitamins and minerals. The root, which contains bitter compounds, is often dried and used to make teas. It smells of putty and has a sweet, nutty flavor.

DRIED BITTER ORANGE The evergreen bitter orange tree is native to Africa, Arabia, and Syria, though it is cultivated around the world. The tree's flowers are incredibly fragrant, while the fruit is very sour and bitter. Bitter orange peel and its oil are used in a variety of foods, liqueurs (such as Triple Sec), sweets, and marmalade.

GENTIAN ROOT Gentian is an herb that originated in Alpine and Himalayan pastures. The root takes several years to mature, and it is one of the world's strongest bitters.

MUGWORT A common flowering plant in the British Isles, mugwort has dark green leaves with a cottony down underneath, which gives dried mugwort a mossy texture. The root smells spinach-like and tastes sweet and acrid.

ORRIS ROOT The orris is a group of two species of European iris. Its rhizomes, resembling ginger, are stripped and dried until they have a chalky appearance. Dried orris root smells floral, sweet, and musky and is used in natural toothpastes, perfumes, and potpourri, as well as gin.

QUASSIA BARK Native to much of South America and the Caribbean, quassia has been used throughout history for curing fevers, malaria, and stomach ailments. The bark is bitter and smells of white pepper, hay, and water chestnut.

SARSAPARILLA There are more than 300 species of this woody perennial found worldwide, including in Asia, Australia, India, and South and Central America. It has a sweet aroma and slightly bitter flavor with hints of tarragon. Sarsaparilla was the original "root" in root beer.
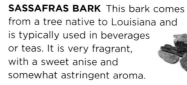

SASSAFRAS BARK This bark comes from a tree native to Louisiana and is typically used in beverages or teas. It is very fragrant, with a sweet anise and somewhat astringent aroma.

WORMWOOD This plant has been long associated with both bitterness and liquor, and it has a reputation for inducing hallucinations. It is well known for its use in making absinthe, but it's also an ingredient in Pernod and vermouth. Its aroma echoes mint and chamomile teas.

Cocktail Bitters

✓ WHY THIS RECIPE WORKS: For cocktail geeks, making your own bitters is akin to getting a prison tattoo: You're in the gang and no one's going to mess with you (read "question your cocktail chops"). Given this comparison, you're probably thinking, wow, making bitters must be difficult, time consuming, and painful. It's not. Grab a bunch of dried barks, roots, spices, and herbs, a quantity of high-proof booze, and a bunch of lidded jars and you're 80 percent there. The rest is simply mixing, waiting, and straining. Homemade bitters will add depth and complexity to cocktails as well as foods (try adding drops to vinaigrettes, sauces, soups, and stews).

Whether I'm cooking dinner or mixing a drink, I always want the ability to season to taste. With that in mind, I've created more of a bitters kit (along with a couple of suggested combinations to get you started). This recipe makes an arsenal of infusions, each a high-proof liquor infused with one ingredient for a specific amount of time—like mint-infused vodka or allspice-infused rum. Then, to create bitters, combine the infusions (which you've strained) in varying proportions. I've found that mixing infusions of lemon, bitter orange, quassia bark, ginger, and coriander creates a delightful blend of Citrus Bitters. After mixing up my Old-Fashioned Bitters recipe, you might decide that it needs more gentian, cardamom, or bitter orange, and while you'll be wrong, you'll at least have the tools to help you realize that mistake. Consider yourself inked.

Good to know: I use readily available high-proof booze, not pure grain alcohol, so these bitters aren't as concentrated as the professionally crafted stuff. As such, it's necessary to use a heavier hand when adding them to drinks (I tend to quadruple the amounts called for in cocktail recipes).

—DAN SOUZA, Associate Editor, *Cook's Illustrated*

BARKS, ROOTS, HERBS, AND SPICES

Cocktail bitters are produced by infusing spirits with a variety of unique barks, roots, herbs, and spices. While some of the herbs and spices can be found in the supermarket, the more unusual barks and roots can be found at specialty health food stores or through online retailers like mountainroseherbs.com. Four-ounce dropper bottles and 8-ounce glass jars are available from sks-bottle.com.

Gather the goods: After some research, I made a list of the most common bitters components—dried barks, roots, spices, and herbs—and assembled my choices. In addition to familiar spices (cardamom, coriander, ginger, allspice, star anise), I also ordered mugwort, gentian root, and quassia bark. Dandelion root, mint (in the form of tea), and citrus peel likewise made the cut. For the spices, I crush and toast them each in a dry skillet to release their flavorful oils.

Pour on the booze: Next, I combine each dried component with alcohol in a jar. After some testing, I matched each dried component with a liquor. Mugwort's grassiness, gentian root's muskiness, and quassia's sweet hay flavor all matched best with bourbon. Citrus' clean flavor made sense with neutral-tasting vodka, while allspice and rum were a good match. Purchase the highest-proof alcohol you can legally get your hands on: 101-proof bourbon, 100-proof vodka, 151-proof rum.

Steeping time: I let the infusions sit for anywhere from 24 hours to five days. My ratio of stuff to booze is pretty high, so infusion times are cut significantly (no month-long wait here). I also skip the annoying (and, thankfully, unnecessary) step of daily agitation. I discovered agitation has very little effect on infusion strength.

Strain and put up: After the infusions have sat for the appropriate amount of time, simply strain them through a coffee filter–lined fine-mesh strainer and transfer them to clean, labeled jars.

Meet your tool kit: Treat your cabinet of finished infusions as you might a spice rack: These infusions are base ingredients that can be combined in varied amounts to create new and interesting flavors. I found that adding a batch of simple syrup to the assembly was a must; if you sample store-bought bitters, you'll notice most have a hint of sweetness, which rounds out the bitters and keeps them from being too harsh. Like making spice blends, the options here are pretty limitless.

Two starter recipes: My potent Old-Fashioned Bitters have a base of gentian and mugwort for depth and bitterness, plus a warm-spice kick and mint for backbone. Anise and bitter orange round things out. Try them in a Manhattan or rye-based classics like a Sazerac or Vieux Carré. My Citrus Bitters, with bitter orange and lemon, plus ginger, coriander, and quassia, are far more complex than the store-bought single-citrus stuff. Use them in cocktails that feature citrus juice or zest as well as those that benefit from a brighter background. Try them in gin-based drinks like an Alaska Cocktail, Bijou, or Martinez.

The bitter finish: Bitters can play a lot of roles in cocktails, but in general they provide background flavor and add complexity. When a cocktail tastes flat or overly sweet there is a good chance that it's lacking bitters. Having an arsenal of bitters and infusions gives you a lot of control over tweaking a cocktail to your liking. Just keep in mind you'll want to use a greater quantity of these homemade bitters than store-bought since they aren't as concentrated. When a cocktail recipe calls for two dashes of bitters, I typically add half a dropper of my homemade bitters.

Cocktail Bitters Tool Kit

Makes 12 infusions and ¾ cup simple syrup

Start today, enjoy in 1 to 5 days

BOURBON INFUSIONS

- ¼ cup dried mugwort, mostly leaves with some stems (½ ounce)
- ¼ cup gentian root (1 ounce)
- ¼ cup quassia bark (¾ ounce)
- 3 cups 101-proof bourbon

VODKA INFUSIONS

- ¼ cup dried lemon peel (¾ ounce)
- ¼ cup dried bitter orange peel (1 ounce)
- ¼ cup mint tea leaves (about 8 tea bags)
- 5½ cups 100-proof vodka
- 2 tablespoons dried dandelion root (½ ounce)
- 8 star anise pods, cracked and toasted
- 2 tablespoons black cardamom seeds, toasted
- 2 tablespoons coriander seeds, cracked and toasted
- 2 tablespoons ground ginger

RUM INFUSION

- ½ cup 151-proof rum
- 2 tablespoons allspice berries, cracked and toasted

SIMPLE SYRUP

- ½ cup boiling water
- ½ cup sugar

1. FOR THE BOURBON INFUSIONS: Place mugwort, gentian root, and quassia bark separately into 3 glass jars with tight-fitting lids. Add 1 cup bourbon to each jar and cover.

2. FOR THE VODKA INFUSIONS: Place lemon peel, bitter orange peel, and mint tea separately into 3 glass jars with tight-fitting lids. Add 1 cup vodka to each jar and cover. Place dandelion root, star anise, cardamom, coriander, and ginger separately in 5 glass jars with tight-fitting lids. Add ½ cup remaining vodka to each jar and cover.

3. FOR THE RUM INFUSION: Combine rum with allspice in glass jar with tight-fitting lid.

4. TO STEEP AND STRAIN INFUSIONS: Strain infusions, one at a time, through coffee filter-lined fine-mesh strainer into glass measuring cup, using rubber spatula to help mixtures filter through, then transfer strained infusions back into individual glass jars (replace coffee filter after straining each mixture) according to following schedule: Strain gentian root, mint tea, star anise, and ginger after 24 hours; strain mugwort, quassia bark, dandelion root, cardamom, and allspice after 48 hours; strain lemon, bitter orange, and coriander after 5 days.

5. FOR THE SIMPLE SYRUP: Stir water and sugar together in glass jar with tight-fitting lid until sugar is fully dissolved. Simple syrup can be refrigerated for up to 1 month. Infusions can be stored in cool, dark place indefinitely.

TO MAKE OLD-FASHIONED BITTERS: Combine 1½ tablespoons simple syrup, 4½ teaspoons mugwort infusion, 4½ teaspoons gentian root infusion, 4½ teaspoons mint tea infusion, 2¼ teaspoons quassia bark infusion, 2¼ teaspoons dandelion root infusion, 2¼ teaspoons cardamom infusion, 2¼ teaspoons bitter orange infusion, 1⅛ teaspoons star anise infusion, and 1⅛ teaspoons allspice infusion in glass measuring cup; transfer to glass dropper bottle. Bitters can be stored in cool, dark place indefinitely. Makes about ¼ cup.

TO MAKE CITRUS BITTERS: Combine ¼ cup lemon infusion, 2 tablespoons bitter orange infusion, 1 tablespoon simple syrup, 2 teaspoons quassia bark infusion, 2 teaspoons ginger infusion, and 2 teaspoons coriander infusion in glass measuring cup; transfer to glass dropper bottle. Bitters can be stored in cool, dark place indefinitely. Makes about ¼ cup.

Citrus-Infused Vodka

✔ **WHY THIS RECIPE WORKS:** The cute names and unwieldy glassware put me off mixed drinks early on. Typically, I'm the person at the cocktail bar asking for the draft list. However, there are times when a pint of suds just won't do—afternoons during a heat wave or in the wake of an imprudently large dinner, for example. In situations like these, cocktails certainly have their place. (Mind you, I still wouldn't be caught dead ordering an "anything-a-tini.")

Infused spirits are a great way to get a flavorful cocktail without having to mess around with too many add-ins. Focusing on citrus as the flavoring agent is a solid choice because citrus peel is packed with aromatic compounds, or essential oils, just waiting to be extracted. These essential oils don't dissolve well in water (no surprise there) but they do dissolve well in alcohol. Vodka's neutral flavor makes it a versatile choice for infusions.

Some people just drop a few strips of citrus zest in a bottle of vodka and call it a day, but they're missing out on maximum flavor. Many of the prized aromatic compounds are isolated in special storage cells. That's why citrus peels release a burst of aroma when you crush them between your fingers: You're breaking open those storage cells. So running the ingredients through the blender is a quick way to release more flavor into the vodka.

You can keep your infusions economical by using citrus peels left over from juicing (any fruit will work). Mix and match with simple syrup, sparkling water, juices, and garnishes for easier-than-they-seem party cocktails. For best results, use organic citrus fruits and wash them thoroughly. Initially, infused vodka will be cloudy but will turn clear with age. Take care not to remove the white pith when peeling the citrus.

—SARAH GABRIEL, Test Cook, *Cook's Country*

> *"Infused spirits are a great way to get a flavorful cocktail without having to mess around with too many add-ins. Focusing on citrus as the flavoring agent is a solid choice because citrus peel is packed with aromatic compounds, or essential oils, just waiting to be extracted."*

Wash it: Citrus-infused vodkas are simple, classic, and easily put together. Plus, you can use fruit peels left over from eating or juicing to keep it economical. Lemon, grapefruit, and orange are my top picks. I try to buy organic to minimize the possibility of pesticide residue in my cocktails. Just make sure to wash your citrus thoroughly.

Peel it and weigh it: Using a sharp vegetable peeler is the easiest way to get the zest while avoiding the bitter white pith. To infuse a 750-milliliter bottle of vodka, I found using 1¼ ounces of zest does the trick. (For rogue cooks or those without kitchen scales, 3 lemons, 2 oranges, or 1½ grapefruits should each yield about the right amount.)

Blanch it: Technically, if you remove all the pith, bitterness should be a non-issue. However, I blanch the strips as insurance. Also, this process removes any waxes or pesticides that might be on the peels. Blanch the strips of zest in boiling water for 30 seconds, then pour the zest in a strainer over a sink and shake off remaining water.

Blend it, stash it: This is the key step. Put the zest in the blender and add the vodka (make sure to save the bottle for storing the finished infusion). Blending exposes more of the zest to the vodka and busts open the cells in which the essential oils are stored. This means a stronger infusion in less time. There's no need to liquefy the mixture; just blend for about 30 seconds to break the zest into small pieces. Then pour the vodka-zest mixture into a wide-mouthed jar. Screw on the lid and stash the jar someplace dark.

Strain it: After four days, your infusion will be ready. Unlike commercially infused vodka, you'll notice your homemade infusions pick up color naturally from the fruit. Now it's time to strain it. Set a funnel inside the empty vodka bottle and line it with a coffee filter. Pour the vodka into the funnel slowly, being careful that it doesn't breach the filter.

Mix and drink: Mix some lemon peel-infused vodka with simple syrup and sparkling water for an easy "limoncello" soda. The infused vodka will keep indefinitely, but for best color and flavor, store your infusion in a cool, dark place.

Citrus-Infused Vodka

Makes one 750-ml bottle
Start today, enjoy in 4 days

13	(3-inch) strips lemon, orange, or grapefruit zest (1¼ ounces; 3 lemons, 2 oranges, or 1½ grapefruits)
1	(750-ml) bottle vodka

1. Bring 1 quart water to boil in small saucepan. Add zest to boiling water and cook until beginning to soften and dull in color, about 30 seconds. Strain zest well and transfer to blender. Add vodka (saving bottle for storage of finished infusion) and process until zest is finely minced, about 30 seconds. Pour into 1-quart jar, cover, and store in cool, dark place until fully infused, about 4 days.

2. Set funnel over empty vodka bottle and line with coffee filter. Strain infused vodka through filter, discarding zest. Infused vodka can be stored in cool, dark place indefinitely.

Brewing Beer **101**

Before you jump into the world of home brewing, it helps to read up on the supplies you'll need and the lingo home brewers use. Making your own beer is a bit of an investment (in terms of both time and dollars), but the payoff of this creative endeavor is the reward of a beer you crafted yourself that you can share with your friends (or not). Our home-brew recipe is perfect for first-time home brewers.

Get Equipped

In addition to some basic kitchen tools (large coarse-mesh strainer, thermometer, scale, and turkey baster or ladle) you'll need some equipment specific to beer brewing. Most of what you need can be found in a starter set sold at home-brewer supply stores and online at northernbrewer.com or midwestsupplies.com (set will likely include some equipment you won't need for our recipe). Equipment is listed in alphabetical order.

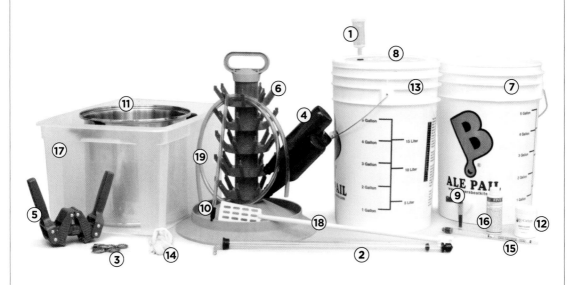

1. **AIRLOCK** This clear plastic three-piece apparatus is filled with boiled and cooled filtered water, allowing carbon dioxide to escape from the fermenting bucket while keeping oxygen and other beer spoilers out.

2. **AUTO-SIPHON** This two-piece apparatus allows you to easily start the transfer of beer from the fermenting bucket into the bottling bucket with a few easy pumps.

3. **BEER BOTTLE CAPS** These caps have a rubber gasket on the underside to help create an airtight seal with the bottles. While this recipe makes about fifty 12-ounce bottles of beer, we always sanitize a few extra caps in case a cap doesn't seal properly.

4. **BEER BOTTLES** Brown glass bottles are typically used for bottling beer, as they limit the beer's exposure to sunlight. This recipe makes

about 5 gallons of beer and will require approximately fifty 12-ounce bottles.

5. **BOTTLE CAPPER** This two-handled crimping tool is used to attach caps to filled bottles. (We use it when bottling our IPA as well as root beer and ginger beer.)

6. **BOTTLE TREE** Each stackable section has sturdy arms that hold bottles upside down to drain and dry after sanitizing.

Get Equipped (continued)

7. **BOTTLING BUCKET** This 6.5-gallon bucket used in the bottling process is made from food-grade plastic. It looks a lot like the fermenting bucket (#13), but the bottling bucket has a hole in the side toward the bottom to accommodate the bottling spigot.

8. **BOTTLING/FERMENTING BUCKET LID WITH GROMMET** A home-brew kit will come with one food-grade plastic lid with a hole in it. This lid is used for covering both the fermenting bucket and bottling bucket. During fermenting, the hole in the lid is fitted with a rubber grommet, and the airlock (#1) is then attached to the lid via that grommet.

9. **BOTTLING SPIGOT ASSEMBLY** This plastic piece is used along with the hose (#19) and wand (#10) in the transfer of beer from the bottling bucket to bottles. To prevent leaking, make sure to attach the spigot with the gaskets in the interior and exterior of the bucket and turn the spigot to the "off" position before filling the bottling bucket with beer.

10. **BOTTLING WAND** This clear plastic tube has a pressure valve on one end so that when you press the tip of the bottling wand onto the bottom of the beer bottle, beer flows into bottle; releasing pressure causes the pressure valve to close and stop the flow of beer.

11. **BREW POT** Make sure to use a sturdy 5-gallon stainless steel pot to maintain even heat and prevent scorching during the brewing process; avoid using an aluminum pot.

12. **EASY CLEAN** Cleanliness is critical throughout the process. We clean all equipment with this oxygen-based powdered cleaner that contains no dyes or fragrances, then follow up with iodophor sanitizer (#16). Be sure to follow the manufacturer's instructions when combining with water before using.

13. **FERMENTING BUCKET** A lot like the bottling bucket (#7) but without the spot for the spigot, this 6.5-gallon food-grade plastic bucket is used for fermentation. It is covered with the grommeted lid (#8) for fermentation.

14. **GRAIN STEEPING BAG** This cloth mesh bag allows you to easily remove cracked grain after making the preboil tea.

15. **HYDROMETER AND TEST TUBE** This glass laboratory instrument has a color-coded scale and comes with a glass vial used to hold a beer sample for measuring specific gravity. Hydrometer readings are used to calculate the beer's alcohol content; be sure to follow the manufacturer's instructions, as these can be very difficult to read.

16. **IODOPHOR SANITIZER** An iodine-based sanitizer, iodophor requires just one minute of contact time to sanitize equipment, bottles, and caps. Iodophor is a no-rinse sanitizer if used in the correct proportions with water, so be sure to follow the manufacturer's instructions when using.

17. **LARGE PLASTIC TUB** To cool the wort before transferring it to the fermenting bucket, you'll need a tub that is large enough to hold the brew pot and plenty of ice water.

18. **LONG-HANDLED SPOON** At several points in the process you'll need to do some stirring. Make sure to use a large stainless steel or plastic spoon that's at least 16 inches long. Don't use a spoon made from wood, since it has a greater chance of holding on to off-flavors and bacteria. Some home-brew kits come with a long paddle called a wort spoon, which works fine for this job.

19. **SIPHON HOSE** A 5-foot clear plastic hose, this piece is used for transferring both beer from the fermenting bucket to the bottling bucket and from the bottling bucket to the bottles. Running the hose under hot water will make it easier to attach to the auto-siphon (#2) and spigot (#9).

Key Ingredients and Terminology

DRY MALT EXTRACT This is a concentrated malt extract that has been spray dried to remove the moisture content. It helps to simplify the brewing process.

EXTRACT BREWING This form of brewing involves the use of concentrated malt extract, which is added directly to the brew pot and boiled with the hops to create the wort. The use of malt extract allows the brewer to skip the process of extracting sugars from a large quantity of grains.

FERMENTATION The process in which yeast converts sugar to carbon dioxide and alcohol.

HOPS These aromatic flower clusters grow on vines and look like miniature green pine cones. Dried hops are used in brewing to impart a bitter, tangy flavor to beer. They also help preserve it. Hops are sold in dried leaf and pellet form. Made by grinding and compressing the leaves, pellets keep longer and take up less storage space. Beer made with pellets may be more cloudy than beer made with leaf hops, but aroma and flavor differences are slight.

IRISH MOSS This dried seaweed is used in brewing to help clarify beer. The Irish moss is boiled with the wort, causing unwanted proteins and other solids to coagulate and settle in the wort after cooling, making them easier to separate out.

MALT GRAINS Barley and other grains are allowed to partially sprout, then are kiln-dried to certain degrees of darkness. Malt grains release the sugars necessary for yeast to produce alcohol. In more involved recipes, you create a "mash" from a large quantity of malt grains; for this recipe we instead rely on dry malt extract (see above). To add color and aroma to our beer, we steep malt grains in water for what's known as a "preboil tea."

PRIMING SUGAR Priming sugar is simply corn sugar (also known as dextrose) that is added to fermented beer before bottling to cause a small refermentation, and thus natural carbonation, in the bottles.

SPECIFIC GRAVITY The relative density of the wort compared to water during various stages of fermentation. Specific gravity is measured with a hydrometer. (See Calculating Alcohol by Volume below.)

WORT This is the sweet unfermented malt-sugar solution that produces beer once fermented. After preparing the wort in the brew pot and cooling it, we strain it into the fermenting bucket, cover it, and leave it to ferment for 2 weeks.

Calculating Alcohol by Volume (ABV)

As beer ferments, yeast consumes the sugar and produces ethanol (i.e., alcohol), lowering the liquid's density. By knowing the specific gravity before and after fermentation (referred to as original gravity and final gravity), you can calculate the beer's alcohol content. (Science refresher: Specific gravity is the ratio of the density of a substance to the density of water taken at a specific temperature. Luckily, your handy hydrometer figures this out for you.) To calculate the ABV, plug your original gravity reading and your final gravity reading from your hydrometer into the following equation:

(Original Gravity - Final Gravity) x 131 = ABV%

With our readings, we got: (1.070 - 1.017) x 131 = 6.9%

If your final gravity reading is off by more than a few hundredths of a decimal point (the original in this recipe is highly unlikely to vary), carefully take another reading. If your number is still off, it likely means the fermentation is incomplete. Place the lid back on the fermentation bucket and measure the final gravity in a few days.

America's Test Kitchen IPA

WHY THIS RECIPE WORKS: I began my love affair with beer (albeit the cheap stuff) in college. Only later would a job at a brewpub change my life, and perspective on beer, forever. I soon became obsessed. I sought out extreme styles, rare beers, and foreign imports. I developed a preference for bars with well-curated beer lists. I started taking detailed tasting notes and researching flavor profiles on malts and different hop varietals.

It suddenly dawned on me that I might be able to brew my own beer. So I did. It turned out to be a perfect marriage of cooking and chemistry. A recipe, a little research, and a trip to my local home-brew store was all I needed to get myself started on my beer-making odyssey. Three years later, I am still making and enjoying my own beer.

Home brewing is a rewarding and versatile hobby that can be as simple or complex as the brewer chooses. America's Test Kitchen IPA is a recipe I wrote for extract brewing. This means the recipe calls for a commercially prepared malt extract. Rather than extracting your own sugars from milled malted grain in a process known as "mashing," you can skip this step entirely by using the store-bought extract—great for beginners. This project still requires a bit of equipment and patience, but successfully making a beer you simply can't find anywhere else makes it all worth it.

Once you've whet your appetite with this recipe, you might want to learn about making different styles or use more involved methods for an even more customized flavor. The possibilities with home brewing are pretty much endless. Before you get started, take a look at pages 336–338 to learn about the equipment you'll need and the lingo used in home brewing.

—JUDY BLOMQUIST, Production and Imaging Specialist, America's Test Kitchen

> *"It suddenly dawned on me that I might be able to brew my own beer. So I did. It turned out to be a perfect marriage of cooking and chemistry. A recipe, a little research, and a trip to my local home-brew store was all I needed to get myself started on my beer-making odyssey."*

Get prepped: Since yeast can be temperamental, remove it from the fridge and let it acclimate to room temperature for a few hours before getting to work. I also weigh out the hop pellets and arrange them carefully in a bowl for each hop addition; hops added early in the boil contribute primarily to bitterness, while later additions provide hop flavor notes and aroma. I chose Warrior hops, with their heavy-hitting alpha acid content, for bittering. For the citrusy flavor and bright, floral aroma that is so characteristic of American IPAs, I went with Amarillo hops.

Get the grains ready: First, make a "preboil tea" by steeping crushed grains in water. American crystal malt 40L imparts caramel color and flavor, while Carapils malt adds body and increases the foamy head. Water accounts for over 90 percent of the final product, so filtered water is key (I run the 6 gallons needed through a filter attached to the faucet head, but you can also just buy the water). Put your brew pot on the stove, add 3 gallons of the water, then fill a steeping bag with the specialty grains.

Steep it: Knot the top of the steeping bag and set the burner under the pot to high. Holding the knotted end of the steeping bag, submerge it in the water, swirl a bit to saturate the grain, then clip the knotted end to the side of the pot, making sure to keep the grain submerged. I like to help the preboil tea along by periodically giving the bag a gentle swirl in the water. As soon as the preboil reaches 170 degrees, pull the bag out and allow liquid from the bag to drain back into the pot before discarding. Don't squeeze the bag; this could introduce astringent tannins into the beer.

Keep it clean: Because the ideal environment for yeast fermentation is also ideal for growth of bacteria and other beer-spoiling varmints, sanitation is of utmost importance. The fermenting bucket and lid, coarse-mesh strainer, long-handled spoon, airlock, turkey baster or ladle, and yeast vial are all going to come in contact with beer after the boil, so wash, sanitize, and air-dry them all. I use Easy Clean for washing and an iodophor sanitizer (prepare both according to the containers' instructions). I also keep some sanitizer handy to dip my hands into periodically throughout the process.

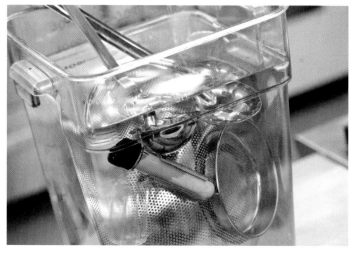

Back to the kettle: Meanwhile, keep heating the preboil tea until it's at a rolling boil. Turn off the heat and dump in the dry malt extract, one bag after another, stirring to prevent caking or scorching. Once it's dissolved, bring this solution, or wort (pronounced "wert"), back to a boil and begin timing for 1 hour. Keep an eye on the pot and stir it frequently—the sugary concoction can quickly boil over. If it begins to, kill the heat (move off heat only if necessary), stir until it settles, then continue boiling.

Hop to it: After the wort has boiled for 15 minutes, stir in an ounce of Warrior hops and let it boil another 25 minutes. Add the second ounce of Warrior hops and let it boil for five minutes. Now add an ounce of Amarillo hops and a teaspoon of Irish moss (for clarifying) and let it boil for five more minutes. Add another ounce of Amarillo hops and let it boil for five minutes. Add a third ounce and let that boil for five minutes. Now you are at the 60-minute mark. Turn off the burner and throw in the fourth and final ounce of Amarillo hops.

Whirlpool, then cool: Use the long-handled spoon to stir the wort in wide circles to create a whirlpool, then remove the spoon and allow the whirlpool to go for 10 minutes or so (I use this time to prepare an ice bath in a bucket big enough for the brew pot). This gathers loose particles, known as "trub," into a pile at the bottom. Once the spinning stops, lift the pot into the ice bath. The quicker the wort cools the better since post-boil wort is vulnerable to bacteria and wild yeast inoculation as long as it's out in the open.

Make a splash: Once the wort hits 75 degrees, put the mesh strainer over the fermenting bucket. Pour the wort through the strainer and into the bucket (you might need a helper or two), making as much of a splash as possible. A heavy pour aerates the wort, which is essential for yeast growth and reproduction. The strainer not only catches any trub that happens to pour out with the wort, but it also aids in aeration. Pour in enough of the remaining 3 gallons of filtered water to bring the quantity of wort to 5 gallons.

Gravity of the situation: As the beer ferments, yeast consumes the sugar and produces ethanol, which lowers the density of the liquid. By knowing the specific gravity before and after fermentation, you can calculate the beer's alcohol content (see formula page 338). Most home-brew kits come with a hydrometer and test tube to get this reading. I use a sanitized turkey baster or ladle to transfer a sample from the bucket to the tube. Insert the hydrometer and record the reading at the bottom of the meniscus. When using a dry malt extract this first reading won't vary much, but taking it is good practice.

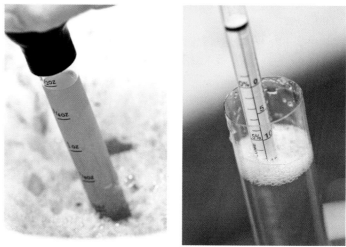

Pitch the yeast: With the wort ready to go, give the unopened yeast vial a gentle shake, then open it up and pour the contents into the fermenting bucket. This step is known in brewer parlance as "pitching the yeast."

Under lockdown: Fit the hole in the fermenting bucket lid with the grommet, then put the lid on the bucket and press down for a good seal. Assemble the airlock, then press its pointed end into the grommeted hole. Fill the airlock to the line with boiled, cooled filtered water, then cap its top. The airlock allows the carbon dioxide produced during fermentation to bubble up through the water and escape without allowing oxygen or bacteria back in. Now shuffle the bucket off to a cool, dark place for two weeks.

Seriously clean: After two weeks of fermenting, the water in the airlock will have stopped bubbling. The bottling process is time consuming due to the sheer volume of stuff you need to clean and sanitize: the turkey baster or ladle, auto-siphon, hose, bottling bucket, spigot, bottling wand, bottle capper, bottles, and caps (I sanitize a few extra caps to account for mess-ups). After cleaning everything with Easy Clean, sanitize it all in an iodophor solution, then let it all air-dry. The bottles you can dry on a bottle tree, and the lid you'll sanitize quickly later since it's on the fermenting bucket at this point.

Primed to go, spigot set to go: I carbonate my beer using a method known as "bottle conditioning," aka natural carbonation. A priming sugar, added to the bottling bucket, provides food for the yeast. The yeast eats the sugar and produces carbon dioxide that remains dissolved in the beer until it's opened. Dissolve the priming sugar in a cup of boiling water, then set it aside to cool. Once it's cool, assemble the spigot in the bottling bucket—making sure the spigot is set to the "off" position—and pour in the cooled priming sugar solution.

Set up for the transfer: It's time to transfer the beer to the bottling bucket. Heft the fermenting bucket onto the counter and place the bottling bucket below on the floor. With sanitized hands, remove the fermenting bucket lid and take a final gravity reading (repeat the process used to measure the original gravity). It should be around 1.017. If you are way off, take a second reading. If it's still off, put the lid back on and let it ferment a few days longer. Calculate the ABV; you should get around 6.9 percent.

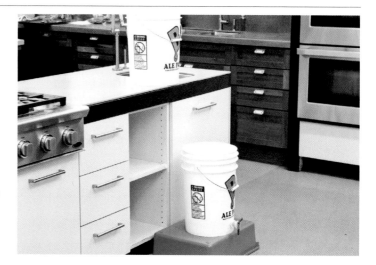

Get pumped: Re-sanitize your hands and attach the hose to the auto-siphon. Plunge the pump end of the auto-siphon into the beer, carefully holding it a few inches above the bottom to keep it out of the sludge (known as "trub") that's settled there, and extend the hose into the bottling bucket with your other hand. A couple of solid pumps on the auto-siphon will send it into action.

Leave the trub: Near the end, you'll need to tilt the bucket to get out as much beer as possible. Even then, leave some liquid behind to avoid picking up the trub on the bottom of the bucket. This sediment isn't harmful to the beer, but the less that finds its way into the beer, the clearer the beer will be. Once it's all transferred, hoist the full bottling bucket onto the counter and sanitize your hands, the hose (again), and the lid, then cover the bottling bucket with the lid.

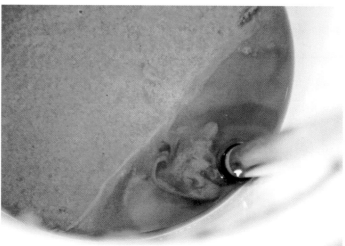

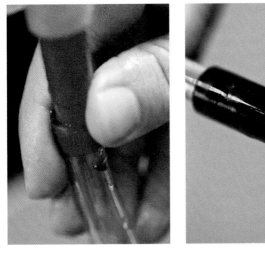

The magic wand: Attach the hose to the spigot on the bottling bucket as you see here on the left, then attach the bottling wand to the other end. Turn the spigot to allow beer to flow into the wand. The gravity valve at the tip of the wand (shown on the right) will keep the beer from spilling all over the place (for the most part). Beer is released when the valve is pressed against the bottom of the bottle, and the flow stops as soon as it is lifted and the valve falls back into place.

Fill 'em up: Holding a bottle with a firm grasp, insert the bottling wand into the bottle and press the tip onto the bottom of the bottle. Once the beer level reaches just below the mouth of the bottle, release pressure from the wand to stop the flow of beer and slide it out of the bottle. Removing the wand creates a bit of headspace at the top of the bottle (about an inch and a half), which is necessary to allow for pressure buildup, but you don't want too much. Excess air inside the bottle can lead to oxidation, which creates a cardboardy off-flavor that is really unpleasant.

The hoppy taste of victory: Cap the bottle, crimping it on with a bottle capper (see page 304 for a visual). Then repeat filling and capping. Once everything is bottled, there's one last round of waiting. Bottles generally take about two weeks to carbonate. If you open one up early just to see how things are developing, remember that young beer can have any number of unattenuated compounds present that affect the flavor profile in big ways. Don't be surprised if your first couple of beers taste overtly butterscotchy or fruity; flavors will mellow with age. Last task: Invite some friends over and celebrate!

America's Test Kitchen IPA

Makes about fifty 12-ounce bottles

Start today, enjoy in 4 weeks

- **1** pound American crystal malt 40L, cracked
- **8** ounces Carapils malt, cracked
- **6** gallons plus 1½ cups filtered water
- **1** vial White Labs California Ale yeast (WLP001), held at room temperature for 3 hours
- **7** pounds light dry malt extract
- **2** ounces Warrior hop pellets
- **4** ounces Amarillo hop pellets
- **1** teaspoon Irish moss
- **4** ounces priming sugar

1. TO BREW: Combine crystal malt and Carapils malt in steeping bag; tie knot in top of bag. Add 3 gallons water to 5-gallon stockpot (brew pot) and completely submerge steeping bag in water; clip knotted end of bag to side of pot. Bring water to 170 degrees over high heat, swirling bag in water periodically. Meanwhile, clean all brewing equipment (fermenting bucket with lid and grommet, large coarse-mesh strainer, long-handled spoon, airlock, turkey baster or ladle) and unopened yeast vial using Easy Clean, then sanitize using iodophor solution prepared following container's instructions, and air-dry.

2. Remove steeping bag from brew pot, allowing liquid from bag to drain back into pot (do not squeeze bag). Discard bag and bring steeped water to boil. Off heat, add dry malt extract, stirring constantly to prevent caking and scorching on bottom of pot.

3. Return mixture (wort) to boil and cook for 15 minutes. (If at any point wort begins to foam and boil over, turn off heat and stir until it settles; return to heat and continue boiling.) Stir in 1 ounce Warrior hops and boil for 25 minutes. Stir in remaining 1 ounce Warrior hops and boil for 5 minutes. Stir in 1 ounce Amarillo hops and Irish moss and boil for 5 minutes. Stir in 1 ounce Amarillo hops and boil for 5 minutes. Stir in 1 ounce Amarillo hops and boil for 5 minutes. Off heat, add remaining 1 ounce Amarillo hops and stir wort in wide circles to create whirlpool; let sit for 10 minutes.

4. Fill large tub with ice water. Place brew pot in ice bath and cool wort, stirring occasionally, until it registers 75 degrees, about 30 minutes.

5. Set coarse-mesh strainer over fermenting bucket. Pour cooled wort through strainer into bucket. Add 3 gallons filtered water to fermenting bucket until wort measures 5 gallons (you may not need all of water). Using turkey baster, remove ½ cup wort, then transfer to hydrometer tube and measure and record wort's original gravity with hydrometer; save reading until needed for calculation in step 8. Give unopened yeast vial a gentle shake and pour entire contents into remaining wort.

6. Bring ½ cup filtered water to boil; let cool to room temperature. Fit lid with grommet and secure lid on fermenting bucket. Assemble and insert airlock through grommet in lid. Fill airlock chamber to line with boiled and cooled filtered water (you may not need all of water) and top airlock with cap. Transfer fermenting bucket to cool, dark place and let sit for 2 weeks.

7. TO BOTTLE: Clean all bottling equipment (turkey baster or ladle, auto-siphon and hose, bottling bucket, spigot, bottling wand, bottle capper, fifty 12-ounce beer bottles, and 60 bottle caps) using Easy Clean, then sanitize using iodophor solution prepared following container's instructions, and air-dry. Bring remaining 1 cup water and sugar to boil in small saucepan and cook, stirring occasionally, until sugar is completely dissolved, about 1 minute. Remove from heat, cover, and let cool.

8. Assemble bottling bucket and spigot (make sure spigot is in "off" position) and attach siphon hose to auto-siphon. Arrange fermenting bucket on counter and bottling bucket on floor directly below it. Using turkey baster, remove ½ cup beer, transfer to hydrometer tube, then measure and record final gravity with hydrometer. Calculate alcohol by volume using original gravity and final gravity readings (see page 338).

9. Pour cooled sugar solution into bottling bucket. Place pump end of auto-siphon into beer and extend siphon hose into bottling bucket. Pump siphon to begin transfer of beer from fermenting bucket to bottling bucket, sucking up as little sediment in bottom of fermenting bucket as possible. Continue to siphon until as much liquid as possible has been transferred to bottling bucket.

10. Remove now-empty fermenting bucket and place bottling bucket on counter. Clean, sanitize, and air-dry lid and siphon hose. Place lid on bottling bucket and attach hose to spigot of bottling bucket and bottling wand to hose. Turn spigot to "on" position and allow beer to flow into wand.

11. Insert wand into bottle and press tip of wand against bottom to begin flow of beer into bottle. Once beer level reaches just below mouth of bottle, release pressure from wand to stop flow of beer and remove wand from bottle (this will leave about 1½ inches headspace). Place cap over mouth of bottle. Center bottle-capper over top of cap and push both handles completely down, applying even pressure around cap. Release bottle capper and twist cap to test for tight fit. If cap is loose or improperly attached, remove and top bottle with new cap. Repeat with remaining beer, bottles, and caps.

12. Transfer sealed bottles to cool, dark place and let sit until fully carbonated, about 2 weeks. Sealed bottles can be stored in cool, dark place or refrigerated for at least 4 months.

Meet the D.I.Y. Test Kitchen

AMANDA AGEE
Executive Editor, *Cook's Illustrated*

Amanda was once a vegetarian for three days. When she's not thinking about giving up meat, she's eating it. She lives in Cambridge, Massachusetts, with her husband, daughter, and two cats.

JACK BISHOP
Editorial Director, America's Test Kitchen

Jack has worked at America's Test Kitchen since 1992. On the television shows, Jack is the "tasting guy," but over the years he has worked on a variety of magazine, book, and web projects. His personal passions are vegetables and anything Italian. In the summer, you will find Jack harvesting radishes or digging potatoes at his community-supported farm.

JUDY BLOMQUIST
Production and Imaging Specialist,
America's Test Kitchen

Judy studied painting and worked in a print shop before joining the production department at ATK. Her job is to make pictures of food look as delicious as possible. She loves making things, so if she's not cooking up home brew, she spends her time drawing, sewing, and baking.

MATTHEW CARD
Contributing Editor, *Cook's Illustrated*

After stints as a bike messenger and cooking his way through restaurants up and down the East Coast, Matthew acquired a Master's Degree in Literature and landed at the magazine more than a decade ago. When he's not developing recipes or writing, Matthew spends as much time as he can cycling in the hills surrounding his adopted hometown of Portland, Oregon, and chasing his two small boys.

ELIZABETH CARDUFF
Editorial Director, Books

After a long career in nonfiction book publishing where she edited many cookbooks, Elizabeth now runs the book program at America's Test Kitchen. She loves every aspect of making cookbooks as well as helping talented test cooks refine their editorial skills while learning more about food from them on a daily basis than she could have ever imagined.

DANIEL CELLUCCI
Assistant Test Cook, America's Test Kitchen

Born of immigrant parents, this son of Italy quickly found his calling cooking next to his grandmother in the apartment upstairs from his childhood home. After graduating from culinary school in 1999, Dan went on a coast-to-coast journey before settling in at America's Test Kitchen as an assistant test cook.

LYNN CLARK
Associate Editor, *Cook's Country*

Lynn worked in editing for a large consulting firm before leaving her job to attend culinary school and embark on a new career. Lynn was formerly responsible for overseeing freelance assignments for *Cook's Country* and was the co-executive chef for the television show. After five years with the magazine, she left ATK to start a family. She enjoys running, watching baseball, and traveling with her husband, Joe.

JULIA COLLIN DAVISON
Executive Food Editor, Books

Julia has done all manner of jobs at ATK, from grocery shopping and dish washing to being an original cast member on both television shows. She graduated from the Culinary Institute of America, Hyde Park, in 1996, but credits much of her food knowledge to her years in the test kitchen. She is in charge of recipe development for books. She met her husband, Ian, on the set during the second season of filming ATK, and together they have a young daughter.

KEITH DRESSER
Senior Editor, *Cook's Illustrated*

Keith has led the *Cook's Illustrated* recipe development process for five years. He also develops content for the America's Test Kitchen television show and co-manages the back kitchen during filming. When not at the test kitchen, he spends his time trying to find foods (other than mac and cheese) that both of his beautiful daughters will eat, watching the Red Sox (beating the Yankees), and reading cheesy mystery novels.

CHRIS DUDLEY
Associate Editor, Special Interest Publications

A graduate of the French Culinary Institute, Chris has contributed to publications including *Gourmet*, *GQ*, and *Time Out New York*. He currently lives in Boston, where he writes stories and edits recipes.

LOUISE EMERICK
Senior Editor, Books

After receiving her journalism degree from UNC-Chapel Hill, Louise returned home to Texas for enchiladas verdes and a post at *Texas Monthly*. Now in Boston, she enjoys four legitimate seasons, biking to work, and the wonders of the local fish share. Louise manages the editorial process for several cookbooks each year and loves cooking simple, seasonal food as much as the classics.

SARAH GABRIEL
Test Cook, *Cook's Country*

Having majored in American Studies at Smith College, Sarah was destined for food service. She fell in love with cooking and baking and did both for years before discovering that there is actually a paying job for cooks with liberal arts degrees: test cook. At home, Sarah's cooking and writing projects begin in her garden.

LORI GALVIN
Executive Editor, Books

Lori's interest in recipes began while digging through her grandmother's recipe box, particularly when she found lasagna listed under "f" for "foreign." She has edited many of the company's landmark cookbooks, including *The New Best Recipe*, *Baking Illustrated*, and *The Cook's Illustrated Cookbook*. She enjoys preparing lasagna and many other dishes, foreign or not, for her husband, Ken.

ANDREA GEARY
Associate Editor, *Cook's Illustrated*

Andrea grew up in the Boston area, but her formative years as a cook were spent in hotels and restaurants in the Scottish Highlands where she cooked on everything from a 1940s-era coal-fired cast-iron stove to a wood-fired pizza oven to a state-of-the-art programmable CVap oven. She is currently trying to master her electric stove in Cambridge, Massachusetts.

AMY GRAVES
Associate Editor, America's Test Kitchen

After eight years at the *Boston Globe*, Amy left newspaper writing for culinary school. A year later, she was working for the *International Herald Tribune* when her mom told her she should apply for a job at America's Test Kitchen. Now she writes about kitchen gadgets and ingredients for the tasting and testing team. She lives for anything good that you can put on bread.

KATE HARTKE
Associate Editor, Books

After 10-plus years in the Boston book publishing world, Kate loves books more than ever. During both her AM and PM commute, you can find her nose buried in a paperback. When not editing recipes or reading a great novel, she enjoys spending time with her husband, Dan, and dog Ollie.

SHANNON HATCH
Assistant Editor, America's Test Kitchen

Raised on gumbo and étouffée, Shannon's adventurous appetite was fed at an early age. As a journalism graduate of the University of Georgia, her career began at national lifestyle and women's interest publications, but her love of food and writing brought her to America's Test Kitchen. Her perfect day is spent in the kitchen with her husband, Nathan, a new recipe, and a bottle of wine.

REBECCA HAYS
Managing Editor, *Cook's Illustrated*

Becky has worked at ATK for more than a decade. In addition to her duties as managing editor, she regularly appears as an on-screen test cook on America's Test Kitchen. At home, Becky cooks constantly for her family, usually with her 3-year-old son at her side.

ANDREW JANJIGIAN
Associate Editor, *Cook's Illustrated*

Prior to ATK, Andrew was an organic chemist, chef, mushroom cultivator, oven builder, and cooking instructor. Which is to say, his job at ATK is the only thing his peripatetic resume is good for. In his spare time, he enjoys long walks on the beach, bread baking, and pining for the day Boston has a decent pizza joint.

SCOTT KATHAN
Managing Editor, *Cook's Country*

As managing editor, Scott edits every page of the magazine about a dozen times before publication. Prior to coming to America's Test Kitchen in 2006, he covered restaurants and nightlife for the Boston Phoenix Media Group and taught at Regis College. His first job was scrubbing sheet pans in a high-volume bakery. Scott is probably cooking tacos for his two young children right now.

JENNIFER LALIME
Test Cook, Books

After a decade in business and corporate training, Jen followed her insatiable appetite and curiosity into the kitchen to indulge her passion for food. Her first professional culinary stint was as an intern at ATK. She went on to join the book team, developing recipes as a test cook and showcasing her digits in much of the ATK food photography by serving as "the hands" for many a recipe.

BRIDGET LANCASTER
Executive Food Editor, New Media, Television, and Radio

Bridget joined the ATK team in 1998 and is an original cast member of both *America's Test Kitchen* and *Cook's Country* television shows, as well as a co-host for the America's Test Kitchen Radio program. She also serves as the lead instructor for the America's Test Kitchen Cooking School.

MARI LEVINE
Associate Editor, Web Editorial

Over the past four years, Mari has been able to combine her journalism and culinary degrees with her restaurant and lifelong eating experience. As an online editorial team member, she generates and maintains content for the websites and blogs. When she's not working hoisin sauce into everything she eats or bingeing on anything sandwiched between two slices of bread, she can be found on her bike, engrossed in a documentary, or playing sports that involve throwing and/or catching a ball.

REBECCAH MARSTERS
Associate Editor, *Cook's Country*

With nothing but an Art History degree, a job in a coffee shop, and a love of all things edible, Rebeccah proceeded to culinary school to learn the finer points of the kitchen. Since then, she's been at ATK working as a test cook for *Cook's Country*. Outside of work, she can be found attempting downward dogs at the gym, traveling as much as possible, and diligently researching where to find the finest cocktails and best burgers in Boston.

SUZANNAH MCFERRAN
Senior Editor, Books

Suzannah fell in love with food while living in Italy during college. After a series of stints in politics, investment banking, and the Internet, she left them all behind and found her way back to food. She helped open a cheese shop in Charlottesville, Virginia, attended culinary school in New York, and spent a few years working in restaurants before landing at ATK in 2006. When she is not working, she is usually chasing after her two kids, eating an avocado, or savoring a good piece of dark chocolate.

REBECCA MORRIS
Test Cook, Books

Rebecca never really appreciated growing up on the warm sandy beaches of Sarasota, Florida, until of course she attended the Culinary Institute of America in the Hudson Valley. Along with learning how to cook, she developed a fondness for the seasons (well, three of them at least), and now craves asparagus in spring, peaches in summer, cauliflower in autumn, braised short ribs in winter, and bacon year round.

CHRISTIE MORRISON
Associate Editor, Books

Armed with a Master's Degree in English and a diploma from the Cambridge School of Culinary Arts, Christie joined ATK in 2009. She enjoys the diversity of cooking in the books she works on, from baking to pressure cooking. A culinary instructor and born-again runner in her free time, Christie craves balance, coffee, and fried egg sandwiches—not necessarily in that order.

CHRIS O'CONNOR
Associate Editor, America's Test Kitchen

Chris began his culinary education working in restaurants throughout Boston and New York City before joining the test kitchen. Chris enjoys exercising his palate several times a day just to keep it in shape. He is an avid Red Sox fan with a love for charcuterie and homemade pizza.

ADDY PARKER
Associate Editor, Books

An academic background in philosophy isn't particularly helpful in a restaurant kitchen, but Addy found that when her structured, logical way of thinking commingled with her passion for cooking, the perfect job was a spot at ATK. Addy started as an intern and had particular affection for the camaraderie of the book team, where she served as a valuable team member for several years.

LAUREN PERKINS
Marketing Assistant, America's Test Kitchen

During her time at ATK, Lauren supported all of the marketing functions, including newsstand sales, direct mail, and e-mail promos. She enjoys running, mostly because she likes baking desserts, always from scratch. Her guilty pleasures are soft-serve ice cream, all varieties of cereal, and Bravo TV.

KELLY PRICE
Test Cook, *Cook's Country*

Kelly graduated from Johnson & Wales in Charlotte and worked for ATK for both the book team and *Cook's Country* over the course of two years. Kelly enjoys being outside, sundresses, country music, dogs, and tomato-based cultures. Her favorite foods are salsa, spaghetti, tomato sandwiches, Cheerwine, and biscuits.

CAROLYNN PURPURA MACKAY
Test Cook, *Cook's Country*

After working for eight years as an engineer, Carolynn traded construction specs for cookie recipes and got her AS in Baking and Pastry from Johnson & Wales. She lives in Jamaica Plain with her husband and two dogs. When she is not in the test kitchen she can be found running very slow marathons, on the competitive barbecue circuit, and doing everything in her power to avoid hugs.

CALI RICH
Senior Editor, America's Test Kitchen

After receiving her journalism degree from UNC–Chapel Hill and a degree in cuisine from the Cordon Bleu in London, Cali returned to the States and joined ATK as a kitchen intern. Several months later, *Cook's Country* was launched and over the next seven years Cali worked up to senior editor. The recent arrival of a baby gal encouraged Cali to restructure her schedule and, as luck would have it, join the online cooking school team.

ADAM RIED
Contributing Editor, America's Test Kitchen

An original cast member in both of ATK's PBS shows and frequent magazine contributor, Adam cut his gastronomic teeth with a culinary certificate from Boston University and 10 years in the test kitchen. An unchecked cookbook addict (and author), he is a regular cooking columnist for the *Boston Globe Magazine*, culinate.com, and *ChopChop* and has written for numerous local, national, and international publications.

BRYAN ROOF
Senior Editor, *Cook's Country*

A chef and registered dietitian, Bryan worked in many of the East Coast's award-winning restaurants before landing at America's Test Kitchen in 2006. During his tenure, he's written for *Cook's Illustrated* and cooked alongside his good friend Christopher Kimball on the ATK television show. When not working, he can be found making happy meals at home with his three budding chefs and lovely wife.

YVONNE RUPERTI
Associate Editor, America's Test Kitchen

Yvonne was an associate editor of photo shoots and a cast member on the America's Test Kitchen TV show. Prior to ATK, she owned her own bakery; she is a mean cake decorator. Though she specializes in desserts, her favorite foods include scrambled eggs, brie, and soppressata.

TAIZETH SIERRA
Assistant Editor, America's Test Kitchen

For a kid whose favorite food growing up was beef tongue and who searched for the marrow bones in the pot of beef soup, a degree in culinary arts and restaurant management was an obvious choice. Though Tai is classically trained, the cuisine of Northern Mexico is still her biggest influence. When she's not trying desperately to re-create her family's recipes she enjoys comic books, video games, and going for walks in the woods with her husband, Lee, and pit bull, Dory.

DAN SOUZA
Associate Editor, *Cook's Illustrated*

Dan cut his culinary teeth in the unforgiving plains and patinaed gulyás pots of rural Hungary. A graduate of the Culinary Institute of America, Dan cooked in restaurants in New York City and Boston before finding his true calling: applying good science to create great recipes. Dan also serves as a guest cook on the television show.

DIANE UNGER
Senior Editor, *Cook's Country*

Diane has been a member of the ATK family for 10 years. When not in the test kitchen, deep frying just about anything, she enjoys baseball, barbecue, and making pizza with her wonderful son Bob.

MARCUS WALSER
Systems Administrator, America's Test Kitchen

A test kitchen refugee, Marcus graduated from Johnson & Wales with a degree in culinary arts. He promptly left all that behind and now designs and implements technology systems at America's Test Kitchen. In his spare time, he exposes food items to unspeakable chemicals and inhospitable environments for the sake of science.

KATE WILLIAMS
Test Cook, Books

Kate's first project in recipe development, at age 11, was a chocolate cake with many secret ingredients. Prior to ATK, she worked in food journalism and held various restaurant positions. When she's not splitting open lobsters or manning an army of slow cookers, she can be found eating falafel, running in circles, and playing German board games (preferably all at once).

JOHN WILLOUGHBY
Editorial Director, Magazines

John (Doc) Willoughby was present at the creation of *Cook's Illustrated* and, after 10 years in New York as Executive Editor of *Gourmet*, he returned to the (now much expanded) organization in 2010. Last February he went back to Uruguay to see if the dulce de leche is still good. It is.

SARAH WILSON
Associate Editor, *Cook's Country*

With a finance degree from William and Mary and time spent in some of New York's, France's, and Boston's finest kitchens, Sarah decided to go into publishing. After winding her way through all of the ATK publications, she is now an instructor for the online America's Test Kitchen Cooking School. Outside of work, Sarah can be found chasing her two daughters and trying to find five undisturbed minutes with her husband.

DAN ZUCCARELLO
Associate Editor, Books

Hailing from the warm, welcoming state of New Jersey, Dan graduated from Johnson & Wales in Rhode Island and spent several years working in a variety of the local restaurants before joining ATK in 2008. He never passes up a seafood dinner and loves all things spicy. He enjoys spending time in his vegetable garden.

Index

NOTE: Page references in *italics* indicate finished recipe photographs.

A

Acids, for cheese making, 137

Agar, buying, 285

Alcohol by Volume (ABV), calculating, 338

Almond(s)

blanched, buying, 315

Butter, 4–5, *5*

Granola with Dried Fruit, 228–29, *229*

Horchata, 315–16, *316*

Torrone, 278–81, *280*

American Cheese, *130,* 132–35, *134*

America's Test Kitchen IPA, 339–47, *345*

Anchovies

Worcestershire Sauce, 26–28

Angelica root, about, 328

Apple Butter, 94–97, *97*

Artichokes, Marinated, 37–39, *39*

B

Bacon

Country-Style Pâté, 214–17, *216*

Homemade, 180–83, *182*

Jam, 77–79, *79*

Balsamic-Fig Jam, 67–69, *69*

Bark, Chocolate-Toffee, 269–71, *270*

Barks, roots, and herbs 101, 328

Bars, Granola, 230–32, *232*

Beans

Dilly, 114–15, *115*

Dukkah, 47–49, *49*

Tofu, 174–77, *176*

Beef bung caps, about, 204

Beef Jerky, 222–25, *224*

Beer

America's Test Kitchen IPA, 339–47, *345*

brewing 101, 336–38

Beets, Pickled, 119–21, *121*

Berries

Blueberry Refrigerator Jam, 59

Raspberry-Peach Spreadable Fruit, 60–62, *62*

Raspberry Refrigerator Jam, 59

Strawberry Refrigerator Jam, 58–59, *59*

Beverages

America's Test Kitchen IPA, 339–47, *345*

Citrus-Infused Vodka, 333–35, *335*

Cocktail Bitters, 329–32, *331*

Coffee Liqueur, 323–24, *324*

Cold-Brew Coffee, 312–14, *314*

Eggnog, 317–20, *320*

Ginger Beer, 306–8, *307*

Horchata, 315–16, *316*

Hot Cocoa, 322, *322*

Hot Cocoa Mix, 321–22, *322*

Iced Coffee, 314

Root Beer, 302–5, *304*

Sweet Vermouth, *300,* 325–27

Tonic Water, 309–11, *311*

Big-Batch Summer Tomato Sauce, 43–46, *46*

Bitters

Citrus, 329–32, *331*

Cocktail, 329–32, *331*

Old-Fashioned, 329–32, *331*

Black cocoa powder, about, 258

Black sesame seeds, buying, 47

Blueberry Refrigerator Jam, 59

Bottles, caps, and bottle cappers, buying, 306

Bourbon

Cocktail Bitters, 329–32, *331*

Eggnog, 317–20, *320*

Brandy

Coffee Liqueur, 323–24, *324*

Bread. *See* Grissini

Bread-and-Butter Pickles, 108–10, *110*

Brewing beer 101, 336–38

Brigadeiros, 272–73, *273*

Butter, Cultured, 170–73, *173*

Butter Crackers, Rich, 249–52, *251*
Buttermilk
    Crème Fraîche, 165–66, *166*
    Paneer, 157–60, *159*
Butter muslin, for cheese making, 138

C

Cabbage
    Kimchi, 127–29, *129*
    Sauerkraut, 124–26, *126*
Cajeta, 295–96, *296*
Calcium chloride, 137
Candied Ginger, 50–52, *52*
Candy
    Almond Torrone, 278–81, *280*
    Brigadeiros, 272–73, *273*
    Chocolate-Toffee Bark, 269–71, *270*
    Marshmallows, *256*, 282–84
    Orange Jelly Slices, 285–88, *287*
    Pistachio-Orange Torrone, 281
    Salted Caramels, 274–77, *276*
Canning 101, 70–71
Caramelized Onion Jam, 75–76, *76*
Caramels, Salted, 274–77, *276*
Carrots
    Giardiniera, 122–23, *123*
    Kimchi, 127–29, *129*
Cauliflower
    Giardiniera, 122–23, *123*
Celery
    Giardiniera, 122–23, *123*
Centaury herb, about, 328
Champagne yeast, buying, 306
Cheese
    American, 132–35, *134*
    Cream, Neufchatel, 138–40, *140*
    Feta, 153–56, *155*
    Fromage Blanc, 161–64, *163*
    Goat, Fresh, 149–52, *151*
    Mozzarella, 141–45, *144*
    Paneer, 157–60, *159*
    Ricotta, 146–48, *148*
Cheesecloth, 138

Cheese making
    acids, 137
    best milk for, 136
    butter muslin for, 138
    calcium chloride, 137
    cheesecloth for, 138
    how milk turns into cheese, 136
    rennet, 137
    starter cultures, 137, 161
Chicken livers
    Country-Style Pâté, 214–17, *216*
    Mousseline, 211–13, *213*
Chile(s)
    dried, buying, 201
    Giardiniera, 122–23, *123*
    Harissa, 29–31, *31*
    Hot Sauce, 15–18, *17*
    Mexican Chorizo, 201–3, *202*
    Red Pepper Jelly, 80–82, *82*
    Spicy Tomato Jam, 72–74, *74*
    Sriracha, 19–21, *21*
Chili powder, Korean, about, 127
Chocolate
    black cocoa powder, about, 258
    Brigadeiros, 272–73, *273*
    couverture, about, 265
    -Hazelnut Spread, 6–7, *7*
    Hot Cocoa, 322, *322*
    Hot Cocoa Mix, 321–22, *322*
    Ice Cream Shell, 293–94, *294*
    -Mint Cookies, Thin, *256*, 265–68
    -Mint Cookies, Thin, with Easy
        Chocolate Coating, 268
    Sandwich Cookies, 258–61, *260*
    -Toffee Bark, 269–71, *270*
Chorizo, Mexican, 201–3, *202*
Chutney
    Green Tomato, 88–89, *89*
    Mango, 86–87, *87*
Cinchona bark
    about, 328
    buying, 309
    Tonic Water, 309–11, *311*
Cinnamon
    Graham Crackers, 255
    Horchata, 315–16, *316*

Citric acid
    buying, 285, 309
    Tonic Water, 309–11, *311*
Citrus Bitters, 329–32, *331*
Citrus-Infused Vodka, 333–35, *335*
Cocktail Bitters, 329–32, *331*
Cocoa
    Hot, 322, *322*
    Hot, Mix, 321–22, *322*
    powder, black, about, 258
Coconut
    Granola Bars, 230–32, *232*
Coffee
    Cold-Brew, 312–14, *314*
    Iced, 314
    Liqueur, 323–24, *324*
Cognac
    Sweet Vermouth, *300,* 325–27
Colby cheese
    American Cheese, 132–35, *134*
Cold-Brew Coffee, 312–14, *314*
Confit, Duck, 208–10, *210*
Cookies
    Chocolate-Mint, Thin, 265–68
    Chocolate-Mint, Thin, with
        Easy Chocolate Coating, 268
    Chocolate Sandwich, 258–61, *260*
    Cinnamon Graham Crackers, 255
    Graham Crackers, 253–55, *255*
    Peanut Butter Sandwich, 262–64, *264*
Corn Chips, 233–36, *235*
Cornmeal
    Corn Chips, 233–36, *235*
Corn Tortillas, 240–42, *242*
Country-Style Pâté, 214–17, *216*
Couverture chocolate, about, 265
Crackers
    Cinnamon Graham, 255
    Graham, 253–55, *255*
    Lavash, 243–45, *245*
    Rich Butter, 249–52, *251*
Cream
    Crème Fraîche, 165–66, *166*
    Cultured Butter, 170–73, *173*
Cream Cheese, Neufchatel, 138–40, *140*
Crème Fraîche, 165–66, *166*
Crocks, buying, 22, 124

Cucumbers
    Bread-and-Butter Pickles, 108–10, *110*
    Kirby (pickling), about, 104
    Pickle Relish, 111–13, *112*
    Sour Dill Pickles, 104–7, *107*
Cultured Butter, 170–73, *173*
Cured, smoked, and terrined
    Bacon, 180–83, *182*
    Beef Jerky, 222–25, *224*
    Country-Style Pâté, 214–17, *216*
    Duck Confit, 208–10, *210*
    Duck Prosciutto, 190–93, *192*
    Gravlax, 194–96, *196*
    Guanciale, 187–89, *189*
    Merguez, 197–200, *199*
    Mexican Chorizo, 201–3, *202*
    Mortadella, 204–7, *206*
    Mousseline, 211–13, *213*
    Pancetta, 184–86, *185*
    Pork Rillettes, 218–21, *220*
Curing salt, about, 180

D

Dandelion root, about, 328
Desserts
    Cajeta, 295–96, *296*
    Chocolate Ice Cream Shell, 293–94, *294*
    Chocolate Sandwich Cookies, 258–61, *260*
    Maple Cream, 297–99, *299*
    Peanut Butter Sandwich Cookies, 262–64, *264*
    Sugar Cones, *256,* 289–92
    Thin Chocolate-Mint Cookies, 265–68
    Thin Chocolate-Mint Cookies with
        Easy Chocolate Coating, 268
Dill
    Dilly Beans, 114–15, *115*
    Gravlax, 194–96, *196*
    Pickles, Sour, 104–7, *107*
Dried bitter orange, about, 328
Dropper bottles, buying, 329
Dry malt extract, about, 338
Duck
    Confit, 208–10, *210*
    fat, buying, 208
    Prosciutto, 190–93, *192*
Dukkah, 47–49, *49*

E

Easy Refrigerator Jams, 58–59
Edible wafer papers, about, 278
Eggnog, 317–20, *320*
Extract, Vanilla, 53–55, *55*

F

Feta Cheese, *130,* 153–56, *155*
Fig-Balsamic Jam, 67–69, *69*
Fish
    Gravlax, 194–96, *196*
Fish sauce
    Kimchi, 127–29, *129*
    Spicy Tomato Jam, 72–74, *74*
    Worcestershire Sauce, 26–28
Fresh Goat Cheese, 149–52, *151*
Fromage Blanc, 161–64, *163*
Fruit
    Dried, Granola with, 228–29, *229*
    see also specific fruits

G

Garlic
    Kimchi, 127–29, *129*
Gentian root, about, 328
Giardiniera, 122–23, *123*
Ginger
    Beer, 306–8, *307*
    Candied, 50–52, *52*
Glass jars, for bitters, buying, 329
Goat's Milk
    buying, 149
    Cajeta, 295–96, *296*
    Feta Cheese, 153–56, *155*
    Fresh Goat Cheese, 149–52, *151*
Graham flour
    buying, 253
    Cinnamon Graham Crackers, 255
    Graham Crackers, 253–55, *255*
Grains. *See* Cornmeal; Oats; Rice
Granola Bars, 230–32, *232*
Granola with Dried Fruit, 228–29, *229*

Grapefruit
    Citrus-Infused Vodka, 333–35, *335*
Gravlax, 194–96, *196*
Greek-Style Yogurt, 167–69, *169*
Green beans
    Dilly Beans, 114–15, *115*
Green peppercorns, about, 214
Green Tomato Chutney, 88–89, *89*
Grissini, 246–48, *248*
Guanciale, 187–89, *189*

H

Harissa, 29–31, *31*
Hazelnut-Chocolate Spread, 6–7, *7*
Hazelnut oil, about, 6
Herbs, barks, and roots 101, 328
Hops, about, 338
Horchata, 315–16, *316*
Horseradish, Prepared, 32–33, *33*
Hot Cocoa, 322, *322*
Hot Cocoa Mix, 321–22, *322*
Hot Sauce, 15–18, *17*

I

Iced Coffee, 314
Irish moss, about, 338

J

Jams
    Bacon, 77–79, *79*
    Blueberry Refrigerator, 59
    Caramelized Onion, 75–76, *76*
    Easy Refrigerator, 58–59
    Fig-Balsamic, 67–69, *69*
    Raspberry Refrigerator, 59
    Strawberry Refrigerator, 58–59, *59*
    Tomato, Spicy, 72–74, *74*
Jelly
    Red Pepper, 80–82, *82*
    Wine, 83–85, *85*
Jerky, Beef, 222–25, *224*

K

Ketchup, 11–14, *13*
Kettle Chips, 237–39, *239*
Kimchi, 127–29, *129*
Korean chili powder, about, 127

L

Lamb
  Merguez, 197–200, *199*
Lavash Crackers, 243–45, *245*
Lemons
  Citrus-Infused Vodka, 333–35, *335*
  Meyer, about, 34
  Preserved, 34–36, *36*
  Tonic Water, 309–11, *311*
Lime
  Tonic Water, 309–11, *311*
Liqueur, Coffee, 323–24, *324*
Livers, chicken
  Country-Style Pâté, 214–17, *216*
  Mousseline, 211–13, *213*

M

Malt grains, about, 338
Mango Chutney, 86–87, *87*
Maple
  Cream, 297–99, *299*
  sugar, buying, 180
Marinated Artichokes, 37–39, *39*
Marmalade, Seville Orange, 63–66, *65*
Marmelada (Quince Paste), 98–101, *100*
Marshmallows, 282–84
Masa harina
  buying, 240
  Corn Tortillas, 240–42, *242*
Masarepa flour
  buying, 233
  Corn Chips, 233–36, *235*
Meat
  Beef Jerky, 222–25, *224*
  Merguez, 197–200, *199*
  see also Pork
Merguez, 197–200, *199*

Mexican Chorizo, 201–3, *202*
Meyer lemons, about, 34
Milk
  Cajeta, 295–96, *296*
  Eggnog, 317–20, *320*
  Feta Cheese, 153–56, *155*
  Fresh Goat Cheese, 149–52, *151*
  Fromage Blanc, 161–64, *163*
  goat, buying, 149
  Greek-Style Yogurt, 167–69, *169*
  Horchata, 315–16, *316*
  Hot Cocoa, 322, *322*
  Mozzarella, 141–45, *144*
  Neufchatel Cream Cheese, 138–40, *140*
  Paneer, 157–60, *159*
  powder, whole, buying, 132
  Ricotta Cheese, 146–48, *148*
Mint
  -Chocolate Cookies, Thin, 265–68
  -Chocolate Cookies, Thin, with
    Easy Chocolate Coating, 268
Mortadella, 204–7, *206*
Mostarda, Peach, 90–93, *93*
Mother of vinegar cultures, buying, 22
Mousseline, 211–13, *213*
Mozzarella, 141–45, *144*
Mugwort, about, 328
Mustard
  Peach Mostarda, 90–93, *93*
  seeds, buying, 8
  Whole-Grain, 8–10, *10*

N

Neufchatel Cream Cheese, 138–40, *140*
Nuts
  Almond Butter, 4–5, *5*
  Almond Torrone, 278–81, *280*
  blanched almonds, buying, 315
  Chocolate-Hazelnut Spread, 6–7, *7*
  Chocolate-Toffee Bark, 269–71, *270*
  Country-Style Pâté, 214–17, *216*
  Dukkah, 47–49, *49*
  Granola Bars, 230–32, *232*
  Granola with Dried Fruit, 228–29, *229*
  Horchata, 315–16, *316*

Nuts *(cont.)*
  Mortadella, 204–7, *206*
  Peanut Butter, 5
  Peanut Butter Sandwich Cookies, 262–64, *264*
  Pistachio-Orange Torrone, 281

O

Oats
  Granola Bars, 230–32, *232*
  Granola with Dried Fruit, 228–29, *229*
Old-Fashioned Bitters, 329–32, *331*
Onion, Caramelized, Jam, 75–76, *76*
Orange(s)
  Citrus-Infused Vodka, 333–35, *335*
  dried bitter, about, 328
  Jelly Slices, 285–88, *287*
  -Pistachio Torrone, 281
  Seville, about, 63
  Seville, Marmalade, 63–66, *65*
  Tonic Water, 309–11, *311*
Orris root, about, 328
Oven-Dried Tomatoes, 40–42, *42*

P

Pancetta, 184–86, *185*
Paneer, 157–60, *159*
Pantry staples
  Almond Butter, 4–5, *5*
  Big-Batch Summer Tomato Sauce, 43–46, *46*
  Candied Ginger, 50–52, *52*
  Chocolate-Hazelnut Spread, 6–7, *7*
  Dukkah, 47–49, *49*
  Harissa, 29–31, *31*
  Hot Sauce, 15–18, *17*
  Ketchup, 11–14, *13*
  Marinated Artichokes, 37–39, *39*
  Oven-Dried Tomatoes, 40–42, *42*
  Peanut Butter, 5
  Prepared Horseradish, 32–33, *33*
  Preserved Lemons, 34–36, *36*
  Sriracha, 19–21, *21*
  Vanilla Extract, 53–55, *55*

Pantry Staples *(cont.)*
  Whole-Grain Mustard, 8–10, *10*
  Wine Vinegar, 22–25, *25*
  Worcestershire Sauce, 26–28
Paste, Quince (Marmelada), 98–101, *100*
Pâté, Country-Style, 214–17, *216*
Peach
  Mostarda, 90–93, *93*
  -Raspberry Spreadable Fruit, 60–62, *62*
Peanut Butter
  Homemade, 5
  Sandwich Cookies, 262–64, *264*
Peanuts
  Peanut Butter, 5
  Peanut Butter Sandwich Cookies, 262–64, *264*
Pecans
  Chocolate-Toffee Bark, 269–71, *270*
  Granola Bars, 230–32, *232*
Pectin, about, 80
Pepitas
  Granola Bars, 230–32, *232*
Peppercorns
  Beef Jerky, 222–25, *224*
  green, about, 214
  Sichuan, about, 222
Pepper(s)
  Giardiniera, 122–23, *123*
  Pickle Relish, 111–13, *112*
  Red, Jelly, 80–82, *82*
  see also Chile(s)
Pickled recipes
  Bread-and-Butter Pickles, 108–10, *110*
  Dilly Beans, 114–15, *115*
  Giardiniera, 122–23, *123*
  Kimchi, 127–29, *129*
  Pickled Beets, 119–21, *121*
  Pickled Watermelon Rind, 116–18, *118*
  Pickle Relish, 111–13, *112*
  Sauerkraut, 124–26, *126*
  Sour Dill Pickles, 104–7, *107*
Pink salt, about, 180
Pistachio(s)
  Country-Style Pâté, 214–17, *216*
  Dukkah, 47–49, *49*
  Mortadella, 204–7, *206*
  -Orange Torrone, 281

Pork
    Bacon, 180–83, *182*
    Country-Style Pâté, 214–17, *216*
    Guanciale, 187–89, *189*
    jowls, about, 187
    Mexican Chorizo, 201–3, *202*
    Mortadella, 204–7, *206*
    Pancetta, 184–86, *185*
    Rillettes, 218–21, *220*
Potatoes
    Kettle Chips, 237–39, *239*
Poultry. *See* **Chicken livers**
Prepared Horseradish, 32–33, *33*
Preserved Lemons, 34–36, *36*
Preserves
    Apple Butter, 94–97, *97*
    Bacon Jam, 77–79, *79*
    Blueberry Refrigerator Jam, 59
    Caramelized Onion Jam, 75–76, *76*
    Fig-Balsamic Jam, 67–69, *69*
    Green Tomato Chutney, 88–89, *89*
    Mango Chutney, 86–87, *87*
    Marmelada (Quince Paste), 98–101, *100*
    Peach Mostarda, 90–93, *93*
    Raspberry-Peach Spreadable Fruit, 60–62, *62*
    Raspberry Refrigerator Jam, 59
    Red Pepper Jelly, 80–82, *82*
    Seville Orange Marmalade, 63–66, *65*
    Spicy Tomato Jam, 72–74, *74*
    Strawberry Refrigerator Jam, 58–59, *59*
    Wine Jelly, 83–85, *85*
Priming sugar, about, 338
Prosciutto, Duck, 190–93, *192*

Q

Quassia bark, about, 328
Quince
    about, 98
    Paste (Marmelada), 98–101, *100*

R

Raisins
    Granola with Dried Fruit, 228–29, *229*
    Mango Chutney, 86–87, *87*
Raspberry
    -Peach Spreadable Fruit, 60–62, *62*
    Refrigerator Jam, 59
Red Pepper Jelly, 80–82, *82*
Relish, Pickle, 111–13, *112*
Rennet, 137
Rice
    Horchata, 315–16, *316*
Rich Butter Crackers, 249–52, *251*
Ricotta Cheese, *130*, 146–48, *148*
Rillettes, Pork, 218–21, *220*
Root Beer, 302–5, *304*
Roots, barks, and herbs 101, 328
Rum
    Cocktail Bitters, 329–32, *331*

S

Salmon
    Gravlax, 194–96, *196*
Salt
    for canning, 70
    curing, about, 180
    Salted Caramels, 274–77, *276*
Sarsaparilla root
    about, 302, 328
    Root Beer, 302–5, *304*
Sassafras bark
    about, 302, 328
    Root Beer, 302–5, *304*
Sauces
    Cajeta, 295–96, *296*
    Chocolate Ice Cream Shell, 293–94, *294*
    Hot, 15–18, *17*
    Sriracha, 19–21, *21*
    Tomato, Big-Batch Summer, 43–46, *46*
    Worcestershire, 26–28
Sauerkraut, 124–26, *126*

Sausage casings, buying, 197
Sausages
    Merguez, 197–200, *199*
    Mexican Chorizo, 201–3, *202*
    Mortadella, 204–7, *206*
Sausage stuffers, buying, 197
Scallions
    Kimchi, 127–29, *129*
Seafood
    Gravlax, 194–96, *196*
Seeds
    black sesame, buying, 47
    Dukkah, 47–49, *49*
    Granola Bars, 230–32, *232*
    Lavash Crackers, 243–45, *245*
Sesame seeds
    black, buying, 47
    Dukkah, 47–49, *49*
    Lavash Crackers, 243–45, *245*
Seville Orange Marmalade, 63–66, *65*
Seville oranges, about, 63
Shrimp, salted, about, 127
Sichuan peppercorns
    about, 222
    Beef Jerky, 222–25, *224*
Simple Syrup, 332
Snacks
    Cinnamon Graham Crackers, 255
    Corn Chips, 233–36, *235*
    Corn Tortillas, 240–42, *242*
    Graham Crackers, 253–55, *255*
    Granola Bars, 230–32, *232*
    Granola with Dried Fruit, 228–29, *229*
    Grissini, 246–48, *248*
    Kettle Chips, 237–39, *239*
    Lavash Crackers, 243–45, *245*
    Rich Butter Crackers, 249–52, *251*
Sour Dill Pickles, 104–7, *107*
Soybeans
    Tofu, 174–77, *176*
Spices
    buying, for cocktail bitters, 329
    Dukkah, 47–49, *49*

Spicy Tomato Jam, 72–74, *74*
Spreads
    Almond Butter, 4–5, *5*
    Apple Butter, 94–97, *97*
    Chocolate-Hazelnut, 6–7, *7*
    Green Tomato Chutney, 88–89, *89*
    Harissa, 29–31, *31*
    Ketchup, 11–14, *13*
    Mango Chutney, 86–87, *87*
    Maple Cream, 297–99, *299*
    Peanut Butter, 5
    Pickle Relish, 111–13, *112*
    Raspberry-Peach Spreadable Fruit, 60–62, *62*
    Red Pepper Jelly, 80–82, *82*
    Seville Orange Marmalade, 63–66, *65*
    Whole-Grain Mustard, 8–10, *10*
    Wine Jelly, 83–85, *85*
    see also Jams
Sriracha, 19–21, *21*
Starter cultures, for cheese making, 137, 161
Strawberry Refrigerator Jam, 58–59, *59*
Sugar Cones, *256,* 289–92
Sunflower seeds
    Granola Bars, 230–32, *232*
Sweets
    Almond Torrone, 278–81, *280*
    Brigadeiros, 272–73, *273*
    Cajeta, 295–96, *296*
    Chocolate Ice Cream Shell, 293–94, *294*
    Chocolate Sandwich Cookies, 258–61, *260*
    Chocolate-Toffee Bark, 269–71, *270*
    Maple Cream, 297–99, *299*
    Marshmallows, *256,* 282–84
    Orange Jelly Slices, 285–88, *287*
    Peanut Butter Sandwich Cookies, 262–64, *264*
    Pistachio-Orange Torrone, 281
    Salted Caramels, 274–77, *276*
    Sugar Cones, *256,* 289–92
    Thin Chocolate-Mint Cookies, 265–68
    Thin Chocolate-Mint Cookies with
        Easy Chocolate Coating, 268
Sweet Vermouth, *300,* 325–27

T

Tamarind
  about, 26
  Worcestershire Sauce, 26–28
Thin Chocolate-Mint Cookies, *256,* 265–68
Thin Chocolate-Mint Cookies with Easy
    Chocolate Coating, 268
Tofu, 174–77, *176*
Tomato(es)
  Green, Chutney, 88–89, *89*
  Jam, Spicy, 72–74, *74*
  Ketchup, 11–14, *13*
  Oven-Dried, 40–42, *42*
  Sauce, Big-Batch Summer, 43–46, *46*
Tonic Water, 309–11, *311*
Torrone
  Almond, 278–81, *280*
  Pistachio-Orange, 281
Tortilla presses, buying, 240
Tortillas, Corn, 240–42, *242*

V

Vanilla
  beans, buying, 53
  Extract, 53–55, *55*
Vegetables
  Giardiniera, 122–23, *123*
  see also specific vegetables
Vermouth, Sweet, *300,* 325–27
Vinegar, Wine, 22–25, *25*

Vodka
Citrus-Infused, 333–35, *335*
Cocktail Bitters, 329–32, *331*
Coffee Liqueur, 323–24, *324*
Vanilla Extract, 53–55, *55*

W

Wafer papers, about, 278
Walnuts
  Chocolate-Toffee Bark, 269–71, *270*
Water-bath canning method, 71
Watermelon Rind, Pickled, 116–18, *118*
White chocolate chips
  Hot Cocoa Mix, 321–22, *322*
Whole-Grain Mustard, 8–10, *10*
Wine
  Jelly, 83–85, *85*
  Sweet Vermouth, *300,* 325–27
  Vinegar, 22–25, *25*
Worcestershire Sauce, 26–28
Wormwood, about, 328
Wort, about, 338

Y

Yogurt
  Cultured Butter, 170–73, *173*
  Greek-Style, 167–69, *169*